THE TEL QUEL READER

'This collection includes the most important essays and gives an excellent picture of *Tel Quel's* work and evolution over time.' Frederic Jameson, Duke University.

The Tel Quel Reader fills a gap in what has until now been unavailable to English readers. In view of the influence of *Tel Quel*, such a collection is long overdue.' Paul Patton, University of Sydney.

The Tel Quel Reader presents for the first time in English many of the key essays that played an instrumental role in shaping the contours of literary and cultural debate in the 1960s and 1970s. (*Tel Quel*, a French literary review and intellectual grouping that ran from 1960 to 1982) published some of the key essays of major poststructuralist thinkers from Michel Foucault to Roland Barthes. Julia Kristeva herself was a member of *Tel Quel's* editorial board.

The Tel Quel Reader fills a crucial gap in the English literature on literary and cultural theory. It includes two essays by Julia Kristeva available in English for the first time. It also includes an essay by Michel Foucault and a fascinating interview with Roland Barthes, both also available here in English for the first time. Two important essays by Philippe Sollers, a co-founder and editor of *Tel Quel*, also afford much-needed insight into this influential but often overlooked figure.

The Tel Quel Reader provides an indispensable resource for students of literary theory, cultural studies, philosophy and French studies. It will also be essential reading for students of art theory, visual studies and film and anyone studying poststructuralist theory today.

Patrick ffrench and **Roland-François Lack** are both Lecturers in French at University College London. Patrick ffrench is the author of *The Time of Theory: A History of Tel Quel 1960–83* (1995). Roland-François Lack is the author of *Poetics of the Pretext: Reading Lautréamont* (1997).

THE TEL QUEL
READER

*Edited by Patrick ffrench and
Roland-François Lack*

London and New York

First published 1998
by Routledge
11 New Fetter Lane, London EC4P 4EE

Simultaneously published in the USA and Canada
by Routledge
29 West 35th Street, New York, NY 10001

Typeset in Garamond by Routledge
Printed and bound in Great Britain by TJ International Ltd,
Padstow, Cornwall

British Library Cataloguing in Publication Data
A catalogue record for this book is available from the British Library

Library of Congress Cataloguing in Publication Data
The Tel Quel Reader/edited by Patrick ffrench and Roland-François
Lack.
Includes bibliographical references and index.
1. Tel quel. I. ffrench, Patrick. II. Lack, Roland-François.
PN5190.T44T45 1998
97–21264
840.9'9995 – dc21
CIP

ISBN 0–415–15713–7 (hbk)
ISBN 0–415–15714–5 (pbk)

CONTENTS

CONTENTS

PREFACE

All of the material from *Tel Quel* included in this volume, except Pleynet's 'Heavenly Glory' and the excerpt from Sollers's *Paradis*, is being published here in English for the first time.

A defining, if somewhat vexing, characteristic of *Tel Quel* writing is a tendency to cite material in the text without indicating a source. In these cases, where we have used an existing translation we have indicated the source, and where the translation is our own, we have not. Where the authors *have* given bibliographical references, we have tried to give the English translation where it exists, although it has not always been possible to use an existing translation for material cited in the text. Problems have arisen particularly where an author uses a French translation from, say, German that foregrounds terms not rendered in the existing English version. This is often the case with Freud, Marx and Lenin. We have adopted the convention of inserting translator's notes or other note material of our own in square brackets. Where titles are referred to in the text we have followed the rule of giving English titles for texts which have been translated, and French titles only for those which have not. Translator's notes relative to the meaning of specific words are given in square brackets either as endnotes or, occasionally, as single explanatory words within the body of the text.

ACKNOWLEDGEMENTS

Although we have made every effort to obtain permission for all of the texts included here, and to acknowledge such permission, in some cases this has not been possible.

We gratefully acknowledge the following for permission to publish translations of material from the French:

Editions du Seuil for *Tel Quel*, 'Division de l'ensemble', Jean-Joseph Goux, 'Marx et l'inscription du travail', Jean-Louis Baudry, 'Freud et la "création littéraire"', Marcelin Pleynet, 'Sade lisible' from *Tel Quel, Théorie d'ensemble* © Editions du Seuil 1968.

Editions du Seuil for Marcelin Pleynet, 'La "folie" thétique' from Marcelin Pleynet, *Art et littérature* © Editions du Seuil 1977.

Editions du Seuil for Roland Barthes, 'Réponses' from Roland Barthes, *Œuvres complètes* © Editions du Seuil 1995.

Editions Gallimard for Michel Foucault, 'Distance, Aspect, Origine' from Michel Foucault, *Dits et Ecrits* © Editions Gallimard 1994.

Guy Scarpetta for *Le corps américain* © Guy Scarpetta 1977.

Columbia University Press for Julia Kristeva, 'Le sujet en procès' and 'Pour une sémiologie des paragrammes' Copyright © 1968 and Copyright © 1976 by Columbia University Press.

We would also like to thank Catherine Grynszpan for permission to use a reproduction of a painting 'D'une peintre chromatique' by Marc Devade for the cover.

We are also grateful to Jacqueline Lesschaeve and Henry Nathan for permission to publish their translation of Marcelin Pleynet's 'La gloire du ciel',

'Heavenly Glory', from *Tel Quel*, 77 (Autumn 1978), and to Carl R. Lovitt for permission to publish his translation of an excerpt from Philippe Sollers's *Paradis*, which appeared in *Tel Quel*, 70 (Summer 1977) and in *TriQuarterly*, 38 (Winter 1977).

We would also like to thank Michael Temple and Vérène Grieshaber for their translations included in this volume.

INTRODUCTION

Patrick ffrench and Roland-François Lack

Literary journal, group, movement, ideology? *Tel Quel* is a protean name which has taken on all of these different modalities. At the material level, it is the name of a periodical published in Paris between 1960 and 1982, appearing four times a year and amassing a total of ninety-four issues. Its editorial committee had a volatile history, becoming stable only in the mid-seventies. The only constant name is that of Philippe Sollers, but the review is equally associated with Julia Kristeva, who became a member of the committee itself in 1970 but had been linked with the review for up to four years previously. Marcelin Pleynet, Denis Roche, Jean-Louis Baudry and Marc Devade were also members of the committee, Pleynet acting as editorial secretary for the review from 1962 until its demise.

The existence of the *Tel Quel* 'group' is less circumscribed, less institutional. If regular involvement in the numerous conferences, seminars and interventions that bear the name *Tel Quel* are signs of belonging, then the group certainly includes Roland Barthes, Guy Scarpetta, Jean-Joseph Goux, and novelists Pierre Guyotat, Maurice Roche, Severo Sarduy. Beyond these confines, *Tel Quel* is associated with a proliferation of star-names: Michel Foucault, Jacques Derrida, Luce Irigaray, René Girard. . . . For these, it is more a question of a discrete intervention, which needs to be addressed on its own terms, and in terms of the individual writer or theorist's work at the time. We look at the 'dissemination' of *Tel Quel*, its engagement with a wider intellectual community, in the last section of this book, though it is also signalled in our opening chronology.

As a movement or ideology, there is also a difficulty of identification, since *Tel Quel* is a phenomenon that, over a twenty-two year history, is often defined punctually in relation to the context of that moment. To identify and define what might be termed *telquelisme* is then either to fix on a particular historical movement, which is usually the 'moment of theory', around 1968, or to describe the quality of a strategy in relation to the context, to attempt to define a continuity running underneath historical contingency. *The Tel Quel Reader* addresses both concerns: by centring largely on texts from the period of *Théorie d'ensemble* (Group Theory), the tactically named

1

collective volume published in 1968 (whose preface is the first piece in our collection); and by including earlier and later texts that signal a development and continuity of strategy. As we propose below, this strategy is identifiable as a practice at the level of rhetoric: an analysis of the given – political, theoretical and literary – rhetoric of a time, and as a transgressive or even transcendent approach to this rhetoric.

The *Reader* is divided into three broad sections, titled 'Science', 'Literature' and 'Art', with a concluding section representing *Tel Quel*'s interaction with the authoritative names of the period. These subdivisions are neither arbitrary nor benign; they relate to a rhetorical practice active typographically on the front cover of each issue of the review, from the moment, around 1967, when it takes on a demarcated identity. In that year the subtitle 'Science/Littérature' is permanently appended. In 1970 it is expanded to read 'Littérature/Philosophie/Science/Politique', with 'Art' added in 1978–9: the final state of the subtitle reads 'Littérature/-Philosophie/Art/Science/Politique'. The order of the words in the subtitle was proposed as a reflection of a movement of causal determination, such that Politics would be the most punctual level on which reality is engaged with, widening out to literature as a discourse which envelops the other four. *Tel Quel*, in this schema, pays at least nominal respect to Marxism, postulating an economico-political level as prior to the superstructural. Our division adds to this paradigmatic narrative a syntagmatic, historical one, suggesting an evolution from a scientific or pseudo-scientific discourse on an object, Literature, a discourse which is subsequently undermined by this object and by its subjective dimensions, and displaced onto the wider and transcendent quality of Art. The division also reflects simpler generic differences: texts in 'Science' relate to the theorization of literature; texts in 'Literature' to *Tel Quel*'s own literary practice or to that of writers which it identifies as canonically important; 'Art' includes material on painting or on non-verbal artistic practices. These generic distinctions are nevertheless characterized by intersections and cross-currents: Kristeva's 'Subject in process' makes substantial appeal to psychoanalysis; Pleynet's '"Thetic" madness' is preceded by a text of poetry, showing how the poetic is considered within *Tel Quel* as carrying equal weight as a vehicle of speculation. The organization of the *Reader* thus serves multiple purposes: it proposes a narrative, it identifies different kinds of discourse at work in *Tel Quel*, and it mimics *Tel Quel*'s own rhetoric of self-justification.

Science

The 'moment' of *Tel Quel*, the period between, roughly, 1966 and 1975 when it was the vehicle of a theory and practice of the text, coincided with the rise and fall of 'science' as a discourse on literature or, more exactly, of science as a discourse emulated by literary theory. The evolution of the review up to this 'moment' shows a gradual displacement from a sense of literature *tel quel*, 'such as it is', through a notion of 'avant-garde' practice, gesturing then towards some form of 'scientific' analysis.

Science, or quasi-science, is a rhetorical move that distinguishes *Tel Quel*'s terroristic take on the materiality of literary practice, an effacement of the mystique of 'literature' and the ideology constructed around it. This scientificity is manifest not only as axiomatic, 'truth-telling' discourse on cultural production (in which respect it differs little from already existing models of cultural analysis): it has a form and a rhetoric of its own. It has immediate visible form in the typographical disposition on the page of numbered sections and subsections, as in Devade's 'theorem' text on chromatic painting, or Julia Kristeva's first article in the review, 'Towards a semiology of paragrams'. In such texts the systematicity of science dissolves the mystique of the object (literature or art), at the risk of installing a new mystique of science, visible in the quasi-mathematical formulae that constellate Kristeva's piece, performing the same typographical gesture as the Chinese characters which also begin to appear in *Tel Quel* from this year (1967). Rhetorically, since the Proper Name is also a marker of a certain kind of discourse, a sign as well as a reference, Kristeva's references to König, Gödel, Bourbaki, Boole in the 'Paragrams' piece, and, in the book Σημειωτική (*Séméiotiké*), to Cantor and Hilbert, also mark out a certain strategic scientificity.

Perhaps the crucial point here is not, however, to fix on this scientificity as characteristic of *Tel Quel*'s discourse, but to identify the strategy which informs the emulation of science. Identifying it as a rhetorical strategy enables us to view the long-term continuity of the movement in terms of a self-conscious play on a rhetorical level, based on a wish to displace the commonplaces of the moment. Science then becomes one aspect of this play.

Tel Quel's quasi-scientificity as rhetorical strategy also functions in relation to its appeal to what Foucault called 'initiatory' discursive practices, the discourses founded by Marx, Freud and Saussure. The moment of *Tel Quel* happily coincides and is often confused with the moment of a re-evaluation of these initiatory discourses, the attempt to erase their humanist, unscientific elements, to re-evaluate them, precisely, as science. *Tel Quel*'s appeal to Marx, to Freud and to Saussure, goes by way of the contemporary proponents of their scientificity – Althusser for Marx, Lacan for Freud, and, for all three, Barthes, Derrida and Kristeva, if in radically distinct ways.

The impression that these discourses of re-evaluation are fixated on personalities is to some degree a retrospective effect: from the broader range of authoritative discourses engaged with by *Tel Quel*, those marked by the names Marx, Freud and Saussure, and relayed by Althusser, Lacan and Derrida, address us now as authoritative still. By insistently reciting these star-names – and also by more proactive means[1] – *Tel Quel* itself became an authoritative relay of discourse, though the 'science' of some other names (such as Joseph Needham, Linnart Mäll and even V.I. Lenin[2]) is, retrospectively, not so authoritative now.

The fixation on personality is also an effect of the time, a quality of the French intellectual context wherein 'master-discourses' are, precisely, those of a master. It is an effect of incarnation, word become flesh, where the word is strategic and, in some sense, 'revolutionary'. For example, Lacan's physical presence in the Seminars is both that of a body in which the master-discourse is incarnated, and that of a strategist, intervening in but necessarily above and beyond the discourse of which he is the master. Reading the Seminar today, our Derridean unease faced with the transcript of a Logos is not the unfortunate effect of an unavoidable contingency, but the trace of that peculiarly authoritative activism that defines the moment of Althusser, Lacan and Derrida. The Ur-text of this trope – written discourse as the trace of an activist performance – is Saussure's *Course in General Linguistics*, the master's Logos reconstructed from disciples' notes; the figure persists when we note that even today a large part of Derrida's textual output is 'merely' the written trace of a masterly performance; and it is ever-present in *Tel Quel*, where so many texts originate in personality-dominated, performative spaces (the 'Group for Theoretical Studies', the many conferences, seminars, discussion groups and dialogues).

The apparent 'corruption' of pure science by personality, here, is mirrored in *Tel Quel*'s discourse by the reconstruction of science as critique. Given that science, from the first, is a function of a rhetorical strategy, the dangers of empiricism, a purely descriptive discourse, are to be avoided. Reconstrued as critique, science – or theory, as it will be called – is also a critique of science. Kristeva's 'Semiotics: A Critical Science and/or a Critique of Science'[3] identifies the 'initiatory' discourses of Marx (with Althusser), Freud (with Lacan) and Saussure (with Derrida and herself) as discourses which initiate an epistemological break with the past and construct themselves through this critique; a rhetorical strategy *the same as* Joyce's enveloping of multiple languages within his writing, or Lautréamont's 'plagiarisms' in the *Poésies*.[4] Recurring in Goux's article on Marx's critique of economics, in Baudry's article on Freud's critique of psychology, and sustained throughout *Tel Quel* by an appeal to a Derridean theory and practice of the text, it is this analogy, this *as*, which is the most problematic aspect of the strategy. If the appeal to science is rhetorical, it is a point of anchorage, a juncture, which must be at the same time fixed and moveable. The relation to literature begins to seem grounded in more than analogy.

Literature

When science becomes, by such means, rhetorical, it shares the ground of literature. The literature that provides science with analogies can itself be construed as scientific (the systematicity of Joyce; Lautréamont's advocacy of a *science nouvelle*) but the significant affect is in the other direction: science becomes undermined by its object. This is happening when, in the theoretical discourse of *Tel Quel*, the twin dimensions of the subjective and the political come increasingly into play. It happens in the writing practice of *Tel Quel* authors when, for example, the typographic marks of scientificity are joined by other textual markers characterized by a kind of irreducibility, affect or excess. From *Nombres* to *Lois* to *H*, the textual space of Sollers's writing becomes organized as much by Chinese ideograms and exclamation marks as by number and sequence, before finally attaining unpunctuated seamlessness; into Pleynet's poetry come Mallarméan spatial dispositions and press cuttings; in Maurice Roche's explosively visual textualizations, from *Compact* through *Circus* to *Codex*, the space of the scientific equation or diagram is invaded by figures and drawings, turning these 'scientific' forms into features of a different, figural space.

Tel Quel is at one and the same time a journal of science *and* literature, of theory and of creative writing. The radical textual practices of Sollers, Pleynet and Roche are an intrinsic part of *Tel Quel*'s theoretical project,[5] both as journal and as series. In the 'Collection *Tel Quel*' (the eighty or so books published under the journal's imprint), no distinction of format or rubric is made between volumes of *écriture* and volumes of theory. Nor is any separation made in the journal: the list of contents gives no clue that Sollers's 'Un pas sur la lune' (A Step on the Moon) (issue 45) is a reading of Derrida, that Denis Roche's 'La poésie est inadmissible' (Poetry is Inadmissible) is a poem, or that Pleynet's 'La matière pense' (Matter Thinks) begins as a critical reading of Artaud to 'degenerate' into poetic fragments.

Our sense of *Tel Quel* as a journal of 'creative writing' is reinforced by the publication, alongside such material by the *Tel Quel* writers, of many literary 'greats'. The roll-call of 'collaborators' is impressive: Antonin Artaud, John Ashbery, Georges Bataille, Jorge Luis Borges, Joseph Brodsky, William Burroughs, Michel Butor, Roger Caillois, T.S. Eliot, Paul Eluard, Jean Genet, Allen Ginsberg, Jean-Luc Godard, Juan Goytisolo, Günter Grass, Hervé Guibert, Pierre Guyotat, Martin Heidegger, Eugene Ionesco, James Joyce, Pierre Klossowski, Lu Hsun, Henri Michaux, Charles Olson, Francis Ponge, Ezra Pound, Alain Robbe-Grillet, Philip Roth, Nathalie Sarraute, Claude Simon, Paul Valéry, Virginia Woolf. . . . How some of these names come to feature in the pages of *Tel Quel* is self-evident. The translation of foreign authors is a conventional function of the literary review, and is characteristic of *Tel Quel* throughout its existence, from Woolf in *Tel Quel* 1 to Joyce in *Tel Quel* 83. The participation of authors from outside an apparent group identity is also common, especially at times when that group identity is less categorically determined: in this respect *Tel Quel* was more receptive towards the beginning and end of its itinerary, publishing Robbe-Grillet in issue 4, for example, and Guibert in issue 94. (On the other hand, Godard's appearance in issue 52 may be read as specifically a function of the group's developing Maoist identity.) And it is a definitive function of a literary review to make available previously unpublished texts by 'great' authors, alive or dead, whatever the intrinsic significance of the texts themselves. The display of names like Artaud, Bataille, Dante, Genet, Joyce, Ponge, Pound and Sade in *Tel Quel* – through special issues or isolated texts by them – was used to declare polemical affinities, and it is clear that from a certain moment such names independently constitute a canon which can be identified as specific to *Tel Quel*, specifying *Tel Quel*'s independence both through theory (in theoretical readings of such authors) *and* practice.

The emergence of this canon is initially articulated with the moment of science in *Tel Quel*, such that the 'limit-texts' identified by Sollers – Dante, Sade, Mallarmé, Lautréamont, Artaud and Bataille[6] – are arranged to each side of the 'epistemological break', with Mallarmé and Lautréamont identified as contemporaries of Marx, Freud and Saussure, participating in the same historical shift. But the historical map projected backwards as a function of *Tel Quel*'s reference to Althusserian epistemology becomes redundant when this reference is dropped in favour of a more heterogeneous – if more interventionist – form of Marxism (i.e., Maoism), and as science is undermined by its object. At the same time, Sollers's proposal of a 'monumental' history, or canon, allows the mutation of this historically defined canon into one justified by an emphasis on the subjective, and on the writer as exceptional subject, as 'monument'. An enlarged canon then comes into place: Joyce and Céline are signalled as primary objects of analysis and celebration, a colloquium in 1972 highlights Artaud and Bataille as subjects of excess, and Kristeva's *Revolution in Poetic Language* (1974) consecrates Lautréamont and Mallarmé as proponents of a radical shift in knowledge. Eventually, this movement of expansion leads to the dissolution of the canon, as the evolution of *Tel Quel*'s political strategy and of its version of psychoanalysis carries it towards dissidence. The canon is exploded, implying a vision of radical literature so wide and at the same time so specific as to include Dostoevsky, Ionesco, Phillip Roth and (in the final issue) André Malraux.

The answer to the question 'Why literature?' changes according to the different versions of canonicity promoted by or ascribable to *Tel Quel*: firstly, because it is the vehicle of an epistemological radicality reflected in social and philosophical change, and of a rhetorical analysis of it which engages the participation of the reader; secondly, because it is the vehicle of a subjective excess which incarnates political and cultural revolution; and thirdly, because it is dissident with regard to any system, exceptional with regard to any rule.

Art

In the articulation of Science and Literature, and whichever of the two is foregrounded, the privileged regime is writing, *écriture*. Through Saussurean linguistics it is the object of an authoritative founding discourse; through Derridean grammatology it is an instrument of radical, activist critique. The 'high' grammatological phase of *Tel Quel*'s activity can be traced very simply in the proliferation of references to *Writing and Difference* and *Of Grammatology*, serving as the key to innumerable 'scientific' constructions. By 1973 the reference to Derrida has diminished, along with the instrumental prestige of writing. *Tel Quel* has gone, in the words of a 1976 photo-text piece by Denis Roche, 'beyond the writing principle'.[7] As the exceptional subject emerges, the importance of writing wanes in favour of a different formulation. The opposition between speech or voice and writing is displaced: writing may operate within another opposition, articulated with the body as in Scarpetta's piece (translated below), but the emergent exceptional subject demands that the whole question be rearticulated as the relation of the phenomenal to the transcendent. This shift is contemporary with the dissolution of the canon and the widening of the field of inquiry marked by *Tel Quel* 71/73, where an aerial photograph of the globe introduces a 'United States' special issue dominated by considerations of non-verbal arts (theatre, performance, music, painting, film). While 'Science' and 'Literature' (Saussure and Mallarmé) grounded the articulation of speech and writing, enabling the subsumption of science and literature in *écriture*, the ground upon which the phenomenal and the transcendent are articulated are these non-verbal practices, eventually to be signalled on the cover of *Tel Quel* by one word: 'Art'.

This is a new regime, and if at times, speaking of presence and absence, it mimics the dialectics of grammatology, the dynamic is different. It is symptomatic of late *Tel Quel* that the American issue proliferates in images; however, in a regime where writing is displaced but where theory survives, such images do not function in relation to theory as the equivalent of text. In a curiously archaic, even redundant way, these images 'speak for themselves'. In fact their presence itself is redundant, except insofar as it signifies transcendence, or irreducibility.

The trace of 'Art' in *Tel Quel* does not figure a kind of practice where theory can merge with its object, as in *écriture*; Denis Roche's photo-text piece is explicitly about the object's boundaries. But even for a journal of writing as practice, this does not imply an impasse, where there would be no further possibility for writing, or no further subject to write about. Two covers of *Tel Quel*, issue 59 in autumn 1974 and issue 67 two years later, dramatize the negotiation of this shift. Both figure writing: on the first, an 'In China' special issue, Chinese characters no longer constellate the text and blank spaces of an *écriture* (*à la* Pound or Sollers), they trace the graphic handwritten flourish of a poem by Mao, an exceptional subject on the verge of transcendence; on the second (the issue featuring Roche's 'Au-delà du principe d'écriture'), a Talmudic image of a seven-branched Menorah – composed entirely from Hebrew characters – signifies the creative labour of a fully transcendent subject, God. Writing takes transcendence as its object, whence the presence of 'God' in the journal from issue 65 onwards, or it persists as undifferentiated infinity (in Sollers's *Paradis*, serialized from *Tel Quel*, 57 [1974], onwards). In *Paradis*, supported by the images reproduced alongside but not 'within' it, writing becomes a totalizing, irreducible block or a sacred body, a sign of the impossibility of meaning, and therefore of transcendence.

This narrative of *Tel Quel* as a writing-practice, leading from Science, through Literature, to end in Art, is in fact a movement towards *l'infini*, the title of the journal in which *Tel Quel* was reborn. It is a movement away from the 'moment' of *Tel Quel* that is the principal object of this reader. The texts from *Tel Quel* that follow date from 1967 to 1976, ten years of the journal's twenty-two year existence. They are selected to present a case for the enduring value of the review's enterprise, an enterprise which we have to some degree explicated here but which, in the final test, demands that they be read for themselves.

Notes

1 By publishing Saussure (his texts on the 'Anagrams') and Derrida.
2 Joseph Needham, authority on Chinese Science, is appealed to in articles by Sollers and Kristeva from 1967, and contributes an article (translated) to the special issue on China in 1972 (48/49). The linguist Linnart Mäll is cited respectfully by Kristeva in her 'Paragrams' piece, and he later publishes in *Tel Quel* an article that returns the compliment, citing the 'Paragrams' piece approvingly. For reference to Lenin see, below, Kristeva's 'The subject in process', Sollers's 'The Bataille act', Devade's 'Chromatic painting', etc.
3 See Kristeva, 'Semiotics: A Critical Science and/or a Critique of Science', in T. Moi (ed.), *The Kristeva Reader* (Oxford, Blackwell, 1986).
4 See also 'Towards a semiology of paragrams', below.
5 Such texts inevitably pose great, perhaps insurmountable, problems for the translator. It is no accident if they are represented here only by a page from Sollers's *Paradis*, translated by Carl R. Lovitt, and Pleynet's poem 'Heavenly Glory', translated by Jacqueline Lesschaeve and Henry Nathan, both published in the journal itself. Similar experiments in publishing translations of *Tel Quel* authors in the review itself are rare.
6 The subjects of the essays in *Writing and the Experience of Limits*, trans. L.S. Roudiez (New York, Columbia University Press, 1983); the book *Logiques* (Paris, Seuil, 1968) spans a slightly larger canon which includes Ponge, Roussel and Joyce.
7 'Au-delà du principe d'écriture', *Tel Quel*, 57 (1974).

CHRONOLOGICAL HISTORY
OF *TEL QUEL*

1957–9

The first committee of the review, established around the principal figures Philippe Sollers, Jean-Edern Hallier and Jean-René Huguenin, is formed. In 1957 Sollers's first text, the short story 'Le défi', is published by the left-wing Catholic publisher Seuil, and praised by François Mauriac, the prestigious Catholic novelist and critic. In 1958 Sollers's first novel, *A Curious Solitude*, is published, and is praised by Mauriac and Louis Aragon, principal literary figure of the PCF (French Communist Party).

1960

The review *Tel Quel* is officially formed, and the first issue published. It includes an opening 'Déclaration', affirming 'literary quality' and the determination to 'place poetry at the highest point of the mind'. The title 'Tel Quel' echoes that of a book by Paul Valéry, who is cited in the 'Déclaration', but an epigraph, from Nietzsche, asserts a will to 'affirm this world such as it is' ('tel quel'). In the same issue Sollers's 'Sept propositions sur Robbe-Grillet' appear, and the review allies itself with the *nouveau roman* at this early point, publishing work by Claude Simon and Robert Pinget. There are also publications by Francis Ponge and Antonin Artaud, marking a will to affirm poetic language. At the end of the year Jean-René Huguenin and his colleague Renaud Matignon leave the committee, after disagreements over the direction of the review. Sollers and Hallier meet Georges Bataille, who gives them a series of lectures from 1950 to publish. There are contacts with André Breton and Louis-Ferdinand Céline.

1961

The review begins to show a distinct orientation towards the avant-garde, in literature and criticism, at the expense of the initial affirmation of 'literary quality'. Publications in the review include texts by Ponge, Bataille, Artaud, Robbe-Grillet, Pound, Hölderlin and Borges. Barthes publishes his first text in the review, 'Littérature aujourd'hui', in which he criticizes the review's pretension to affirm 'literature such as it is'. Sollers's second novel, *The Park*, shows an orientation towards the *nouveau roman*, but with decisive differences. Marcelin Pleynet approaches *Tel Quel* after Sollers reviews his poetry favourably. The novelist and dramatist Jean Thibaudeau joins the committee.

1962

The review begins to publish new poetry of an experimental nature, by Marcelin Pleynet and Denis Roche, as well as work by Michaux and Ponge. Pleynet's first text, *Provisoires amants de nègres*, is published. The review continues its association with Georges Bataille, publishing an excerpt from *The Tears of Eros*. An interest in James Joyce is shown with a long text by Umberto Eco, later to form part of *The Open Work*. The poet and philosopher Michel Deguy and the *nouveau romancier* Jean Ricardou join the committee. At the end of the year Jean-Edern Hallier is excluded from the committee after attempting to gain complete control. The 'Collection *Tel Quel*' at Seuil is begun with Denis Roche's poetry collection *Récits complets*. There are contacts between Derrida and Sollers. Death of Bataille.

1963

Poetic language continues to be affirmed in the review with publications by Pleynet, and a translation of Charles Olson's 'Projective Verse'. The review's orientation towards the avant-garde across the arts is shown with a text by Pierre Boulez. Robbe-Grillet is interviewed in 'Littérature aujourd'hui', while criticism of the *nouveau roman* begins to emerge in Sollers's review of Foucault's book on Roussel, and Sollers's essay 'Logique de la fiction'. Foucault publishes 'Language to Infinity' in the review, which compares its textuality with the writing of Blanchot. The committee is substantially reformed when Pleynet, Denis Roche, Jean-Pierre Faye and Jean-Louis Baudry join, with Pleynet as editorial secretary. Michel Deguy leaves the review. Michel Foucault chairs a *Tel Quel* conference at Cérisy on 'Une littérature nouvelle?', with debates on the novel and poetry, and writes an article in *Critique* which analyses the novels of Sollers, Thibaudeau, Baudry and Faye, and the poetry of Pleynet, distinguishing them from the *nouveau roman* and identifying their radical difference. Sollers, Barthes and Foucault contribute articles to a special issue of *Critique* on Bataille, alongside Leiris, Klossowski and Blanchot.

1964

The review allies itself with the Italian neo-avant-garde with publications by the poet and novelist Eduardo Sanguineti. Barthes's text 'Literature and Signification' is published in the review. Pleynet writes two important articles on poetic language, 'La pensée contraire' and 'L'image du sens', which identify the need for an analytic approach to the notion of the avant-garde. Sollers writes a critical review of Robbe-Grillet's *Pour un Nouveau Roman*.

1965

A special issue on Artaud includes Derrida's first article in the review, 'La parole soufflée'; Sollers's essays on Artaud and on Dante begin to establish a form of criticism which identifies a canon of 'limit-texts' and begins to define a theory of literature specific to the review. Sollers's third novel, *Drame*, shows a definitive departure from the *nouveau roman* and the establishment of a textuality specific to the review. Barthes writes an important essay on *Drame* in the journal *Critique*. Pleynet's *Comme* also develops a specific practice of poetic language. Todorov's collection, *Théorie de la littérature*, of texts by the Russian Formalists associates the review with literary formalism and affirms its place at the forefront of critical innovation. Julia Kristeva arrives in Paris and attends Barthes's seminar. Sollers and Baudry attend Lacan's seminar. Sollers meets Lacan.

1966

In 'Problèmes de l'avant-garde' Pleynet refers to Barthes, Lacan and Derrida as allies in an analytic approach to the limits of literature and language, criticizing the notion of the avant-garde. Derrida publishes 'Freud and the Scene of Writing' in an issue devoted to psychoanalysis and linguistics. Sollers's essay 'Literature and Totality', given as a paper at Barthes's seminar at the *Ecole Pratique des Hautes Etudes*, identifies Mallarmé as a powerful precursor of a theory of radical textuality. The 'Collection *Tel Quel*' publishes formally innovative novels by Maurice Roche, and critical works by Barthes and Genette. Pleynet's book *Lautréamont* is critical of Bachelard and Blanchot's approach to this writer, and identifies Lautréamont/Ducasse's texts as a crucial destruction of the edifice of 'literature', via an 'underwriting' (*souscription*) of the laws of rhetoric. An important conference on Sade is organized by the review, with contributions by Barthes, Klossowski, Sollers, Hubert Damisch and psychoanalyst Michel Tort. The 'Lacano-Althusserian' review *Cahiers pour l'analyse* is launched, publishing Althusser, Lacan and Derrida and constituting a vital reference (for a time) for *Tel Quel*.

1967

Sollers's article 'The Roof', on Bataille, links a theory of textuality to a critique of society and culture of Marxist dimensions. Kristeva's first article, 'Towards a semiology of paragrams,' is published, crucial in outlining a theory of intertextuality and the notion of a paragrammatic text running underneath the surface of the text as phenomenon. Sollers writes 'Programme', a radical platform for textual, theoretical and ideological revolution. Derrida's *Writing and Difference* is published in the 'Collection *Tel Quel*'. Sollers's 'Lautréamont's Science' completes the series of essays on 'limit-texts' which will make up *Logiques* [*Writing and the Experience of Limits*]. The review engages in dialogues with the PCF review *La Nouvelle critique*. There are contacts with PCF writers Daix, Houdebine, Scarpetta, Henric. A split in the committee emerges at the end of the year: Jean-Pierre Faye leaves; Jacqueline Risset and Pierre Rottenberg join. The subtitle 'Science/Littérature' is permanently appended.

1968

Derrida's 'Plato's Pharmacy', published in the review, associates its radical textuality with an ideological critique of Western logocentrism. Baudry's 'Freud and "Literary Creation" ' is critical of Freud's phantasmatic approach to literature. Kristeva's 'Distance et anti-représentation' identifies non-Western traditions as powerful references for a non-representative textuality. Sollers's 'critical machine' *Logiques* and the novel *Nombres* are published, the latter breaking new ground in the use of structural motifs of generation (the square) and the introduction of Chinese characters. The review, in the midst of dialogue with the PCF, supports its policy on May 1968, that it is a petty-bourgeois revolt. The Group for Theoretical Studies is created, a forum for the presentation of work; Sollers, Kristeva, Derrida, Jean-Joseph Goux and others contribute. A conference at Cluny with *La Nouvelle critique* links the review's theory and practice of the text to Marx's critique of the economy and the Marxist conception of ideology, with reference to the work of Althusser.

1969

The review continues to affirm innovative writing, with publications by Pierre Guyotat, Jean Genet and William Burroughs. Sollers's 'Survol/rapports (blocs)/conflits' sketches out an ideological strategy and resumes the review's theory and practice of the text. Starobinski's 'The Text in the Text', in the review, analyses Saussure's 'Anagrams', which are a crucial reference for Kristeva. Kristeva publishes a long essay on Sollers's novel *Nombres*, 'L'engendrement de la formule', in which the notions of geno-text and pheno-text are introduced. Kristeva's *Séméiotiké* is published in the 'Collection *Tel Quel*', collecting her articles from 1967; it will become a permanent theoretical reference for the review. *Théorie d'ensemble*, a compendium of theoretical essays produced in and around the review, is published, featuring earlier essays by Foucault, Barthes and Derrida, and the Marxist-oriented work of 1967. The review is the site of a polemic with Jean-Pierre Faye over his letter in the PCF newspaper *L'Humanité* accusing Derrida of complicity with Heidegger's alleged complicity with Nazism. Sollers and Kristeva occupy the office of Robert Flacelière, Director of the *Ecole Normale Supérieure*, when Lacan's seminar at the ENS is suspended. The reviews *TXT* and *Cinéthique* are created, in the wake of *Tel Quel*. *Cahiers pour l'analyse* folds and some of its members join the militant *Gauche prolétarienne*.

1970

Translations of Mao Tse-tung in the review show a movement towards Maoism. Derrida's 'The Double Session', at the Group for Theoretical Studies, continues the critique of logocentric, idealist philosophy in the review. Sollers's 'Lénine et le matérialisme philosophique' establishes dialectical materialism as a crucial philosophical reference for the review, but again suggests a movement towards Maoism. Pleynet's *Painting and System* in the 'Collection' is a powerful critique of an idealist conception of painting, focusing on Cézanne and Matisse as proponents of a materialist practice. Kristeva joins the committee, as does the painter Marc Devade, associated with the materialist, 'Derridean' painting group 'Support/Surfaces'. The review *Peinture, cahiers théoriques* is created by artists of the Supports/Surfaces group, and is closely associated with *Tel Quel*. Polemics arise with Jean-Pierre Faye's new review *Change* over accusations of early right-wing tendencies in *Tel Quel*. Serge Leclaire's Department of Psychoanalysis at Vincennes is criticized in *Tel Quel*. The words 'Philosophie/Politique' are added to the subtitle. Guyotat's *Eden, Eden, Eden* is banned, resulting in a polemic over its censure and a petition circulated and published in *Tel Quel*. At the second Cluny colloquium, 'Littérature et idéologie', Kristeva and Derrida are criticized by members of *Change* and *Action poétique*, and the alliance with the PCF becomes strained. The review *Poétique* is founded by Todorov, Cixous, Richard and Genette, ostensibly as a review of formalist and structuralist criticism, a role long since abandoned by *Tel Quel*. The *Nouvelle revue de psychanalyse* is created.

1971

A special issue on Surrealism analyses and criticizes its psychoanalytic theories and condemns its reference to occultism. A special issue on Barthes, the first of its kind, links his work to *Tel Quel*'s political and ideological radicality. Sollers's 'Sur la Contradiction', a reading of Mao's essay of the same name, solidifies the review's reference to Maoist Marxism. Pleynet's 'Lautréamont politique' engages in a debate about the political use-value of Lautréamont/Ducasse. Sollers's *Lois* shows a less structurally austere, more parodic and violent form of writing, closer to Rabelais, Joyce and Céline than to Blanchot. *Tel Quel* signs a manifesto with the film reviews *Cinéthique* and *Cahiers du cinéma* against the review *Positif*, but criticizes *Cinéthique* for its criticism of the PCF. The Maoist splinter group the 'The June 1971 Movement' is created and 'occupies' the offices of *Tel Quel*. *La Nouvelle critique* publishes a note criticizing the review for its addition of the 'Philosophie/Politique' subtitle and Pleynet's critique of Aragon. *Tel Quel* replies, defending its position. Sollers publishes a letter in *Le Monde* protesting against the interdiction of Maria-Antonietta Macciocchi's *De la Chine* at the Communist *L'Humanité* Festival. Sollers intervenes at the festival. The November issue announces the formal break with PCF, the review is declared in crisis and the Group for Theoretical Studies is suspended. The crisis is resolved when Thibaudeau and Ricardou leave the committee, leaving the Maoist core in control. Sollers and Cuban novelist Severo Sarduy translate the latter's novel *Cobra* into French, a parodic and heterogeneous novel which marks a different orientation in the review's textual practice.

1972

A special issue on 'La pensée chinoise' annexes *Tel Quel*'s materialist, antirepresentative textual practice to Chinese philosophy and the Chinese language. Denis Roche publishes his 'destruction of poetry' *Le mécrit*. Derrida's *Dissemination* is published in the 'Collection *Tel Quel*', but Derrida marks out his will to distance himself from the review, after interviews with *Tel Quel* associates Houdebine and Scarpetta, who press him on the question of Marxism. The Althusserian notion of ideology is criticized in a polemical interchange in the review between Bernard Sichère and Marie-Claire Boons (of the group 'Yenan'). A conference on Artaud and Bataille, organized by the review, links these writers to the Maoist politics of the review, but also constitutes a powerful analysis of their work. The review *Art Press* is launched, which will be closely associated with *Tel Quel*. *Tel Quel* is critical, in editorials, of the alliance between the PCF and the PS (Parti socialiste).

14

1973

Special issues on Artaud and Bataille publish the papers of the 1972 confer-ence. In her article on Artaud, Kristeva develops the notion of the 'subject in process', and shows a decisive orientation towards psychoanalysis. A special issue on Joyce brings him out as a proponent of a plural and heterogeneous, materialist textuality. Sollers's unpunctuated novel *H* is essentially a fore-runner of *Paradis*. Barthes's *The Pleasure of the Text*, in the 'Collection', enlarges the scope of *Tel Quel* textuality to a more 'corporeal' register. Denis Roche leaves the committee. Kristeva lectures in the USA. The review condemns the fascist coup in Chile and PCF–PS alliance in France. Sollers, Kristeva and Pleynet participate in a conference on 'Psychoanalysis and Politics' in Milan, organized by psychoanalyst-entrepreneur Armando Verdiglione.

1974

The first instalment of *Paradis* marks the beginning of the serial publication in the review of Sollers's unpunctuated epic, parodically treating society, politics, ideology, sexuality, literature and theology. A special issue on China focuses on its political status. Sollers's *Sur le matérialisme* and Kristeva's *Revolution of Poetic Language* are published, two extensive texts which repre-sent the review's theory or philosophy in the early seventies. Marxism is investigated further in Macciocchi's *Pour Gramsci*, and an initial link to the feminist movement (particularly to the group 'Psych et Po' and the Editions des Femmes) is made with Kristeva's *About Chinese Women*. The alliance will not last long. Editorials criticize Derrida and Althusser for proposing philosophies of idealism. In April and May, Sollers, Kristeva, Pleynet, Barthes and François Wahl visit China, invited there by the Embassy. On their return letters in *Le Monde* by Barthes and Wahl criticize or remain silent on the political situation in China. Sollers affirms the philosophical 'Criticize Confucius' campaign in China.

1975

Marxism is criticized for its overly systematic, economic basis, and the review focuses more and more on forces of excess and violence, articulated in the review as a 'radical evil' which entails a consideration of theology, of sexuality and of obscenity, for example in the writings of Sade or Guyotat.

1976

Editorials and texts identify a 'crisis of rationalism', as feminism, movements of youth revolt, random violence and fascism proliferate. The review adopts a strategy of 'analysis' of this excess, which links it to Lacan's ideas. A critique of Marxism as repressing the forces of violent excess which constitute the social link is suggested and developed. In discussions with Maurice Clavel, Sollers shows his disillusionment with Marxism and with the 'tragedy' in China. Sollers makes his first trip to USA, and meets de Kooning. By now Kristeva has begun practising psychoanalysis.

1977

A special issue on the USA affirms the heterogeneous and plural forms of artistic practice in the States, and recognizes the less institutional, but also less radical, situation of intellectuals and artists. Barthes's *A Lover's Discourse: Fragments*, in the 'Collection', shows an apparent shift on Barthes's part to less ideological concerns. Macciocchi's *Après Marx, Avril* analyses the revolt of the Italian Movement.

1978

A special issue on 'Recherches féminines' interrupts the serial publication of Sollers's *Paradis* and, with articles by Kristeva and others, affirms woman's position as dissident. A special issue on dissidence, collecting papers from a conference organized by Armando Verdiglione, establishes dissidence as a key term for the review: dissidence with regard to theory, ideology, institution. Literature is seen as essentially dissident with regard to any system.

1979

Publications by René Girard, Philippe Muray, Shoshana Felman and Sollers show *Tel Quel*'s intention to analyse religion, sexuality and psychoanalysis in relation to literature. The subtitle 'Art' is added to the list.

1980

Barthes's last text, 'Deliberation', on diary writing, is published in the review. Sollers's 'Socrate en passant', 'Le Pape' and 'On n'a encore rien vu' offer playful, vocal deliberations on a number of different subjects. Another special issue on Joyce establishes that writer as the principal focus of this period. Kristeva's *Powers of Horror* establishes a psychoanalytic reading of abjection, particularly focused on Céline, which is closely articulated with the work of Sollers and others, and identifies Céline as a principal area of interest. Pleynet's *Voyage en Chine*, a long awaited account of the 1974 trip, recounts it on a personal level, showing how the subjectivity of the writer has now become more important than ideological considerations. Death of Roland Barthes. Sollers welcomes Lacan's dissolution of the *Ecole Freudienne de Paris*. Sollers, Jean-Marie Benoist and Bernard Henri-Lévy, in *Tel Quel*, criticize the 'hegemony of philosophy' centred on *Critique*. Louis Althusser strangles his wife at the *Ecole Normale Supérieure* and is committed without a trial. Papal visit to France.

1981

In 'Le GSI', 'Pourquoi j'ai été chinois' and 'Histoire de femme' Sollers continues his critique of the intellectual 'spectacle', affirming the importance of theology and focusing specifically on the issue of sexuality. Sollers's novel *Paradis* is published by Seuil, collecting the numerous excerpts published in the review. Sollers will give virtuoso readings from the text. Pleynet's collection of poems *Rime*, is published, abandoning the structure of *Stanze* and adopting an aggressive, fragmented style. Philippe Muray's *Céline* is published in the 'Collection *Tel Quel*'. Death of Jacques Lacan.

1982

Sollers's articles 'Je sais pourquoi je viens' and 'L'Assomption' continue to develop the vision of previous texts, arguing for a view of sexuality as determined by language and a reading of theological texts as materialist critiques of the phenomenal world. Special issues on Picasso, psychoanalysis. Publication of a text by Malraux. Barthes's posthumous *The Responsibility of Forms* is the last text to be published in the 'Collection *Tel Quel*'. Final issue of the review. Sollers's novel *Women*, which shifts to a heterogeneous, conversational narrative style and contains thinly veiled parodic portraits of Barthes, Lacan and Althusser, is published by Gallimard. *Tel Quel* shifts publisher to Denoë and changes name to *L'Infini*. In 1983 the first issue of *L'Infini* begins with an affirmation of the continuity with *Tel Quel*, but not with its myth, and states the intention to 'rewrite the history of the twentieth century'.

Part I

SCIENCE

1

DIVISION OF THE ASSEMBLY[1]

Tel Quel

Nothing is easier than overtaking, purely, through abstraction, the certainties of the future, which only arise from the sluggishness in conception of the mass.

(Mallarmé)

Ideas are not transformed in language such that their particularity is dissolved or their social character appears beside them in language, like prices on merchandise. Ideas do not exist separately from language.

(Marx)

Perhaps it is too early, although already possible, to precisely date the efficiency and the force with which a general theoretical thrust has become evident around a certain number of decisive concepts, reexamined, echoed or constructed over the last few years. *Writing, text, unconscious, history, work, trace, production, scene*: none of these intersection-words is in itself a theoretical novelty, since what is at stake, in the way in which they will henceforward intervene in specific areas of our research, is not a series of inventions destined to be added to the market of knowledge, but a specific constellation playing a role both of delimitation and of transformation. A while ago it was possible for there to appear a book titled *Theory of Literature*,[2] which, in recalling the experience of a 'formalism', linked to the birth of 'structuralism', suggested after the event the site of a radical break in the approach to the so-called 'literary' text. The three words in quotation marks just read have since been singularly displaced by those in italics above. But one should not conclude that an 'overcoming' of the literal, of the formal, or the structural is now in course, through a simple mutation. More profoundly, it seems, to mark out an operation also verifiable in the history of science, that *a fundamental reorganization always occurs, not in the movement which immediately precedes the revolution, but in the movement which precedes this movement*. It is thus that, to specify the historical dimension of

21

what is 'happening' now, we have to go back beyond effects situated in the 1920s and 1930s (surrealism, formalism, the development of structural linguistics) in order to more correctly situate a more radical break inscribed at the end of the last century (Lautréamont, Mallarmé, Marx, Freud). This initial principle is pertinent if we want to realize – without effacing them – the areas in relation to which this volume [*Théorie d'ensemble*] acquires its active function and the divisions which make those areas exist as a heterogeneous whole, and intended as such. Only then can the new movement which disturbs and puts back into play both the movement and the *après-coup* that follows it be understood. Only then can be calculated and foreseen which movement this new movement will itself precede.[3]

This book, then, is an organization of reminders and appeals to the other side of a closure, a circle of which the circumference will have appeared a hundred or so years ago, and 'the other side' only recently. One had to avoid both the metaphysical trap of reunification and synthesis (falling back inside the closure) and the ignorance of the structural *après-coup* which only displaces the circle (whence the necessity of interrogating the foundations of several methods arising out of this displacement, the ideology of linguistics, for example). These are the lines of force of a work of assembly which has been operating, as far as *Tel Quel* is concerned, from 1963 (date of the Cérisy conference, see issue 17) to 1968 (date of the Cluny conference, see *La Nouvelle critique*, Nov. 1968), The names of Foucault, Barthes and Derrida suffice to underline this temporal shift. Those of Lacan and Althusser will be found, positioned as *levers*, within the various studies.

Consequently, what is at stake is:

– *to recognize a specific milieu* in which the signifying practice called, within the closure, 'poetry' or 'fiction', and which explicitly includes its own reflection, is active. This is what Foucault recognized very quickly in the figure of the *network* (outside the library) producing the emergence, in the distance, of the 'interior folds of language', a 'volume in perpetual disinsertion', an 'arrowshot' whose effects of isomorphism constitute a space and a limit relating to a topology of the fictive, defined by Foucault as 'the verbal nervure of what does not exist, such as it is'.[4] WRITING IN ITS PRODUCTIVE FUNCTIONING IS NOT REPRESENTATION;

– *to regulate an analysis* of which the example is given by Barthes in an inaugural text,[5] as concerns the approach to the practice of new writings of the network, their consequences of decentring not only in relation to the 'subject' but also, and perhaps especially, to history: 'History itself is less and less conceived as a monolithic series of determinations; we know, more and more, that it is, just as is language, a play of structures, whose respective interdependence can be pushed far further than one had thought; History is also a writing.' . . . 'What is at stake is to increase the rupture of the symbolic system in which the modern West has lived and will continue to live . . . to decentre it, withdraw from it its thousand-year-old privileges, such that a new writing (and not a new style) can appear, a practice founded in theory is necessary.' On this level, it is pertinent to plug analysis into an excess which is precisely that of the *text* in which the 'heart of all languages' would function. As Barthes also writes, regarding Japanese, the 'subject' (classical substantive element of Western reflection closed in and on language) becomes 'not the all-powerful agent of discourse, but rather a large obstinate space which envelops the statement and displaces itself within it.' WRITING SCANS HISTORY;

– *to inscribe a theoretical 'jump'* in relation to which Derrida's 'Differance' situates a position of reorganization. Derrida's text indicates acutely but discretely the place and the object of this theoretical overturning – critical site of all the metaphysical sediments left in the 'human sciences' –, site of appearance of the text through the detour of the 'pyramidal silence of graphic difference' which redistributes the relations between writing and speech, space and representation. Text: 'Figures without truth, or at least a system of figures not dominated by the value of truth, which then becomes only an included, inscribed, circumscribed function.'[6] WRITING NO LONGER SIGNIFIES WITHIN TRUTH;

– *to unleash a movement* which displaces the axes of reference of a discontinuous history identified at the level of the texts, their differences and their points of juncture. A process of rewriting able to sift through the mass of cultural objects;

– *to elaborate concepts* capable of regulating this space ('signifying practice', 'paragram', 'intertextuality', 'ideologeme' – Kristeva), as well as methods permitting a figuration of its transformative double;

– *to unfold a history/ies* – a plural history – formed by the differences between writings – communicating theory and practice through a series of radical breaks precisely identifiable in their time;

– *to articulate a politics* logically linked to a non-representational dynamic of writing, that is: an analysis of the misunderstandings provoked by this position; an explanation of their social and economic characteristics; a construction of the relations of this writing to historical materialism and to dialectical materialism.

Such a project, of which we are only sketching out the plan here, emerges clearly from the texts presented in this volume. It must be added that a work as marginal and risky as this – of which the Group for Theoretical

Studies formed by *Tel Quel* is the social materialization – would not have been thinkable without an anonymous reality at work between the individuals whose ambition is to disappear as soon as possible in the transfers of energy provoked by the pursuit of a practice without rest and without guarantees. For now, this is where the experience has led: we allow it to formulate itself, from one level to another, from one background to another, with the necessity but also the always suspended chance of a game.

October 1968
Translated by Patrick ffrench

Notes

1   [This unattributed text opens *Théorie d'ensemble* and refers to that volume in its title 'Division de l'ensemble' and in its text. While it refers specifically to the three opening texts of that volume, by Foucault, Barthes and Derrida, it also functions as a 'programme' for *Tel Quel* at this moment (1968–9). Its reference to 'this volume' can, with a certain liberty, be read both in reference to *Théorie d'ensemble* and to *this* volume, *The Tel Quel Reader*.]
2   [T. Todorov, *Théorie de la littérature* (Paris, Seuil, 1965).]
3   We call the cultural fall-out phenomena of, for example, 'existentialist' phenomenology, the *nouveau roman*, etc., *après-après-coup*.
4   [See M. Foucault, 'Distance, aspect, origin' in this volume, p. 104.]
5   [Barthes, 'Drame, poème, roman', in *Sollers écrivain* (Paris, Seuil, 1979), 15–16.]
6   [J. Derrida, *Margins of Philosophy*, trans. A. Bass (Hemel Hempstead, Harvester Wheatsheaf, 1982), 18.]

2

TOWARDS A SEMIOLOGY OF PARAGRAMS

Julia Kristeva

The simple expression will be algebraic or will not be. . . .
We arrive at theorems that require demonstration.
(Saussure, 1911)[1]

First principles

I.1 Literary semiology[2] is already going beyond what are thought to be the inherent limitations of structuralism, its 'staticism'[3] and its 'non-historicism',[4] by setting itself the task that will justify it: the discovery of a formalism that corresponds isomorphically to literary productivity's thinking itself. Only two methodologies could serve as a basis for such a formalism:

1 Mathematics and metamathematics – artificial languages that, due to the freedom of the signs they use, are more and more able to elude the constraints of a logic based on the Indo-European subject–predicate relation, and that as a consequence are better adapted to describing the poetic operation of language.[5]

2 Generative linguistics (grammar and semantics), insofar as generative linguistics conceives of language as a dynamic system of relations. We reject its philosophical foundation, derived from a scientific imperialism that grants generative grammar the right to establish rules for the construction of new linguistic, and by extension poetic, variations.

I.2 The application of these methods to a semiology of poetic language presupposes, first of all, a revised general conception of the literary text. We accept the principles stated by Saussure in his 'Anagrams':[6]

(a) Poetic language 'adds a second mode of being, an artificial, supplementary mode of being, so to speak, to the original mode of the word'.
(b) There is a correspondence between elements, through pairing and through rhyme.
(c) These *binary* poetic laws go so far as to transgress the laws of grammar.

(d) The elements of a *theme-word* (even a letter thereof) can 'extend over the entire text or be concentrated in a tiny space, such as one or two words'.

This 'paragrammatic' conception of poetic language (the word 'paragram' is used by Saussure) suggests three major theses:

A Poetic language is the only infinity of code.
B The literary text is double: writing-reading.
C The literary text is a network of connections.

I.3 These propositions should not be read as a hypostasis of poetry. On the contrary, they will serve to situate poetic discourse within the ensemble of signifying gestures that make up collective productivity, underlining the following points:

1 A general and radical analogy informs all of these gestures. Social history seen as a space, not as a teleology, also structures itself *paragrammatically* at each of its levels (including poetry which, like the other levels, exteriorizes the general function of the ensemble) – nature–society, law–revolution, individual–group, class–class struggle, linear history–tabular history being the non-exclusive oppositional pairings wherein are played out those never-finished *dialogical* relations and 'transgressions'.

2 The three particularities of poetic language described above put an end to the isolation of poetic discourse (considered, in our hierarchized society, as 'ornament', as 'superfluous', or 'anomalous') and accord it a status as social practice which, when seen as paragrammatic, is manifest at the level of the text's articulation as well as at the level of its explicit message.

3 Paragrammatism being more easily described at the level of poetic discourse, that is where semiology must first of all apprehend it, before extending it to all reflexive productivity.

Poetic language as infinity

II.1 Describing the operation of poetic language (which here means the language of both 'poetry' and prose) is today an integral (if perhaps the most troubling) feature of linguistics in its efforts to explain the mechanism of language.

The value of this description lies in two facts that are among the most striking characteristics of the 'human sciences' today:

1 Its more evident formalism (in the mathematical sense) makes of poetic language the only complementary structure among the practices of the linguistic totality.

2 The avowal of the limits of the scientific enterprise, a constant feature of the history of science, is for the first time made in terms of scientific logic's inability to formalize, without distortion, the functions of poetic

discourse. A divergence becomes apparent: an incompatibility between the scientific logic developed by society to explain itself (to justify its passivity *and* its disturbances) and the logic of a marginal, subversive discourse, a discourse more or less excluded from social utility. It is clear that poetic language as a complementary system obeying a logic different from that of the scientific enterprise requires, if it is to be described, an apparatus that takes into account the characteristics of this poetic logic.

So-called everyday discourse and especially its rationalization by linguistic science disguise this logic of complementarity, without destroying it, by reducing it to logical categories that are limited both socially (in terms of hierarchized society) and spatially (limited to Europe). (The social and linguistic reasons for this effacement will not be discussed here.)

II.2 The prejudices that derive from this process have had their influence on studies of the specificity of the poetic message. Stylistics, growing, in the words of Vinogradov,[7] like a weed between linguistics and literary history, tends to study 'tropes' or 'styles' as just so many deviations from normal language.

Researchers think of the specificity of poetic language as a 'particularity' of the ordinary code (see Bally, Marty, Spitzer, Nefile, etc.). Definitions given either derive from the literary or linguistic domain while adopting the premises of a philosophical or metaphysical system unable to solve the problems posed by the linguistic structures themselves (see Vossler, Spitzer, Croce or Humboldt), or else, excessively broadening the field of linguistic study, they transform the problems of poetic language into a problematic of the study of any linguistic phenomenon (see Vossler in particular). The most interesting Russian Formalist studies of the poetic code have considered it to be a 'violation' of the rules of ordinary language.[8] Many recent and very interesting studies are nonetheless premissed on such a conception. The notion of poetic language as a deviation from normal language ('novelty', 'putting out of gear', 'transcendence of the automatism') has replaced the naturalist conception of literature as reflection (expression) of reality, and this notion is becoming a cliché that prevents the study of specifically poetic morphology.

II.3 That linguistic science which pays heed to poetic language and the basics of stochastic analysis has arrived at the idea of the *convertibility* of the linguistic code, contesting the concepts of deviation and irregularity applied to poetic language.[9] But the conception of the linguistic system as a hierarchy (need the linguistic and social reasons of such a conception be dwelt upon?) prevents poetic language (e.g. metaphoric creation) being seen as anything other than a 'sub-code of the total code'.

The empirical results of the studies mentioned above can only be of value within a non-hierarchical conception of the linguistic code. It is not simply a matter of reversing the perspective and postulating, *à la* Vossler, that ordinary language is a particular instance of that larger formalism represented by poetic language. For us poetic language is not a code encompassing all others, but a class A which has the same power as the function ϕ $(x1 \ldots xn)$ of the infinity of the linguistic code (see the theorem of existence), and all 'other languages' ('ordinary' language, 'metalanguages', etc.) are quotients of A over more limited fields (limited by the rules of the subject–predicate construction, for example, as the basis of formal logic), which disguise, as a consequence of this limitation, the morphology of the function ϕ $(x1 \ldots xn)$.

II.4 Poetic language[10] contains the code of linear logic. Moreover, we could find in poetic language all the combinatory figures that algebra has formalized into a system of artificial signs and which are not exteriorized at the level of the manifestations of ordinary language. In the operation of the modes of conjunction of poetic language we can observe, furthermore, the dynamic process whereby signs take on or change their significations. Only in poetic language is found the practical realization of the 'totality' (though we prefer the term 'infinity') of the code at man's disposition. In this perspective, literary practice is revealed to be the discovery and the exploration of the possibilities of language; an activity that frees man from certain linguistic (psychical, social) networks; a dynamism that breaks the inertia of language-habits and offers the linguist a unique opportunity to study the *becoming* of the signification of signs.

Poetic language is an unbreakable dyad of the *law* (the law of ordinary discourse) and its *destruction* (specific to the poetic text), and this indivisible coexistence of the plus and the minus is the *constitutive complementarity* of poetic language, a complementarity that arises at every level of non-monological (paragrammatic) textual articulation.

Poetic language cannot, therefore, be a sub-code. It is the ordered infinite code, a complementary system of codes from which can be isolated (as a functional abstraction, for the purposes of demonstrating a theorem) an ordinary language, a scientific metalanguage and all the artificial systems of signs – which are all no more than sub-sets of this infinity, exteriorizing the rules of its order within a limited space (their power is less in proportion to that of the poetic language that is cast over them).

II.5 Such a notion of poetic language demands that the concept of the *law* of language be replaced by that of linguistic *order*, so that language is considered not as a mechanism governed by certain principles (pre-established in terms of certain restricted applications of the code), but as an organism whose complementary parts are interdependent and come successively to the fore according to their different applications, without thereby foregoing the particularities of their place in the total code. This *dialectical* notion of language resembles the physiological system, and we are grateful to Joseph Needham for suggesting the term 'hierarchically fluctuating'[11] to describe the system of language. We should also remember that the transformational method has already galvanized the specific study of grammatical structure: Chomsky's ideas[12] on the rules of grammar have their place in this vaster conception of poetic language sketched out here.

II.6 The *book*, on the other hand, situated within the infinity of poetic language, is *finite*: it is not open, but closed, constituted once and for all; it has become a principle, *one*, a law, but it is only readable as such within a possible opening onto the infinite. This readability of the closed opening onto the infinite is only *completely* accessible to the one who writes, that is, from the point of view of that reflexive productivity which is writing. 'He sings for himself and not for his fellows', writes Lautréamont.[13]

For the writer, then, poetic language is a *potential infinity* (in Hilbert's sense of the phrase[14]): the infinite set (of poetic language) is considered as a set of realizable possibilities; each of these possibilities is separately realizable, but they are not realizable all together.

For its part, semiology could include in its reasoning a notion of poetic language as a *real infinity* that cannot be represented, allowing it thereby to apply the procedures of set theory, which, if somewhat doubtful, can be employed within certain limits. Guided by the finitism of Hilbert, axiomatizing the articulations of poetic language would avoid the difficulties posed by set theory and at the same time would include, in the approach to the text, that notion of the *infinite* without which, it has become clear, it is impossible to deal satisfactorily with problems of precise knowledge.

The objective of 'poetic' research is at a stroke displaced: the task of the semiologist will be to try to read the finite in relation to an infinity by uncovering a signification that would result from modes of conjunction within the ordered system of poetic language. To describe the signifying operation of poetic language is to describe the mechanism of conjunction within a potential infinity.

The text as writing-reading

III.1 The literary text inserts itself into the set of all texts: it is a writing-response to (a function or negation of) another text or other texts. By writing while reading the anterior or synchronic literary corpus the author lives in history, and society writes itself in the text. Hence paragrammatic science must take account of an ambivalence: poetic language is a *dialogue* between two discourses. A foreign text enters the network of writing: the network absorbs the text according to specific laws that are yet to be discovered. Hence all of the texts in the space read by the writer function within the paragram of that writer's text. In an alienated society, in consequence of their very alienation, writers *participate* by means of a paragrammatic writing.

The verb 'to read' had, for the Ancients, a signification worth remembering and valorizing for an understanding of literary practice. 'To read' was also 'to bring together', 'to gather', 'to watch for', 'to discover the trace of', 'to take', 'to steal'. 'To read', then, denotes an aggressive participation, an active appropriation of the other. 'To write' would then be 'to read' as production, as industry; writing-reading, or paragrammatic writing, would then be the aspiration towards aggressivity and total participation. ('Plagiarism is necessary' – Lautréamont.[15])

Already Mallarmé knew that to write was 'to claim in accordance with a doubt – the drop of ink married to the sublime night – some duty to recreate it all, with reminiscence to prove that one is really there where one should be. . . . ' 'To write' was for him 'a summons to the world that it should equal its fear with rich figured postulates, as a law, on the pallid paper of such audacity. . . . ' [16]

Reminiscence, a summons of figures to 'prove that one is there where one should be'. Poetic language appears as a dialogue of texts: every sequence is *made* in relation to another sequence deriving from another corpus, such that every sequence has a double orientation: towards the act of reminiscence (the evocation of another writing) and towards the act of summation (the transformation of this writing). The book refers to other books and by the modes of summation (of *application*, in mathematical terms) gives those books a new way of being, elaborating thereby its own signification.[17] See Lautréamont's *Chants de Maldoror* and, above all, his *Poésies*, which present a declared polyvalence unique in modern literature. They are dialogue-texts, that is: firstly, as much by the conjunction of their syntagms as by the character of their semic and phonetic 'grams', they address another text; secondly, their logic is not that of a system *submissive* to the law (God, bourgeois morality, censorship), but the logic of a broken, topological space, proceeding by oppositional dyads in which the 1 is implicit but transgressed. They read the psychological, romantic code, parodying and diminishing it. Another book is always present in the book, and it is on the basis of that book, over it and despite it, that the *Chants de Maldoror* and the *Poésies* are constructed.

Since the interlocutor is a text, so too is the subject: a personal-impersonal poetry arises from which, with the person-subject, are banished man, 'the description of passions without moral conclusion', 'the phenomenon', 'the accidental'. 'The coldness of the maxim shall come first!' Poetry will be constructed as an axiomatic network both indestructible ('the indestructible thread of impersonal poetry') and destructive ('the theorem is mocking of its nature').[18]

Consequences:

III.2 The poetic sequence is at least *double*. But this doubling is neither horizontal nor vertical: the paragram is neither a message sent by the writing subject to an addressee (which would be the horizontal dimension), nor is it a matter of signifier–signified (the vertical dimension). The double of writing-reading is a *spatialization* of the sequence. A third dimension is added to the two dimensions of writing (i.e. subject and addressee; subject of enunciation and subject of utterance): that of the 'foreign' text.

III.3 The double being the minimal sequence of paragrams, their logic is different from that of 'scientific logic', from the *monologic* that evolves in the binary space of 0–1 and proceeds by means of identification, description, narration, the exclusion of contradictions, the establishment of truth. It can be seen why, in the *dialogism* of paragrams, the laws of grammar, syntax and semantics (which are laws of 0–1 logic, i.e. Aristotelian, scientific or theological logic) are transgressed while remaining implicit. This transgression, by absorbing the 1 (the prohibition), announces the *ambivalence* of the poetic paragram: there is a coexistence of the monological (scientific, historical, descriptive) discourse and the discourse that destroys this monologism. Without the prohibition there would be no transgression; without the 1 there would be no paragram based on the 2. The prohibition (the 1) constitutes meaning, but at the very moment of constitution meaning is transgressed in an oppositional dyad, or, more generally, in an expansion of the paragrammatic network. Hence, through the poetic paragram we see that the *distinction* censorship–liberty, conscious–unconscious, nature–culture, is historical. We should speak of their indivisible cohabitation and of the *logic* of this cohabitation, a logic of which poetic language is a visible realization.

III.4 The paragrammatic sequence is a *set* of at least two elements. The modes of conjunction of its sequences (Mallarmé's *summation*) and the rules that govern the paragrammatic network can be expressed by set theory, by the operations and theorems that are derived from or relate to them.

III.5 The problematic of the minimal unit as *set* replaces that of the minimal unit as *sign* (signifier–signified, Sr–Sd). The set of poetic language is formed by sequences in relation; it is a spatialization and a putting into relation of sequences, distinct thereby from the sign, which implies a linear division between signifier and signified. Thus postulated, this basic principle leads semiology to seek a formalization of relations within the text and between texts.

31

The tabular model of the paragram

The way that is truly the way is other than a constant way.
Terms that are truly terms are other than constant terms.

(Tao Tö King, 300 BC)

IV.1 In this perspective, the literary text presents itself as a system of multiple *connections* that could be described as a structure of paragrammatic networks. By paragrammatic network we mean a *tabular* (non-linear) model of the elaboration of the literary image, in other words, the dynamic and spatial graphism designating, in poetic language, the multi-determination of meaning (different from the semantic and grammatical norms of ordinary language). The term *network* replaces univocity (linearity) by encompassing it, and suggests that each set (sequence) is the outcome and the beginning of a plurivalent relation. In this network, the elements will be presented as the *peaks* of a graph (as in König's theory), enabling us to formalize the symbolic operation of language as a dynamic mark, as a moving 'gram' (hence as a *paragram*) which *makes* rather than *expresses* a meaning. Hence each peak (phonetic, semantic, syntagmatic) will refer to at least one other peak, so that the semiological problem will be to find a formalization of this dialogical relation.

IV.2 Such a tabular model will be highly complex. To make representation easier, we shall have to isolate certain *partial grams* and distinguish *sub-grams* within them. The stratification of the text's complexity is an idea to be found in Mallarmé: 'The buried sense moves and disposes the pages into a choir.'[19]

We should note straightaway that the three types of connection (within the sub-grams, between them, and between the partial grams) are not different by nature and are not distinguished hierarchically. They are all expansions of the *function* that organizes the text, and if this function is manifest at different levels (phonetic, semic, sequential, ideological) that does not mean that one of these levels is dominant or primordial (in time or as a value). The differentiation of *function* is an operative diachronization of a synchrony: the expansion of the *theme-word* described by Saussure. This function is specific to every type of writing. In all poetic writing, however, it has an invariable property: it is dialogical and its minimal interval is 0 to 2. Mallarmé had already formulated this notion of the Book as a writing organized by a topological dyadic function, discernible at every level of the *transformation* and of the structure of the text:

> The book, which is a total expansion of the letter, must find its mobility in the letter; and in its spaciousness must establish some

nameless system of relationships which will embrace and strengthen fiction.[20]

Words rise up unaided and in ecstasy; many a facet reveals its infinite rarity and is precious to our mind. For our mind is the centre of this hesitancy and oscillation; it sees the words not in their usual order, but in projection (like the walls of a cave), so long as that mobility which is their principle lives on, that part of speech which is not spoken. Then quickly, before they die away, they all exchange their brilliancies from afar; or they may touch, and steal a furtive glance.[21]

This phenomenon can be formalized by the theorem of existence.

IV.3 If we take as an example a paragraph or even a sentence from Lautréamont's text (and from any text), we can read, at each level, the global function of the book. In other words, if the general function of the text as infinity ε is $\varphi\,(x_1 \ldots x_n)$ the set appears in the form of several sub-sets that have the same power (are equivalent to $\varphi\,(x_1 \ldots x_n)$).

$$<a_1a_2>\varepsilon A \;\dot{\equiv}\; <b_1b_2>\;\varepsilon B$$

$$<b_1b_2>\;\varepsilon B \;\dot{\equiv}\; <c_1c_2>\;\varepsilon C$$

$$<abc>\;\varepsilon E \;\dot{\equiv}\; <c_1c_2>\;\varepsilon C^{21}$$

It is possible to find for the infinite $\varphi\,(x_1 \ldots x_n)$ a class E such that whatever the sets $x_1 \ldots x_n$ might be, $<x_1 \ldots x_2>\;\varepsilon E \;\dot{\equiv}\; \varphi\,(x_1 \ldots x_n)$. This class, which is not the only possible class, but which in its fundamental nature is identical to the other possible classes, is the sentence (the passage) written by Lautréamont.

By this means we formulate the famous metatheorem of existence whose value for poetic language is specific, hence different from its value for mathematics.

In poetic language this theorem denotes the different sequences as equivalent to a function encompassing them all. Two consequences follow: firstly, the non-causal sequence of poetic language is stipulated; secondly, emphasis is placed on the impact of a literature that develops its message in small sequences; signification (φ) is contained in the mode of conjunction words and phrases. To shift the centre of the poetic message onto its sequences is to become conscious of the functioning of language and to *work* on the signification of the code. No $\varphi\,(x_1 \ldots x_n)$ can be realized if we have not found the class E (and its sets A, B, C ...), such that $<x_1x_2>\;\varepsilon E \;\dot{\equiv}\; \varphi\,(x_1 \ldots x_n)$. Any poetic code that confines itself to postulating a function $\varphi\,(x_1 \ldots x_n)$ without realizing the theorem of existence, without constructing sequences equivalent to ε, is a failure. (This explains, among other things, the flagrant failure of 'existentialist' literature at the level of its metaphysical writing, which testifies to the complete incomprehension of the functioning of poetic language on the part of the authors of that school.) Lautréamont was one of the first consciously to practise this theorem.

The theorem of existence in poetic language refers to the axiom of selection stipulating that there is a univocal correspondence, represented by a class, that associates one of its elements with each of the non-empty sets of the theorem (of the system).

$$(\exists A) \{Un\,(A)\,(x)\,[\sim Em(x) > (\exists y)\,[y\,\varepsilon\,x\cdot< yx > \varepsilon A]\}$$

In other words, we may simultaneously select an element from each of the non-empty sets that concern us. Thus expressed, the axiom is applicable within our universe E. It also explains how every sequence carries the message of the book.

IV.4 The tabular model has two partial grams:

A   The text as writing: writing-grams.
B   The text as reading: reading-grams.

It should be emphasized again that these different levels, far from being statically equivalent, are correlated between themselves so as to be reciprocally transformed.[23] Writing-grams can be examined as three sub-grams: phonetic, semic and syntagmatic.

A.1 *Phonetic writing-grams.*

Our arbitrary selection of a paragraph from the *Chants de Maldoror* is justified by the theorem of existence.

> There are moments in existence when lousy-headed [*à la chevelure pouilleuse* – A] man, his eyes staring, casts wild glances [*l'oeil fixe, des regards fauves* – B] into the green membranes of space [*les membranes vertes de l'espace* – C]; for he thinks he hears before him the ironic hooting of a ghost [*les ironiques huées d'un fantôme* – D]. He staggers and bows his head; what he has heard is the voice of conscience [*c'est la voix de la conscience* – E].[24]

The function that structures the global text is equally manifest at the phonetic level of paragrams. We need only listen to the phonetic aspects of these sets and examine their graphic form to perceive the correspondences $f(v) - al(oe) - s(z)$: the morpheme 'phallus' emerges as the function-word at the base of the utterance. Like those names of chieftains that Saussure finds embedded in vedic and saturnian verses, the function-word in the Maldoror passage is spread out in a spatial diagram of correspondences, of combinatory play, of mathematical graphs and self-permutations in order to add complementary significations to the fixed (effaced) morphemes of ordinary language. This phonetic network joins the other levels of the paragram to communicate a new dimension to the poetic image. Thus, in the multivocal totality of the paragrammatic network, the signifier–signified distinction is diminished and the linguistic sign emerges as a dynamism that proceeds by quantum force.

A.2 *Semic writing-grams.*

Here is how a static semic analysis would have defined the sets of our paragrammatic network:

A   body ($a1$), hairs ($a2$), flesh ($a3$), filth ($a4$)
B   body ($b1$), tension ($b2$)
C   matter ($c1$), loud colour ($c2$), sinister ($c3$), abstraction ($c4$)
D   sinister ($d1$), fear ($d2$), spiritualization ($d3$)
E   spirit ($e1$), idealization ($e2$)

Yet the poetic image is constituted in the correlation of semic components by means of a correlational interpretation within the message itself, by a transcoding internal to the system. The operations of set theory (applications, bijections, surjections, etc.) will show the curves that constitute the paragrams. The complexity of the applications at every level of the network explains the impossibility of translating a poetic text (ordinary and scientific language prohibits such semic permutations).

The equivalence that is established between semes in the network of poetic language is radically different from the equivalences of simple semantic systems. Application unites sets that are not equivalent at any primary linguistic level. Application unites semes that are radically opposed ($a1 \equiv c4$; $a4 \equiv e1, \ldots$ etc.), referring to different denotations, in order to signal that in the semantic structure of the literary text these semes can coincide.

The notion of constructability (which implies the axiom of selection), associated with our other observations on poetic language, explains the impossibility of contradiction within the space of poetic language. This is close to Gödel's statement concerning the impossibility of proving contradiction within a system using means formalized within that system. But despite the similarities between these two statements and despite the consequences thereof regarding poetic language (e.g. metalanguage is a system formalized within the system of poetic language), we shall insist on their difference: the specificity of the *prohibition* in poetic language and its functioning make of poetic language the only system where contradiction is not a non-sense but a definition; where negation is determinate and where empty sets are a particular significant mode of sequence. It would not be an exaggeration to postulate that all relations within poetic language can be formalized by functions simultaneously employing two modes: *negation* and *application*.

Made up of oppositions that have been overcome, poetic language is an undecidable formalism that does not seek to be resolved. Meditating on the possibility of discerning contradiction within set theory, Bourbaki[25] finds that 'an observed contradiction would be inherent to the very principles that are at the basis of set theory'. Projecting this reasoning onto a linguistic background we arrive at the notion that at the basis of mathematics (i.e. the structures of language) there are contradictions that are not only inherent but indestructible, constitutive and non-modifiable, the 'test' being a coexistence of oppositions, a demonstration of the conclusion that $0 \neq 0$.

A.3 *Syntagmatic writing-grams.*

'When I write down my thought, notes Lautréamont, it does not escape me. This act make me remember my strength that I always forget. I learn in proportion to the connection of my thoughts. I mean to know only the contradiction between my mind and nothingness.'[26] The connection of writing and nothingness, that writing transforms into *totality*, seems to be one of the laws of the syntagmatic articulation of paragrams. ('The way is empty', Tao Tö King, IV).

There are two striking syntagmatic figures in the topological space of the *Chants de Maldoror*:

1. The empty sets: $A \cap B = \varnothing$ (A and B have no common elements); 2. The disjunctive totals $S = A \oplus B$, where $D = A \cap B$ (the total is made of elements to either A or B).

The formalism $A \cap B = \varnothing$ would apply to the oppositional dyads tears–blood, blood–ash, lamp–angel, vomit–happiness, excrement–gold, pleasure–bodily disgust, dignity–contempt, happiness–horror, rhinoceros–fly, baobab tree–pin, etc. The images of the cruel child, of childhood and ugliness, of the hermaphrodite, belong within this formalism. They can also be described by the formalism $S = A \oplus B$, if we consider that, for example, the couple tears–blood share the semes 'liquid', 'matter', but that the poetic function of the dyad is constituted by the disjunctive total of all the elements (peaks) that they do not have in common. It may be that the common peaks of two syntagms are only their phonemes, and the disjunctive total is constituted by the union of all the other divergent peaks.

Thus the law of empty sets organizes the sequence of phrases, of paragraphs and themes in the *Chants*. Each phrase is attached to the preceding one as an element that doesn't belong to it. No 'logical' causal ordering organizes this sequence. We couldn't even speak of negation, since it is simply a matter of elements belonging to different classes. The result is a chain of empty sets turning on itself, resembling Abel's rings: a semic set, already mentioned and included in an empty set, reappears to enter another empty set (see the 'glow worm' episode). There is no limit to this chain except 'the border of this sheet of paper'. Only a logic that appeals to the 'appearance of phenomena' can bring a 'chant' to a close (can close a $0 \neq 0$ sequence). Laughter as a means of censure is refuted along with the means employed by rationalism: irony ('to laugh like a cock') and Voltaire ('the great Voltaire's abortion') are enemies of the same order. Everything that recalls, suggests or imposes the monolithic unity of logical discourse, suppressing the oppositional dyad, is the equal of a 'stupid God' and (in Lautréamont's words) lacks *modesty*. Consequently: '*Laugh*, but weep at the same time. If you are unable to weep with your eyes, weep with your mouth. If it still be impossible, *urinate*. . . . '[27] Once again the intersection of the italicized sememes forms a chain of empty sets in which is manifest the writer's 'modesty': his refusal to codify.

Each sequence is thus annihilated, the couples form zeros that signify and the text, structured as a chain of signifying zeros, contests not only the system of the code (romanticism, humanism) with which it is in dialogue, but also its own texture. We realize then that this emptiness is not *nothing* and that the paragram has nothing to do with 'nothingness': silence is avoided by the *two* in opposition to each other. The zero as non-sense doe not exist in the paragrammatic network. The zero is two which are *one*: in other words, the one as indivisible and the zero as nothingness are excluded from the paragram, whose minimal unity is both an (empty) all and an (oppositional) two. We shall examine more closely this paragrammatic numerology, where there is no 'one' or 'zero' but only 'two' and 'all'. *Unity* is empty, does not count, the one is zero but it signifies: it controls the space of the paragram, it is there to fix the centre, but the paragram does not give it a value, a *stable meaning*. This 'unity' is not the synthesis of A and B; but it has the value of *one* because it is *all*, and at the same time it cannot be distinguished from *two*, because within this unity come together all the contrasting semes, both opposed to each other and united. At once *unity* and *couple*, the oppositional dyad, to apply a spatial expression, is realized in the three dimensions of volume. The numerical game of paragrams played by Lautréamont goes from even (2) to odd (1–3). This is not a passage from the unlimited to the limited, or from the indeterminate to the determined. It is a passage from the symmetrical to the centred, from the non-hierarchized to the hierarchized. In the numerical game of disjunctive totals and empty sets is revealed the mutation of the paragram from between prohibition and transgression: the sequences are disjointed ($A \oplus B = S$), differentiated, but above this difference poetic language creates unities that transform differences into non-exclusive oppositional dyads. The paragram is the only space of language in which the 1 does not function as a *unity*, but as a *whole*, as all, because it is double. How are we to interpret this code of numbers? Writing refuses to become system; being double, its denial is a denial of itself . . .

Marx accused Hegel of betraying the dialectic by proposing a form – that of his own system. Lautréamont's paragrammatic writing avoids the trap of 'form' (in the sense of fixity) as well as the trap of *silence* (which had even tempted Mayakovsky: 'The name of this/theme/ . . . !', in 'For That'), by being constructed through empty sets and disjunctive totals.

Type B grams (reading-grams) can be examined under two sub-headings:

B1 The foreign text as reminiscence.
B2 The foreign text as citation.

Lautréamont writes: 'When, with the utmost difficulty, I was taught to speak, it was only after reading what someone had written on a sheet of paper that I could in my turn communicate the thread of my reasoning.'[28] His *Chants* and his *Poésies* are readings of other writings: his communication is communication with another writing. Dialogue (the second person is frequent in the *Chants*) takes place not between the Subject and the Addressee, the writer and the reader, but within the act itself of writing, where the one who writes is *same* as the one who is, while remaining an other to himself.

The foreign text, object of 'mockery', is absorbed by the poetic paragram either as *reminiscence* (Baudelaire's ocean? Musset's moon, child and gravedigger? Lamartine? Musset's pelican? the entire code of Romanticism dismantled in the *Chants*) or as *citation* (the foreign text is literally taken up and dismantled in *Poésies*). The transformations through citation and reminiscence in the paragrammatic space could be formalized through the procedures of formal logic.

Since the paragram is the destruction of another writing, writing becomes an act of destruction and self-destruction. This is clearly apparent as theme, and even explicitly stated through the image of the ocean (*Chant* I.9). The writer first of all refuses the romantic image of the ocean as idealization of man. He then refuses the image itself as sign, dissolving its *fixed meaning*. After destroying man, the paragram destroys the *name*. ('This something has a name. That name is: ocean. You inspire him with such a fear that he respects you . . . '[29]). If Lautréamont salutes the 'wild, magnetic' ocean, it is insofar as the ocean is for the poet a metaphor of a fluctuating, negative network, touching the limits of all possible negations, i.e. it is a metaphor of the book.

This construction-destruction is all the more flagrant in *Poésies*. Poetry denies, and is a denial of itself, by refusing to be systematized. Discontinuous, fragmented, contestatory, poetry exists as a series of *juxtaposed maxims* that can only be read as *Moralism* (as 1) and as *Double* (as 0).

Affirmation as the negation of a text reveals a new dimension to the double unity of the paragram, and reveals a new signification to the work of Lautréamont. The modes of negation employed by him replace the ambiguity of the texts read by a proposition where negation and affirmation are distinct, set apart and incompatible; expressions of nuance in passing from one to the other are effaced, and in place of a dialectic synthesis (as in Pascal and Vauvenargues) Lautréamont constructs a Whole, which is nonetheless 'two'. For example:

> I shall write my thoughts without order, and not perhaps in unplanned confusion; this is the true order, whereby my object will always be marked by disorder itself. I would be according my subject too much honour if I treated him with order, since I wish to show that he is incapable of order. (Pascal).

And Lautréamont:

> I shall write my thoughts with order, to an unconfused plan. If my thoughts are just, the first to spring to mind will be a consequence of the others. This is the true order. It marks my object with calligraphic disorder. I would be according my subject too much dishonour if didn't I treat him with order. I wish to show that he is capable of order.

This paragraph sums up the law of reflexive production in Lautréamont's work. *Order*, established by *'calligraphic* disorder' (is this untoward word, forcing its way into the text, not the dynamism of paragrammatic development in a broken space?) – this order is the writing of a *maxim*, of a *moralism* ('to write in order to subject to a high morality', *Poésies* I.15), of a categorical *one*, a *one* that exists only insofar as it implies its contrary.

IV.5 Our reflections on the sequences of the paragrammatic network lead to a conclusion regarding the different types of semiotic practice at society's disposition. For the moment we can identify three, defined in relation to social (sexual, linguistic) prohibitions:

1 The semiotic *system* based on the *sign*, hence on *meaning* (the 1) as predetermining and presupposed element. This is the semiotic system of scientific discourse and of all representational discourses. It constitutes a large part of literature. We shall characterize this semiotic practice as *systematic* and *monological*. This semiotic system is conservative, limited, it is

oriented towards what is denoted, it is logical, explanatory, unchanging and does not seek to modify the other (the addressee). The subject of this discourse identifies with the law and refers univocally to an object, repressing its relations with the addressee, as well as the relation between the addressee and the object.

2 *Transformative* semiotic practice. The sign as basic element becomes blurred: 'signs' are disengaged from their denotations and are oriented towards the other (the addressee), who is modified by them. This is the semiotic practice of magic, of yoga, of the politician in a revolutionary period, of the psychoanalyst. Transformative practice, unlike the symbolic system, is changing and seeks to transform, it is not limited, explanatory or logical in the traditional sense. The subject of transformative practice remains subject to the law, and relations within the triangle object–addressee–law (=subject) are not repressed, though they still appear univocal.

3 The semiotic practice of *writing*. We shall call it dialogic or paragrammatic. Here the sign is eliminated by the correlative paragrammatic sequence that is *double* and *zero*. The sequence could be represented by a tetralemma: each sign has a denotation; each sign has no denotation; each sign both has and has not a denotation; it is not true that each sign both has and has not a denotation. If the paragrammatic sequence is π and the Denotation is D, we could express this as:

$$\pi = D + (-D) + [D + (-D)] + \{- [D + (-D)]\} = 0$$

or, in mathematical logic, $A \bigcirc B$, which designates a non-synthetic union of different, often contradictory, formulae. The triangle of the two preceding systems (the symbolic system and transformative practice) changes here, in paragrammatic practice, into a triangle where the law occupies a place at the centre: the law is identified with each of the three terms of the triangle's permutation at a given moment of the permutation. The subject and the law are differentiated and the grams that link the points of the triangle become bi-univocal. As a consequence they neutralize each other and are reduced to signifying zeros. The writing daring enough to follow the complete trajectory of the dialogic movement represented by our tetralemma above, daring enough to be the description and negation of a text, effected within the text being written, such writing does not belong within what is traditionally called 'literature', which is dependent on the symbolic semiotic system. Paragrammatic writing is a continuous reflection, a written contestation of the code, of the law and of itself, a *way* (a complete trajectory) that is *zero* (which denies itself); it is the contestatory philosophical enterprise become language (discursive structure). It is illustrated in the European tradition, by the writing of Dante, Sade and Lautréamont.[30]

IV.6 The operations that will serve to formalize relations within this para-grammatic space are derived from isomorphic systems: set theory and metamathematics. The formalisms of symbolic logic could also be used, while avoiding the limits symbolic logic might set against poetic language because of its rationalist code (the 0–1 interval, the principles of the subject–predicate phrase, etc.). The result will be an *axiomatics* whose appli-cation to poetic language needs to be justified.

Before proceeding to that justification, with in mind the possibility of formalizing the paragrammatic network, we shall refer to a key testimony provided by Chinese antiquity: the Yi-king, the *book of mutations*. In the 8 trigrams and 64 hexagrams of this book, mathematical operations and constructions of linguistic meaning are intermingled, proving that 'the quantities of language and the relations between them can be expressed *in their basic nature* by mathematical formulae' (F. de Saussure)[31]. Among the several merits of this text, which only a mathematical *and* linguistic enter-prise can fully represent, we shall signal two:

1 Chinese linguists seem to have been genuinely preoccupied by prob-lems of permutation and combination, so that many mathematicians (Mikami) point out that the hexagrams have been composed with long and short marks (rods) and that these are linked to the *graphic* form of their calculations. The rods (phonemes) and the calculations (morphemes) can be considered anterior to any signifier. In the same way, esoteric mathematics ('Mi Suan') deal with problems of linguistic combination and the famous 'San Tchaï' method, whereby answers are provided to such questions as: 'how many ways can nine letters be arranged of which three are "a", three are "b", three are "c".'

2 Chinese 'grams' refer back not to some obsession (God, chief, sex) but to a universal algebra of language as the mathematical operation of differ-ences. Taken from two extremes in time and space, Lautréamont's text and the Yi-king each in their own way expand on the significance of Saussure's anagrams on a scale that touches the essence of the linguistic function. To these writings we can add a contemporary book, Philippe Sollers's *Drame*, whose structural grid (the alternating combinations of continuous and frag-mented passages – 'he writes' – that total 64 squares) and pronominal permutations link the serene numerology of the Yi-king to the tragic drives of European discourse.

Axiomatization as caricature

The phenomenon passes. I seek laws.

(Lautréamont)

V.1 The true history of the axiomatic method begins in the nineteenth century and is marked by the passage from a substantial (or intuitive) conception to a *formal* construction. This culminates in Hilbert's work (1900–1904) on the foundations of mathematics, where the tendency towards the formal construction of axiomatic systems reaches its peak and inaugurates the current phase: the conception of the axiomatic method as a method for the construction of new formalized signifying systems.

Obviously, however formalized the method, it must still today be based on certain definitions. The definitions employed by the current axiomatic method are, however, *implicit*: there are no rules of definition and a term achieves a determined significance only as a function of its context (the totality of axioms). Since the basic terms of an axiomatic theory are implicitly defined by the totality of axioms (and not by reference to the elements they denote), the axiomatic system describes not a concrete objective domain but a class of abstractly constructed domains. Consequently, the object studied (scientific theory or, here, poetic language) is transformed into a kind of *formalism* (a formal calculation based on fixed rules) composed of the symbols of an artificial language. This is made possible by:

1 a symbolization of the language of the object studied (the theory in question, or poetic language): the replacement of the signs and expressions of natural language (which are polyvalent and often lack precise signification) with the symbols of a rigorous and functional artificial language;

2 a *formalization*: the construction of an artificial language as formal calculation, discounting its significations outside of formalization; a distinct differentiation is evident between artificial language and the referent it describes.

V.2 Applied to mathematics, the limits[32] and the advantages[33] of the axiomatic method are revealed. Applied to poetic language, the method avoids certain difficulties that have hitherto been insoluble (linked above all to the notion of real infinity). We should note once again that language is practically the only *real infinity* (i.e. an infinite set made of rigorously distinct acts). This concept is naturally idealized: we would be dealing with a real infinity if we read the entire natural sequence, but this is beyond our consciousnesses, even when it comes to literary language. The application of mathematics (of set theory), dominated by the idea of the infinite, to that infinite potentiality which language is for the writer, will make every user of the code aware of the concept of the infinity of poetic language, the role of the axiomatic method being to provide the mode of connection of the elements of the objective domain under analysis.

V.3 It could be objected that the extreme formalization of the axiomatic method, though its use of set theory rigorously describes relations between elements of the poetic code, leaves aside the signification of each of its elements, i.e. literary 'semantics'. We believe that the semantics of linguistic elements (including literary semantics) *are* these relations between elements in the linguistic organism, and that, consequently, these semantics can be mathematized. In the current state of research, however, we would have to use classical semantic analyses (the division into semantic fields; semic and distributional analysis) as the starting-point (as implicit definitions) for a symbolization and formalization of the modes of these functions.

V.4 The alliance of two theories (semantics + mathematics) demands a reduction of the logic of the one, semantics, in favour of the other, mathematics. The subjective judgement of the information-processor continues to play an important role. Nonetheless, the axiomatics of poetic language will be constituted as a branch of symbolic logic allowing it to go beyond the limits of syllogism and of problems posed by the subject–predicate sentence (the problem of truth being at a stroke dispensed with), in order to embrace other methods of reasoning. For the analysis of the literary text, the axiomatic method has the advantage of seizing the pulsations of language, the lines of force in the field wherein the poetic message is developed.

The use of notions derived from new mathematics is obviously only metaphorical, insofar as an analogy can be established between on the one hand the relation of ordinary to poetic language, and on the other the relation finite/infinite.

A modification of mathematical logic also follows, because of the differences between the types of relations that underpin poetic language and the type that constitutes the language of scientific description.[34] The first difference, obvious to anyone who tries to formalize poetic language, concerns the sign '=' and the problem of truth. These are at the basis of the intellectual abstractions of symbolic logic, of mathematics and metamathematics, whereas poetic language resists these structures. It seems impossible to use the sign '=' in a formalization without distorting poetic language (the reason being, precisely, the correlative applications and negations that organize the level of its semic manifestation, in Greimas's terms), and if we use that sign, it is because modern mathematics (scientific thought) offers no other system of reflection. Likewise, the problem of truth and of logical contradiction is differently posed by poetic language. For us, formed by the school of Greek abstraction, poetic language constructs its message by means of relations that seem to presuppose logical (Aristotelian) truths, and to operate despite those truths. Two kinds of explanation seem 'reasonable': either poetic language, and everything that is known as 'concrete thought', is a primitive level of thought, incapable of synthesis (see Lévy-Bruhl, Piaget), or it is a deviation from normal logic. The linguistic evidence refutes these two interpretations. Poetic language preserves the structure of classes and relations (multiplicatory series and correlations), as well as a group connecting the inversions and reciprocities within elementary groupings (that constitute 'the sum of the parts'). It therefore seems impossible to distinguish, as Piaget does, between a concrete logic (the child's relational logic) and a verbal logic (the logic of scientific abstraction). It is hard to conceive of a logic outside language. Relational logic is verbal, it takes the word in its articulation and its originary functioning, and if our civilization obscures its structures in ordinary or scientific language, it doesn't efface those structures: they subsist in the immanence (in Greimas's sense of that term) of our linguistic (logical, scientific) universe.

V.5 The polyvalent logic presupposing an infinite number of values in the interval false–true $0 \leq x \leq 1$ is a part of bivalent (0–1), Aristotelian logic.

Poetic logic is inscribed on a different surface. It remains indebted to Aristotelian logic not in being a part thereof, but insofar as it contains and transgresses that logic. Since poetic unity is constructed in relation to an other as *double*, the problem of *truth* (of the 1) does not concern it. The poetic paragram bypasses the one, and its logical space is 0–2, the 1 existing only virtually. Can we speak of logic in a domain where truth is not an organizing principle? We would say yes, under two conditions:

A Following G. Boole, logic as science is not a part of philosophy, but a part of mathematics. It seeks, then, to express mental operations without concerning itself with ideological principles (including the principles of truth), but by furnishing models for the articulation of elements within the sets studied. Assimilated to mathematics, logic avoids the obligation to '*measure* by *comparison* with predetermined *standards*' (which is one of the faults of contemporary structuralism): logic refuses to be a *numerical ratio*. To pursue this path opened up by Boole is to free logic from the (historically determined and limited) principle of truth and to construct logic as the *formalization* of *relations*. Boole made the first break by detaching symbolic logic from philosophy and connecting it to mathematics, which he thought of not as a science 'of magnitudes' but as the formalization of *combinations*. This initiative was due to the fact that 'logical theory is intimately bound up with the theory of language', itself considered as a network of combinations. Boole's reflections lead to a further break: the connection of logical formalization to the new mathematics and to metamathematics. This enterprise is justified by the discovery of the fragmented topological scene of writing, where the poetic paragram is developed as a double in relation to an other. Such a paragrammatic logic – closer to Boole than to Frege – would stand in relation to symbolic logic as the new mathematics stand in relation to arithmetic.

Situated methodologically between symbolic logic and structuralism, this paragrammatic logic will provide the general formulae enabling us to understand the *particularities* of a *law* and of a symmetry, i.e. to test them. 'The pleasures promised by such an approach are inconceivable.'[35]

B Applied to 'art', this network of *numbers* will destroy the illusory, idealist notion of art as 'prophetic and projective' (Plato, Philebus). A logic constructed as a science for the understanding of art (without reducing it to the monologism of the traditional scientific approach, based on 'the truth') will take the structure of this art to reveal that *all art is an applied science*; the science that the artist possesses *with* (or *after*, or *in advance of*) his period.

V.6 It seems paradoxical that signs can explain the functioning of words. What justifies the claim is that in our society the word is become clarification, petrifaction, straitjacket; it fixes, it ossifies, it brings to a close. Even after Rimbaud, Lautréamont and the Surrealists, it seems surprising when in someone's work the word engages with spaces, attracts those vibrations that describe a rhythm. We have had to counter the restrictions of rationalism and seize the palpitating life of gesture, of the body, of magic, in order to rediscover that man possesses languages that do not confine him to the line, that allow him to extend himself into space. There followed a revolt against speech: with Artaud, for example, its inferiority to movement or colour was demonstrated. Today's linguistic science is determined to show how the word fixes and breaks down this momentum of distance and relation: this flight of the object that is language. As product of a rationalist and logical abstraction, linguistics has difficulty responding to the violence of language as movement across space where, in the pulsation of its rhythm, it establishes significations. We need a mathematical formalism to soften a 'monologic' science and to expose the skeleton, the graphic form of those dispositions in which the dialectic of language is manifest: an infinity of uninterrupted ordered permutations. And who knows, perhaps one of the strongest purposes of linguistics is to purge language of these layers of 'signification' and 'interpretation', of *a priori* concepts and of ready-made logic, and to make its order blank: reflexivity and transitivity; not transitivity, symmetry and asymmetry. Then we might realize that there are words that do not fix, because significations do not simply exist [ne *sont*], they are made [se *font*], and that poetic language offers its infinity in order to substitute new sequences for worn-out language: graphic spasms that call into question man, his image of the universe and his place therein. The order of this discourse, written by man in space as a disassociative, vibratory act, is discovered in mathematical symbolism: a metaphoric product which, when returned to the discourse from which it sprang, would clarify that source.

V.7 These formulae can only grasp a few very limited dimensions of a paragrammatism that would envisage the poetic text as a social, historical and sexual complex.

Furthermore, formalization only reveals *reflective productivity* in reverse; the semiologist comes after the writer to *explicate* (conceptualize) a synchrony and to find only *mental operations* where the whole functions *en bloc* (language, body, social affiliation).

But a (monological, gnosiological) scientific enterprise has been, is and will be necessary to any society, since *explication* (the 'abstraction' that Lenin calls a 'fantasy',[36] and which in modern terms is called *différance*[37]) *is* the *gram*, something fundamental and indispensable to the social (to exchange). 'In real exchange,' writes Marx, 'abstraction must be in turn reified, symbolized, realized by mean of a certain sign.'

If 'the sign' is a social imperative, the problem of its choice in the 'human sciences' ('a *certain* sign') remains open.

Formalized abstraction has, in our view, several advantages over the discursive symbolization of abstraction, including the following:

1 Formalization makes present an otherwise indiscernible structure. Mathematics 'throw a light upon the ordinary language from which they derive', writes Quine:

> in each case a special function which has hitherto been only accidentally and inconspicuously performed by a construction in ordinary language now stands boldly forth as the sole and express function of an artificial notation. As if by *caricature,* inconspicuous functions of common idioms are thus isolated and made conspicuous.[38]

The word *caricature* evokes an initial meaning (Latin *carrus, um*, Low Latin *carricare*, Italian *caricare*) involving notions of weight, load, burden, but also of strength, credit, authority, gravity. Axiomatization is an effect of gravity, an order and an authority imposed on the complex fluidity of the object studied (poetic language). But this strength does not disfigure its object; it seizes the lines of force of this object ('its grimaces'), grimacing as the object itself would grimace, if it went to the extremes of its grimaces. Proustian imitation has been described as load, the body as 'caricature'. In this series of powerful 'caricatures', paragrammatic axiomatization is a bold initiative, 'exaggerated' and 'eccentric', proceeding by *traits* and by *choice of detail* (caricature without its pejorative sense) to resemble its object more closely than could a discursive description (a portrait).

2 Since axiomatic formalization remains a *symbolic* semiotic practice, is not a *closed system*; it is, then, open to all semiotic *practices*. If, like every signifying operation, it is ideological, the ideology that impregnates it is the only one it cannot escape, because any explanation (any 'gram', science, society) is *constituted* by that ideology; it is the ideology of *knowledge* (of a difference that tends to return to that from which it is originally differen-

tiated). Formalization is also ideological insofar as it leaves the semiologist 'free' to choose his object and to make his divisions according to his political position.

3 Confronting the contemporary discoveries of metamathematics and of mathematical logic with the structures of modern poetic language, semiology will encounter the two culminating points of two inseparable human enterprises – the *grammatic* (scientific, monologic) and the *paragrammatic* (contestatory, dialogic) enterprise. And thereby, semiology acquires a social position, a dynamic and revolutionary politics.

This paragrammatic science, like any science, cannot render the complexity of its object, even less so when it comes to literary paragrams. We are no longer under the illusion that an abstract and general structure can provide a total reading of a personal writing. And yet, the effort to grasp the logic of paragrams at an abstract level is the only means of crushing that vulgar psychologism and sociologism which sees poetic language as mere expression or reflection, and effaces thereby its particularities. The problem facing the semiologist is then to choose between *silence* and a *formalization* that has the prospect, as it tries to constitute itself as paragram (as destruction and as maxim), of corresponding isomorphically to the paragrams of poetry.

Translated by Roland-François Lack

Notes

1 [F. de Saussure, from R. Godel (ed.), *Les sources manuscrites du cours de linguistique générale* (Paris: Droz, 1957), 49.]

2 [The version of this essay published in *Tel Quel*, 29 (1967) differs significantly from the later version in Kristeva's book *Séméiotiké: recherches pour une sémanalyse*. In particular, within the body of the text the structuralists' term *sémiologie* is systematically replaced by the post-structuralist 'sémiotique', dramatizing the contingencies marking the development of *Tel Quel* theory out of a structuralist context. In the same way, *l'homme* is replaced by *le sujet*. We translate here the first version of the essay.]

3 See the dynamic model of structure in Roland Barthes, 'Introduction to the Structural Analysis of Narratives', in *Image–Music–Text*, trans. S. Heath (London, Fontana, 1977).

4 See the integration of natural culture in myth in A.J. Greimas, 'The Interpretation of Myth: Theory and Practice', trans. K. Clougher, in P. Maranda and E. K. Maranda (eds), Structural Analysis of Oral Tradition (Philadelphia: University of Pennsylvania Press, 1971).

5 'This function which brings to light the palpable side of signs intensifies thereby the fundamental dichotomy of signs and objects.' R. Jakobson, *Essays in General Linguistics*.

6 Partially published by J. Starobinski in *Words upon Words: The Anagrams of Ferdinand de Saussure* (New Haven, Yale University Press, 1979).

7 V. Vinogradov, *K Postroeniju teorii poetitcheskovo jazika* (Poetika, 1917).

8 V. Zirmonsky, *Vedenije v metiku, Teorija stixa* (Leningrad, 1925); B. Tomachevsky, *Ritm prozy. O stixe* (Leningrad, 1929). [Texts by Tomachevsky were included in

the 'Collection *Tel Quel*' anthology of Russian Formalists edited by T. Todorov, *Théorie de la littérature* (Paris, Seuil, 1965).]

9 R. Jakobson, 'Structure of Language in its Mathematical Aspects', *Proceedings of Symposia in Applied Mathematics*, vol. 12 (1961), 242–52.

10 [At this point Kristeva proposes to designate 'le langage poétique' by means of the quasi-algebraic expression 'lp'; for reasons of clarity this translation has not followed the practice.]

11 Professor Joseph Needham (of Cambridge) borrows the term from comparative physiology, specifically from the terms for the 'endocrinal orchesta' of mammals.

12 [*Idées* are replaced by 'théories' in the *Séméiotiké* version of this essay.]

13 [Translation adapted from John Rodker, *The Lay of Maldoror by the Comte de Lautréamont* (London, The Casanova Society), 186.]

14 ['[T]he role of the infinite in mathematics, according to Hilbert, is similar to the Idea of Reason in Kant, – it transcends all experience and in a way completes it,' W. Neale and M. Neale, *The Development of Logic* (Oxford, Clarendon, 1962), 684.]

15 [Lautréamont, *Poésies* II.59.]

16 [S. Mallarmé, 'Villiers de l'Isle Adam'.]

17 The concepts developed here and below concerning writing as 'lecturology', as 'double', and as 'social practice' were presented *for the first time* and as a *writing-theory* by Philippe Sollers in 'Dante and the Traversal of Writing' (*Tel Quel*, 23 [1965]) and 'Literature and Totality' (*Tel Quel*, 26 [1966]). [See Sollers, *Writing and the Experience of Limits*, trans. L.S. Roudiez (New York, Columbia University Press, 1983).]

18 [Kristeva is quoting from *Poésies* I.15, II.75, II.76, II.82, I.46 and II.103 respectively.]

19 [S. Mallarmé, 'The Book: Restrained Action'.]

20 [S. Mallarmé, 'The Book: Spiritual Instrument', in *Selected Prose Poems, Essays, Letters*, trans. Bradford Cook (Baltimore, Johns Hopkins University Press, 1956), 26–7.]

21 [S. Mallarmé, 'Mystery in Literature', ibid., 33.]

22 [$<x1x2>$ signifies 'ordered set'; ε = 'element of'; $\cdot\equiv\cdot$ signifies 'of equal power'.]

23 A Russian Formalist had already posed this problem (Y. Tynianov, *Problema stixotvornovo jazika*, Leningrad, 1924, 10): 'We must conceive of the form of the literary work as dynamic. . . . The factors of the word do not have the same value, the dynamic form is constituted neither by their union or their mixture, but by their interdependence, or rather by the valorization of a group of factors at the expense of an other group. The valorized factor deforms those subordinate to it.' [Extracts from this book also featured in the 'Collection *Tel Quel*' reader of Russian Formalists, *Théorie de la littérature*.]

24 [Translation adapted from Rodker, *The Lay of Maldoror*, 123. I have reproduced the French to make clear Kristeva's point about the phonetic reference to the word 'phallus'.]

25 [Nicolas Bourbaki: collective *nom de plume* for a group of French mathematicians, dating from the 1930s. The title *Théorie d'ensemble* is an echo of their book *Théorie des ensembles* (Set Theory).]

26 [*Poésies* II.25.]

27 [Translation adapted from Rodker, *The Lay of Maldoror*, 185.]

28 [Translation adapted from ibid., 82.]

29 [Translation adapted from ibid., 23.]

30 With the author's permission we follow here the considerations of L. Mäll in 'The Zero Way', in *Works on Semiotics* (Tartu, USSR, 1965). Mäll studies the

fundamental problems of 'Buddhology' from the semiotic point of view and invokes the Buddhist notion of 'the vanity of all signs' ('Sarva-dharma-sunyatà').

31 [F. de Saussure, from R. Godel (ed.), *les sources manuscrites du cours de linguistique générale* (Paris: Droz, 1957), 44.]

32 J. Ladrière, *Les limitations internes des formalismes* (Louvain, E. Nowelaerts/Paris, Gauthier Villars, 1957).

33 J. Porte, 'La méthode formelle en mathématiques. La méthode en sciences modernes', special issue of *Travail et méthode*, 1958.

34 E. Benveniste, *Problems in General Linguistics*, trans. M.E. Meek (Coral Gables, FL, University of Miami Press, 1971), 12: 'It is not enough to observe that one allows itself to be transcribed in a symbolic notation and the other does not, or does not immediately; the fact remains that both one and the other proceed from the same source and that they contain the same basic elements. It is language itself that suggests the problem.'

35 G. Boole, *The Mathematic Analysis of Logic* (Oxford, Blackwell, 1948), p.7. The French cited by Kristeva appears to be a very loose version of the following passage in Boole: 'Now I do not dare to say to what extent the same sources of pleasure [which we derive from the application of analysis to the interpretation of external nature] are opened in the following essay.'

36 V.I. Lenin, 'Conspectus of Aristotle's *Metaphysics*', in *Philosophical Notebooks*, volume 38 of *Collected Works* (London, Lawrence & Wishart/Moscow, Foreign Languages Publishing House, 1961), 372.

37 See J. Derrida, 'De la grammatologie', *Critique*, December 1965–January 1966 [in English in *Of Grammatology* (Baltimore, Johns Hopkins University Press, 1974)], and 'Freud et la scène de l'écriture', *Tel Quel*, 26 (1966) [in English in *Writing and Difference*, trans. Alan Bass (London, Routledge & Kegan Paul, 1978).] Derrida defines the 'gram' as the fundamental mechanism of 'human' functioning and substitutes this term for the idealism-charged notion of *sign*.

38 W.V. Quine, 'Logic as a source of syntactical insights' in *The Ways of Paradox and other essays* (Cambridge, Mass. and London: Harvard UP, 1966), 44.

3

MARX AND THE INSCRIPTION OF LABOUR[1]

Jean-Joseph Goux

> This logocentrism, this epoch of the full speech, has always placed in parenthesis, suspended, and suppressed for essential reasons, all free reflection on the origin and status of writing.
>
> (Derrida, *Of Grammatology*)

> When they thus assume the shape of values, commodities strip off every trace of their natural and original use-value, and of the particular kind of useful labour to which they owe their creation.
>
> (Marx, *Capital*)[2]

Use-value and exchange-value

In privileged, often exclusive ways language (in the history of the West) is conceived as a set of signs of exchange. Whether in its communicative or expressive aspects, or, more subtly, in the choice of translatability as the characteristic of all language, the sign is always seen as an element of a commercial transaction. The emphasis is unanimously (from Aristotle to André Martinet[3]) on the *exchange-value* of signs – their function in the process of circulation.

We will propose that the sign (*like any product*) also has a use-value, which historically has gone unrecognized, passed over in silence. By the use-value of a product is understood not simply that it can be put 'directly' to use as an object of consumption, but also (from the outset more crucial in establishing the analogy between sign and product) that it serves 'indirectly' as a *means of production*.[4] Just as every product is a means of producing other products (the 'indirect' route whereby other products are made – given a certain expenditure of labour), so signs (series of signs or parts thereof) form the means of production of other signs (of other combinations of signs).

Hence the misrecognition of the *use-value* of signs amounts to nothing less than the occultation of their productive value, concealing the work or play of signs upon and with other signs. The functional value, the efficiency of signs in the production of meaning, the *calculation*, the purely combinatory instance, what we might call, with appropriate ambiguity, the fabric of the text (labour and structure, fabrication and fashioning), is effaced (or rather forgotten/repressed) beneath negotiable transparency (that of meaning).

On the basis of the opposition, borrowed from political economy, between use-value and exchange-value we can establish a fundamental distinction, implicating the entire field of language and writing, one that should prove its relevance through the expansions and rapprochements it seems to allow with the instance of economy.

But what, more precisely (in the economic domain), fixes the relation between use-value and exchange-value? Examine for a moment Marx's analysis.

The basic starting-point is that 'the exchange relation of commodities is characterized precisely by its abstraction from their use-values'.[5] Every product exchanged is reduced to a common measure, 'is reduced to an expression totally different from its visible shape'. Hence, firstly, if 'the material constituents and forms which make the product of labour a use-value' disappear, then at the same stroke disappear (and this double effacement is crucial) 'the different concrete forms' that distinguish one form of labour from another. What is implicated, then, in the process of exchange is only 'the residue of the products of labour'. 'There is nothing left of them in each case but the same phantom-like objectivity.' As far as the domain of circulation is concerned, every product of labour is 'metamorphosed into an identical *sublimation*'.[6] And, generally speaking, 'the common factor in the exchange relation of the commodity is its *value*'.

It is clear that this process, described here in the economic field, has an exact homologue in language and writing. The opposition between signifier and signified is nothing less (this will be firmly established and analysed in its consequences) than this division between use-value and exchange-value. What remains after a translation (after an exchange of signifiers) is the signified. The signified is understood in a general sense as that which (ideas, meaning, concept) remains intact (unchanged) despite the different *forms* of its *expression*. It is *content* ideally conceived as separable from form. And we can say that, just as the exchange of products, i.e. social assimilation and disassimilation, is effected through a formal metamorphosis that reveals the 'dual character' of the commodity, 'possessing both use-value and exchange-value', so the exchange of signs (dialogue, translation – linguistic assimilation and disassimilation) is effected through a formal metamorphosis revealing the dual character of the sign, the apparently irreducible dichotomy of signifier and signified.

If, historically, whatever the form and the content of the activity and the product, we are dealing (in the economic domain) with value – (inasmuch as exchange overrides all relations of production) – then in the linguistic domain (forgetting the differences) we are dealing with that other 'ghostly' 'sublimation', meaning. Just as, according to Marx, the body of the commodity and 'the different concrete forms' that distinguish one form of labour from another are abstracted in the process of bourgeois production dominated by value, so the body of the letter (and everything that in the letter signals its irreducibility to translation) is abstracted and reduced in the element of meaning (within the specific historical period in which we find ourselves).

On the basis of this parallel hegemony of linguistic *meaning* and the exchange-*value* of commodities, our specific task will be to trace the contours described by this homology, and to discover the crucial implications thereof. What, in effect, is at stake here is the principle behind the hierarchy of signifier, signified and referent (whose genealogy, we shall see, can be illuminated by the process of commodity-circulation); at a deeper level, it concerns the effacement of *writing* – a process indissolubly bound up with the occultation and exploitation of *labour*.

Speech and money: general equivalents

Marx's analysis of commodities in the first book of *Capital* demonstrates one thing above all: if, 'originally', the series of commodities formed 'a motley mosaic of disparate and unconnected expressions of value', little by little the values of all of these commodities found expression 'through a single kind of commodity set apart from the rest'. One commodity became 'the general expression of value', the 'general equivalent'. 'All other commodities express their value in the same equivalent.'[7] And, more precisely, 'the specific kind of commodity with whose natural form the equivalent form is socially interwoven now becomes the *money-commodity* or serves as money. It becomes its specific social function, and consequently its social monopoly, to play the part of universal equivalent within the world of commodities.'[8] Following this analysis faithfully, we can immediately affirm (and this parallelism is crucial, as is the homologous *genesis* it presupposes) that if, in the economic domain, 'the form of direct and universal exchangeability, in other words the universal equivalent form, has now by social custom finally become entwined with the specific natural form of the commodity gold',[9] in the domain of signs, it is entwined with, identified by the form of *speech-signs*. It should be pointed out that the *use* of signs does not in some privileged way mean the use of linguistic signs. Be they gestures, drawings, signals, 'symptoms' or just objects, nothing limits the notion of the *use* of signs. It appears, however, that of all these signs a certain very particular type has acquired a privileged importance: the signs of speech. These have been invested in a very particular way with the power to retain *meaning*. They can stand for, are equivalent to, any other sign. And this has happened, as regards both commodity-money and speech, for reasons of social convenience. Commodity-gold (or money) must be 'capable of purely quantitative differentiation, it must therefore be divisible at will, and it must also be possible to assemble it again from its component parts'.[10] Similarly, to agree with Merleau-Ponty (before refuting his text on another point, below), 'the verbal gesture' is only one gesture amongst many, 'but it is a gesticulation so varied, precise and systematic' that it is capable of more differentiations than any other gesture or sign. We would add: than any other sign so readily *available* on all occasions. The signs of speech are characterized by their *availability*.

Consequently, and this is essential, just as 'the money-form is merely the reflection thrown upon a single commodity by the relations between all other commodities',[11] we can say that spoken language, as sign-system, is merely the reflection, thrown upon a single type of sign, by the relations between all other signs. In each case the movement is the same. For the economy it is 'necessary that value, as opposed to the multifarious objects of the world of commodities, should develop into this form, a material and non-mental one, but also a simple social form' (i.e. money). And this is possible despite the fact that 'in monetary appellations all trace of the relation to value disappears', just as 'the name of a thing is entirely external to its nature', and that 'I know nothing of a man if I merely know his name is Jacob'.[12] 'From the mere look of a piece of money, we cannot tell what breed of commodity has been transformed into it. In their money form all commodities look alike. Hence money may be dirt, although dirt is not money.'[13] Similarly, at the end of a process that makes speech the general equivalent of all other signs, there is no relation between linguistic signs and what they represent. If the 'money-form of commodities is, like their form of value generally, quite distinct from their palpable and real bodily form', 'a purely ideal or notional form',[14] so the *speech form* of signs is an ideal form, distinct from their non-linguistic form, but in which, nonetheless, are reflected their relations.

It is noteworthy that Marx's critical analysis, considered in its relation to writing, undermines the system of the sign. It denounces not only the assured distinction between linguistic and non-linguistic signs but above all the linguistic (and political) mystification behind the hierarchy of signifier, signified and referent. So, as we have said, since 'the money-form is merely the reflection thrown upon a single commodity by the relations between all other commodities', we should consider speech to be only the *reflection* (and here we need to propose a formal theory of reflection), thrown upon a *single* type of sign, by the relations between all other signs. Money and speech enjoy the privilege of having converge in them, respectively, the whole commodity system and the whole system of all signs whatever. And yet, fundamentally, just as there is no opposition between money (silver or gold) and other commodities, since silver or gold are themselves commodities (if more easily handled, divided up, etc.), so there is no opposition between words (the graphic or phonic material) and other signs (other *things*). But what does the system of value do? It gives the *illusion* that silver or gold, far from being themselves products (of labour), commodities, *and having as such value only as crystallizations of a specific social labour*, are in fact 'merely signs' of value. The role of gold or silver becomes displaced. From being the material and privileged incarnation of value they become mere signs of this value which thereafter transcends them. Mere *representation*. Since, 'money can, in certain functions, be replaced by mere signs of itself', writes Marx, one would imagine 'it is itself a mere sign'.[15] But,

> if it is declared that the social characteristics assumed by material objects, or the material characteristics assumed by the social determinations of labour on the basis of a definite mode of production, are mere signs, then it is also declared at the same time that these characteristics are the arbitrary product of human reflection.[16]

This same gesture forms the system of the linguistic sign. Scriptural or phonic materials are given as 'mere signs', mere *signifiers* (of an external, transcendent meaning); their functional character (as means of production) and their character as result of a function (as product) are both denied. This conceals the fact that meaning is only a product of the labour of real signs, the result of the fabrication of a text, just as the character of money as commodity (worked metal, having value only as a result of this work) is concealed, making it an arbitrary, second-degree, 'mere' sign.

Saussure does exactly the same thing. The correspondence is remarkable.

> It is impossible for sound alone, a material element, to belong to language. It is only a secondary thing, substance to be put to use. All our conventional values have the characteristic of not being confused with the tangible element which supports them.[17]

He adds, in a comparison that reveals his complicity with monetary ideology (and his ignorance of the function of metallic coinage):

> It is not the metal in a piece of money that fixes its value. Its value will vary according to the amount stamped upon it and according to its use inside or outside a political boundary.

It is clear, then, that the same ideological position constitutes silver as 'mere sign' of an ideal value and constitutes the signifier (in its secondary materiality) in relation to the signified. In both cases the fact that there are only products, that there is no value (no meaning) except through productive labour, is concealed. The movement that distinguishes money from other commodities (by taking it as a general equivalent), and makes of it a fetish beyond the realm of production, is homologous to the movement that distinguishes speech from other *signs*, separates speech from the set of all social signs in order to constitute these signs as things exterior to the system of signs (i.e. as *referents*). The triple structure of signifier, signified and referent exposes its radical complicity with the monetary illusion that categorially separates money from value and value from commodities. But value has no transcendent existence; nor does it relate to a natural object (natural objects have no value[18] – contrary to the naïve illusion that sees gold as naturally precious); value relates only to a product of labour. Similarly, meaning is not transcendent to the signs that manifest it; nor does it relate to a referent in itself (the thing itself, in its natural existence): it relates to other signs, to the writing of the totality of social signs.

One further remark. The fact that in certain historical conditions silver or gold (which represent abstracted materialized labour) can be replaced by currency (by scriptural, paper money, or by some ordinary metal) adds nothing new or different to the process just described. It merely confirms (and encourages) the illusion that money is a 'mere sign'.

> That the circulation of money itself splits the nominal content of coins away from their real content, dividing their metallic existence from their functional existence, this fact implies the latent possibility of replacing metallic money with tokens made of some other material, i.e. symbols.[19]

Furthermore,

> in this process which continually makes money pass from hand to hand, it only needs to lead a symbolic existence. Its functional existence so to speak absorbs its material existence. Since it is a transiently objectified reflection of the prices of commodities, it serves only as a sign of itself, and can therefore be replaced by another sign.[20]

However, this passage from gold or silver money to a scriptural money is not insignificant. It explains, in passing, the second-degree nature and the *discredit* of writing (in the restricted sense) in relation to speech. Just as currency is a 'mere representative' of the gold money it 'replaces', writing is conceived of as a mere system of replacement which has value only inasmuch as it is *covered* by speech. The moralizing and psychologizing approach to writing (to literature) that inquires into the sincerity of the author refers us quite specifically to the problem of *credit* and *inflation*. Do the writer's gold-reserves (his speech) correspond to his writing? Do his *funds*, his content [*fonds*] *cover* his form? The relation of content to form evoked by moralizing readings comes down to the fear of a cheque bouncing, a fear of the counterfeit. This fear is possible only insofar as the writing in question is not itself functional or productive, and is restricted, according to the same ideology, to the simple role of a currency replacing the fullness of speech. The suspicion of possible falsification that attaches to the material signifier, as opposed to the basic honesty of the signified, whose transparency and vital immediacy cannot deceive, along with the monetary metaphor that dominates this opposition, can be found in Hegel:

> Brass instead of gold, counterfeit instead of genuine coin may doubtless have swindled individuals many a time; . . . but in the knowledge of that inmost reality where consciousness finds the direct certainty of its own self, the idea of delusion is entirely baseless.[21]

And Schopenhauer writes:

> the wise man has the advantage of possessing a treasure of examples and facts, etc. But he lacks intuition; so his head resembles a bank whose promissory notes far exceed its actual reserves.

The abstraction of labour

The consequences of the monetary illusion are striking not only in that they separate money from value and value from commodities. This triple hierarchy finds its function in the fundamental dissimulation that it makes possible: the dissimulation of concrete production.

But what of language, firstly.

> The means by which the sign is produced is completely unimportant, for it does not affect the system. . . . Whether I make the letters in white or black, raised or engraved, with pen or chisel – all this is of no consequence with respect to their signification.[22]

This point is essential. The system of meaning is indifferent to the production of meaning. The working trace, as productive use, is not part, as such, of the domain of meaning. This same effacement of the trace by value occurs in the production and circulation of commodities. Marx writes, strikingly: 'When they thus assume the shape of values, commodities strip off every trace [*Spur*] of their natural and original use-value, and of the particular kind of useful labour to which they owe their creation.'[23] But it is not only productive labour that is effaced when meaning (value) is crystallized in speech (money); it is also the relations of production.

56

Since every commodity disappears when it becomes money it is impossible to tell from the money itself how it got into the hands of its possessor, or what article has been changed into it. *Non olet* [it has no smell], from whatever source it may come.[24]

Meaning, like money, has no smell. It is impossible to follow its trace. Labour (the labour of writing) and the modalities of the exchange-process vanish in the transparency of meaning. 'The movement through which this process has been mediated vanishes in its own result, leaving no trace behind.'[25] This effacement of the trace is at the same time the effacement of differences, since in this process, 'different products of labour are in fact equated with each other'.[26] Value is manifest only as an equalization, a levelling, a homogenization, a wearing down (in that sense of the word *usury*). 'Capital is by its nature a leveller.'[27]

This levelling takes place at the level of labour itself, at the root of production. Value is the expression not of concrete labour (which value conceals) but of *abstract labour*. The reduction of all commodities to a quantity of abstract labour. This is the *principle of the general exchangeability of commodities*. And this same figure, crucially, can be found in respect of language. Abstract labour constitutes the common measure of different commodities, whatever their particular substance or properties, and 'the determination of the magnitude of value by labour-time is a secret hidden under the apparent movements in the relative values of commodities'; similarly, Derrida's *archi-trace* or *archi-writing*, constituting the schema uniting form to any graphic or other substance, is what makes possible a signifying system indifferent to the substance of expression – and is what remains as the invariant in all substitutions between different types of sign. Put differently, just as the quantity of abstract labour is the basis of the possibility of value and regulates substitutions between commodities regardless of their substance, a certain *de jure* pre-established systematicity is the precondition of that general translatability of signs (exchanges, substitutions) which (through the arbitrariness of their empirical manifestations) is the basis of the possibility of meaning. The figure is identical. Forms 'which stamp products as commodities' must be considered as pre-existing 'the circulation of commodities'[28] – just as the archi-trace refers, in its irreducible originality, to the possibility of a total system, open to all possible investments of meaning.[29] The homology is complete at every level, since just as speech (or graphic forms) are constituted in the effacement of this *archi-writing* ('from the occulted movement of the trace'[30]), it can be said that abstract labour is the *archi-writing* (the abstract trace) which is the basis of the value of commodities and which is effaced by monetary writing.

The complicity between logocentrism and the fetishism of money and of the commodity is thus exposed. In a general way, just as 'circulation bursts through all the temporal, spatial and personal barriers imposed by the direct exchange of products'[31] and so makes possible the hypostasis of value, hypostatized meaning (the Logos) results not only from the occultation of the productive value of signs, but also from the bracketing of the relations of production of signs.

> This division of the product of labour into a useful thing and a thing possessing value appears in practice only when exchange has already acquired a sufficient extension and importance to allow useful things to be produced for the purpose of being exchanged, so that their character as values has already been taken into consideration during production,[32]

hence when exchange has superseded the relations of production; similarly, logocentrism appears when the use-value of signs is concealed by exclusive consideration of their exchange-value. Logocentrism is the linguistic name of a universal and dominant principle of venality, whose basis is abstract labour.

The detour of production

Thus far the economic product has only been envisaged inasmuch as it requires a certain abstract labour, labour whose mathematical quantification, expressed in units of time, supplies the 'law' that regulates the exchange of commodities.[33] This law, we have said, plays the same role in respect of commodities as the transcendental synthesis of *archi-writing* invoked by the arbitrariness of the sign. But the time of labour, like *archi-writing* (considered as a 'given structure'), the regulatory principle of general translatability, does not involve *concrete labour*, 'whose utility is represented by the use-value of its product, or by the fact that its product is a use-value'.[34] We have seen how Saussure eliminates the means of production (and thus the labour of production itself) from the system of language. But here too, if labour is to be considered not only as abstract (as the quantity of labour-time), but also in its concrete aspect, so 'the immotivation of the trace ought now to be understood as an operation and not as a state, as an active movement, a demotivation, and not as a given structure'.[35] At this point the concept of differance comes in. 'Differance, an economic concept designating the production of differing/deferring.'[36]

What is this active movement as regards political economy? The product as use-value can, according to Marx, have an 'immediate' usefulness or else be consumed 'indirectly as a means of production'.[37]

> Labour consumes products in order to create products, or in other words consumes one set of products by turning them into means of production for another set.[38]

It follows that

if we look at the whole process from the point of view of its result, the product, it is plain that both the instruments and the object of labour are means of production and that the labour itself is productive labour.[39]

The means and the object of labour are thus caught in a *detour*, and labour itself has a *detour* as its basis. It represents an indirect use, and the means of production in themselves are the instruments of a *detour of production*.

Here we come upon the related concepts of differance and of the reserve: differance – production of the deferred; reserve – 'accumulation, capitalization, the security of the delegated or deferred decision'.[40] Labour defers. It defers the consumption of products 'as means of subsistence [*de jouissance*]' in order to consume them as the means of labour's functioning.[41] This is a difference, then, between the pleasure-principle and the reality-principle, 'the possibility, within life, of the detour, of deferral'.[42] Concrete labour is trace, reserve, differance. All labour is a detour; all *jouissance* is a short-cut. That which is reserved, in the differance of communication, is *paid out* [*versé*] to labour. But 'there is no life [*vie*] present *at first* which would *then* come to protect, postpone, or reserve itself in *differance*'.[43] It is the condition of *survival* [*survie*]. The movement of differance is not the postponement of a possible (already present) pleasure, but the avoidance, by a strategy of production, of certain death. It is a deviation that *discounts* a long-term *jouissance*, without which no *jouissance* would at that instant (without delay) be possible. The opposition between the detour (of suffering and of production) and the short-cut (of *jouissance*) is not, then, the theme of sexuality nor that of labour, but the basis of their establishment and of their separation.

The *interdiction* – to be more precise – is only a legislation of labour, the management of the detour.

> The motive of human society is in the last resort an economic one; since it does not possess enough provisions to keep its members alive unless they work, it *must* restrict the number of its members and *divert* (*détourner*) their energies from sexual activity to work.[44]

There is thus a complete *correlation* between the economic necessity of the detour of production and the prescriptions of the interdiction – which are basically just prohibitions of the short-cut (incest, onanism). This is a correlation, then between *l'embauche* [the taking on of labour] and *la débauche* [debauchery].

We should note also that the production of means of production diminishes the detour of labour in the long term. In redirecting labour from its immediate end (by the construction of tools) the *productivity* of labour is increased. Whether it is a machine-tool or a writing-machine, the productivity of the machine is measured by the proportion in which it replaces man.[45] For example, journeys between the home and the source of water are replaced by a drainage system whose construction, according to a modified timetable, has introduced indirect labour as a kind of sub-clause with the medium-term aim of diminishing general labour. This is how classical political economy defines the means of production (or *constant capital*, which it takes to represent the whole of capital, so as to better conceal the role of the force of labour – *variable capital*) – as 'a stock of intermediary and reproducible goods whose use through *detours of production* allows the productivity of labour to increase' (Barre).

The exploitation of labour

Concrete labour, the movement of production (trace, differance, reserve) is this 'violent inscription of a form, tracing of a difference in a nature or a matter which are conceivable as such only in their *opposition* to writing'[46] – to concrete labour. 'Labour is, first of all, a process between man and nature'.[47] The object of labour becomes *raw material* 'only when it has already undergone some alteration by means of labour'.[48] But, 'through this movement', man 'acts upon external nature and changes it, and in this way he simultaneously changes his own nature'.[49]

'The trace is the absolute origin of sense in general. Which amounts to saying once again that there is no absolute origin of sense in general.'[50] If this is the case, then, in the same way, 'labour is the substance, and the immanent measure of value, but it has no value in itself'.[51] To put it differently again (the point needs emphasizing): for Derrida 'the trace is the differance which opens the appearance of signification',[52] but this 'originary' position places the trace *outside of* all those conceptions that are regulated by the trace alone – places it in an outside that only a transcendentality (placed under erasure) could, in a provisional moment, designate. Similarly, for Marx, 'the magnitude of the value of a commodity represents nothing but the quantity of labour embodied in it',[53] but, precisely, 'this value-creating property of labour distinguishes it from all other commodities and precludes it, as formative element of value, from the possibility of having any value itself'.[54] The origin of the meaning of all signs in the movement of differance transcends the world of signs. Concrete labour, the active force in the detour of production, is the basis of the value of all commodities, but is not itself a commodity.

The figure, let us say once more, is the same. The homology is for the moment difficult to sound exactly. If, once proposed, the meaning or the origin of the trace must be place under erasure, if everything begins with the trace but the trace has no meaning, in an identical way 'in the expression "value of labour", the concept of value is not only completely extinguished, but inverted, so that it becomes its contrary. It is an expression as imaginary as the value of the earth.'[55] This essential non-belonging to the system of signification of the 'production of the trace', of the 'labour of writing', and of the 'force of writing', demands to be investigated as a whole.

In following the same problematic, the same figure, we open up the question of the signification of the trace and that of the value of labour. Or rather the question of their non-signification, of their non-value. And we open up that which covers unceasingly (by an identical movement) the impossibility of their *translation*.

What Derrida forcibly underlines is that the force of writing, as breaching [*frayage*], inscribes in a material an engraving that is not translatable. 'An untranslatable engraving.' This writing, this production of the trace,

> is not a displacement of meanings within the limpidity of an immobile, pregiven space and the blank neutrality of discourse. A discourse which might be coded without ceasing to be diaphanous. Here energy cannot be reduced; it does not limit meaning, but rather produces it.

In this way 'the metaphor of translation as the transcription of an original text would separate force and extension, maintaining the simple exteriority of the translated and the translating'.[56] If the labour of writing cannot bring about 'the transparency of a neutral translation', concrete labour, as force and as body, as use and as creation of use-value, is also a *hieroglyphic inscription* which suffers no substitution, no exchange. 'The materiality of a word cannot be translated or carried over into another language. Materiality is precisely that which translation relinquishes.' In the same way, concrete labour cannot be evaluated without being *refined*. In the process of creating value, the labour-process

> consists in the useful labour which produces use-values. Here the movement of production is viewed qualitatively, with regard to the particular kind of article produced, and in accordance with the purpose and content of the movement. But if it is viewed as a value-creating process the same labour-process appears only quantitatively. Here it is a question merely of the time needed to do the work.[57]

The basis of selling the force of labour (its exploitation) is the establishment of a code of translation. The domain of circulation *imposes* a code for the translation of labour. Circulation translates the untranslatable. It turns labour into wage-labour. From a linguistic perspective,

> translation, a system of translation, is possible only if a permanent code allows a substitution or transformation of signifiers while retaining the same signified, always present, despite the absence of any specific signifier. This fundamental possibility of substitution

would thus be implied by the couple concepts signified/signifier, and would consequently be implied by the concept of the sign itself.[58]

An identical movement can be discerned at the economic level. 'The difference between labour, considered on the one hand as producing utilities, and on the other hand as creating value' (which only appears through forced translation, the labour market) 'resolves itself into a distinction between *two aspects* of the production process' (my emphasis). The difference between use-value/exchange-value is thus the principle of the same occultation (this is surely demonstrated) as the difference signifier/signified. That the commodity appears to us as two-sided, use-value and exchange-value, and that the sign appears as a two-sided reality are not unconnected phenomena. By the concept of the sign discursive language conceals the 'labour of writing' (the indistinction of force and meaning) that makes it possible, just as the commodity-form masks labour – and exploits the labour that produces it. In the domain of circulation, to transcribe the non-transcriptive writing of labour as money-value, and conversely to convert a sum of money into the force of labour, this transaction is the basis of (capitalist) *profit* and of the assignation, the exploitation of the labourer. Similarly, to transcribe non-transcriptive writing (functional writing) into the commercial element of meaning and language is to profit from the labour of writing by concealing it. Certainly, 'the laws of commodity exchange' appear to have been rigorously observed, 'the seller of labour-power, like the seller of any other commodity, realizes its exchange-value, and alienates its use-value',[59] but 'we must understand the possibility of writing advanced as conscious and as acting in the world (the visible exterior of the graphism, of the literal, of the literal becoming literary, etc.) in terms of the labour of writing', of this production of the trace.

The notion of value, we should say, is superimposed on the founding notion of labour by masking it (through the intermediary of money), as the notion of meaning is superimposed, by masking it (through the intermediary of speech), on the founding notion of the production of the trace.

The exploitation of writing

A man in the public sphere, a Minister, isn't able to, and needn't, spell correctly. His ideas should flow more quickly than his hand; he only has time to mark out the path; he must put words down as letters and phrases as words; it's up to the scribes to sort it out afterwards.

(Napoleon Bonaparte)

operarius: labourer, workman, secretary, scribe

Writing has always been regulated, constricted, taxed by the fullness of speech. These terms signify in this context the erasure [*rature*], the occultation (through political force) as well as the exploitation of the force of labour. Speech taxes writing just as labour is taxed by the dominant ideology. (Labour is condemned, but at the same time *serves*; it is mere piecework.) The historical dissimulation of the text, the change in writing's *class-status* [its de-classification], is the condemnation levelled at the manufacture (as labour, as structure) of the use-value that sustains value and meaning. This signifies the (political) domination of a one class over a *labouring* class.

We can now state more specifically that the meaning-effect is born in the concealed gap between labouring inscription (operative writing) and monetary or linguistic pseudo-transcription. Just as capitalism situates itself within 'the difference between the price of labour-power and the value which its function creates',[60] within logocentric discourse it appears that the signified *profits* from the signifier in order to manifest itself – but that the signified could make do without the signifier. The signified is the *revenue* of the signifier, the *surplus-value* of the labour of signs. To say, as Merleau-Ponty does, that the virtue of the signifier lies in enabling the signified to go beyond the signifier is to point out, at the linguistic level, that 'the means of production have been converted into commodities whose value exceeds that of their component parts'.[61] As Merleau-Ponty, better than anyone, has said: 'the wonderful thing about language is that it promotes its own oblivion'. Writing is only 'the minimum setting of some invisible operation. Expression fades out before what is expressed, and this is why its mediating role may pass unnoticed.'[62] The labour of words is sublimated in the element of meaning. Whatever the labour, the operation of writing, there is a content [*fond*] (revenue – reserves [*fonds*]) that can become independent of signs (of form). To believe that content can be separated from form is to know, as the capitalist knows, 'that all commodities, however tattered they may look, or however badly they may smell, are in faith and in truth money', 'and what is more, a wonderful means for making still more money out of money'.[63] The medium of the passage from money to commodity and from commodity to money matters little. 'Events which take place *outside the sphere of circulation*, in the interval between buying and selling, do not affect the form of this movement.'[64]

All labour with words, then, that envisages nothing more than a revenue of meaning detachable from its function (discursive, expressive language) corresponds to the value-giving movement of industrial capital. Writing is put to work to produce as much meaning as possible. We could add that, within limits (those of idealist philosophy), the absorption of all traces (of all labour) by the full presence of meaning corresponds exactly to the value-giving movement of usurers' capital or more generally to the ignorance (to the expenditure) of all labour, of every medium between one value and another. 'In usurers' capital the form M–C–M is reduced to the unmediated extremes M–M, money which is exchanged for more money'.[65] Just as the money-form, detached from any trace of labour, from any relation to commodities, enables financial *speculation*, the hypostasis of the exchange-value of words enables philosophical *speculation*.

> Value therefore now becomes value in process, money in process, and, as such, capital. It comes out of circulation, enters into it again, preserves and multiplies itself within circulation, emerges from it with an increased size, and starts the same cycle again and again. M–M, money which begets money.[66]

This 'abridged' circulation, 'in its final result and without any intermediate stage',[67] is the basis of speculative idealist philosophy, which short-circuits the use-value of signs (the labour of writing) to situate itself within the Logos that reabsorbs (evaluates, appreciates) everything – just as, 'since money does not reveal what has been transformed into it, everything, commodity or not, is convertible into money'.[68]

But if 'nothing is immune from this alchemy', this alchemy does not in itself create value. It displaces and concentrates value (it accumulates value) but doesn't create it. Just as non-operative (non-written) speculation remains empty and unproductive, so circulation and exchange create no value.[69] And if meaning appears in exchange, it is not *by means of* exchange that meaning is created; it is by means of an operation (a use) that remains removed from it. Just as 'surplus-value cannot arise from circulation', and as, 'for it to be formed, something must take place in the background which is not visible in the circulation itself',[70] so language *profits* from an operation that is made invisible by the brilliance of meaning.

Algebra and (speculative idealist) philosophy appear to be two *economic* modes. But one is realized in the sphere of use (algebraic abbreviation enabling operations that increase the productivity of signs) and the other (usurious exploitation, 'abridged' circulation) in the sphere of exchange. More generally, two *formalisms* can be defined: the first linked to the use-value of signs, to their production and productive consumption, an *operative formalism* (mathematics, logic, 'poetry'); the second linked only to the exchange-value of signs, corresponding to a purely monetary function, confusing the formal use-value of signs, arising out of their 'specific social function',[71] with real, productive use-value. This is the formalism that, in language and in the economic sphere, can give rise to *inflation*. The economy of the cursive and discursive, of the financial and the monetary, is not an algebraic abbreviation but only a (non-operative, non-combinatory) steno-graphic abbreviation, one that can, through extrapolation and interpolation beyond any *function*, generate fluidity, the flowing and transparent discursivity of dilution, the currency of monetary flux (of *liquidity*) as a revenue detached from the operation.

Textual de-enunciation (Sollers[72]) is, on the other hand, a movement of *deflation*, of generalized devaluation, that should, after logocentrism's *crash* and *bankruptcy*, reveal the scriptural operation that was masked by speculation and which speculation profited from thereby.

Discursive language is the occultation of the detour of production that sustains it. It dispenses with the scriptural operation while secretly exploiting it. What is masked thereby is the use-value of *combinatory elements* both as product (the result of labour) and as the means of production of other products. The concept *sign* belongs only to the sphere of (specular) exchange, just as the concept commodity designates a product only in the market-place (that stage on which exchanges are performed).

The occultation of use implicates not only the (algebraic) labour of elements, i.e. 'indirect' use; it also concerns the (sexual) play of elements, i.e. 'direct' use (as immediate object of consumption, *jouissance*), the combinatory short-cuts of (material) word-play. The dissimulation of the sphere of use by the sphere of circulation (of writing by meaning) concerns both labour and sex. Hence it affects the two poles that, in a generalized combinatory-system of elements, represent labour and sex: mathematics and poetry.

Capital/labour

'Writing, labour.' 'Meaning, value.' 'Exploitation of writing, exploitation of labour.' . . . It is true that the ins and outs of this correspondence, of this close homology, are difficult to grasp. But there is no doubt about the complicity between the terms. 'The subordination of the trace to full presence taken up in Logos, the abasement of writing beneath a word dreaming of its plenitude', 'the logocentric repression which organized itself to exclude or debase, to put outside and underneath, as a didactic and technical metaphor, as servile matter or excrement, the body of the written trace'[73] . . . has the same figure as the exploitation of the labour force by the dominant political class, and it corresponds in every detail to the extortion of surplus labour that sustains that class (an extortion more or less disguised depending on the historical period). The taxation of labour, the absorption of its product by value, is indistinguishable from the effacement of the trace by the Logos (law, reading, ligature). Plato's open contempt for writing signifies the open extortion (in slavery) of surplus labour. The philosopher is openly dispensed from writing just as the dominant class is dispensed from working. Dispensation from the detour of production sustains political speech (which evolves within the immediacy and self-evidence of meaning) and by return taxes, imposes upon, productive labour. In the same way, the misrecognition of the specific use-value of writing and its dissimulation in the universal transparency of exchange (its relative change in class-status, its de-classification) corresponds to the capitalist moment of disguising the extortion of surplus labour in the guise of the free contract (effected in the sphere of exchange).

Logocentrism situates itself within the short-cut effect produced by the detour it imposes. Thus the scriptural compromise between the short-cut and the detour (poetic writing) is prohibited by the scission between a labour ignorant of the thing to which it is a detour, and a short-cut (a dispensation) ignorant of the detour from which it has escaped. Logocentrism is, then, the effect of the detour's deviation [*détournement du détour*] (for the benefit of a class that 'consumes without producing').

Hegelian thought can be interpreted, after the event, as a heroic but unilateral attempt to loosen the covering of logocentrism (before being crushed by it). We arrive at science (posits Hegel) by covering every part of the path via which the concept of knowledge is reached. For 'truth is not like a stamped coin that is issued ready from the mint and so can be taken up and used'.[74] The Hegelian *path* is the trace (the detour) which will give meaning (value) to truth (to the stamped coin). It is the dream of a labouring trace that would nonetheless remain within Marx's monetary *sublimation*. Hegel also writes that truth should not be like a product detached 'from the instrument that shapes it',[75] but it is, in the end, 'the suppression of differences'. Truth finds itself in its element. Whereas, by taking literally the long path, the trace of labour, the painful detour (of production), by denouncing the monetary illusion of value as the dissimulation of the exploitation of the force of labour, by exposing the secret of money-fetishism and commodity-fetishism, Marx's analysis strikes at the very root of the *system of the sign*.

The relations between *capital* and *labour*, on the one hand, and between conscious and unconscious, on the other, are *revealed* (and brought together) in the relations between speech (meaning) and writing (the scriptural operation). Just as, according to Freud, 'the unexplained phenomenon of consciousness appears, in the system of perception, *in the place of* lasting traces', so the dominant ideology puts itself *in the place of* the productive labour that sustains it. So meaning profits from the writing that makes it possible.

This is an essential *usurpation*, operating at every level. With the same gesture, a certain economy of exploitation absorbs the signifier in the signified (by setting up that distinction), reduces the fabrications of writing to its meaning, reduces the inscription of labour to the value of its workmanship.[76]

But thereafter, to force open the closure that restricts the efficacy of the trace (which regulates and taxes it) is to aim towards the other side, where the force and the product of labour will undergo no translation (no fixing of a price, no speculation). Thereafter the gap between inscription (the labouring trace) and pseudo-transcription (value, money), which is part of the same system as the opposition of unconscious and conscious, labour and capital, will head towards its own annulment. The force of labour will enter into its own space of generalized writing, of compromise between the short-cut and the detour, of textual history, excluding all hypostases of meaning.

Translated by Roland-François Lack

Notes

1 [This article appeared originally in *Tel Quel*, 33 (1968), alongside texts by Ponge, Pleynet, Rottenberg and the first part of Derrida's 'Plato's Pharmacy'. A modified version was republished in *Théorie d'ensemble*.]
2 Derrida, *Of Grammatology*, trans. Gayatri Chakravorty Spivak (Baltimore, Johns Hopkins University Press, 1976 [1967]), 43; Marx, *Capital: A Critique of Political Economy*, trans. Ben Fowkes, volume 1 (Harmondsworth, Penguin, 1976 [1867]), 204.
3 [Contemporary French linguist.]
4 Marx, *Capital*, 125.
5 Ibid., 127.
6 [The English translation of Marx has 'congealed quantities of homogeneous human labour', the French translation used by Goux has a quite different resonance: 'métamorphosés en sublimés identiques'.]
7 Ibid., 156 and 158.
8 Ibid., 162.
9 Ibid.
10 Ibid., 184.
11 Ibid.
12 Ibid., 195.
13 Ibid., 204.
14 Ibid., 189.
15 Ibid., 185. [Fowkes's English translation of Marx has 'mere *symbol*', but the French text used by Goux has *sign*, making the passage from Marx to Saussure so much easier.]
16 Ibid., 185–6.
17 Saussure, *Course in General Linguistics*, trans. Wade Baskin (New York, McGraw-Hill, 1966 [1916]), 118.
18 'Uncultivated land is without value because no human labour is objectified in it', Marx, *Capital*, 197.
19 Ibid., 223.
20 Ibid., 226. [Again Goux's text has 'sign' where the English translation has 'symbol'.]
21 Hegel, *The Phenomenology of Mind* trans. J. B. Baillie (London, Allen & Unwin, 1971), 570. [Baudrey's French has the more abstract 'mis en circulation d'une façon isolée' for Baillié's 'swindled individuals many a time', drawing out the economic metaphor, and 'dans le savoir de l'essence' where Baillié's translation gives 'in the knowledge of that inmost reality'.]
22 Saussure, *Course in General Linguistics*, 120.
23 Marx, *Capital*, 204.
24 Ibid., 205.
25 Ibid., 187.
26 Ibid., 181.

27 Ibid., 520.
28 Ibid., 168.
29 Derrida, *Of Grammatology*, 45.
30 Ibid., 47.
31 Marx, *Capital*, 209.
32 Ibid., 166.
33 Ibid., 268.
34 Ibid., 132.
35 Derrida, *Of Grammatology*, 51.
36 Ibid., 23.
37 Marx, *Capital*, 125.
38 Ibid., 290.
39 Ibid., 287.
40 Derrida, *Writing and Difference*, trans. Alan Bass (London, Routledge & Kegan Paul, 1978), 190.
41 Marx, *Capital*, 290. [The syntax of Goux's Marx differs greatly from the English version, and there is an essential difference between the English phrase 'means of subsistence' and the French 'moyen de jouissance'. Though 'jouissance' is a respectable currency in economic and legal discourse, the Barthesian resonance is not out of place. This is a further illustration of how the French Marx can appear more a contemporary of French theory than does his English equivalent.]
42 Derrida, *Writing and Difference*, 198.
43 Ibid., 203.
44 [S Freud, *Introductory Lectures on Psychoanalysis*, in J Strachey (ed.) *Standard Edition*, vol. XVI (London: Hogarth Press, 1953), 312, Goux's emphasis.]
45 See Marx, *Capital*, 557.
46 Derrida, *Writing and Difference*, 214.
47 Marx, *Capital*, 283.
48 Ibid., 285.
49 Ibid., 283.
50 Derrida, *Of Grammatology*, 65.
51 Marx, *Capital*, 677.
52 Ibid., 65. [Derrida wrote 'appearance *and* signification', not *of*.]
53 Marx, *Capital*, 136.
54 [We have translated Joseph Roy's French version of Marx used by Goux as it differs so markedly from Fowkes's English version: 'That this same labour is, on the other hand, the universal value creating element, and thus possesses a property by virtue of which it differs from all other commodities, is something which falls outside the frame of reference of the everyday consciousness' (*Capital*, 681).]
55 Ibid., 677.
56 Derrida, *Writing and Difference*, 213.
57 Marx, *Capital*, 302.
58 Derrida, *Writing and Difference*, 210.
59 Marx, *Capital*, 301.
60 Ibid., 682.
61 Ibid., 709.
62 Merleau-Ponty, *Phenomenology of Perception*, trans. Colin Smith (London, Routledge, 1992), 401.
63 Marx, *Capital*, 256.
64 Ibid., 256 [our emphasis].
65 Ibid., 267.
66 Ibid., 256.

67 Ibid., 257.
68 Ibid., 229.
69 We should add here that as *value* any commodity belongs to a set marked by *internal relations of equivalence*, the properties of which are: *reflexivity* (any element *a* is equivalent to itself); *symmetry* (if *a* is equivalent to *b*, *b* is equivalent to *a*); and *transitivity* (if *a* is equivalent to *b*, and *b* is equivalent to *c*, then *a* is equivalent to *c*). Furthermore, as commodities (determined by a value) all products can figure on a *unique scale*. The only determination that counts being quantitative (a quantity expressible in common units), the set of commodities is defined, to use once again the language of set theory, by an *internal relation of order*. Thus the bourgeois code, insofar as it is subject to the logic of money and commodities (i.e. subject to a reduction to the same *order* within the linearity of the quantitative), is particularly impoverished. Hence all those types of complex relation between *several sets* (applications: surjections, bijections, injections, etc.) and delinearized modes of junction (networks, trees, etc.) that, as Kristeva has shown, intervene in poetic language cannot be manifest at the usual level of the poetic code unless an economic prohibition taxes them with being unreadable irregularities.
70 Marx, *Capital*, 268.
71 Ibid., 184.
72 Sollers, 'The Science of Lautréamont', in *Writing and the Experience of Limits*, trans. L.S. Roudiez (New York, Columbia University Press, 1983).
73 [Quotation, no doubt from Derrida, unattributed.]
74 Hegel, 'Preface' to *The Phenomenology of Mind*, 98.
75 Ibid., 99.
76 [Goux is exploiting a number of double-meanings that are difficult to reproduce (e.g., *fabrique* as 'factory' and as 'invention'; *facture* as 'workmanship' and 'invoice'). The overall effect is to illustrate the gesture of 'usurpation' at work at every level.]

4

FREUD AND 'LITERARY CREATION'[1]

Jean-Louis Baudry

The essential contribution of Freud's discovery, conferring on psychoanalysis its importance and relevance today, seems by most of Freud's successors to have gone unnoticed, to have been incomprehensible, or at least misread, due to the central obsession that haunts Western thought, and haunts Freud himself: the obsession with the subject and the more or less general inability to think beyond this reference. And yet Freud, from his work on neuroses, affirms that there is a diminution of the text due in the first place to the repressive organization of society,[2] and that the lost text may be recovered, but in a deformed state (a suspect notion, in fact, since it suggests the existence and permanence of an initial text); this recovered text has been worked on, transformed, subjected to operations analogous to those at work in the production of a properly literary text. The 'unconscious', a functional concept linked to a certain state of the text, serves to define both the site of the lost text's recuperation and the transformative mechanisms to which the text is subjected. In the *Project for a Scientific Psychology* (1895), Freud reveals his interest in what we may call the dynamic of the text, the process of inscription and apparition where we recognize the specific characteristics of writing: 'trace', 'frayage', 'effraction', 'après-coup'.[3] The *Traumdeutung* and the *Psychopathology of Everyday Life* are first and foremost textual analyses enabling us to discover the grammar, the adjustments to and the redistribution of the lost text. In the field that is psychoanalysis's proper concern, the recuperation of a text lost because of the system of Western society (a system of thought and an economic system[4]), and before the development of linguistics, Freud displayed a remarkable knowledge of textual production and textual dynamics, of the slippages, permutations, reinvestments, to which the text is subjected, as inter-textual exchanges (organic conversions, symptoms of displacement, of substitution, etc.). We seem to have before us all the procedures and textual organizations of which the written text (literature) is the privileged site. We could, then, expect Freud to be as perceptive regarding the literary event as he is in deciphering the 'unconscious' text. It is true that he is a keen reader, 'tireless', as he himself says of Leonardo. He is able, moreover, in the manner of the cultivated bourgeois of his period, to spice his correspondence and his writings with appropriate citations. But there is more. A literary character gives his name to one of the fundamental concepts of psychoanalysis and, starting in *The Interpretation of Dreams*, the analysis of a dramatic character, Hamlet, contrasted with this first character, will demonstrate the reinforcement of repression in our society and the resulting neurotic effects.

Literature provides the reference points and confirms the hypotheses of analytic research; it will also become, through a necessary rotation, an object of inquiry. The continuity of the same movement leads Freud to seek in literature an exemplary support for analytic investigation (all the more exemplary through the text's accessibility), to ask literature for an explanation of this support, to make literature an area of exploration, of analytic 'curiosity'. It will not be surprising to find Freud using such concepts as 'artist', 'creative writer', 'novelist', 'poet', the literary 'work' and the process of 'creation', reading and the reader, clearly inter-dependent concepts.

Freud's written commentary on Jensen's *Gradiva* is more than a simple analysis of dreams or delusion, and seems above all to raise theoretical problems. From his first remarks, Freud announces the givens of the problem when he says that his curiosity was

> aroused one day by the question of the class of dreams that have never been dreamt at all — dreams created by imaginative writers and ascribed to invented characters in the course of a story. The notion of submitting this class of dreams to an investigation might seem a waste of energy and a strange thing to undertake; but from one point of view it could be considered justifiable.[5]

And Freud spends a large part of his analysis attempting to justify it. The question he seems to ask himself is this: How is it that dreams imagined by an author and attributed, according to the demands of fiction, to a character are susceptible to analytic interpretation in the same way as 'real' dreams? And how is it that fictional characters are described in such a way that they seem to be subject to the same psychical forces as real people? Freud firstly establishes a distinction between reality and imagination. However, this distinction does not observe the bounds of classical psychology, according to which dreams belong to the imagination and cannot be called 'real'. Freud opposes real dreams (*wirklichen Träume*) — dreams lived by a real subject — and imagined dreams ('Real dreams were already regarded as unrestrained and unregulated structures — and now we are confronted by unfettered imitations of these dreams!'[6]). The conceptual field that determines this distinction is not established from the outset. Is it the opposition of conscious and unconscious? But the novelist's productions are still subject to the 'unconscious' that always oversees 'conscious' production. Is it the state in which these dreams are realized, waking and sleeping? Possibly, and we shall see how Freud establishes the intermediary term whereby we can pass from one to the other. But it is already important to note that this distinction leaves to one side what they have in common, that is, their textual character, allowing writing, the written text, to undergo without mediation the same reading to which dreams are susceptible; and also important to note that the founding of this distinction on the central position occupied by the 'subject' is at the origin of Freud's difficulties. The difference between 'real dream' and 'imagined dream' puts the emphasis not on the textual differentiations that might arise from their comparison, hence not on a reading of the text itself, but on a state or a faculty (the imagination) attributed to the 'subject'. On the contrary, using the real/imaginary opposition, Freud is obliged to have recourse to mediations if he is to demonstrate that 'imaginary' dreams are interpretable in the manner of 'real' dreams. And from the outset, imperceptibly, he adopts uncritically the theory of art as imitation. *Mimesis* is implied by the terms of his question: if literary work and reality are interchangeable as objects of a new knowledge (psychoanalysis) that the novelist could not have been aware of, this can only be because the one is an imitation of the other, and that the imitation is perfect. But then where does this perfection come from? 'My readers will no doubt have been puzzled to notice that so far I have treated Norbert Hanold and Zoe Bertgag, in all their mental manifestations and activities, as though they were real people [*wirklichen Individuen*] and not the author's creations [*Geschöpfe eines Dichters*].'[7] And Freud insists so strongly on the work's conformity to reality that when the *Gradiva* twice seems to go against verisimilitude he makes an effort to demonstrate that there is no incompatibility with reality, not least because reality can be expanded to involve 'the sources in the author's mind'. [8] This expansion of the notion of reality to include the unconscious is essential because it enables Freud to preserve his realist conception of 'art'. Freud affirms that between the work and its 'creator' there is a relation such that if the work evinces a certain knowledge, this knowledge must be referred to a 'subject' who would be, deliberately or not, consciously or unconsciously, the dispenser thereof. We might ask whether, put in these terms, the question in fact exposes the grounds of the 'science' that poses it. These are *metaphysical* grounds, because of the dualisms implied: real and imaginary, sign and meaning, signified and representation, etc.; *theological* grounds, relating a creator to his creature, a subject to its predicate in a relation such that if $P \in S$, S would never be reducible to the sum of its predicates, in other words, the 'subject' is never an effect of the text, but exists before it as the causal substance necessary to its production; they are *ideological* grounds, lastly, insofar as the presuppositions that found this discourse are not themselves questioned. These metaphysical and theological presuppositions are, in fact, clearly inscribed in Freud's text: poets and novelists

> know a whole host of things between heaven and earth of which our philosophy has not yet let us dream. In their knowledge of the mind they are far in advance of us everyday people, for they draw upon sources which we have not yet opened up for science.[9]

And further on he speaks of the poets 'whom we are accustomed to honour as the deepest observers of the human mind'.[10] But as soon as Freud introduces the relation – a relation of causality, of belonging – between the 'poet' or 'novelist' and his 'work', we see him hesitating as to the specifics of this relation. Though he seems inclined to see the 'poet' as a privileged 'subject' connected to the *Creator*, placed between heaven and earth, having access to knowledge denied the profane layman, and thereby destined to be the object of proper veneration, he also slips in another response:

> There is far less freedom and arbitrariness in mental life, however, than we are inclined to assume – there may be none at all. What we call chance in the world outside can, as is well known, be resolved into laws. So, too, what we call arbitrariness in the mind rests upon laws, which we are only now beginning dimly to suspect.[11]

At this point Freud suggests that the work is not so much the site of an unexplainable, supernatural knowledge, as the object of a knowledge to be applied to it. Freud doesn't risk deciding between these two possibilities. He is unable to consider artistic production as just another production of the mind, but he can't abandon it to aesthetic appreciation alone. There are several signs of this hesitation: the frequent use of the interrogative form, paragraphs interrupted a little too quickly. The term *profane* acquires its full significance. Freud's enterprise is peculiarly prudent and respectful, too little inclined to upset a few idols. 'Since our hero, Norbert Hanold, is a fictitious person, we may perhaps put a timid question to his author, and ask whether his imagination was determined by forces other than its own arbitrary choice.'[12] A timid question, and for the moment left unanswered (though the answer was implied when a little earlier Freud had invoked the unity of psychical life and the laws that are its basis), indicating some mental reservations and revealing the procedure Freud intends to apply. It is also an insistent question, one that can be formulated in several different ways: What knowledge does the author have at his disposal? What are its 'sources'? What is the relation between this knowledge and that of science (the old science, classical psychiatry, and the new science, psychoanalysis)? We should remember that Freud is seeking to validate the analytic method and its results through works of fiction, he wants to arrive at a confirmation of his views on the 'unconscious' and on dreams through conclusions established by the study of literary works. This confirmation is important on methodological grounds: the novel is a synthesis where psychoanalysis, in effect, is an analysis. The object is to show that the same elements, the same psychical processes, are encountered whichever route is taken, whether a patient is being treated or a character is being 'created'. Freud seeks to understand the status of the work, to determine its place among other products of the mind, to recover the processes of 'artistic creation' and to discover why some men are capable of such production and others not (Freud shared the conventional view on this subject according to which, contrary to what Lautréamont affirms, poetry can only be made by one, not by all[13]). Doubtless, novelists and poets 'know a whole host of things between heaven and earth of which our philosophy has not yet let us dream' (and here Freud's conception is no different from the Romantic, bourgeois, Christian vision of the poet), yet in another passage Freud writes: 'If the insight which has enabled the author to construct his "phantasy" in such a way that we have been able to dissect it like a real case history is in the nature of knowledge, we should be curious to learn what were the sources of that knowledge.'[14] The commentary on *Gradiva* was written in 1906–7. Though Freud has by this time emerged from his 'proud isolation' and though psychoanalysis is beginning to be recognized, psychoanalysis still has to struggle against the prejudices of classical psychiatry and to effect the conquest of new territories. We can sense that 'Delusions and Dreams' is a response to these two objectives. In the first place, Freud is quite happy to establish a firmer footing in the literary domain – the Postscript to the Second Edition is a declaration of victory in this enterprise ('In the five years that have passed since this study was completed, psycho-analytic research has summoned up the courage to approach the creations of imaginative writers'[15]). And secondly, he is pleased to be able to demonstrate that psychoanalysis is in agreement with a literary work and is capable of giving a correct interpretation of the dreams and delusions of a fictional character, whereas the simplistic notions of the old science, psychiatry, could only place delusion within a faulty and inappropriate classification, formulating clearly moral judgements upon the hero ('a strict psychiatrist would at once stamp him as a *dégénéré* '[16]). The result is that, thanks to psychoanalysis, the novelist acquires something approaching scientific status.

> Perhaps, too, in most people's eyes we are doing our author a poor service in declaring his work to be a psychiatric study. An author, we hear them say, should keep out of the way of any contact with psychiatry and should leave the description of pathological mental states to the doctors. The truth is that no truly creative writer has ever obeyed this injunction. The description of the human mind is indeed the domain which is most his own; he has from time

immemorial been the precursor of science, and so too of scientific psychology. . . . The creative writer cannot evade the psychiatrist nor the psychiatrist the creative writer, and the poetic treatment of a psychiatric theme can turn out to be correct without any sacrifice of its beauty.[17]

But Freud goes further. The comparison between science (the old science) and the novelist distinctly favours the latter:

It is science that cannot hold its own before the achievement of the author. Science allows a gulf to yawn between the hereditary and constitutional preconditions of a delusion and its creations, which seem to emerge ready-made – a gulf which we find that our author has filled. Science does not as yet suspect the importance of repression, it does not recognize that in order to explain the world of psychopathological phenomena the unconscious is absolutely essential, it does not look for the basis of delusions in a psychical conflict, and it does not regard their symptoms as compromises. Does our author stand alone, then, in the face of united science? No, that is not the case (if, that is, I may count my own works as part of science).[18]

Freud here signals the relation that can be established between the novelist and the new science – psychoanalysis – and how the knowledge of psychoanalysis can bring to the fore the other unnoticed knowledge of the novelist.

When, from the year 1893 onwards, I plunged into investigations such as these of the origin of mental disturbances, it would certainly never have occurred to me to look for a confirmation of my findings in imaginative writings. I was thus more than a little surprised to find that the author of Gradiva, which was published in 1903, had taken as the basis of its creation the very thing that I believed myself to have freshly discovered from the sources of my medical experience. How was it that the author arrived at the same knowledge as the doctor – or at least behaved as though he possessed the same knowledge?[19]

This seems like another too timid question, since Freud prefers not to answer it. We should, however, note the slight error in this passage. Freud didn't wait for Jensen's Gradiva to appear before seeking confirmation of his results in the poets. In The Interpretation of Dreams, dealing with 'Dreams of the Death of Persons of whom the Dreamer is Fond', Freud analyses at some length Sophocles' Oedipus Rex, which he describes as 'nothing other than the process of revealing, with cunning delays and ever mounting excitement – a process that can be likened to the work of psycho-analysis', and he follows the trace of Oedipus to reach the character of Hamlet. This is where we might perhaps find a tentative answer to the question Freud asks so timidly, but so insistently. Having demonstrated that, in *Hamlet*, the desires of the child are repressed, unlike what happens in *Oedipus Rex*, Freud proceeds to explain in terms of this same repression the hero's reluctance to avenge his father:

> The loathing which should drive him on to revenge is replaced in him by self-reproaches, by scruples of conscience, which remind him that he himself is literally no better than the sinner whom he is to punish. Here I have translated into conscious terms what was bound to remain unconscious in Hamlet's mind; and if anyone is inclined to call him a hysteric, I can only accept the fact as one that is implied by my interpretation. The distaste for sexuality expressed by Hamlet in his conversation with Ophelia fits in well with this: the same distaste which was destined to take possession of the poet's mind more and more during the years that followed, and which reached its extreme expression in *Timon of Athens*. For it can of course only be the poet's own mind which confronts us in Hamlet. I observe in a book on Shakespeare by Georg Brandes (1896) a statement that *Hamlet* was written immediately after the death of Shakespeare's father (in 1601), that is, under the immediate impact of bereavement and, as we may well assume, while his childhood feelings about his father had been freshly revived. It is known, too, that Shakespeare's own son who died at an early age bore the name of 'Hamnet', which is identical with 'Hamlet'. Just as *Hamlet* deals with the relation of a son to his parents, so *Macbeth* (written at approximately the same period) is concerned with the subject of childlessness. But just as all neurotic symptoms, and for that matter dreams, are capable of being 'over-interpreted' and indeed need to be, if they are to be fully understood, so all genuinely creative writings are the product of more than a single motive and more than a single impulse in the poet's mind, and are open to more than a single interpretation. In what I have written I have only attempted to interpret the deepest layer of impulses in the mind of the creative writer.[20]

So lengthy an extract is needed in order to highlight the curious dislocation that occurs in the course of the demonstration.

> The distaste for sexuality expressed by Hamlet in his conversation with Ophelia fits in well with this (i.e. Hamlet's hysteria): the same distaste which was destined to take possession of the poet's mind

more and more during the years that followed, and which reached its extreme expression in *Timon of Athens*.

So the distaste in question is not Hamlet's but Shakespeare's. Before this sentence, Freud has not mentioned Shakespeare, and only the mention of another one of his plays makes it clear that the 'poet' referred to is not Hamlet (why couldn't it be?) but Shakespeare himself. It is as if for Freud, who doesn't trouble to alert us to the fact, the analysis of a fictional character and the determination of his neuropathic symptoms naturally coincide with the analysis of the symptoms of the author, without need of justification. Applying Freud's own method, we might ask whether his hurried approach and unusually careless style do not betray a sudden 'timidity' faced with a sense of 'profanation' (just as we might easily relate the Shakespeare described by Freud to Freud's own biography, to the *Traumdeutung* that arises from the auto-analysis begun just after the death of Freud's father). A certain notion of 'literary creation' can be discerned in this passage: through its themes a literary work refers us to the biography of the author, the death of the father, the absence of children. The work then springs forth from the author's emotions. The author expresses his own feelings, and in such a way that through the work it is possible to interpret the deepest proclivities of the poet's soul (his 'unconscious', his conflicts). The work is the expression of a mind. It is haunted by an invisible but present character who is both concealed and revealed by the work. The work eludes him, as the dream eludes the dreamer and the symptom eludes the patient, but it denounces and betrays him. Hamlet's distaste for sexuality *is* Shakespeare's own distaste. The proof is, we could say, without over-stretching Freud's text, that the subject of *Macbeth* is the absence of children. The work refers to a situation outside of it and designates not the text itself, but the author of the text. Sketched out here is the whole of psycho-analytical literary criticism, its ideological domain and its methods. Though its point of arrival is slightly different from that of simple biographical criticism (the author's 'unconscious', his motives and conflicts, that which, though hidden from him, determines his themes and images – rather than the simple reduction of the work to events in the author's life, to sentimental episodes, etc.), the fundamental relation of the 'work' to the 'author', of the text to a 'subject', remains the same. As expression of an author, signifier of a signified that it is intended to represent, the text still comes second; it is, finally, reducible to another, more essential text. The only power accorded the text in its own right, as we shall see, is to supply the 'secondary benefit' of pleasure, an 'incentive bonus'.[21] From this passage of *The Interpretation of Dreams* we conclude that a fictional character is assimilable to a real person. There is the same mechanism of illusion and hypostasis that determines the entire discourse of literary criticism. And yet in 'Delusions and Dreams' Freud manifests a degree of prudence on this matter and seems anxious to show he is conscious of the slippage effected: 'My readers will no doubt have been puzzled to notice that so far I have treated Norbert Hanold and Zoe Bertgag, in all their mental manifestations and activities, as though they were real people and not the author's creations', and he ends his study on a reminder of the fictional nature of the characters he has nonetheless analysed: 'But we must stop here, or we may really forget that Harold and Gradiva are only creatures of their author's mind.'[22] But, as we have seen, it is the possibility of treating fictional characters as real that, among other things, creates problems for Freud in this text. His position in 'Delusions and Dreams' seems to be a withdrawal from the one taken up in *The Interpretation of Dreams*, but the same schema is in evidence: Freud hypostasizes the characters and it is they who are analysed. The subject of *Gradiva*, the neuropathic nature of the hero, serves Freud in this purpose. To begin with he looks only at the characters' symptoms, then effects a reversal, giving us to understand that the characters and the work together can be read as symptoms. A particular type of symptom, admittedly, according the 'novelist', 'poet' or 'artist' a specific status within – or at the margins of – neurosis. Freud says that Hamlet is a hysteric, but if the character's distaste for sexuality is Shakespeare's, Freud gives us to understand, without saying it, that Shakespeare too is a hysteric. The expected conclusion of what appears to be a syllogism[23] is 'forgotten'. Has the conclusion been involuntarily missed out (censoring an act of profanation) or has Freud voluntarily suppressed it because it still poses problems for him, while perhaps initiating a question that he will attempt to resolve in the future? Describing Jensen's hero, Freud comments: 'This separation between imagination and intellect destined him to become an artist or a neurotic; he was one of those whose kingdom is not of this world.'[24] Hence, having affirmed that 'the creative writer cannot evade the psychiatrist nor the psychiatrist the creative writer', having acknowledged that poets and novelists 'know a whole host of things between heaven and earth of which our philosophy has not yet let us dream', and that the novelist 'has from time immemorial been the precursor of science, and so too of scientific psychology', Freud seems very close to saying that, like the neuropath, the novelist or poet, i.e. a person attributed texts that define him as novelist or poet, is, by virtue of those texts, a suitable subject for analytic investigation. This is clearly stated in the Postscript to 'Delusions and Dreams':

> In the five years that have passed since this study was completed, psycho-analytic research has summoned up the courage to approach the creations of imaginative writers with yet another purpose in view. It no longer merely seeks in them for confirmation of the findings it has made from unpoetic, neurotic human beings; it also demands to know the material of impressions and memories from which the author has built the work, and the

methods and processes by which he has converted this material into a work of art.[25]

The *neurotischen Menschen*, the neurotics, would appear – as a rather ambiguous implication of Freud's remarks – to divide into *poetischen* (creators) and *unpoetischen* (non-creators). This classification is no different from that used within the banal ideological conception of 'artistic creation'; both are determined by the same presuppositions: creators have a particular relation to madness;[26] their work is the manifestation of a delusion that possesses them. 'Creation', 'madness', 'possession', 'delusion', are terms that can be permutated. The 'delusion' that afflicts the hero of *Gradiva*, destined by virtue of his imagination to be poet or neuropath, gives Jensen's book the air of an abyssal composition, as Freud points out on several occasions: the character's delusion serves as a distorting mirror of the mechanisms at work in the elaboration of the work as a whole. That this madness of the 'creator', possessed by an 'other speech', is exalted by Romanticism, or serves as justification for writers lacking a social role, or that, from a Freudian perspective, based on its pathological finality, it is defused by the production of a work, the pertinent structure of the related terms remains unchanged: i.e. the necessary relation existing between the production of text (the work) and the indispensable presence of a neuropathic condition in the individual producer of the text.

However, even though it is useful to reveal certain analogies and uncover an implicit ideological ground, the Freudian concept shouldn't be reduced to this too simple formulation, nor should it be forgotten that above all Freud is seeking to understand better the mechanisms and forms of neurosis, and to demonstrate that neurosis doesn't just concern 'some poor sick individual' (as Janet described Roussel), but covers an immense domain. Freud's later texts on 'literary creation' will confirm and prove the dependence of creation on neurosis, and establish more precisely the mechanism, the schema of 'artistic creation', while taking up again the themes exposed in *Gradiva*.

In his commentary on *Gradiva*, Freud asks what are the 'sources' of the novelist's knowledge, a knowledge enabling the novel to be analysed in the manner of a genuine medical study. He followed the question with the beginnings of an answer:

> We probably draw from the same source and work upon the same object, each of us by another method. And the agreement of our results seems to guarantee that we have both worked correctly. Our procedure consists in the conscious observation of abnormal mental processes in other people so as to be able to elicit and announce their laws. The author no doubt proceeds differently. He directs his attention to the unconscious in his own mind, he listens to its

possible developments and lends them artistic expression instead of suppressing them by conscious criticism.[27]

This formulation is paradoxical, even obscure. Freud does not define this operation whereby the author's attention is directed to his 'unconscious', nor does he say what are the 'possible developments' to which the 'artist' lends 'artistic expression'. We might, rather, envisage a radical distinction between neurosis and the act of writing, and even a principle of exclusion, if neurosis in effect results from conflicts generated by the repression of the 'unconscious' text, whereas the literary work results from its admission and inscription (its double inscription). We have already underlined this ambiguity in the Freudian position. Is the work on the side of science or can it be compared to neurotic formulations? We might wonder whether reference to sublimation has its origin here, whether sublimation is not a means of eluding a problem insoluble in its own terms, a speculative solution to dispel contradictions.

In the text translated as 'Creative Writers and Daydreaming' (*Der Dichter und das Phantasieren*; *das Phantasieren* poses problems of translation), and at the end of Chapter 23 of the *Introductory Lectures on Psycho-Analysis* ('The Paths to the Formation of Symptoms'), Freud completes his concept of 'creation' and 'creative' labour, and explains what he meant by 'possible developments'. He also details certain aspects of his formulation in the *Gradiva* that we have not gone into here.

> We laymen have always been intensely curious to know . . . from what sources that strange being, the creative writer, draws his material, and how he manages to make such an impression on us with it and to arouse in us emotions [*Erregungen*] of which, perhaps, we had not thought ourselves capable.[28]

The terms of the question, the profane[29] layman and the distinct personality of the 'creator', are those employed in 'Delusions and Dreams', and they recur in the *Introductory Lectures on Psycho-Analysis*. But the question is displaced: whereas in 'Delusions and Dreams', it concerned the knowledge of the novelist and was addressed to the man of science, here it refers to pleasure and is addressed to the reader. Just as the knowledge contained in the work would be revealed by the knowledge of the man of science, so it is the pleasure of the reader that will reveal what fixes the work of the novelist, and also what is at stake in the reader's mind. This question accords a specific function and effect to reading: generating emotions, determining pleasure (*Genuss* [*jouissance*]). This notion of the work as source of pleasure and emotion, on the basis of which Freud undertakes to elucidate the process of 'creation', clearly is little different from the role assigned by the bourgeoisie to 'art'. In the same way, applying the tired distinction of form and content, this notion privileges themes, content, assigning them the representative function that will enable the reader's identification with the 'hero'. The German term *Stoff* (cloth, material) might allow of a certain ambiguity, but the rest of the text shows that 'theme' is the proper translation. Themes and pleasure, these are the inductive materials of Freud's demonstration. The text should be read closely because only a word-for-word reading allows us to uncover the unconscious ideology that can permeate a scientific discourse. It is manifest, for example, in terms such as 'profane' or 'distinct personality' of the 'creator'. Here we shall point out its principal articulations.

Freud relates poetic activity to children's play. This comparison might be fruitful insofar as an analysis of games could elucidate the operations of distribution and permutation etc. that control the production of text, and also and above all insofar as play reverses the accepted relation of inscription to expression. 'The advent of writing', writes Derrida, 'is the advent of this play.'[30] This thinking about play, akin to the more daring propositions of Nietzsche, a thinking of the 'game of the world'[31] that seems to announce an exit from the space of Platonic metaphysics,[32] clearly explodes all reference to the subject and exposes all its modes of defence (to the point that we might ask whether the very possibility of neurosis is initially determined by a system of thought that proposes the subject as its origin. This is why even Freud's thinking, despite the 'third narcissistic wound it has inflicted on humanity', in not genuinely calling into question the supremacy of the subject, has effectively maintained the rule of neurosis – or so we might conclude from observing the worldwide development of psychoanalysis, its results and the role assigned it by society. But Freud avoids this direction, immediately re-establishing the opposition between play and reality. 'The opposite of play is not what is serious but what is real. . . . The creative writer does the same as the child at play.'[33] For Freud play seems to mean simulation and representation.

> A child's play is determined by wishes: in point of fact by a single wish – one that helps in his upbringing – the wish to be big, to be grown up. He is always playing at being 'grown up', and in his games he imitates what he knows about the lives of his elders.[34]

Play would then be an activity intended to correct an unsatisfying reality by an imaginative representation, the reproduction and transformation, in the mode of the unreal, of a reality that is an obstacle to satisfaction. By emphasizing that certain literary works – those that are, precisely, destined to be put on stage [*représentées*] – are named from the German word *Spiel* (play) – *Trauerspiel* (tragedy), *Lustspiel* (comedy) – Freud seems to insist on this notion of representation – *Darstellung* – that we shall come upon again. We might note in passing that the French word for play, *jeu*, and the verb associated with it, suggests a productive activity attesting not so much to the opposition of play and reality but to their complicity, insofar as reality can be considered a product of labour and of knowledge. It would be interesting to examine Freud's concept of reality (*Wirklichkeit*). It is no doubt directly opposed to the *Trieb*, the drive. We might find a pertinent opposition between drive and reality, the one defined in relation to the other. Reality would seem connected to the idea of necessity, *Ananké*, the force of things. It would be what forces the 'subject' to renounce satisfaction, and would in this sense be close to the notion of reality promoted by bourgeois ideology and morality. Reality is what obliges the child, the 'subject' (and the proletariat), to renounce the satisfaction of its desires (but also of its needs).[35]

The analysis of renunciation will allow Freud to establish an analogy between infant-play and phantasy, the waking-dream. 'We can never give anything up; we only exchange one thing for another. What appears to be a renunciation is really the formation of a substitute or surrogate. . . . Instead of playing, [the adult] now phantasizes.'[36] Freud is interested in studying the characteristics of and conditions under which the phantasm appears. But it is through neurotics, not through writers, that we have access to the phantasm. On several occasions Freud regrets that writers are so discreet when asked about the sources of their work, and he had already shown his unhappiness at Jensen's silence on this matter. Freud seems to make of this silence, this reticence, a symptom available to interpretation (his interpretation of creativity) and not a sign of incapacity; not, in fact, the impossibility of answering a question inadequate to its object: textual reality.

Phantasm, Freud says, is the realization of a desire – showing thereby its relation to dream and to neurotic symptoms, which are formations of substitutive satisfaction. Freud makes an extraordinary remark: 'The happy man has no phantasms.' We might come to suspect that artistic activity, if it is linked to the production of phantasms, is the business of individuals who suffer particular difficulty in achieving satisfaction. In the *Introductory Lectures on Psycho-Analysis* Freud's position on this subject is explicit:

> An artist is once more in rudiments an introvert, not far removed from neurosis. He is oppressed by excessively powerful instinctual needs. He desires to own honour, power, wealth, fame and the love of women, but he lacks the means for achieving these satisfactions. Consequently, like any other unsatisfied man, he turns away from reality and transfers all his interest, and his libido too, to the wishful construction of his life of phantasy, whence the path might lead to neurosis.[37]

And in 'Creative Writers and Day-Dreaming': 'If phantasies become over-luxuriant and over-powerful, the conditions are laid for the onset of neurosis or psychosis.'[38] This remark is striking, since elsewhere Freud says that the novelist 'listens to all possible developments and lends them artistic expression instead of suppressing them by conscious criticism'.

Phantasms 'fit themselves in to the subject's shifting impressions of life' and hover, 'as it were, between three times – the three moments of time which our ideation involves (*unseres Vorstellens* [*notre faculté représentative*])'.[39] The temporal analysis of phantasm-formation is important because it will demonstrate the identity between the process of production of the 'waking-dream' and that of literary 'creation'. Freud does not define this *Vorstellen*, but we might imagine that it is connected to the notion of time. It would reside in the ability of the 'subject' to use representations to make present the past and the future. Memories and projections would then be 'representations' generated by desire ('past, present and future are strung together on the thread of the wish that runs through them'). But as for the present, how is it to be represented? Freud gives no answer to the nonetheless important question of the representation of the present in the present. We might find that the question opens onto the model of the mirror, which occupies metaphysical and psychological thinking as a necessary function of knowledge, be it the self-knowledge the 'subject' acquires through consciousness and introspection, or the knowledge theorized as reflection of the thing-in-itself, or, from a more strictly psychoanalytic viewpoint, the knowledge at stake in the problems posed by the 'subject' and his identifications. Must we conclude that the third moment of time of our 'representative faculty', the present, is defined and exhausted by perception? But then where do we situate the phantasm that brings together these three moments? Is this not the kind of difficulty that arises with a system of thought bound up with linearity, itself implicated in the problematic of the subject? Doubtless we have to completely rethink, down to its basic terms and beyond an insistent phenomenological temptation, this 'representation' of the present as the inscription of textual articulation, as the very possibility of writing within 'spacing' and 'difference'. We refer to Derrida's essential analyses.[40] Derrida has shown that such a thinking is at work in Freud, and perhaps it can just be discerned here in the capacity of 'an occasion in the present' to awaken a desire already inscribed in 'an earlier experience (usually an infantile one) in which this wish was fulfilled'. The phantasm, says Freud, 'carries about it traces [*Spuren*] of its origin from the occasion which provoked it and from the memory'.[41] It is their articulation that has to be rethought as that which, when doubled, only allows of a doubled presence, i.e. which destroys the present as presence.

The mechanism of phantasm-formation is described as follows:

Mental work is linked to some current impression, some provoking occasion in the present which has been able to arouse one of the subject's major wishes. From there it harks back to a memory of an earlier experience (usually an infantile one) in which this wish was fulfilled; and it now creates a situation relating to the future which represents [*darstellt*] a fulfilment of the wish. What it thus creates is a day-dream or phantasy, which carries about it traces of its origin.[42]

A suspect origin, according to Freud in the *Introductory Lectures on Psycho-Analysis*: ambitious desires and erotic desires, these last concerning women above all ('In young women erotic wishes predominate almost exclusively, for their ambition is as a rule absorbed by erotic trends').[43]

Freud had already provided an analysis of phantasm in 'Delusions and Dreams' and, from the slippage effected in *The Interpretation of Dreams*, we could deduce that through the character of Norbert Hanold, it was the writer and his 'sources' who was at issue, just as Shakespeare was there in Hamlet. Phantasms have a double determination: one that is conscious, apparent to Norbert Hanold himself and derived entirely from the representations of archaeological science, the conscious intentions of the novelist and the work as it is thought by the novelist; another that is unconscious, derived from repressed childhood memories and from affective drives attached to them. Perhaps the writer's silence is to be explained by his inability to know the 'sources' of his novel, since these are determined by the unconscious and effectively inaccessible to him. This is a familiar ideological schema. A psychological subject is asked to account for the text and then the non-pertinence of the question, the impossibility of receiving a satisfactory answer, is exploited to make this 'subject' the site of another speech, of a full speech expressing an unjustifiable meaning. This is how the oracular figure of the poet was imposed, as messenger of a truth he himself could not master or understand. Once again a notion is established at the expense of the text, which is made transparent by the privilege accorded the meaning it carries, with no account taken of the operations necessary to the text's production.

Phantasms

> are substitutes for and derivatives of repressed memories which a resistance will not allow to enter consciousness unaltered, but which can purchase the possibility of becoming conscious by taking account, by means of changes and distortions, of the resistance's censorship. When this compromise has been accomplished, the memories have turned into phantasies, which can easily be misunderstood by the conscious personality.[42]

There have been divergent interpretations of the Freudian concept of the phantasm.[43] For some there is a primary phantasmatic operation upon which the play of drives depends. In the texts studied here phantasms are unambiguously presented as formations of substitutive satisfaction, derivative, hence secondary substitutes for repressed memories. They depend on the *Vorstellen*. This representative function that Freud assigns them is carried over to the function of literary 'creation': 'May we really attempt to compare the imaginative writer with the "dreamer in broad daylight", and his creations with daydreams?'[44] The assimilation, even if put as a question, is immediate, though Freud will be obliged to distinguish between two categories of author, those 'like the ancient authors of epics and tragedies, who take over their material ready-made', and 'writers who seem to originate their own material'.[45] He discounts the former, despite his greater respect for them, to concentrate on 'the less pretentious authors of novels, romances and short stories who nevertheless have the widest and most eager circle of readers of both sexes'.[46] By taking no account of authors who receive their themes, their materials, 'ready-made', Freud appears to exclude not only the particular nature of writing in its specificity and in its production, but also its literariness, its specifically literary aspect, i.e. (and Freud's attention should have been alerted to this by his analysis of dream-writing) that all inscription is double, that every text doubles and effaces another text, and that all literature, even the literature Freud draws on for his examples, is only readable through other texts, and depends in its production and in its reading on a general 'intertextuality'. When Freud returns a little later to the class of works excluded from his demonstration, those that consist in the 'refashioning of ready-made and familiar material', and which for him seem to have a superior literary value, he ignores the problems posed by this 'refashioning'. Once again, he neglects textual production as the possibility of refashioning and acting upon another text, he removes the 'themes' from the context of their inscription. He goes through the text to see only the 'subjects' it expresses, the 'distorted vestiges of the wishful phantasies of whole nations, the secular dreams of youthful humanity', expressed in myths, legends and stories.[47] Which is to say that these 'subjects' are merely representative, mere 'vestiges'. The term may or may not have a pejorative sense for Freud. Perhaps, in his analyses, he is simply under the sway of the 'logocentrism' that, according to Derrida, inevitably reduces writing to a secondary, instrumental role. So secondary a role, in effect, that in all of his writings on literary creation Freud never once mentions that the object of his attention is a *written* object. His entire demonstration follows from this. Enclosed within the perspective of the subject, he assimilates text-production to the mode of phantasm-formation, explaining one by means of the other, without thinking (although the relation of phantasm to memory seems to suggest this) that the study of the text as inscription would enable an elucidation of the phantasmatic mechanism, a reversal that would allow him, among other things, to bypass the difficulties relating to the temporality of phantasm.[48] Freud's choice of 'the less pretentious authors of novels, romances and short stories' is thus determined by the 'forgetting', the denial of the written, and hence by the privilege accorded themes insofar as these are representatives of 'something' not dependent on inscription. The trace of this 'something', of this 'always elsewhere', will be followed below. Themes are evidently the thing most easily grasped by a reading directed towards meaning; but they are also what correspond best to the order of representation and to the activity that in our society is seen as supplying harmless substitutive objects for the satisfaction of desire. Freud sees this process of substitution and derivation, but he doesn't see, and for good reason, that this is the process whereby writing is occulted. This preference is supported by the idea that themes are immediately given over to the subject, without the intervention of intermediary textual matter, without bringing into play the effect upon them of other themes (of other texts). It is supported by the fiction of an original purity of the theme (the fiction of a psychical apparatus producing its own language; but is the system of reception reproduced by this apparatus, the history of the subject, not part of the general text?), allowing Freud to consider themes as objects better suited to scientific observation. It is true that Freud says of his authors that they 'seem' to create their themes spontaneously, but if this creation is not spontaneous, it is not very clear what would distinguish from authors who receive their themes 'ready-made', unless it be the fact that in one case the textual refashioning is manifest and regulated, and in the other it is not. By privileging the representative order, Freud excludes the specifically literary event and attempts to reduce the set of operations in play within literature to those operations regulating the production of a popular narrative, his summary of which is supposed to express its specific character: the story of a hero who loses blood from many deep wounds, of a ship on a stormy sea, of a wreck, etc. The narratives described by Freud belong to the category of works 'treated' by Lautréamont, subjected by him to logical operations[49] that bring out and negate their representative system, giving them over to scriptural practice alone. Freud specifies the dominant character of these works, the presence of the hero, who is nothing less than 'his majesty the self'. The presence of the self, whether identified with the hero, divided into partial selves to generate a multiplicity of characters, or simply attributed the role of spectator (narrator), is in the end responsible for the effect produced by these works: pleasure. The relations of 'creator' to 'creation', of the author to his life, here come into play, relations that are not so simple, says Freud, as is usually thought, because they are determined by the phantasm as intermediary link. 'A strong experience in the present awakens in the creative writer a memory of an earlier experience (usually belonging to his childhood) from which there now proceeds a wish which finds its fulfilment in the creative work. The work itself exhibits elements of the recent provoking occasion as well as of the old memory.'[50] And all that distinguishes phantasm from work is that the work gives us pleasure, rather than inspiring disgust, repulsion or indifference, as directly communicated phantasms would. Through the *ars poetica*, through technique, we overcome the feeling of repulsion that 'is undoubtedly connected with the barriers that rise between each single ego and the others'.

The creative writer

> bribes us by the purely formal – that is aesthetic – yield of pleasure
> which he offers us in the presentation of his phantasies. We give the
> name of an *incentive bonus*, or a fore-pleasure, to a yield of pleasure such
> as this, which is offered to us so as to make possible the release of still
> greater pleasure arising from deeper psychical sources. In my opinion,
> all the aesthetic pleasure which a creative writer affords us has the char-
> acter of a fore-pleasure of this kind, and our actual enjoyment of an
> imaginative work proceeds from a liberation of tensions in our
> minds.[51]

This passage is determined by dualist thought and by the persistent opposition within Freudian discourse between form and content (and also between
interior and exterior, essential and inessential, etc.). As product of technique,
form seems to serve the purpose of making 'deeper psychical sources' accessible, readable; it is marked by the supplementarity and exteriority that result
from 'phonologism' (Derrida), a self-presence independent of the form whose
purpose is specifically to arouse attention. The form/content distinction leads
to and explains the discrimination between pleasures, their hierarchization. A
fore-pleasure comparable to the pleasure brought on by foreplay, which
enables the 'release' of a 'still greater pleasure', of a higher *jouissance*, liberating
'certain tensions' in the subject. An incentive bonus as salary-supplement.
Without insisting any further on analogies that are certainly inscribed in the
literality of Freud's terms, it should be pointed out that the signifier–signified
distinction has rarely been so emphatic, and within this, that the demotion of
the signifier, reduced to the role of lure, has rarely been so radical.

There are analogies between phantasm and creation, but there is also a
more intimate relation between them, a necessary relation, even, an engendering. The work is a representation of the phantasm, the 'yield of pleasure
which the creative writer offers us in the representation [*Darstellung*] of his
phantasms'. In the *Introductory Lectures on Psycho-Analysis*:

> The true artist knows first of all how to give his waking dreams a
> form such that they lose any personal character. . . . He knows just
> as well how to embellish them in such a way as to hide their *suspect
> origin*. He possesses moreover the *mysterious power* of modelling his
> given material so as to turn it into the faithful image of the repre-
> sentation existing in his phantasy, and of attaching to this
> representation – an unconscious phantasy – a sum of pleasure suffi-
> cient to mask or to suppress, provisionally at least, repression.[52]

In this way, after the event, he justifies the relation between the work as
representation and play. Works that are called *Lustspiel*, *Trauerspiel*, manifest

objectively, on a stage accessible to the senses, the essential representative character of all works. Freud's choice of a particular type of novel is explained: in the novels he draws on for examples, the writing and the rhetoric of clichés, of pre-existent (and not 'refashioned') utterances, of tired metaphors, of predictable effects, have to attain a perfect transparency in order to produce the illusion of reality – however extravagant their deviations, even because of their extravagance. Their procedures are determined by the representative form to which they aspire. Need we add that textual practice begins at the point where such a representative function is subverted, a subversion that Lautréamont, in the *Chants de Maldoror*, brings about at the expense of the same novels that Freud considers best able to instruct us in the process of literary creation.

Freud's entire conception is permeated, marked and conditioned by the idea of representation. Representation determines the order of the conception's demonstration and provides its materials, since the phantasm represented by the work is itself a representation: mental work 'now creates a situation relating to the future which represents (*darstellt*) a fulfilment of the wish. What it thus creates is a day-dream or phantasy.' We could already have learned this from a closer reading of 'Delusions and Dreams'. On the one hand the work is representation, *Darstellung*. Freud insists upon this: 'And it is really correct – this imaginative picture [*Darstellung*] of the history of a case and its treatment.'[53] 'We have to render the novelist's exact representation [*Darstellung*] in the technical terms of psychology.'[54] In Marie Bonaparte's French translation, *représentation* translates *Darstellung* but also *Schilderung*: 'the representation of human psychical life is the proper domain of the novelist [*Die Schilderung des menschlichen Seelenbens*]'. *Schilderung* designates the properly literary activity of description and *Darstellung* the act of making present, the representation of something that will occupy the scene, the way a theatrical play is represented, put on. *Darstellung* carries with it the sense of something actualized which already existed in the same state before being represented. And if the work is a representation, the *Darstellung* of a phantasm, the phantasm is itself the representation of representations, the *Darstellung* of *Vorstellungen*, of repressed representations. To pick up Freud's text again:

> We remain on the surface so long as we are dealing with memories and ideas [*Errinerungen und Vorstellungen*]. What is alone of value in mental life is rather the feelings. Ideas [*Vorstellungen*] are only repressed because they are associated with the release of feelings which ought not to occur. It would be more correct to say that repression acts upon feelings, but we can only be aware of these in their association with ideas [*Vorstellungen*].[55]

And a little further on, when Freud indicates the double nature of the determination of the phantasm:

One [determinant] was derived wholly from the circle of ideas [*Vorstellungenkreis*] of the science of archaeology, the other arose from the repressed childhood memories that had become active in him [Hanold] and from the emotional instincts attached to them.[56]

Elsewhere, phantasms are:

substitutes for and derivatives of the phantasies which are the precursors of delusions. They are substitutes for and derivatives of repressed memories which a resistance will not allow to enter consciousness [*darstellen*] unaltered, but which can purchase the possibility of becoming conscious by taking account, by means of changes and distortions, or the resistance's censorship. When this compromise has been established, the memories have turned into the phantasies . . . [57]

And again:

I indicated, in most detail in connection with the states known as hysteria and obsessions, that the individual determinant of these psychical disorders is the suppression of a part of instinctual life and the repression of the ideas by which the suppressed instinct is represented . . . [*und die Verdrängung der Vorstellungen, durch der Unterdrücktetrieb vertreten ist*].[58]

This montage of citations shows *how, through the analysis of a novel, Freud is sketching out the working of the psychical apparatus.*

Freud's conception, his representation, we might say, of 'literary creation' (identifiable in his use of the words 'creation', 'creative writer', 'work', etc.) is dominated by the idea, the ideologeme, of representation. This ideologeme, marking Freud's class affiliation and period, permeates the bourgeoisie's conception of 'art' and is diffracted onto the texts themselves, so that their own textuality is dissembled by it. In Freud's wake, but furthering itself from the paths he had traced, the psychoanalytic movement, and the thinking inspired by it, has manifested the same lack of understanding and a remarkable inadequacy faced with the written, no doubt because of its representatives' attachment to the metaphysics, ideology and interests of their class.

In the light of questions raised by these texts on literary creation, we might ask if the determining model of representation has not contaminated the whole of psychoanalysis, if the functioning of the mind as imagined by Freud has not been entirely understood as a dynamic of representation – whether it is called *Repräsentanz, Vertretung, Vorstellung, Darstellung,* since whatever 'object' comes into play and whatever the particular functioning of its representation, it is always the making-present of something other that is understood by these terms. The biological hypostasis of the system marks the end-point of the series.

Taking these texts on literary creation as a basis, we could construct the following model of the psychical apparatus:[59]

		Affect	Repression		
somatic X	*Trieb* (drive) *psychische Repräsentanz*	*Vorstellung* (representation of the drive)	*Darstellung* (compromise formations)	dreams, symptoms, phantasms → *Darstellung* (work)

We should emphasize the limitations of the above and insist on the fact that Freud's thought cannot be reduced to or summed up by such a model. It simply indicates one of the currents of Freudian thinking, the current discernible in the writings on literary creation.

We could, furthermore, inquire into the representation of a representation of representation, etc., whose origin remains hypothetical and unattainable. The question opens onto another aspect of Freudian thinking, complementary but opposed to the category of representation: the category of interpretation as an interminable process of referral from one signifier to another, inseparable, in this sense, from textual production within an inter-textual organism.

Unsatisfied desires, said Freud, promote phantasms, and every phantasm is the realization of a desire. Is desire then linked, or should it be linked, to representations? Or is representation that which undoes desire, turns it away from being the desire for that practice, textual production, within which the term 'desire' may itself be improper or useless. Is representation not, in the end, in its opposition to such practice, that which keeps intact the closed and repetitive cycle of meaning, of the sign, of presence, of the subject, of neurosis? Could we not say that desire itself is an effect of representation, of a bringing-to-presence, and that insofar as desire is always desire for something (something that would be God or a representation thereof), it is bound up with the teleological thought of meaning? This would allow us to understand the complicity between neurosis itself and a system founded on representation; and to understand how neurosis is obliged to block and occult writing for the same reason that makes neurosis a defence-mechanism against sex. The same reason: there can no more be a 'subject' of writing than a 'subject' of sex. The same defence, if sex and writing depend on the same operation of inscription, of rupture, of expenditure. At issue is the relation to death that Freud defines for sex in *Beyond the Pleasure Principle* but which he was unable to conceive of for writing, just as he could not go beyond (and think the questions posed by) the 'scene of writing' as metaphor for the psychical apparatus.[60] The impossibility of thinking the text, of reading writing, determines the system of representation in the same way that representation results in the dissimulation of writing. 'There is no writing which does not devise some means of protection, *to protect against itself*',[61] says Derrida. Which surely suggests that neurosis is this surface of protection – the irreducible thinking of a 'subject' – whereby sex and writing are at the same time dissimulated, covered over, effaced, and protected, stored up, removed momentarily from inevitable effacement. But obviously Freud could not see that the apparatus he had given himself for the understanding of neurosis was a part of the very system by which neurosis is instituted.

Translated by Roland-François Lack

Notes

1 [This article originally appeared in *Tel Quel*, 32 (1968), and subsequently in *Tel Quel*, *Théorie d'ensemble* (Paris, Seuil, 1968).]

2 Whether or not this repression is inevitable is another problem. It is nonetheless interesting to note that this repression in Freud is marked by the term *renunciation*: the child is obliged to renounce his satisfactions (to defer them); it is also interesting that the term is fundamental to Christian ideology and a privileged ideological weapon of the dominant class.

3 See Derrida, 'Freud and the Scene of Writing', in *Writing and Difference*, trans Alan Bass (London: Routledge & Kegan Paul, 1978).

4 It seems that any movement, any system of thought determined by the dimension of *meaning* and *truth*, inevitably leads to a loss of text.

5 [S. Freud, 'Delusions and Dreams in Jensen's *Gradiva*', in J. Strachey (ed. and trans.), *The Standard Edition of the Complete Psychological Works of Sigmund Freud*, vol. IX (London, The Hogarth Press, 1975), 7.]

6 [Ibid., 9]

7 [Ibid., 41]

8 [Ibid., 43]

9 [Ibid., 8]

10 [Ibid., 9]

11 [Ibid.]

12 [Ibid., 14–15]

13 [A *détournement* of Lautréamont's famous maxim in *Poésies* that 'poetry should be made by all, not by one'.]

14 ['Delusions and Dreams', 91]

15 [Ibid., 94]

16 [Ibid., 45]

17 [Ibid., 43–4]

18 [Ibid., 53]

19 [Ibid., 54]

20 [*The Interpretation of Dreams*, in J. Strachey (ed. and trans.), *The Standard Edition of the Complete Psychological Works of Sigmund Freud*, vol. IX, (London, The Hogarth Press, 1953), 265–6.]
21 ['Creative Writers and Day-Dreaming', in *Standard Edition*, vol. IX, 153]
22 ['Delusions and Dreams', 93]
23 A syllogism that clearly reveals the metaphysical presupposition, the faulty reasoning, and the empiricism on which it is grounded: if A is a part of B and if A is C, B must also be C.
24 ['Delusions and Dreams', 14]
25 [Ibid., 94]
26 The definition of which, because of the domination of linguistics within the 'human sciences', within psychiatry in particular, seems more and more to be based on deviations of language, on a difference from another (ideal) supposedly normal language. Until we can establish or accept a satisfying theory of the text and its production, a text's 'normality' will be decided according to whether it belongs to one or other institution. For example, a text has merely to elude the aesthetico-literary institution, or not to acknowledge it, to be immediately called delusional.
27 ['Delusions and Dreams', 92]
28 ['Creative Writers and Day-Dreaming', 143]
29 [The French has *nous autres profanes* for 'we laymen'] The term 'profane' is to be insisted upon all the more given that, as Freud avows, 'not even the clearest insight into the determinants of his choice of material [*thèmes*] and into the nature of the art of creating imaginative form alone will ever help to make creative writers *of us*', even if 'creative writers themselves like to lessen the distance between their kind and the common run of humanity.' (Ibid.)]
30 Derrida, *Of Grammatology*, trans. Gayatri Chakravorty Spivak (Baltimore, Johns Hopkins University Press, 1976 [1967]), 7.
31 Ibid., 50.
32 Nietzsche: 'When I see the world as a divine game placed beyond good and evil, my precursor is the philosophy of Vedantas and Heraclitus.' [We have not been able to trace the source of this quotation].
33 ['Creative Writers and Day-Dreaming', 144]
34 [Ibid., 146]
35 Is it necessary to point out that we do not intend to undermine the validity of Freudian discourse, not least because Freud himself insists on the deeply illusory aspect of such renunciation, and on the subsequent damage done, inevitable damage, whether unconscious or not. We are simply pointing out the implications of such a discourse. (We might think, for example, of the initial sacrament of baptism centred on the renunciation of 'Satan, his pomp and all his works'.)
36 ['Creative Writers and Day-Dreaming', 145]
37 [S. Freud, 'Introductory Lectures on Psycho-Analysis', in J. Strachey (ed. and trans.), *The Standard Edition of the Complete Psychological Works of Sigmund Freud*, vol. XVI (London, Hogarth Press, 1963), 376.]
38 ['Creative Writers and Day-Dreaming', 148]
39 [Ibid., 147]
40 Derrida, *Of Grammatology*, 65ff.
41 ['Creative Writers and Day-Dreaming', 147]
42 ['Creative Writers and Day-Dreaming', 147]
43 ['Introductory Lectures on Psychoanalysis', translation adapted from *Standard Edition*, vol. XV, 98, where Strachey has: 'In young men, the ambitious phan-

tasies are most prominent, in women, whose ambition is directed to success in love, the erotic ones.']

44 ['Delusions and Dreams', 58]

45 See Michel Tort, 'Le concept freudien du "Représentant"', *Cahiers pour l'analyse*, 5.

46 ['Creative Writers and Day-Dreaming', 149]

47 [Ibid.]

48 [Ibid.]

49 [Ibid., 152]

50 We refer the reader especially to the textual operations presented by Julia Kristeva in 'Pour une sémiologie des paragrammes', *Tel Quel* 29 [see Chapter 2 of this reader].

51 See Philippe Sollers, 'La Science de Lautréamont', *Critique*, 245 (1967).

52 ['Creative Writers and Day-Dreaming', 151.]

53 [Ibid., 152]

54 [Baudry's emphasis. Freud, 'Introductory Lectures', our translation. Strachey's translation, given below, is significantly different from the French so as to lose the sense which Baudry intends it to have: 'A man who is an artist has more at his disposal. In the first place, he understands how to work over his daydreams in such a way as to make them lose what is personal about them and repels strangers. . . . He understands, too, how to tone them down so that they do not easily betray their origin from proscribed sources. He possesses the mysterious power of shaping some particular material until it has become a truthful image of his fantasy, and he knows, moreover, how to link so large a yield of pleasure to this representation of his unconscious phantasy that, for the time being, at least, repressions are outweighed and lifted by it' (376).]

55 Freud, *G.W.*, VII, 70. ['Delusions and Dreams', 44].

56 *G.W.*., VII, 73 [our translation, Strachey's translation is markedly different, see 'Delusions and Dreams', 44.]

57 *G.W.*, VII, 75. ['Delusions and Dreams', 49. Marie Bonaparte's translation gives 'représentations' where the English (Strachey) gives 'ideas'.]

58 ['Delusions and Dreams', 52; Bonaparte gives 'pulsions' where the English gives 'emotions'.]

59 *G.W.*, VII, 85. ['Delusions and Dreams', 58]

60 *G.W.*, VII, 80. ['Delusions and Dreams', 53–4]

61 Based on Tort's 'Le concept freudien de "Représentant"'.

62 Derrida, 'Freud and the Scene of Writing'. In this essential text can be read: 'In that moment of world history subsumed by the name of Freud, by means of an unbelievable mythology (be it neurological or metapsychological . . .), a relationship to itself of the historico-transcendental stage of writing was spoken without being said, thought without being thought: was written and simultaneously erased, metaphorized; designating itself while indicating intrawordly relations, *it was represented*' (229).

63 Ibid., 224.

Part II

LITERATURE

5

DISTANCE, ASPECT, ORIGIN[1]

Michel Foucault

The importance of Robbe-Grillet is measured by the question which his work poses to any work contemporary to it. It is a fundamentally *critical* question, bearing on the possibilities open to language: a question which in their leisure critics turn into a malign questioning of the right to use any other language, or even one close to that of Robbe-Grillet. The objection is usually made to the *Tel Quel* writers (the existence of this review has altered something in the space in which one speaks, but what?) that Robbe-Grillet was there before them and is there in front of them, not perhaps to reproach them or to show their presumption, but to suggest that several of these writers who thought they might escape it have found themselves in the labyrinth of this sovereign, obsessive language, that they have found in this father a trap which captures, captivates them. And since they themselves, after all, hardly speak in the first person without referring and leaning on this prominent third person . . .

To the seven propositions which Sollers has advanced on Robbe-Grillet[2] (placing them almost at the beginning of the review, like a second 'Declaration', close to the first but imperceptibly advanced) I am not, of course, going to add an eighth, which, final or not, would judge the seven others as good or bad; I am rather going to try, in the clarity of these directly enunciated propositions, to bring to light a relation which is a little withdrawn from them, interior to what they propose, and as if diagonal to their line.

It is said that in Sollers's writing (or in Thibaudeau's) there are figures, a language, a style and descriptive themes which are imitations or borrowings from Robbe-Grillet. I would rather say: there are objects woven into the tissue of their words and present under their eyes which owe their existence and the possibility of their existence to Robbe-Grillet. I am thinking of the iron balustrade of which the black, rounded forms ('with its foliage trans-fixed along rounded, blackened stems that move symmetrically now one way, now another'[3]) limit the balcony of *The Park* and form an openwork through which can be seen the street, the city, trees, houses: a Robbe-Grillet-object which is a dark outline against the still luminous evening, an object constantly in view which articulates the visual spectacle, but also a negative object through which the gaze moves towards a depth which appears slightly floating, grey and blue, those leaves and those shapes without branches which can hardly be seen, a little further back, in falling darkness. And it is perhaps not indifferent that *The Park* unfolds its own distance around this balustrade, nor that it opens onto a nocturnal landscape in which the values of light and shadow, which in Robbe-Grillet trace out the outline of forms in full daylight, are inversed in a distant scintillation. On the other side of the street, at a distance which is not certain and which the darkness makes even more doubtful, a 'vast and very bright apartment' hollows out a luminous, mute, accidental and uneven gallery – an interior of theatre and enigma beyond the iron arabesques obstinately maintaining their negative presence. From one work to the other there is the image not perhaps of a mutation, or a development, but of a discursive articulation; and it will become crucial one day to analyse phenomena of this type in a vocabulary which does not use the curiously bewitched terms of influence and exorcism familiar to the critics.

Before coming back to this theme (which I confess is the basis of my concerns) I would like to say two or three things about the coherence of this language which is common, to a certain extent, to Sollers, to Thibaudeau, to Baudry, and perhaps to others. I am not unaware of the injustice of speaking in such general terms, or that one is immediately caught in the dilemma of the opposition: author or school. It seems to me, however, that the possibilities open to language in a given period are not so numerous that isomorphisms cannot be found (thus enabling the possibility of reading several texts against each other) or that the frame should be closed for those who have not yet written or those one has not yet read. Because these isomorphisms are not 'visions of the world', but folds interior to language; the words pronounced, the sentences written, pass through them, adding their own specific lines.

1 Perhaps certain figures (or perhaps all) of *The Park*, of *Une cérémonie royale*[4] or *Les images*[5] are without interior volume, lightened of this dark, lyrical kernel, of that insistent yet withdrawn centre whose presence Robbe-Grillet had already conjured. But in a quite strange sense they do have their own volume, beside them, above and below, around them; a volume in a state of perpetual non-insertion, which floats or vibrates around a figure which is outlined but never fixed, a volume which advances or withdraws, hollows out its own distance and thrusts itself right up in front of the eyes. In fact, these satellite, wandering volumes do not make manifest either the presence or the absence of the object, but rather a distance which at the same time maintains the object far from the gaze and separates it irreducibly from itself: a distance which belongs to the gaze (and seems therefore to be imposed on the objects from the outside) but which renews itself at every

moment in the most secret heart of things. These volumes, which are the interior of the objects outside them, intersect, interfere with each other, tracing composite forms which have only one face and which slip around each other consecutively: thus, in *The Park*, under the eyes of the narrator, his room (he has just left it to go out onto the balcony and it is thus floating beside him, outside, in an unreal and interior dimension) communicates its volume to a small painting which is hanging on one of the walls: the latter opens in its turn behind the canvas, pouring its interior space out towards a seascape, towards the masts of a boat, towards a group of characters whose clothes, physiognomies and slightly theatrical gestures unfold according to a scope so excessive, so unmeasured in any case to the dimensions of the frame which encloses them, that one of these gestures imperiously returns us to the present position of the narrator on the balcony. Or to someone else perhaps making the same gesture. For this world of distance is in no sense that of isolation, but of a proliferation of identity, of the Same at the point of bifurcation, or on the curve of its return.

2 The milieu, of course, makes us think of a mirror – of the mirror which gives things a space outside them and transplanted from them, which multiplies identities and mixes differences in an impalpable knot which cannot be unknotted. Let's remind ourselves precisely of the definition of the park, 'the composite of very beautiful and very picturesque places', each has been taken from a different landscape, has been displaced from its natal site, transported itself, or a close version of itself, to that disposition where 'everything seems natural except the whole assemblage'. Park: mirror of incompatible volumes. Mirror: subtle park where the distant trees are interwoven. Under these two provisional figures it is a difficult (despite its lightness), regular (under its uneven appearance) space which is in the process of opening out. But what is it made of, if it is not completely a reflection, nor a dream, nor an imitation or a reverie? A fiction, Sollers would say, but let's leave aside, for a moment, this word, which is so heavy and yet so thin.

For the moment I would rather borrow from Klossowski a very beautiful word: simulacra. One could say that if, in Robbe-Grillet, objects persist and are obstinate, in Sollers they simulate each other; that is, following the dictionary, they are the image (the vain image) of themselves, the inconsistent spectre, the deceptive thought of themselves; they represent themselves outside their divine presence, while nevertheless signalling it – objects of a piety addressed to distance. But perhaps we should listen to etymology with more care: does not 'to simulate' mean 'to come together', to be at the same time as oneself, but shifted slightly from oneself? To be oneself in a different place, which is not the place of birth, the native ground of perception, but at an unmeasurable distance, in the most proximate outside? To be outside oneself, with oneself, in a 'with' where distances intersect. I am thinking of the simulacra without depth, perfectly round, of *Une cérémonie royale*, or of another also arranged by Thibaudeau, of the *Match de football*: the football game hardly unstuck from itself by the voices of the reporters finds in this sonorous park, in this noisy mirror, its meeting place with so much other reflected speech. It is perhaps in this direction that we should understand what Thibaudeau says when he opposes to the theatre of time, another, in space, as yet sketched out only by Appia or Meyerhold.

3 We are dealing, therefore, with a displaced space, at the same time behind and in front, never completely present, and in fact no intrusion into that space is possible. The spectators in Robbe-Grillet are men upright and on the move, or still hiding out, watching out for shadows, traces, breaches, displacements; they penetrate, have already penetrated, right to the heart of the objects which are presented to them in profile, turning as they move around them. The characters of *The Park*, of *Les images* are sitting, immobile, in areas a little uncoupled from space, as if suspended, on café terraces or balconies. Areas which are separated, but by what? Perhaps by nothing more than a distance, their own distance: an imperceptible empty space, but one which cannot be reabsorbed, nor furnished, a line which is constantly crossed without being effaced, as if, on the contrary, it is in constantly crossing it that it is all the more marked out. For this limit does not isolate two parts of the world: a subject and an object, or objects positioned opposite thought; it is rather the universal relation, the mute, laborious and instantaneous relation by which everything is knotted and unknotted, by which everything appears, sparkles and is extinguished, by which, in the same movement, objects propose themselves and efface themselves. Perhaps it is this role that is played out by the obstinately present form of the division in the novels of J.-P. Faye (lobotomy, frontier within a country) or the impenetrable transparency of windows in Baudry's *Les images*. But the essential aspect of this infinitesimal distance, like that of a line, is not what it excludes, it is more fundamentally what it opens out; it liberates, on either side of its lance, two spaces whose secret is that they are the same, that they are totally here and there, that they are where they are at a distance, that they offer their interiority, their warm cavern, their dark face outside themselves and nevertheless in the nearest proximity. Around this invisible knife all beings pivot.

4 This torsion has the marvellous property of focusing time: not to make its successive forms cohabit in a space of traversal (as with Robbe-Grillet) but to allow them to converge in a sagittal dimension – as arrows penetrating the density in front of us. Or otherwise they are overhanging, the past no longer being the ground on which we are, nor a surging up in the form of memory, but on the contrary arising in spite of the oldest metaphors of memory, arriving from the depth of the most proximate distance and with it: time takes on a vertical stature of superimposition where the oldest level

is paradoxically the nearest to the summit, ridge-pole and flight line, high place of reversal. A precise and complex sketch of this curious structure is given at the beginning of *Les images*: a woman is sitting on a café terrace, with in front of her the large framed windows of a building which dominates her; and through these glazed surfaces come a continuous flow of images which are superimposed on one another, while on the table there is a book whose pages she rapidly flicks through between her finger and thumb (from bottom to top, thus backwards): appearance, effacement, superimposition, which echoes in an enigmatic mode, when her eyes are lowered, the framed images which accumulate above her when she raises her eyes.

5 Stretched out beside itself, the temporality of *Jealousy* and *The Voyeur* leaves traces which are differences, thus ultimately a system of signs. But the time which arises and superimposes makes analogies flicker, shows nothing other than the figures of the Same. Such that with Robbe-Grillet the difference between what has happened and what has not happened, even though (and to the extent that) it is difficult to establish, remains at the centre of the text (at least in the form of a lack, a white page or a repetition): it is a limit and an enigma: in *La chambre secrète* the descent and the re-ascent of the man up and down the staircase to the body of the victim (dead, wounded, bleeding, struggling, dead again) is after all the reading of an event. Thibaudeau, in the sequence of the assassination attempt, seems to follow a similar course: but in fact, in this circular procession of horses and carriages, it is a question of unfolding a series of virtual events (movements, gestures, shouts, cries which perhaps arise or do not arise) and which have the same density as 'reality', neither more or less than it, since they are carried along with it up to the final moment of the parade when in the dust, the sun, the music and the cries, the last horses disappear behind the closing gate. Signs are not deciphered through a system of differences; isomorphisms are followed through a depth of analogies. Not a reading, but rather a drawing together of the identical, an immobile advance towards a state lacking difference. There, the distinctions between real and virtual, perception and dream, past and fantasy (whether they are static or moved across), have no more value than being moments of the passage, relays more than signs, traces of steps, empty surfaces where the Same, from the beginning, does not linger, was announced in the distance and is already insinuating itself (and time, the gaze, the discernment between things, is turned around on the horizon, but also here and now, in each instant, the other side of things always appearing). This, precisely, is the *intermediary*. Sollers writes:

> Here you will find a number of texts which appear contradictory, but whose subject, in fact, turns out to be the *same*. Whether it is a question of paintings, or of real events (but at the same time at that limit where the real turns into dream), of reflections or of rapid

descriptions, it is always the intermediary state in a movement towards an overturning which is provoked, suffered, or pursued.[6]

This almost static movement, this focused attention on the Identical, this ceremony in the suspended dimension of the Intermediary, reveal not so much a space, nor a region or a structure (words which are too embroiled in a mode of reading which is no longer applicable), but a constant and mobile relation, interior to language itself, which Sollers designates by the decisive word 'fiction'.[7]

If I have insisted on these slightly meticulous references to Robbe-Grillet, it is because it was not a question of deciding on originalities, but of establishing, from one work to another, a visible relation, namable in each of its elements, which would not be of the order of resemblance (with the whole series of badly thought and frankly unthinkable notions of influence and imitation), nor of the order of replacement (of succession, development, of schools): a relation such that the works might define each other against, beside and at a distance from each other, taking support at the same time from their difference and their simultaneity, and defining, without privilege or culmination, the scope of a *network*. Even if history makes the short-term movements of this network appear, its intersections and knots can and must be apprehended by criticism according to a reversible movement (a reversal which changes certain properties, but does not contest the existence of the network, since it is precisely one of its basic rules); and if criticism has a role, I mean if the necessarily secondary language of criticism can cease to be a derived, aleatory language, fatally effaced by the work, if it can be at the same time secondary and fundamental, it is to the extent that it brings in to play for the first time, at the level of words, this network of works which, for each of them, is their own silence.

In a book whose ideas will play a leading role for a long time to come, Marthe Robert[8] has shown what relations *Don Quixote* and *The Castle* had woven, not with such and such a story, but with the conditions of the very existence of Western literature, with its conditions of possibility in history (conditions which are works, thus permitting a *critical* reading in the most rigorous sense of the term). But if such a reading is possible, it is thanks to the works produced now: Marthe Robert's book is of all books of criticism the closest to what literature is today: a certain self-relation which is complex, multilateral and simultaneous, where the fact of coming afterwards (being new) is not in any sense reducible to the linear law of succession. Perhaps a historically linear development, from the nineteenth century to the present, appears in the forms of existence and coexistence of literature: it had its highly teleological place in the both real and fantastic space of the Library: in which each book is made to include all others, to consume them, reduce them to silence and finally to take its place beside them, outside them and within them (Sade and Mallarmé with their books, with The

Book, are by definition the Library's damned books). In an even more archaic mode, at the time of the great transformations contemporary to Sade, if literature reflected on itself and criticized itself in the mode of Rhetoric, it was because it relied, at a distance, on a withdrawn yet demanding Word (Truth and Law), which it had to restore to figural language (whence the indissociable opposition of Rhetoric and Hermeneutics). Perhaps one could say that today (since Robbe-Grillet, which is what makes him unique), literature which had ceased to exist as rhetoric has disappeared as a Library. It is in the process of constituting itself as a network – and as a network where neither the truth of the word nor the series of history can function, where the only *a priori* is language. What seems important to me in *Tel Quel* is that the existence of literature as a network never ceases to be more clearly defined, ever since the liminary moment when it was pronounced that:

> What must be said today is that writing is no longer conceivable
> without a clear predication of its powers, a *sang-froid* to the measure
> of the chaos in which it awakes, a determination which puts poetry
> at the highest place of the mind. The rest will not be literature.[9]

We must finally come back to this word fiction, brought up several times and then abandoned. Not without some trepidation. Because it sounds like a term from psychology (imagination, fantasy, reverie, invention, etc.) because it has the appearance of belonging to one of the two dynasties of the Real and the Unreal. Because it seems to lead back – and this would be so simple after the 'literature of objects' – to the inflections of a subjective language. Because it offers so much to the grasp but escapes it. Cutting diagonally across the uncertainty of dreams and of waiting, of madness and wakefulness, does not fiction designate a series of experiences which the language of Surrealism has already expressed? The attentive glance which *Tel Quel* brings to bear upon Breton is not one of retrospection. Yet Surrealism had engaged these experiences in the search for a reality which made them possible and gave them an imperious power over any language (playing upon it, or with it, or in spite of it). But what if, on the contrary, these experiences can be maintained where they take place, at the level of their surface without depth, in that indistinct volume from which they come to us, vibrating around their unidentifiable kernel, on their ground which is an absence of ground? What if dream, madness and night do not mark out the stakes of any solemn threshold, but ceaselessly trace and efface the limits which wakefulness and discourse cross over, when they come towards us and reach us already doubled? What if the fictive was precisely not the beyond nor the intimate secret of the everyday, but the flight of the arrow which hits us right in the eyes and offers us everything which appears. In that case the fictive would be also that which names things, makes them speak and gives them in language their being already split by the sovereign power of words:

'landscapes split in two', writes Marcelin Pleynet. This is not to say, then, that fiction is language: this trick would be too simple, despite its familiarity. It is rather to say with more prudence that between them there is a complex adherence, a dependence and a contestation, and that, maintained for as long as it can keep to its word, the simple experience which consists in taking up a pen and writing, disengages (in the sense of liberates, un-buries, takes back a pledge or goes back on a word) a distance which belongs not to the world nor to the unconscious, nor to the gaze, nor to interiority; a distance which, in its naked state, offers a grid of lines of ink and at the same time a labyrinth of streets, a city being born, always having been there:

> Words are lines, facts when they intersect
> we would represent in this manner a series of straight lines
> cut at a right angle by a series of straight lines
> A city.[10]

And if I was asked in the end to define fiction I would say, without skill: the verbal nervure of what does not exist, such as it is.

I would efface, in order to leave this experience to what it is (in order to treat it, therefore, as a fiction, since it does not exist, that we know), I would efface all the oppositions by which it might be easily dialecticized: confrontation or abolition of the subjective and the objective, of the interior and the exterior, reality and imaginary. This whole vocabulary of dualism needs to be replaced by one of distance, thus allowing the fictive to appear as a distancing specific to language – a distancing which has its place within it, but which, at the same time, stretches it out, disperses it, divides it up and opens it. Fiction does not arise because language is at a distance from things; language is their distance, the light in which they appear and their inaccessibility, the simulacra where only their presence is given; and any language which rather than forget this distance maintains itself within it and maintains it within itself, any language which speaks about this distance in advancing within it, is a language of fiction. It can therefore cut across any prose and any poetry, any novel or any reflection, indifferently.

Pleynet designates the bursting out of this distance in one phrase: 'fragmentation is the source'. In other, less felicitous words: a first, absolutely original enunciation of faces and of lines is never possible, no more so than that primitive appearance of things which literature has often given itself the task of focusing upon, in the name or under the sign of a diverted phenomenology. The language of fiction inserts itself into an already spoken language, into a murmur which never began. The virginity of the gaze, the attentive step which raises words to the level of discovered and circumvented things, do not concern it; what does is usury and distance, the pallor of what has already been pronounced. Nothing is spoken at dawn (*The Park* begins in the evening; and in the morning, another morning, it starts again);

what would be said for the first time is nothing, is not said, loiters in the confines of words, in those rifts in white paper which Pleynet's poems sculpt and ornament, open to the daylight. There is however in the language of fiction an instant of pure origin; it is that of writing, the moment of the words themselves, in scarcely dry ink, the moment when is sketched out what by definition and in its most material being can be nothing but trace, sign, in the distance, to the anterior and the ulterior:

> As I write (here) on this page with uneven lines
> justifying prose (poetry)
> the words designate words and relate each to the
> other what you understand[11]

On several occasions, *The Park* invokes the patient gesture of filling the pages of an orange exercise book with blue-black ink. But this movement is only totally present, in its precise, absolute present tense, at the last moment: only the last lines of the book bring it forward and join up with it. Everything said before, and by this writing (the tale itself) is sent back to an order commanded by this present minute or second: it is resolved in this origin which is the only one present and also the end (the moment of becoming silent), it folds in on itself completely, but at the same time, in its unfolding and its itinerary it is at every moment upheld by this moment, distributed across its space and its time (the page to complete, the words which are aligned), the writing finds there its constant present tense.

It is not a case, then, of a linear series running from the past which is remembered to a present defined by the return of a memory and the moment of writing. But rather a vertical and arborescent relation in which a patient present tense, nearly always silent, never given as itself, supports figures which, rather than ordering themselves according to time, are distributed according to different rules: the present itself only appears once the present tense of writing is finally given, when the novel ends and language is no longer possible. Before, and everywhere else in the book, another order reigns: between the different episodes (but this word is too chronological, perhaps it would be better to say 'phases', with close attention to its etymology), the distinction of tenses and modes (present, future, imperfect or conditional) only relates very indistinctly to a calendar: it sketches out references, indices, relays in which the categories of completion, incompletion, of continuity, iteration, immanence, proximity, distancing, come into play, categories which grammarians would define as those of *aspect*. Perhaps emphasis should be given to this sentence of discrete appearance, one of the first of Baudry's novel: 'I arrange what is around me for an indeterminate length of time.' This is to say that the division of time, of tenses, is not made imprecise in itself, but entirely relative and ordered according to the play of aspect – to that play which is concerned with distancing, the movement away, arrival and return. What secretly inaugurates and determines this indeterminate time is a network which is more spatial than temporal, but one would still have to strip from the word spatial that which attaches it to an imperious gaze or a successive approach; it is more a question of that space below space and time, which is that of distance. If I have deliberately fixed on the word aspect, after that of fiction and simulacra, it is at the same time for its grammatical precision and for a whole semantic kernel which turns around it (the *species* of the mirror and of analogy; the diffraction of the spectre; the doubling of spectres; the exterior aspect, which is not the thing itself nor its definite circumference; the aspect which is modified with distance; the aspect which sometimes misleads but is not effaced, and so on).

A language of aspect which attempts to bring up to the level of words a play more sovereign than that of time: a language of distance which distributes spatial relations according to a different foundation. But distance and aspect are interrelated in a much closer manner than space and time; they form a network which no psychology can untie (aspect offering not time itself but the moment of its *coming forth*; distance offering not things in their place, but the movement which presents them and makes them pass). And the language which brings to the light of day this profound adherence is not one of subjectivity; it opens and, in the strictest sense, 'gives rise' to something which might be designated by the neutral word experience: neither true nor false, neither wakefulness nor dream, neither madness nor reason, it removes everything which Pleynet calls the 'will to qualify'. Because the space of distance and the relations of aspect do not relate to perception, nor to things themselves, nor to the subject, neither to what is deliberately and strangely called 'the world'; they belong to the dispersion of language (to that originary fact that one never speaks at the origin but in the distance). A literature of aspect such that the latter becomes interior to language; not in that it treats it as a closed system, but because it is sensitive to the distancing of the origin, its fragmentation, its scattered exteriority. It finds its landmark and its contestation in literature.

Whence several characteristics specific to such works:

Effacement to start with of any proper name (even reduced to its initial letter), to the profit of the personal pronoun; effacement, that is, of a simple reference to the already named in a language which has always already begun; and characters who are designated only have the right to an indefinitely repeated substantive (the man, the woman), modified only by an adjective buried far off in the depth of familiarities ('the woman in red'). Whence also the exclusion of the unheard of, of the never seen; precautions are taken against the fantastic, the fictive existing only in the support, the sliding, the arising of things (not in things themselves) – in the neutral elements devoid of any oneiric prestige which lead from one surface of the story to another. The fictive has its place in an almost mute articulation:

large white interstices which separate the printed paragraphs or the thin almost punctual particle (a gesture, a colour in *The Park*, a ray of sun in *Une cérémonie royale*) around which language pivots, disintegrates, recomposes itself, assuring passage through its repetition or its imperceptible continuity. A figure opposed to the imagination which opens fantasy at the very heart of things, the fictive lives in the vectoral element which little by little is effaced by the central precision of the image – a rigorous simulacra of what can be seen, a unique double.

But the moment before the dispersion can never be restored; the aspect can never be led back to the pure line of time; the diffraction which is signi-fied in *Les images* by the thousand framed openings cannot be reduced, no more than that which *The Park* recounts in alternatives suspended from an 'infinitive' (to fall from the balcony and to become the silence which follows the sound of the body *or* to tear the pages of the exercise book into little pieces, to watch them flutter in the air for a moment). The speaking subject thus finds him- or herself pushed back to the exterior limits of the text, leaving only an intersection of wakes (I or He, I and He at the same time), grammatical inflections among the other folds of language. Or again, with Thibaudeau, the subject watching the ceremony, and also watching those who are watching it, is probably situated nowhere else but in the 'spaces left between the passing figures', in the distance which makes the spectacle distant, in the grey caesura of the walls which hide the preparations and the queen's secrets. In all of these spaces one can recognize, but as if blindly, the essential empty space which language takes as its own; not a lack, like those that Robbe-Grillet's narratives never cease covering over, but an absence of being, a whiteness which for language is paradoxical milieu and at the same time unerasable exteriority. The lack is not, outside language, what it must mask, nor, within it, what tears it irreparably open. Language is the empty space, that exterior in the interior of which it never ceases to speak: 'the eternal streaming of the outside'. Perhaps it is in such an empty space that echoes, to such an empty space that is addressed, the central gunshot of *The Park*, which arrests time at the mid-point of night and day, killing the other and also the speaking subject (according to a figure which is not without relation to *communication* in the sense intended by Bataille). But this murder does not affect language; perhaps even, at this moment which is neither shadow nor light, at this limit of everything (life and death, day and night, speech and silence), it opens the issue of a language which had always begun before any time. Because, perhaps, it is not death which is at stake in this rupture, but something as if withdrawn from any event. Might one say that this gunshot, which hollows the most hollow place of the night, designates the absolute withdrawal of the origin, the essential effacement of the morning in which things are present, when language names the first animals, when to think is to speak? This withdrawal dooms us to a sharing out, a division (an initial sharing constitutive of all others) of thought and language; in this fork in which we are caught is sketched out a space onto whose surface the structuralism of today proposes a gaze whose meticulousness cannot be doubted. But if this space is interrogated, if we ask of it from whence it comes along with the mute metaphors on which it obstinately rests, perhaps we will see sketched out figures that are no longer those of simultaneity, but the relations of aspect in the play of distance, the disappearance of subjectivity in the withdrawal of the origin; or, inversely, that retreat bestowing a language already scattered in which the aspect of things shines out of the distance right up to us. More than one writer is watching out, at dawn, for these figures, in the morning in which we exist. Perhaps they announce an experience where a single *sharing* will reign (a law and a reckoning of all others): to think and to speak, this 'end' designating the *intermediary* which falls upon us shared and within which a few works are presently attempting to maintain themselves.

'Of the earth which is only a sketch', writes Pleynet on a white page. And at the other end of this language which is one of the thousand-year-old signs of our earth and which also, no more than the earth, has never begun, a last page, symmetrical and also intact, allows another phrase to come before us: 'the background wall is a wall of chalk', thus designating the whiteness of the background, the invisible empty space of the origin, that pale burst from which words come to us – these words precisely.

Translated by Patrick ffrench

Notes

1 [This article originally appeared in *Critique*, November 1963, and was republished in *Théorie d'ensemble* (Paris, Seuil, Coll. *Tel Quel*, 1968).]
2 See *Tel Quel* 1 (1960).
3 Philippe Sollers, *The Park*, trans. A.M. Sheridan Smith (London, Calder & Boyars, 1968), 12.
4 Jean Thibaudeau, *Une cérémonie royale* (Paris, Minuit, 1960).
5 Jean-Louis Baudry, *Les images* (Paris, Seuil, Coll. *Tel Quel*, 1963).
6 Sollers, *L'Intermédiaire* (Paris, Seuil, Coll. *Tel Quel*, 1963).
7 Sollers, 'Logique de la fiction', in *Logiques* (Paris, Seuil, Coll. *Tel Quel*, 1968).
8 Marthe Robert, *L'Ancien et le Nouveau* (Paris, Grasset, 1963).
9 'Déclaration', *Tel Quel*, 1 (1960). Since then, J.-P. Faye has actually joined *Tel Quel*, Faye being a writer who wishes to write novels not 'in series', but establishing between each of them a certain relation of proportion.
10 Marcelin Pleynet, *Paysages en deux* followed by *Les Lignes de la prose* (Paris, Seuil, Coll. *Tel Quel*, 1963), 121.
11 Marcelin Pleynet, *Comme* (Paris, Seuil, Coll. *Tel Quel*, 1965), 19.

6

THE READABILITY OF SADE[1]

Marcelin Pleynet

> . . . in the state wherein we live today, let us always start from
> this principle: when man has weighed and considered all his
> restrictions, when, with a proud look his eyes gauge his
> barriers, when, like the Titans, he dares raise his bold hand to
> heaven and, armed with his passions, as the Titans were armed
> with the lavas of Vesuvius, he no longer fears to declare war
> against those who in times past were a source of fear and trem-
> bling to him, when his *aberrations* now seem to him naught
> but errors rendered legitimate by his studies – should we then
> not speak to him with the same fervor as he employs in his
> own behavior?
>
> (Sade, 'Reflections on the Novel'[2])

Whether we like it or not, whether we are ready or not to acknowledge it,
we are not completely innocent of the various censorings which Sade's work
has suffered, and I would even go as far as to say that even today it is our
more or less widespread complicity with these various modes of censorship
that characterizes how we read Sade, that makes this reading more or less
possible. Soon it will be two centuries since this work first became an issue,
and two centuries since our culture has excluded it. In other words, it is
impossible to address this reading without first of all addressing the cultural
code which refuses it, without first of all acknowledging that we are nothing
but the products of this code, and that, in the course of our reading of Sade,
whether we like it or not, we are actually complicit, even in our desire to
understand, with the various types of censure we might have set ourselves
against to begin with. Whosoever is not prepared to question the normality
(and the objective justification of this normality) of the codes of cultural
understanding before even taking on a reading of Sade is sure to find themselves at one moment or another stopped or limited in their reading
(legislatively, as it were) as sure as they would stop at that point in their
experience. It is important to remember that, on the level of this cultural

code, Diderot himself will be accused of indulging himself in a 'dirty and lubricious physiology' (Paul Albert, *Introduction aux œuvres de Diderot*).

It is only slightly surprising to see the importance accorded Sade's biography while practically no critical study has been devoted to the cultural references which inform and authorize the work. Sade has not been read; if he had been one would have recognized that what was shocking in his work (shocking for good taste, morality, sensibility) was conditioned [*souscrit*] by a precise culture, and that it should have been taken into consideration not as a monstrous epiphenomenon, but as an example of a particular cultural activity. This has been particularly guarded against for the good reason that it would thereby have been necessary to address the scientific and materialist philosophy of the eighteenth century, which bourgeois culture has systematically attempted to obscure. One only has to look at the way that Enlightenment philosophy in France is largely given over to the glory of the deists Rousseau and Voltaire, while the atheists are practically never mentioned. It is precisely the most virulent and the most systematic of these atheists, d'Holbach, whom Sade recognizes as an authority. At the end of November 1783, from the Château of Vincennes where he is incarcerated, Sade writes to his wife:

How do you think I can appreciate the *Refutation of the System of Nature*[3] if you do not send me, with the *Refutation*, the book which is being refuted, as if I were to judge a case without seeing the evidence of the two sides? You must see that this is impossible, although *the 'System' is acutely and incontestably the basis of my philosophy*,[4] and although I am its adherent *to the point of martyrdom*,[5] if it were necessary, you must see that it is impossible, seven years after having seen it, for me to remember enough of it to appreciate its refutation.[6] I am willing to consider that I might be wrong, but give me the means. . . . Ask Vilete to lend it to me for only 8 days, and no stupidities over this, please: it would indeed be one to refuse me a book which I have had read to the Pope, *a frankly magnificent book, a book which should be in every library and in every mind, a book which saps and destroys for ever the most dangerous and the most odious of myths*,[7] which has led to more bloodshed on the earth than any other, and which the whole universe would unite to topple and to annihilate without remainder, if the individuals which composed this universe had the least idea of their happiness and of their tranquillity.

Sade will return to this demand during the same month: 'It is impossible for me to appreciate the *Refutation of the System of Nature* if you do not send me the *System* itself' (letter of 23 November 1783). Another letter also from 1783 shows how far Sade was conscious of the transgressive value of his philosophical culture, and how far this consciousness was more coherent than that of his censors; in June 1783, he writes to his wife:

> To refuse Jean-Jacques' Confessions is an excellent thing, above all after having sent me Lucretius and the dialogues of Voltaire; that demonstrates great judiciousness, profound discernment in your spiritual guides. Alas they do me much honour in reckoning that the writings of a deist can be dangerous reading for me. I would indeed like to be in that position.[8]

One can see that as far as his own culture was concerned Sade had very clear ideas, infinitely more clear than his censors who forbade the reading of Rousseau under the pretext that these were works which would 'overheat his mind, and make him write unsuitable things'.[9] And without speaking of Rousseau the deist, it was and still is in effect the case that the materialist philosophy of the eighteenth century overheats Sade's mind and makes him write unsuitable things. It remains to be seen how to view this overheating. Our culture has got rid of the problems that Sade's work might have caused it, by individualizing them: Sade's work has no other signification for it than to characterize or signify a monstrous individual: the sadist. Must we then conclude that minds overheated by certain readings can only produce monsters? It is certain that for contemporary society scepticism and materialism are 'overheating' and criminal doctrines to the extent that they produce those monsters who come to transform the very bases of society. Perhaps for this society there is every benefit (and in any case it cannot do otherwise) in incarnating these doctrines in a type of individual lacking in the social qualities which it recognizes, and in thus displacing the field of activity of this doctrine from the order of a productive knowledge (which is criminal from the legislative point of view) to that of the legislative (which is criminal from the point of view of the production of knowledge). It then becomes clear that this society has every interest in making an example of a thinking which appears to it to be criminal, and reducing it to an individual that it can condemn (and who becomes condemnable from that point on). For it we look closely, the overheated mind of Sade is the exact opposite of a mad mind, it is a rational mind which never fails to situate its reasoning historically and theoretically (see 'Reflections on the Novel'), and which knows it is more logical in its acts than the legislators who censure it, allowing the reading of Lucretius and forbidding the reading of Rousseau.

Thus situated, re-situated in the cultural context which produced it and to which it does not cease referring, the work of Sade authorizes a series of questions which will not reduce its transgressive violence, for sure, but will permit an approach to and the reading of a text which has a demystifying force equal to any other. The philosophy of the Enlightenment which gives birth to it is not in fact without ambiguity,[10] shared as it is between d'Holbach and Rousseau, between atheists and deists, its most immediate activity and practice being the revolution of '89, the triumph of Rousseauist morality and deism. We should note here in passing that the decree recognizing the existence of the Supreme Being and immortality of the soul is unanimously voted in by the Convention on 7 May 1794, while Sade finishes *Philosophy in the Bedroom* in 1795. The contradictions between d'Holbach and Rousseau, for example, are not unfamiliar to Sade, who will summarize whole passages from the *System of Nature*[11] throughout his work, and who will never stop writing specifically against Rousseau. In one of the most important essays published today about Sade,[12] which needs to be reread, Philippe Sollers remarks precisely that Sade's most important characters, Justine and Juliette, are

> feminized masculine names – the one infallibly evoking right and justice, the other appearing as a counterpart not only to *Romeo and Juliet*, but to Rousseau's *Julie ou la Nouvelle Héloïse* as well, Rousseau the inventor of education, of Natural origin, Good, Sacred Interiority, Discourse, Individuality and Belles Lettres in all their glory, in short the representative of Neurosis itself (thus Saint-Fond corresponds to Saint-Preux, Clairwil to Claire).[13]

We should indeed not forget that Rousseau's *La Nouvelle Héloïse* was presented from its first publication as a diatribe against atheist philosophers; Rousseau writes: 'Julie devout is the philosophers' demon'[14] and that the character of Wolmar was seen by all as a psychologized portrait of Baron d'Holbach.[15] We can see that Sade is working in full knowledge of a precise cultural space that he intends to disengage from any deist ambiguity (and from any Rousseauist exploitation), a space from which his thought unfolds. Because if Rousseau is exemplary in this case, the thought of the *philosophes* is also not without contradictions precisely concerning morality; it is necessary for Sade to highlight the work of the most radical among them (d'Holbach) and to guard himself as much as possible against any metaphysical interpretation, even from those which Marx denounces when he writes: ' . . . man, turning against the existence of God, turns against his own religiosity'.[16] Sade comes after those for whom this 'religiosity' is a problem (Diderot, d'Holbach) and he overtakes them in deriving consequences from his atheism that none of his contemporaries were able, historically, to follow or to understand. To recognize the work done by Sade on and beyond the scientific philosophy of the eighteenth century the latter would have to be reconsidered, and it would be necessary to emphasize the contradictions (which for this philosophy are insoluble) which determine it, contradictions which the revolution of '89 illustrates: mechanistic materialism can describe historical phenomena, but it cannot think through the forces which produce these phenomena. Remarks such as 'the brain secretes thought as the liver secretes bile' are conditioned by this philosophy in the same way as the following remark about the order of matter:

> It follows that I will not die completely, and that a part of myself will escape the ruin of my moral existence, without my being able to flatter myself of having any consciousness or any notion after my death of what I am or of what I might have been, since I have no consciousness or notion of the previous existence of each of the particles of matter of which I am now composed, which also existed as concretely before I existed as they will do after I no longer exist.[17]

This is an exemplary remark which Sade will take up and generalize in exemplary fashion in his turn:

> Never lose sight of the fact, said the Pope, that there is no real destruction: that death itself is not such a destruction, and that philosophically and physically viewed death is nothing but a different modification of matter in which the active principle, or if you prefer, the principle of movement does not stop acting, although in a less apparent way. The birth of man is no more the start of his existence than death is its cessation; and the mother who gives birth to him is no more the giver of life than the murderer who kills him is the giver of death. One produces a species of matter organized in one way, the other provides the opportunity for the reorganization of matter in another sense, and both create. Nothing is born, nothing essentially dies, everything is action and reaction of matter.[18]

This is a remark, or a principle, should I say, in which I see, within the limits specific to mechanistic materialism, that which gave Sade the opportunity to trangress those limits. Thought, specifically dialectic in this instance ('Men have thought dialectically long before knowing what the dialectic was . . . ', Friedrich Engels, *Anti-Dühring*), will oppose Sade in a general sense to the order which cannot think the dialectic. I mean that this principle of the negation of the negation which produces (through its global consequences, through its global execution) the work of Sade had to be absolutely and on every point irreducible to the bourgeois order which conditions mechanistic materialism and the revolution of '89. This is an order which is not yet that of our culture and one against which, today, the work of Sade does not cease inscribing itself. I refer once more to Sollers's essay: 'As universal – and atemporal – project, the Encyclopedia of Sade annuls that of the Enlightenment, which is limited to a certain mode of reading.'[19] The order which I am underlining and to which the work of Sade is absolutely irreducible is first of all that of this 'mode of reading'.

The contradictions which materialist mechanism presents for the order which justifies it are obviously not restricted to the work of Sade, but the timidity with which they are proposed everywhere else makes them practically unreadable. Diderot writes to Sophie Volland:

> Nothing is indifferent in a system linked and entailed by a general law; it seems that everything is equally important. There is no small or great phenomenon. The *Ugenitus* is as necessary as the rising and setting of the sun. It is certain to abandon itself blindly to the universal torrent, and it is impossible to resist it. Impotent or victorious efforts are also of this order. If I think that I love you freely, I am wrong. It is not so.

One can see that everything which is trying to show itself here hardly dares to be said, and is retracted as soon as spoken, commanded in its weakness by the same order which will make Diderot write in a different letter: 'I prefer baptism to circumcision, it hurts less.'[20] What is only expressed very timidly and marginally by the *philosophes* is radically, completely and centrally exposed by Sade, instituted as the only writing possible, as the very reality of writing, and constitutes the very body in relation to which any reality will be determined. His 'Idea on the Novel' (we should note that *idea* is in the singular)[21] cannot not put into question the phantasmatic representational kind of reading to which the novels of Sade are too often submitted. Instead, we might read:

> . . . bear ever in mind that the Novelist is the child of Nature, that she has created him to be her painter; if he does not become his mother's lover the moment she gives birth to him, let him never write, for we shall never read him.[22]

It is clear that Sade proposes incest as the only possible condition for novelistic writing, as the act after which writing becomes possible. It is not necessary to emphasize that such an enterprise is fundamentally transgressive (and even more so if it is proposed as theory). Starting from this condition, one might think that everything becomes possible, but it is still necessary to stipulate that everything becomes possible only to the extent that everything becomes readable . . . We should not forget that the work of Sade is fiction; the 'crimes' that are committed are 'written' crimes, and that it will depend on the liberality, the generality of the reader as to whether these crimes are taken as phantasms or as methods of reading . . . Incest is a taboo, an order which no less than any other is to be read (and which to the extent that a society sees it as the most criminal of crimes is to be read more than any other). Its situation in the order which is ours today is nonetheless such that its reading produces a hole, and precipitates the destructive expenditure of all possible readings – readings which are all just so many crimes (in relation to the legislative structures), a situation in which there is no reader who will feel unconcerned, that is to say, stopped by what concerns him, finding his limit there, or produced by the reading of his limits.

The structures and the order of this 'judiciary'[23] society have to be powerful for the majority of readers to find themselves stopped in the open relation they would like to have with the text, and as if forced to recognize that one of the readings that this text proposes is criminal[24] or insane, which, in the present order comes down to the same thing. The passage from awareness to non-awareness of the text depends essentially on this point of rupture that the more or less powerful mark of legislative knowledge institutes in each reader; this is a knowledge whose specific contradictions, even today, are extremely difficult to articulate. It is only on this basis that it will be possible to reveal its regressive activity. It is clear that over the matter with which we are concerned here (Sade and the order of reading), psychoanalysis, among other things, the texts of Freud, should have long ago familiarized us with the reality repressed by the judiciary structure (seen as unconscious), and which as we know writes itself out in prisons, in asylums and in dreams. When Sade writes: 'the simplest movements of our bodies are enigmas as difficult to decipher as thoughts, for whoever thinks upon them', we can of course read this only with reference to mechanistic materialism, but if we situate it in the context of the functioning of Sade's work, if we relate it to what was said above regarding incest, a displacement is effected which pulls out whatever in this question relates to mechanistic materialism and introduces it into the context of a questioning of the normality of this code. 'The simplest movements of our bodies' obey structures which can only be articulated as normality to the extent that they support the structures of moral legislation; 'the simplest movements of our bodies are enigmas for whoever thinks upon them', to the extent that whatever exceeds moral legislation (the excesses) can only be thought after a putting into question of this legislation. The prudish stupidity against which Freud had to struggle is well known. But at the same time I do not want to imply that I consider the work of Sade as the illustration of a phantasmatic reading. The reading of the work of Sade, like the reading of Freud, is one which, for us today, 'reveals the essence of fantasy',[25] that is to say that it no longer presents itself as a 'criminal' reading, but only to the extent that it can be received outside that dual space which up until now has condemned it to a representative mode (representation/reality = reading), to the extent that it can be received outside of this dual space which up to the present has condemned the reader to live his life in the representative mode of the (transcendent) Subject. The problems which the work of Sade poses for moral legislation can be revealed in a more or less precise manner in the multiple forms that a society employs to resolve (without posing them) the contradictions that it produces (myths, religions, etc.). And there again it is not by chance that Sade (like Freud) returns to and so often cites archaic religions or old myths.[26] The work of Sade, in the order of our culture, is one of the 'monumental' contradictions which are there to be read and to be rendered productive by all those who want to understand what possible future this culture holds for them, and to what fields of activity the dialectic of contradictions is obliging them . . .

Philosophy in the Bedroom is one of the most systematic texts written by Sade, much less violent (monstrous) than his epic novels (*Justine, Juliette, The One Hundred and Twenty Days of Sodom* . . .) this small book echoes Sade's first text *Dialogue between a Priest and a Dying Man*, in being, like this *Dialogue*, the only dialogic text in all of Sade's work, and specifically in being, like the *Dialogue*, engaged with a knowledge which is intended to be taught before convincing (which is not always the strategy of the novel). The title, if we focus on it, points clearly to the site of the Sadean project: philosophy IN the bedroom. In the eighteenth century 'philosophy' is understood as materialist philosophy: what is retiring here to the bedroom is that aspect of the thought of the century which cannot be taught in public, and which will be taught in the private space. We should hear, then, '*materialist* philosophy in the bedroom' – or even the *effects*, in what we call private space, of materialist philosophy – or even not the superficial effects, those of the surface, but the *consequences* of materialist philosophy in all its ramifications. We should not forget that the text is written at the moment when the revolution of 1789 is concerned with the moral structures of the nation and at the moment when it re-establishes a deistic morality. In the context of the public good, philosophy, from this point onwards, cannot 'say everything' and it is only in a reserved space, a space withdrawn, so to speak, from revolutionary and Rousseauistic jurisdiction that it will disseminate its lessons.

As an epigraph to the 1795 edition of *Philosophy* we read: 'Mothers will prescribe this reading for their daughters', which, taking into consideration what the philosophers' pupil (Eugénie) does to her mother at the end of the book, gives a quite wide dimension to this lesson, and emphasizes again the double strategy of Sade's text and the complexity of his method. This method, which it would be necessary to show at work throughout Sade's entire œuvre, consists first of all in the drawing together of texts whose totality (or multiplicity) has to be read. *Philosophy in the Bedroom* offers numerous examples of this; among others, the epigraph 'Mothers will prescribe this reading for their daughters', put in relation or in equation with the use which Eugénie makes of her mother at the end of the book: relation, multiplication, which makes any realistic reading of the story impossible, makes it impossible to read the text as a description of a reality exterior to it, and obliges the reading to widen itself, transporting and playing it out from one text to another, multiplying its effects from one text to another.

Simply on the level of the construction of the book we can find in *Philosophy in the Bedroom* the following modes: a specifically didactic, educational dialogue (the pupil Eugénie receives a lesson which starts with an explanation of vocabulary to then pass on to textual exegesis before introducing her to the cultural and philosophical approach); the more theatrical application of the dialogue which obliges the author to accompany his text with stage directions ('To make Eugénie understand what is at stake he socratizes Augustin himself . . .'[27]), these directions being in italics; the author's own interventions appearing as footnoted references to the cultural order ('See Suetonius and Dion Cassius of Nicea') or again as textual indications ('This aspect will be dealt with further on it having been understood that here we have only laid down some of the basic principles of the system'), without forgetting the famous and very important 'Yet another effort, Frenchmen, if you would become Republicans', which amounts to about seventy pages of the *Philosophy* and which is present inside the book as a brochure bought by Dolmancé at the palace of Equality, a brochure which is thus not supposed to form part of the fiction of the dialogue and which must answer, from outside the didactic fiction, the question that Eugénie poses from the inside: 'I would like to know if morals are really necessary in a government, if their influence is of any weight as concerns the genius of the nation?' The position of this speech 'Frenchmen just one more push . . .' as exterior to the fiction is very important, in fact, as it brings up what I have already underlined several times, that is, the way in which Sade's text finds itself willingly determined by and destined for the historical text (its reading functions through multiplying each of the texts which are proposed to it without forgetting the historical reality which determines these texts). Even a less attentive reading of *Philosophy* cannot not convince us of this. In fact it is more than improbable that at the moment that *Philosophy* was written, and even more so at the moment it was published, that one would have been able to find such a brochure as the one Dolmancé has the Chevalier read. And it's precisely the impossibility of having such a brochure to read which will lead Sade to title it: 'Yet another effort, Frenchmen, if you would become Republicans' (the strategy operated from fiction to reality is clear: fiction must act upon reality, transform it in order to become real, but before this transformation, it is already more real than reality, as it marks its own will to transform, 'just one more push', while without it reality would be stopped in its tracks and thus completely fictive). It is necessary to know in fact that from 7 May 1794 the French Republic declares itself deist, first of all in a report presented to the Committee of Public Safety 'On the Relation of Religious and Moral Ideas to Republican Ideals', in which one can read:

Who then gave you the mission to announce to the people that the divinity does not exist, you who are passionate about this arid doctrine and not about the nation? What advantage do you find in persuading men that a blind force presides over their destiny and strikes crime or virtue at random, that man's soul is nothing but a light breath which blows itself out at the entrance to the tomb?

and further on:

I cannot say how nature might have suggested to man more useful fictions; and if the existence of God, and the immortality of the soul were nothing but dreams, they would still be the most beautiful conceptions of man's mind. I do not need to add that it is not a question here of putting any particular philosophical opinion on trial, neither of contesting the virtue of such and such a philosopher, whatever his opinions, and even in spite of them, through the strength of a happy nature and of superior reason. It is simply a question of seeing atheism as a national phenomenon, and linked to a system which conspires against the Republic.

These remarks which clearly target the materialist philosophers ('the virtue of such and such a philosopher' might point to d'Holbach) cannot have left Sade indifferent, and if it is added that they were followed by a decree unanimously voted in by the Convention, and whose first paragraph declares: 'The French people recognizes the existence of the Supreme Being and the immortality of the soul', we can understand Sade's demand for one more push if the French people are to become republican – an effort which will enable them to reject the consolations of this 'puerile religion'. If we compare Robespierre's speech to Sade's, all the rigor is on Sade's side, for example when he declares:

Annihilate for ever, then, whatever might one day destroy your work. . . . One more push: since you are attempting to destroy all prejudice, do not let any remain, if one part remains it is enough to bring all of them back. How much more certain it is that they will return if you allow to remain the one which is the very source of all the others.[28]

Prophetic phrases in relation to the fate of Robespierre and the Revolution. The complexity of the Sadean discourses which make up *Philosophy in the Bedroom* is illustrated here at its simplest level and it shows clearly that the sentence cited above about d'Holbach's *System of Nature*: 'I am its adherent to the point of martyrdom, if necessary' was taken very seriously by Sade.

A theory is at work in the writing of Sade which, at whatever level, never lets past an opportunity to reconsider whatever might betray it (Rousseauism, republican deism). This theory, which can be seen as a consequence, a systematic extension, of the materialist philosophy of the eighteenth century, has to be read from the starting-point of the multiplicity of texts which it calls into play. To only read one text is not to read Sade: Sade thus becomes unreadable. To read only the fictional text, its postural form, is a neurotic reading. To read only the didactic text, to refuse or not be able to read the fictional text, is a neurotic reading. The reading of Sade moves from one to the other without ever letting itself fall into the cultural trap which consists in reducing each text to a unit and in adding unit to unit. Sade is only readable for a reading which thinks through the multiplicitous articulations of textual contradictions and which thinks its own insertion into the order of these contradictions. Sade is not perhaps readable for all, and Sade does not lead us to say this:

> so much for those who can only see the evil in philosophical opinions, susceptible of corrupting everything, who knows if they would not become gangrenous themselves after reading Seneca or Charron! It's not to them that I speak, I am only addressing people capable of hearing me, and they will read my work without danger.

To say of Sade that he is readable, is to say that he is *still* to be read, and by all.

Translated by Patrick ffrench

Notes

1 [This article appeared originally in *Tel Quel*, 34 (1968), destined to serve as an introduction to the Italian translation of *Philosophy in the Bedroom*. It was reprinted in *Théorie d'ensemble* as Part II of an article titled 'The Underwriting (*souscription*) of Form', the first part consisting of an article titled 'Eugène Sue's Practices', about Marx's analysis of Sue's *The Mysteries of Paris*.]
2 Translated as D.A.F. de Sade, 'Reflections on the Novel', in *The One Hundred and Twenty Days of Sodom*, trans. Austryn Wainhouse and Richard Seaver (London, Arena, 1989), 113–14.
3 The book which Sade mentions, the *Refutation of the System of Nature*, could be either that of the Abbé Bergier published in 1771, or that of Holland published in 1773.
4 [Pleynet's emphasis.]
5 Sade's emphasis.
6 D'Holbach's *System of Nature* was published for the first time in 1770, with a second edition also in 1770, and subsequent printings in 1771, 1774, 1775, 1777. Following this letter, Sade would have read it in 1776.
7 [Pleynet's emphasis.]
8 D.A.F. de Sade, letter to his Wife of June 1873, in D.A.F. de Sade, *Three Novels: Justine, Philosophy in the Bedroom, Eugénie de Franval*, trans. Austryn Wainhouse and Richard Seaver (London, Arrow, 1991), 133.

9 'My friend, I brought a package of books to the authorities which was not permitted. M. Noir, explaining, said that they had taken away all your books because they overheated your mind and made you write unsuitable things.' (Letter from Madame de Sade to her husband, August 1782).

10 In order to understand what I emphasized earlier concerning the bourgeois recuperation of the scientific philosophy of the eighteenth century, one might, for example, read the following excerpt from Cassirer's book *The Philosophy of the Enlightenment*, trans. Fritz C.A. Koelln and J.P. Pettegrove (Princeton, Princeton University Press, 1951): 'It is customary to consider the turn towards mechanism and materialism as characteristic of the philosophy of nature of the eighteenth century, and in so doing it is often believed that the basic trend of the French spirit has been exhaustively characterized . . .'(55) and further on: 'Yet in truth this materialism, as it appears in d'Holbach's *System of Nature* and La Mettrie's *Man as Machine* (*L'homme machine*), is an isolated phenomenon of no characteristic significance. Both works represent special cases and exemplify a retrogression into that dogmatic mode of thinking which the leading scientific minds of the eighteenth century oppose and endeavor to eliminate. . . . '. And: 'The *System of Nature* played a relatively unimportant part in the general development of Diderot's thought. Even the thinkers closest to d'Holbach's circle not only rejected the radical conclusions of his work but denied his very premises. Voltaire's sure judgement appeared when he at once attacked d'Holbach's book at its weakest point. With ruthless clarity he pointed to the contradiction in the fact that d'Holbach, who dedicated his banner to the fight against dogmatism and intolerance, in turn set up his own thesis as dogma and defended it with fanatical zeal. Voltaire refused to permit his viewpoint as a free thinker to be based on such arguments, and he was unwilling to receive from the hands of d'Holbach and his followers the "patent of an atheist" (*le brevet d'athée*). And Voltaire was even more critical of d'Holbach's presentation of his views and of the literary value of the book. He classified the work as belonging to the only literary genre he could not tolerate, namely, the "boring genre" (*le genre ennuyeux*). In fact, d'Holbach's style, apart from its prolixity and digressiveness, is particularly harsh and dry. Its objective is to eliminate from the philosophy of nature not only all religious but all aesthetic elements as well, and to neutralize all the forces of feeling and phantasy' (72). The length of this quotation is justified if one thinks of it as an exemplary representation of the kind of judgement which professes to displace the activity of d'Holbachian materialism in eighteenth-century culture. To focus only on the 'fanatical zeal' with which d'Holbach defends his work, it would be pertinent to recall the degree of aggression with which works like the *System of Nature* were persecuted (see the *Encyclopaedia*), persecutions which the criticism of the deist Voltaire only serve to justify, in objective terms.

11 Thus, in *Philosophy in the Bedroom*, we find the following: 'If they absolutely insist that you speak of a Creator, tell them that things having always been as they are, having never had a beginning and not destined to have an end, it becomes as useless as it is impossible for man to return to an imaginary origin which would explain nothing and move toward nothing. Tell them that it is impossible for mankind to have true ideas regarding a being who does not appear to any of our senses.' [Translation adapted from D. A. F. de Sade, *Three Novels*, 304.] And in the *System of Nature* one can read the following: 'The notions of nothingness or of the *creation* are only words, which cannot render us any knowledge about the formation of the universe, they do not present any meaning upon which the mind can alight. This notion becomes even more

obscure when one attributes the creation or the formation of matter to a spiritual being, that is to say, to a being which has no analogy, nor point of contact with matter. . . . Moreover, it is agreed that matter cannot totally annihilate itself or cease to exist; and so how is one going to understand how that which cannot cease to exist can ever have had a beginning? Therefore, when one asks from whence matter arose, we shall say that it has always existed' (edn of 1821).

12 Philippe Sollers, 'Sade in the Text', in *Writing and the Experience of Limits*, trans P. Barnard (New York, Columbia University Press, 1983).

13 Ibid., 55–6. The characters Saint-Fond and Clairwil are from *Juliette*. Sollers reads Clairwil as 'clear will, she teaches Juliette', but might it not also be possible to read 'Clairwil' as 'clear' and 'vile', which would introduce, within her teaching, the contradiction (which remains for Sade irreducible: 'It is impossible to formulate any collective term for two opposites, as it will not be any more distinct to the understanding' (*Opuscules on the Theatre*) of the clear and the dark, the high and the low . . . The collective term escapes the understanding, but *marks* the activity of the text. Sade will often come back to the problems caused by language, to the problems that his writing poses, as if he found this problem of contradiction crucial to his practice, and insoluble for whoever was unable to think dialectically. For example, in *Philosophy* we can read: 'The poverty of the French language compels us to employ words which, today, our happy government, with so much good sense, disavows; we hope our enlightened readers will understand us well and will not at all confound absurd political despotism with the very delightful despotism of libertinage's passions.' Sade, *Three Novels*, 344 [translation adapted].

14 Rousseau, letter to Vernes, 24 June 1761.

15 On the relations between d'Holbach and Rousseau, see Pierre Naville, *D'Holbach et la philosophie scientifique au XVIIIe siècle* (Paris, Gallimard, 1943).

16 Karl Marx, 'The Holy Family', in David McLellan (ed.), *Selected Writings* (Oxford, Oxford University Press, 1977), 141.

17 Henri de Boulainvillier, *L'Essai de métaphysique dans les principes de B. de Spinoza* (1707).

18 D.A.F. de Sade, *Juliette*, trans. A. Wainhouse (New York, Grove Press, 1968), 772, [Pleynet's emphasis, translation adapted.]

19 Sollers, 'Sade in the Text', 56.

20 Diderot, letter of 24 September 1767.

21 [We should note that Pleynet's insistence on the singular *idée* in Sade's title conflicts with the practice of the translators of the English edition of the text, Wainhouse and Seaver, who translate it as 'Reflections on the Novel'.]

22 Sade, 'Reflections on the Novel', 110. [Pleynet's emphasis.]

23 'All the bourgeois economists are aware of is that production can be carried on better under the modern police than e.g. on the principle of might makes right. They forget only that this principle is also a legal relation, and that the right of the stronger prevails in their "constitutional republics" as well, only in another form.' Karl Marx, *Grundrisse: Foundations of the Critique of Political Economy*, trans. M. Nicolaus (Harmondsworth, Penguin, 1973), 88.

24 For example, Gilbert Lely, Sade's biographer, finds himself blocked by the coprophagic aspect of *The One Hundred and Twenty Days of Sodom*. [Gilbert Lely, *Sade* (Paris: Gallimard, 1967).]

25 See, in relation to this, Michel Tort's essay 'L'effet Sade' in issue 28 of *Tel Quel* (1967). In *Philosophy in the Bedroom*, for example, it is the transgression of the didactic discourse, which, 'exciting' the character, suddenly blocks, interrupts speech, discourse. At the end of one of his lessons Dolmancé realizes that his

remarks have put Eugénie beside herself: 'O, heavens, what is wrong my angel? Madame, see what a state our pupil is in! Eugénie (masturbating): Ah: Heavens, you're making my head spin'. Dolmancé interrupts, and finds himself 'forced' to interrupt his speech: 'Fuck! I'm hard!.. Call Augustin back, I beg you.' Sade, *Three Novels*, 346 [translation adapted]. The structure of transgressive discourse, meeting the structure of the law in the subject, blocks discourse, interrupts thought, which then repeats itself in the formal structure and in the transgressive 'economy' of the text, without being able to dialectically sublate what stops it and conditions it via a productive 'expenditure'. We see the same thing happen for the reader who limits his or her reading to the simple naturalist 'representation' of what he or she is reading (the form), unable from that point to think through, dialectically the various articulations of the text. The book thus contains in its fiction a 'limit' for the reader, *and* the possible reading of this limit. The lesson and the explanation of all of this can moreover be found in a final note to the first text written by Sade: *Dialogue between a Priest and a Dying Man*: 'The dying man rang, the women entered and in their arms the preacher became one whom Nature has corrupted, all because he had not succeeded in explaining what a corrupted nature is.' Ibid., 175.

26 *Philosophy in the Bedroom*: 'We shall look at nations which, even more ferocious, were only satisfied by immolating their children. . . . In the Greek republics, all the children who arrived into the world were carefully examined, and if they were not found to conform in such a way as to be able one day to defend the republic, they were immediately immolated. . . . The ancient legislators had not scruples about sending children to their deaths. . . . Aristotle recommended abortion. . . . ' Ibid., 334–5 [translation adapted].

27 Ibid., 267 [translation adapted].

28 Ibid., [translation adapted].

7

THE BATAILLE ACT[1]

Philippe Sollers

No-one *knows* what it is to swim.

I am picturing Georges Bataille in an office which he used to drop in to. The office opens onto a walled garden, which you get to through a window. Bataille wants to visit the garden. Being tired, he finds it difficult to get through the window. I take him by the arm, we fall onto the earth and the grass. The leaves are black. It's fine weather.

I am telling this story as if I was starting a classic narrative, as if I accepted the relaxed coherence of a book that no-one will ever write. There are traditional beginnings like this in Bataille's narratives, something like a memory, getting more and more eroded and distant, of what existed without ever being able to. But I am not hallucinating. I know that I have to give my talk a theoretical turn.

The most insignificant anecdote, in the system of the non-system, brings in the infinitesimal mark of the instant, that is, the non-dissolution, total or abstract, of the non-system in the system. The system takes place; it is insuperable, exact, rigorous, but at the same time, and as if it does not want to know it, it is a moment. There is always, within it, a concrete detail which seems useless, which seems to be there to prove that, at a certain point, the system founders, collapses, has a lack hollowed out in it, a hole. A hole which imprints a non-seriousness in the system. Apparently, an expense for nothing, a move to nothing. Knowledge is absolute on condition that it deny its fiction.

In one sense, this beginning makes me laugh. Several times I gave up on it. It worries me, I feel that it's worrying. It's definitely beside the point, annoying, subjective, without interest, regressive, nostalgic. Imagine a lecturer who, instead of developing his speech, logically, would tell random anecdotes interspersing them with contradictory theses, drinking more and more while doing it, until, in the end, he was dead drunk in front of you. That's not my intention here, of course. But the rest of what I will say is meant to show why it must and it mustn't be like this. As if the sly and tacit complicity of control and non-control had to be broken. Both are in fact only traces. The subject is a movement *outside* these traces. One of his masks is a character in fiction, an author of fiction. Let's suppose that he passes 'through the window': he becomes the exorbitant detail in the real that makes a hole in the circle. A circumference intact *except for at one point?* Perhaps. I can hear Bataille saying, with a cardiac, muffled voice: 'It's certain that it would be difficult to go further in wisdom than Blanchot.' His eyes, at that moment, were saying nothing exactly, but they had laughed. I can hear him replying to a question I asked him about *Inner Experience*, 'I forget.' The question was without interest, moreover. Myself, I don't remember.

> On a roof I saw some large and solid hooks, standing up half way down. Suppose that a man fell from the crest of the roof, he could by chance be caught by one of them, by his leg or arm. Precipitated from the rooftop of a house, I would crash into the ground. But if a hook were there, I could stop on the way down! Afterwards I might say: 'Someday an architect conceived this hook, without which I would be dead. I should be dead; but it's not true, I am alive, someone had put in a hook.'
>
> My presence and my life would be ineluctable: but something strangely impossible and inconceivable would be their principle.[2]

The question I wanted to ask could also take this form: so Hegel's move is to reveal the true or the absolute no longer as substance but as subject. We are more and more aware of how and why substantialism is trying to move back into Marxism. And how and why the problem of the subject has been withdrawn, so to speak, into the unconscious or into the explosive excess of the Nietzsche-limit. In a sense, the two areas have remained and remain separated, even though they tend more and more to rub up against each other, or even to attack one another. Materialist dialectics has to deal with madness, and it knows it. Psychoanalysis's internal contestation has to deal with historical materialism. Process without subject, subject without process, there we are; the two scenes are juxtaposed, unequally run through by one another, but I would like to make it understood that they get carried away by one another, at the same time.

I propose this: the Marxist overturning or overcoming through and beyond Hegel, the Nietzsche-effect and the Freud-effect relative to what bursts out or falls from the subject in the operation of this overturning and overcoming, can themselves, at once in relation to Hegel and outside him, but very deeply in the most interior interior of Hegel, signify that the overcoming of the exposition as substance, then as subject, then as materialist dialectic, including the non-resolved, gnawing question of the subject, signify, then, that the exposition must logically take hold of itself and overcome itself as the matter of the altered subject. This means: introduction of a discordant dialectic, including at the same time 'the whole perspective' and the 'eruption–disappearance' of what allows the whole perspective but prevents it from closing up.

We are immediately in complete contradiction, since we start off from a subject immersed in substance as a false subject, and we obtain from above it a lack of subject issuing from the subject as absolute but in which substance returns as truth, and, moreover, so to speak, from the above or elsewhere, decentred, 'surplus' of the subject. But this time: impossible. The interlocking of the question of the subject 'expresses', if you like, the question of the masses *making* history. But this making implicates itself somewhere as the practical experience of the concrete impossibility of the subject who, if it is not exposed, will come to block or to delay or to falsify the process. All this is schematic, but designates the difficulty that Bataille never stopped imposing, playing. Playing, since it is immediately apparent that no finished exposition, finished and complete especially in its form and right up to the smallest part of its form, can by definition eliminate this difficulty without eliminating itself from the impossible truth, or if you prefer from the *corner*, which leaves open not the process itself (it stays open anyway) but its activity of reflection. This is not about social practice which is regulated directly without logical difficulty, but about what I would call the experience of self-consciousness in which *there is no* self-consciousness. This affirmation, if it is stopped, that is, dogmatically affirmed by the system, in fact becomes *false*. There is self-consciousness, and it occurs in the movement in which this self-consciousness *is not*. Hegel, says Bataille, 'moves the furthest away from those who act wildly'. The situation I have just described, that I have just decomposed, is in truth *comic*. It is especially comic, and this is important to grasp as soon as possible, because it is impersonal. If it were personal, it would be simply tragic, ridiculous or pitiable (which it can be too, at an inevitable but not decisive moment of repression), it would not be comic, I mean comic in itself and for itself, for nothing or no-one else.

Here I could suddenly stop and pass to an act, denying the problem and maintaining this negation in action. This is done all the time. The action would be right, it would have a correct or contradictory class line, but one which would ultimately be practical, I would be in agreement with science and with a revolutionary conception of philosophy, that much is evident, but the *rest*, the remainder would irresistibly return, and inasmuch as somewhere a point of the circle had not acted as a point outside the circle, I would end up somewhere in neurosis in choosing, or not, to say: 'it's nothing'.

A common joke has it that the difference between a neurotic and a psychotic is that for the psychotic two and two make five, while for the neurotic two and two make four, and it hurts.

If one divides into two, then, in a place outside place, this division must emerge in the 'five' of two plus two.

'Truth', wrote Bataille,

> has rights over us. It even has total rights over us. But we have to answer to *something* which, not being God, is stronger than any rights: this *impossible* to which we only accede in forgetting the truth of all these rights, in accepting to disappear.

It's clear: what 'accedes' to the impossible is not the subject *himself* (he can even die in an insignificant way like a child in the dark). What accedes is excess, which can moreover be reduced and survive poorly within the subject as a forgotten or unrecognized thing. Excess accedes as communication, that is to say, nine times out of eleven as a relapse into denial. That's why there are always at least two subjects to respond to the operation. But this two is not 'two individuals', the two comes from division itself, which does not affect a subject in advance, but in a sense produces the subject in expending it.

The subject *himself*, as *other*, is a double unproductive expenditure.

Of this subject, we can say in general that we want to *know nothing*.

It is useless to debate Bataille's non-knowledge if one does not start off from the fact that this non-knowledge (1) supposes absolute knowledge (the system) and (2) takes account of a not-wanting-to-know within knowledge, analysable, perhaps, but irreducible.

Non-knowledge introduces itself into this inequality, that is to say, that it is expenditure in the place where knowledge and the resistance to knowledge expose the difference of the remainder in loss without remainder. There is always remainder, the remainder *is*. 'Total' expenditure *is not*. We'd have to go back to Bataille's opposition in *Beyond the Serious*, between 'what happens' and 'what doesn't happen'. What happens is always an expenditure in the place of another. Simply because expenditure is death, and no-one would imagine that his skeleton represents him (except in Christian paintings or in some of the natural sciences).

So, production is not everything. And to propose as an 'absolute' limit of the dominant world of production, in an overproductive hero, a super-machine, to plug desire into the blaze of totality, is great, it's even really great, to the extent that it unlocks the archaic economy that haunts production right up to its imperialist limits, but it tells us nothing about raw expenditure, or, more exactly, about the dance that risks a cliff fall.

There is not only flux *or* lack. There is also, when it wants, 'what is this it?', the subject of which we want to know nothing, gusts of wind or intakes of air. It's perhaps what Bataille calls *chance*:

Too much light too much joy too much sky
the too vast earth a swift horse

One day I will *test chance*, and, moving like a sylph over eggs, I will
make it believed that I am walking: my wisdom will seem magical.
Maybe I will close the door to others – supposing that trying chance
demands that one *knows nothing about it*. Man holds onto a line of
chance visible in 'customs', a line that he is himself, a state of grace,
an unleashed arrow. Animals are in play, man is in play, like the
arrow parting the air, I don't know where it will fall, I don't know
where I will fall.

The subject of which we want to know nothing: effect and intersection of
matter in movement? You can't say that it's through a hasty move that
Hegel makes a mistake about expenditure without remainder in transforming it into abstract negativity; it's by *idealism*, and it's through a *dualist*
and *materialist* reaffirmation (thus objectively a movement towards the
extension of dialectical materialism) that Bataille gets into his 'exit' from
Hegel. As such, it takes a good dose of simplicity to reproach him, as Sartre
does, for 'suppressing the synthetic moment of the Hegelian trinity'.

What happens? The external cause of the subject brings him to experience, without being able to master it, the effect of his determining internal
cause, in other words to consume himself in consuming it. The subject
becomes a play which side-steps his cause through and by his cause, the
(external) *condition* rendering the (internal) *base* naked. Bataille gives a name
to this short-cut operation: laughter. We could find other names for the
operation, they would always be fringed by laughter. Minor laughter opens
in an atmosphere of disappearance into major laughter: the transmutation
that results – the negative as the beyond of the serious affirmative – engages
an accelerated contradiction, as if the struggle, identity and conversion of
opposites, were felt directly in the subject's element. The negative is no
more, as in Hegel, 'opposite', you don't 'reside' in its proximity, it does not
become a 'being' emerging out of a 'magical power', even though the experience can *also* be described in this way – the negative *laughs*. It laughs (at) the
subject trembling with laughter. One jump, and it's infectious.

For Bataille, in the unfolding of time Hegel therefore misses the 'sacrifi-
cial' materiality of the operation, its 'moment'. It's not without interest to add
why, according to Bataille, this is the case: through the lack of an experience
of the 'Catholic' type (closer, in Bataille's eyes, to pagan truth than to the
Reformation). In other words, it's a question of the historical variations of
repression (but here the repressed base of materialist thought is of prime
importance). However, it is pointless to proceed to a repression of the forms of
repression: this gesture would move away from a central de-simplification,

the question must be asked at *the heart* of all stratifications. This is why Christianity cannot be circumvented:

> Christianity is nothing other, at bottom, than a crystallization of language. The solemn affirmation of the fourth gospel: *Et verbum facto est*, in a sense, the following profound truth: the truth of language is Christian. If man and language double the world in another imaginary – available through the means of evocation – Christianity is necessary. Or, otherwise, some other affirmation of this kind.

Which, by the same token, signifies that the buried truth of eroticism is Christian, to the extent that it leaves the investigation of sexual reproduction as an unresolved problem. 'Excess is the principle of sexual reproduction.' 'Exuberance is the point at which we let go of Christianity.' It's at this point – Dionysus against Christ – that an effraction must take place in order that the matter in movement of the subject takes place in its place, that is, in its very disappearance. 'Mark the day you read with a burning stone, you who grew pale while reading the philosophers. How can the one who shut them up make himself understood, except in a way incomprehensible to them?'

For Nietzsche's eternal return, which is like the finished and relaunched anticipation, the explosion of the Hegelian summit, Bataille substitutes the experience of the instant, and it's *there*, at that point, that a certain mark sticks out, without return. Sade made it appear in Cartesian idealism but also in the materialism of the Enlightenment. Bataille implicates it at the same time within Hegel and Nietzsche, and, by the same move, asks a question of science and its deviated productions, the question of its underside, the expenditure of the subject, 'unemployed negativity'. If the essence of man becomes the totality of social relations, with all the *true* consequences which this implies (class struggle), what then appears, disengaged but at the same time invisible, so to speak, is the definitive shadow of the negative subject. Which has no recognizable 'right' but must in spite of everything 'answer' to something stronger than rights: to a *fact*, which is always deniable, denied, negated, but which founds negation itself. A fact, an act which is equal to originary repression, an instant equal to the atemporality of the unconscious process, that other name for the sleep of time within the system: 'on the contrary, I am wakefulness itself'. 'If I had to put myself into the history of the world of thought, it would be for having distinguished the effects in our human life of the vanishing of discursive reality, and for having derived a blinding light from the description of these effects.' The instant is that innumerable subject of present loss as lost plaything of all the streaming ruptures of time: not a full presence, nor a deferral, nor an absence, nor a developing retention, the instant, simply, the striated, doubled instant. The instant for Bataille is the reversed, positive, economic form of trauma, so to speak, the trace which succeeds the loss of consciousness, in the same way that consciousness appears where the mnesic trace ends. The instant is a short-circuit in the constitution of the *après-coup*, a move [*coup*] within a move [*coup*]. Bataille's joy is to the joke what solar irradiation is to a pocket torch. Ten thousand jokes per second, ten thousand lapsus per overturned proposition.

> Language lacks because language is made with propositions which bring in identities and from the moment when, because of the excess of amounts to spend, you have to stop spending for profit, and start spending for its own sake, you can't stay on the level of identity. You have to open notions beyond themselves.

'The amount of energy produced is always more than the amount necessary for production.' This excess is trans-invested, against a background of 'a wave of the wasting of life', not only in the form of 'flux' but as affirmative waste, to the depths: 'In the flux, there was no cry, but from the projected "point" existence faints in a cry.' This trans-investment is separate from the causal register of the register of possible effects: 'The sovereign operation is arbitrary and even though its effects legitimate it from the point of view of subordinate operations, it is indifferent to the judgement of this point of view.' The external cause passing through the internal cause undergoes a kind of exposure which makes it, 'at a point', completely heterogeneous to its effects, its effects are its own but it is not their *cause*. Which can be summarized in this imperative but non-dogmatic formula: 'Leave the possible to those who are attached to it.' The only tissue or exit from the tissue is in the possible: the possible is the separation of life and death. In impossible excess, where double expenditure causes and does not cause the possible, that is: comes back as a 'visible' expenditure but at the same time disappears like any expenditure, there is no exit, nor any 'beyond' from which, dead, you might see the exit, but an immediate infinity of moves [*coups*] hooking into a reloading and, without having anything to do with it, increasing, through expenditure, the consciousness of the self that *is not*.

A subject who took it upon himself to say: 'I am the infinite' would immediately have to cope with the law, with the concept: in the sphere of religion the result is exclusion, execution, in science it is internment. Religion or science cannot admit that in 'I am the infinite' in reality it is the infinite that is speaking. If the infinite says it, in spite of everything, as an impossible subject, it's clear that the operation is comic in itself, comic in the sense that Bataille means it, which is to say that this qualification, in its most banal sense, is also true, in another mode, at the highest level, while applicable to any other possible qualification. The laugh is equal to anything else and 'since the most ancient times, laughter laughs at the joker'. In reality, what? You could also say that 'in truth it's only about the possible, but suppressing everything which annihilates it'. This contradiction supposes that 'in heterogeneous reality . . . the part is equal to the whole'. When the part is equal to the whole, the part opens up, the subject is the ball or rather the prey of the unknown, but keeps the faculty of expression (contrary to Oriental methods), and the unknown is laughable, albeit tragi-cally, and this laugh is also a 'supplication without response' from the part in which the faculty of expression subsists. Bataille underlines this: 'the uncon-scious is one of the aspects of the heterogeneous', while the sacred is a 'restrained form' of it. The unconscious and the sacred are themselves inserted into the operation, to the same extent as eroticism, poetry, etc., inserted, in short, into a naked constellation of 'moments' escaping from the system of homogeneous production, 'moments' of which no one moment can move ahead of the others without falsification, that is, without pretending to retain *the* heterogeneous cause of the homogeneous and thus arresting the discordant dialectic of contradiction. Sexuality therefore has no privilege in this schema other than that of a 'teaching' outside teaching, definitely not holding all rights (only truth has total rights). Otherwise, 'you may as well say that we should ultimately go for a complete *tabula rasa* and go back to the time of animality, of free cannibalism and indifference to excreta'. No 'moment' can put itself in the place of truth, that is not *its* place. By defini-tion, consummation can have no place, no more than the impossible subject (which does not mean the imaginary, unreal, abstract subject: on the contrary). Truth, here, is not that of science, but a 'violent refutation'. It's truth that has total rights (especially in that it says the truth of history or of science). But it lets go of any hold on the operation.

> Science is an attention, the totality of attention, given to the object. There is and there cannot be any science of the subject. But if I affirm, starting off from science, that the subject is important for me, I cannot load it up with religious truths (the dogmas), I can only know it strangely, negatively first of all, but I have the right to say that I *want* to lose myself in it.

There is evidently a cash moment in the operation, a moment when, in a sense, the subject *unloads*, and what it unloads is the corpse of the subject of the possible. 'If there is nothing which goes beyond us, which goes beyond us *in spite of us*, not existing *at any price*, we don't reach the insane moment.' The involuntary instance is irreducible here. It's involuntarily, but with total decisiveness, that an instant's throw [*coup*] abolishes chance. You only need a gob on your own limit, a movement breaking the possible within you: 'The most miserable cunt comes by spitting on his own limitations.'

the rebel, the rebel against the play neither minor nor major
who is obliged to reduce the play to the minor state
must envisage the necessity of major play
which is essentially revolt against minor play
the limit of play
Without that the minor man dominates reason

This leads to the recognition that the worst is a play
to the negation of power of suffering and death
Cowardice before such a perspective.

At this point I would say: why is this self-confessed 'cowardice' the guarantee of experience? Why does it constitute the non-complete and always restarted element of the operation? Why does the operation resist the argument of courage, of virility, of knowledge, which become grotesque in it? Why is the grotesqueness of the apology for mastery dominant in discourse and destitute in the play of the major? The possible, the minor, commanded by the hysteric, built up by her, demands position, denies movement, denies the negation of the negation of a 'mobile, fragmentary, ungraspable' reality. Cowardice before the perspective which consist in denying the power of suffering and of death in the same move unmasks the hysteric, the master, the slave of the play of the minor. Here, the man who wants mastery, who wants the maternal, is inflated, but the operation deflates him like a windbag. The destitution of mastery, as of non-mastery, opens onto a different play which reveals, inexcusably, power attained over the terror of suffering, of death. It puts power *completely* in question. Without any possible reinvestment in the sublime; without 'superman', without revelation. 'The universe is FREE, it has nothing to do.' 'Putting in question also wants failure, it wants the success of failure.' In supplication, LAUGHTER ITSELF: 'He refused the inscription on his tomb "At last I attain INFINITE HAPPINESS". The tomb [*tombe*] itself would disappear, one day [*jour*].'

So night falls [*le jour tombe*]. We walk in the garden. I've forgotten how we got back in, what came after.

Translated by Patrick ffrench

Notes

1 [This article originated as a presentation at the 1972 conference 'Artaud/Bataille: Towards a Cultural Revolution', held at Cérisy-la-Salle, and was published in *Tel Quel*, 52 (1973) and subsequently in a volume edited by Sollers, *Bataille* (Paris, 10/18, 1972), where it was followed by the conference discussion after Sollers's intervention, not included here.]

2   [Sollers has not attributed any of the quotations in his text, leading at moments to an undecidability as regards their author, Bataille or Nietzsche, for example. Supposing this to be a deliberate gesture, related to the matter and style of the article, and to its performative nature, we have followed Sollers's example in the translation.]

8

THE SUBJECT IN PROCESS[1]

Julia Kristeva

A theoretical discourse can only attempt to 'take account' of a signifying function refused by our culture by consigning it to the domain of art, that is, to libraries or conferences. At the very most it can try to intervene in the accepted and operating conceptual systems on the basis of the experience that the subject of theory might herself have of this functioning. The following is thus concerned, on the one hand, with an intra-theoretical attempt with ideological consequences (which in no sense provides a comprehensive account of Artaud's experience), and, on the other hand, with an invasion of the positivist neutrality of theory by the subjective experience of the theorist, by her capacity to put herself 'on trial', to move out of the enclosure of her individuality, be it split, to then return to the fragile site of metalanguage so as to utter the logic of this process, suffered if not understood.

Within these limits, the following theses will be presented:

1 In its most audacious moments current (Lacanian) psychoanalytic theory proposes a theory of the subject as a divided unity which arises from and is determined by lack (void, nothingness, zero, according to the context) and engages in an unsatisfied quest for the impossible, represented by metonymic desire. This subject, which we will call the 'unitary subject', under the law of One, which turns out to be the Name of the Father, this subject of filiation or subject-son, is in fact the unvoiced part, or if you like the truth, of the subject of science, but also of the subject of the social organism (of the family, the clan, the state, the group). Psychoanalysis teaches us this: that any subject, inasmuch as he or she is social, supposes this unitary and split instance, initially proposed by Freud with the Unconscious/Conscious schema, while it also points to the role of originary repression in the constitution of the subject. If originary repression institutes the subject at the same time as the symbolic function, it also institutes the distinction between signifier and signified in which Lacan sees the determination of 'any censorship of a social nature'.[2] The unitary subject is the subject instituted by this social censoring.

However, despite being constitutive, this censoring and the subject which

133

it installs do not behave according to a universal law. We cannot yet undertake the history of the institution of the subject or of the development of the forces of production and the modes of production which correspond to them across human history, although Deleuze and Guattari's *Anti-Œdipus*[3] is a first step in this direction. We can only recognize, empirically for the moment, the existence of signifying practices which seem to point to the existence of *another economy*. To take only a few examples: pre-Socratic Greece (Heraclitus, Anaxagoras, Empedocles), the China of the 'Asiatic mode of production', and, particularly, capitalist society since the end of the nineteenth century; all propose texts remarkable for a practice in which the unitary subject, as an indispensable pole assuring the capacity to verbalize (putting into words), is annihilated, liquefied, exceeded by what we will call the 'process of *signifiance*',[4] that is, by pre-verbal drives and semiotic operations logically if not chronologically anterior to the phenomenon of language. In this process, the unitary subject discovered by psychoanalysis is only one moment, a time of arrest, a stasis, exceeded and threatened by this movement. The process in question is not only a 'topologization', or a spatial dynamic which remains subsumable by One (or Unity). It goes as far as rejecting even the Unconscious/Conscious division, the Signifier/Signified division, that is, even the very censoring through which the subject and the social order are constituted.

The process dissolves the linguistic sign and its system (word, syntax), dissolves, that is, even the earliest and most solid guarantee of the unitary subject: Artaud's glossolalia and 'eructations' reject the symbolic function and mobilize the drives which this function represses in order to constitute itself, drives whose organization on and across the body of the subject constitute a fragmented topography, an investment without delay and without *différance*[5] in an asymbolic biological and social matter which is nevertheless already organized.

This pulsional network, which is readable, for example, in the pulsional roots of the non-semanticized phonemes of Artaud's texts, represents (for theory) the *mobile-receptacle site of the process*, which takes the place of the unitary subject. Such a site, which we will call the *chora*,[6] can suffice as a representation of the subject in process, but it should not be supposed that it is constituted by a break (castration); it is more pertinent to see it as functioning by way of the reiteration of the break or separation, as a multiplicity of ex-pulsions, ensuring its infinite renewal. Expulsion[7] rejects the discordance between the signifier and signified to the extent of the dissolution of the subject as signifying subject, but it also rejects any partitions in which the subject might shelter in order to constitute itself: 'One must speak now of the disembodiment of reality, of that sort of rupture that seems determined to multiply itself between things and the feeling they produce in our mind, the place they should take.'[8]

As well as being a-subjective, the process, set in movement and renewal by expulsion, is also a-familial, a-filial, a-social. Only movements of social subversion, at times of change or revolution, can offer a field of social action to this process of expulsion.

2 However, the Marxist conception of the subject does not concern itself with this multiplicity of expulsions which pulverize the unitary subject. Deriving from the Hegelian dialectic, Marxism dismisses Hegelian negativity, which represented the pulverization of subjective unity and its mediation towards the objective order, retaining only an already reified negativity under the guise of 'social relations'. The subject is not a process, but an atom (non-existent, in the end) in relation to others within the objective process. The negativity internal to the subject which takes over from the external process, as a process 'itself', is coagulated and conflated in relations of 'need' or 'desire' between punctual subjects. The Marxist conception of the subject is inherited directly from Feuerbach, whom, on the other hand, Marx refutes as far as social relations and human practice are concerned. We should therefore look more closely at Feuerbach's conception of the subject. Wishing to get rid of the mysticism of self-consciousness (which would be developed by the right-wing Hegelians), and proposing nature and society as the productive bases of mankind, Feuerbach also rejects the negativity which Hegel had proposed as active within unitary conscience, maintained but threatened. The notion of man as defined by 'desires' (according to Feuerbach's terminology) replaces the *process* which founded the Hegelian dialectic, in the name of a realist demand for the limited, finite and real. But at the same time, Feuerbachian realism, which Marxism will inherit, turns out to be a 'pious atheism' (in Marx's words), and this piety appears most transparently in the reduction of negativity by the following gesture of anthropomorphization: first of all, the process of negativity intrinsic to self-consciousness is limited, blocked and bound in one unity, 'man';[9] then negativity is posed as exterior to this unity, as desire for others, thus as foundation of the community, the possibility of the subversion of this community having disappeared.[10] Consequently, the positivistic, socialist overturning of Hegel makes explicit only one of the moments of the process of the dialectic: the thetic, positivistic moment, affirming unity (that of the social subject or of the state). This overturning inaugurates the unitary subject in the place where Hegel saw an objective process of which the unitary subject was but one moment. 'Hegel objectifies what is subjective, I subjectivize what is objective', writes Feuerbach.[11] The desiring unitary subject, the basis of social order, finds its representative in the head of state; the reduction of negativity leads to the hypostasis of oppression.[12]

Marx's dialectical materialism moves decidedly away from Feuerbach's naturalist metaphysics through the reintroduction of the dialectic: the notions of struggle, contradiction and practice. In 1868 Marx wrote to Engels (about Dühring): 'The gentlemen in Germany believe that Hegel's dialectic is a "dead duck". Feuerbach has much on his conscience in this respect.'[13] Nevertheless, Marxism will inherit two essential moments of the Feuerbachian operation:

(i) The anthropomorphization or rather the subjectal unification of the Hegelian dialectic in the form of human unity, the man of desire, the man of lack; this turns into the notion of the proletariat as the way towards total mastery and the absence of human conflict.[14] The complicity of the philosopher and the proletariat expresses this conception of the subject as unitary subject – a Janus of metalanguage and desire: 'Philosophy is the head of this emancipation [i.e. of man] and the proletariat is its heart. Philosophy can only be realized by the abolition of the proletariat and the proletariat can only be abolished through the realization of philosophy.'[15]

(ii) The direct and exclusive anchoring of man in the state or more generally in the social machine and in social relations which are regulated by need and suffering among men. In the machine of social conflicts and contradictions, of production and class, man remains an untouchable unity, in conflict with others but never with 'himself', and in this sense, man remains neutral, an oppressed or oppressive subject, exploiter or exploited, but never a subject in process corresponding to the objective process which was brought to light by dialectical materialism, in nature and society.[16]

If such, according to Marx, is the status of the individual in the bourgeois system, we can say, reading this in the light of recent ideas, that, in and by the state and religion, capitalism demands and consolidates the paranoid moment of the subject: a unity foreclosing the other and putting itself in the place of the other. But if the proletariat resolves the contradiction between subject (as atom) and unalienable subject, after having brought it to the limit, and if it realizes philosophy, its status as subject supposes one or other of two eventualities: either it remains as unity and thus leads back again to the paranoia of the speculative, static or religious subject, or one understands by 'realization of philosophy' its completion, that is, the realization of its moments of rupture, of scission, of the putting into process of unity; the proletariat would then represent a factor disseminating and dispersing subjective and state unity, their bursting apart in a movement towards a heterogeneity irreducible to the instance of conscious mastery. Far from simple hypotheses, these two eventualities are in fact two antagonistic conceptions of society and *a fortiori* of socialist society, and are concerned with the difference between nature and culture itself, in other words with the very status of the 'social animal'.

In such a context, which has been in place since the nineteenth century, it falls upon the 'artistic avant-garde' to exemplify the materialist overcoming of the process of negativity which dissolves subjective unity. Through a specific practice affecting the mechanisms of language itself (in Mallarmé,

Joyce or Artaud) or affecting mythical or religious systems of representation (Lautréamont, Bataille), the 'literary avant-garde' presents society – even if only in its margins – with a subject in process, attacking all the stases of the unitary subject. It thus attacks closed ideological systems, but also the structures of social domination (the state), and accomplishes a revolution which, while remaining distinct and up until now ignored by socialist and communist revolutions, is not its utopian or anarchistic moment, but in fact points to the revolution's own blindness to the very movement which carries it. The 'schizophrenic' process of avant-garde practice introduces a new historicity, a 'monumental history' which cuts across the myths, rituals and symbolic systems of humanity, declaring itself either detached from immediate history (like Artaud) or closely following it, opening it out to the process of negativity which is its motor (like Bataille).

3 A few remarks are necessary on the notion of negativity which we use to formulate a third thesis: that negativity represents for theory the logic of the process which the texts of Artaud, for example, put into practice.

The notion of negativity (*Negativität*) that seems to provide the 'pattern' or the organizational principle of the 'process' derives from Hegel. Distinct from Nothingness (*Nichts*), as well as from negation (*Negation*), negativity is the concept which represents the irreducible relation of an 'ineffable' moment and its 'singular determination': it is the mediation, the overcoming of the 'pure abstractions' of *Being* and *Nothingness*, and their suppression in the concrete, of which they are only moments. In becoming a concept, and thereby belonging to a contemplative (theoretical) system, negativity reformulates into the process, and thereby dissolves and binds, the *static* terms of pure abstraction in a law of mobility. It therefore re-situates not only the stases of *Being* and *Nothingness*, while maintaining their dualism, but also all the categories of the contemplative system: the universal and the singular, the indeterminate and the determinate, quantity and quality, negation and affirmation, etc. It is the logical impulse behind the stases of negation and negation of the negation, but it is not identical with them, being the representation, in logic, of the movement which produces them.

As a logical expression of an objective process, negativity can only produce a subject in process, in other words, the subject constituted according to the law of this negativity, and therefore according to the law of objective reality, can only be a subject which this negativity runs through, a subject opened onto and by this objectivity, a mobile, non-subjectal and free subject. A subject immersed in negativity ceases to be an entity exterior to objective negativity, a transcendent unity, a specifically regimented monad, but is situated as 'the most interior and the most objective moment of life and of spirit'. As the ferment of dialectical materialism, this Hegelian principle was able to realize its materialist potential in the concept of *human activity* as revolutionary activity, and in the social and natural laws which this activity discovers as objective laws. Hegel writes:

Now the negativity just considered constitutes the *turning* point of the movement of the Notion. It is the *simple point of the negative* relation to self, the innermost source of all activity, of all animate and spiritual self-movement, the dialectical soul that everything true possesses and through which alone it is true; for on subjectivity alone rests the sublating of the opposition between Notion and reality, and the unity that is truth. The *second* negative, the negative of the negative, at which we have arrived, is this sublating of the contradiction, but just as little as the contradiction is it an *act of external* reflection, but rather the *innermost, most objective* moment of life and spirit, through which a *subject*, a *person*, a *free being*, exists.[17]

Lenin notes in the margins of this passage: 'the kernel of dialectics, the criterion of truth (the unity of the concept and reality)'.[18]

The *negativity* inseparable from Hegelian *being* is also precisely that which cracks open and hollows out the imprisonment of being in an abstract and superstitious interpretation, and it is negativity also which points to an outside which Hegel would otherwise only have been able to conceive as the complicit opposite of belief. Phenomenological posterity would posit this opposite as negative theology. But the logic thereby exposed will achieve its materialist realization when, with the help of Freud's discoveries, the thought is dared that negativity is the movement of heterogeneous matter itself, inseparable from its differentiation in the symbolic function. If the material movement of division, of expulsion (which we will come to later) remains 'negative' in a Kantian sense, the dialectic thinks it as fundamentally positive, because of its inseparability from being: ' . . . it would be better to say [instead of unity] only unseparatedness and inseparability, but then the affirmative aspect of the relation of the whole would not find expression.'[19]

Thus, while retaining the Kantian opposition, the Hegelian dialectic moves towards its total overcoming, which in the place of 'being' and 'nothingness' installs an *affirmative negativity*, a *productive dissolution*. The theology inherent in this overcoming is nevertheless identifiable in the teleology which its implies, which is a teleology of becoming subordinating or even effacing the moment of rupture.

We must insist on the fact that the *negativity* in question is not to be confused with the *negation* inherent in judgement, with the 'great negatives' which Kant introduces into philosophy in the form of 'polarity' and 'opposition', and which modern philosophy takes upon itself to uncover, substituting for them the notions of difference and repetition. Operative within Hegelian *Vernunft* (Reason) and not within *Verstand* (Understanding), functioning with a reason which is not that of Kant but which accomplishes the synthesis of the theoretical and the practical orders,[20] Hegelian negativity aims at a site transversal to *Verstand*, disturbs its positioning (*stand*) and points towards the space of production. Hegelian negativity is not a composite of the Kantian Idea, an oppositional element interior to judgement, in other words more or less an operation of the understanding or a limit constituting oppositional couples within discourses running from Kant to structuralism. Moreover, a materialist reading of Hegel allows a thinking of this negativity as the trans-subjective and trans-semiotic moment of the separation of matter which is constitutive of the conditions of symbolicity, without confusing it with this symbolicity itself or with the negations internal to it. The term negativity is perhaps unsuitable to designate the movement which produces the semiotic and continues to work on it 'from within'. It may carry the ineffable trace of the presence of the judging subject, but has the advantage of leading this trace and this presence into an outside where a struggle of *heterogeneous opposites* (we will return to this) produces them. The notion of negativity bears the trace of a 'roof'[21] already constituted along with the symbolic function, as a function of the subject, a 'roof' from which, in Artaud's texts for example, the pulsional process of production is made to burst out: the roof of the heterogeneous subject, an impossible unity. To get rid of this 'roof' implies an abandonment of the materialist perspective in the consideration of semiotic functioning: in the place of the heterogeneous dialectic of its process one then installs the presence of the Spinozist substantified Idea, structuring itself across a multiple and opaque flux, or one installs a movement of traces in which the Idea is dispersed, thus missing the moment of practice and of history. Identifying Meaning with Nature or Nature with Meaning, or neither one nor the other, idealism guards itself from thinking of the *production* of the symbolic function as a *specific formation* of the contradictions of matter within matter itself.

We can add that while negation articulates an opposition, that is, a *dichotomy*, *negativity* proposes a *heteronomy*; it proposes the production of the linguistic and logical signifying system of the unitary subject from the objective laws of the materiality which produces them, through a *qualitative* (heterogeneous) *leap*, as one of the moments of this materiality.

The terms of *expenditure* or *expulsion* are therefore more adequate to specify the movement of material contradictions which engenders the semiotic function; the pulsional or more generally psychoanalytic implications that these terms cover make them preferable to the term negativity. But for a dialectical approach and its materialist extension, the concept of *expulsion* should apply to the *practice of the subject*, in this case a signifying practice which supposes an 'experience of limits' on the part of the subject. The term negativity, or the sense which we give it, functions only to indicate the process exceeding the signifying subject in order to link it to 'objective' struggles in nature and society.

Among logicians, Frege is probably alone in conceiving of two types of negation. One, hypothetically situated in impersonal thought, is dismissed; the other, internal to the judgement possessed by a solid and indestructible subject, is also dismissed, but this time as inconsistent, since the judgement of an indestructible subject is itself indestructible – so what can a negation internal to judgement be other than an affirmation of this indestructibility?[22]

These reflections bear out an insight which Freudian psychoanalysis will return to and interpret, without suspecting its proximity with Frege: 'true negation' (which we can call negativity) supposes an 'impersonal thought', a disappearance of the unitary subject, while symbolic negation, the 'No', is nothing other than the symbolic function itself posing the unitary subject. Lacan says that it is the Father who says 'No'. Let us suppose that the process as practised by Artaud, which rejects filiation, 'speaks' negativity; the movement of an 'impersonal thought' which is the destruction of thought as such, the only possible destruction of thought (as opposed to the cutting up of texts, as Frege proposed), without losing the process of the subject, since the subject is not thereby lost but multiplied. Negativity is the repulsion which the subject represses in saying 'No', which returns by attacking this 'No': the Name of the Father, the superego, language itself and the originary repression which imposes it.

Frege says that the negation internal to judgement is implicated in the predication of the affirmative proposition, while also adhering to it. This is an important insight, which signals that the negation internal to judgement is the supplementary and explicit mark of the predicate and/or of the symbolic function. Chinese grammarians define the word in the same way, as 'that which can be denied'. Moreover, it has been demonstrated that any negative transformation, including the lexical, is already a syntactic transformation, or can be imbricated in a syntactic transformation.[23] It has been revealed that, in the course of language learning, signified negation, that is, not only kinetic refusal but the semantic 'No', appears towards the fifteenth month,[24] and coincides with the 'mirror stage' and with the learning of a holophrastic language already featuring certain syntactic links, but that it generally precedes the manifestation of syntactic competence with syntactically formed statements. This is to say that if the symbolic function is essentially syntactic and if it consists essentially in linking a nominal and a verbal syntagm, the formation of the symbol of negation precedes this function, or coincides with its genesis. To be able to say 'No' is to know already how to form syntactically oriented sentences (which are more or less grammatical). In other words, the negation internal to judgement is a mark of the symbolic and/or syntactic function; it is the first mark of sublimation. This kind of observation and linguistic analysis confirms Frege's position, that negation is a variant of the predication internal to judgement. As a result, we have to move out of the enclosure of language in order to grasp what is going on in the genetic temporality which logically precedes the constitution of the symbolic function, in which the negative is absorbed in the predicative. We have to move out of the verbal semiotic field towards that which produces it, in order to grasp the process of *expulsion* which is animated by the drives of a body caught in the tissue of nature and society. It is *pre-verbal gesturality* which marks the *operation* preceding the positioning of the static terms, the symbol-terms of language and its syntax. Certain psycholinguists speak of the 'concrete operations' which are concerned with the practical relations of the subject to objects, to be destroyed, arranged, organized, etc. These are 'forms of knowledge which consist in modifying the object to be known in such a way as to attain such transformations and their results'.[25] These concrete operations include 'sensory-motor actions, interior actions prolonging them, and actions which properly speaking belong to this area',[26] preceding the acquisition of language. It is at this level of 'concrete operations' that Freud perceives, in the *Fort/Da* of the infant, the movement of repulsion (*Austossung* or *Verwerfung*) which indicates a fundamental biological operation, of division, separation, scission, and at the same time produces a relation of the body (always already in division) to the outside, as a relation of expulsion. It is in this precise, corporeal and biological, but already social space (as a link to others) that a non-symbolized negativity is active, a negativity not arrested by the terms of judgement, nor predicated as a negation internal to judgement. This negativity of expenditure poses an object as separate from the body proper and at the same moment fixes it as absent: as a sign. The relation to the sign thus established by expulsion in a dimension which we might call vertical (speaking subject/outside) will find itself projected, within the signifying system, into a horizontal, linguistic dimension (syntactic subject/predicate). The outside, become graspable object, and the function of predication thus appear as points of arrest of negativity or of expulsion, and are indissociable and complicit with one another. Negativity – expulsion – is therefore a functioning only distinguishable across *positions* which absorb and camouflage it: the real, the sign, the predicate, are presented as differential moments, milestones in the process of expulsion.

Expulsion exists only in the trans-symbolic materiality of the process, in the material drives of the body subject to the biological operations of the division of matter and to its social relations. Any prefabricated verbalization will only register expulsions as a series of differences; expulsion is defined and thereby lost. Negativity can only be a dialectical notion specific to the process of *signifiance*, at the hinge of the biological and social orders, on the one hand, and the thetic, signifying phase of the latter, on the other.

Negation, as well as predication, of which it is an aspect, thus witness the passage of the expulsion which constitutes them, inasmuch as it constitutes the real and the sign which designates it. The negation internal to judgement, as well as predication, are illusory points of arrest, pauses or knots in the specific movement of expulsion. They will be the targets of expulsion when it is not restrained by speculative identification and the concomitant symbolic function. In certain schizoid phenomena and in the 'poetic language' of the modern text, negation and syntactic structure will have their status transformed, or their normativity disturbed. These textual phenomena bear witness to a specific pulsional economy, an expenditure or a freeing up of the 'pulsional vector', and thus to a modification of the relation of the subject to the outside. The negativity arrested and absorbed in the negation of judgement only appears, then, through modifications in the function of negation, or modifications in syntax or lexis, aspects specific to 'mad speech' or to 'poetry'. Frege's scissors, cutting up the text, will not damage indestructible thought; what will do so is the return of a surplus expulsion, readable in the modifications of the phenotext. The philosopher suspected as much, it seems, since he excluded poetry from 'thought'; Frege's 'thought' 'does not belong to poetry'.[27]

Expulsion and negativity lead in the last instance to a 'fading' of negation; the surplus of negativity destroys the coupling of opposites and substitutes for this opposition an infinitesimal differentiation of the phenotext. This negativity is insistent – the frequency of morphological procedures (*not . . . this*) is remarkable in Lautréamont, for example, a factor which tends to lend an active, incisive and abrupt character to negation – and in this sense it *affirms* the *position* of the subject, its thetic, positioning phase, that of the subject mastering the verbal function. In psychosis, this affirmation – the insistence of negation – signals the struggle, constitutive of symbolicity, between *stasis* and *expulsion*, a struggle which can end up in the extinction of any symbolic capacity: negativism is then followed by a freeing up of syntactic linkages, simultaneous with a loss of the fixed sign and the reality which corresponds to it. On the other hand, the text, as an 'experience of limits', translates this struggle, constitutive of symbolicity or of the verbal function, but constitutes a *new organization of reality*, which, in the Academy, is called 'the author's world'. The expulsion marked in the abundance of negative *énoncés* in *Maldoror*, or by the syntactic distortions of *Un Coup de dés*, is the product of a *subject in process* who has succeeded, for biographical and historical reasons, in remodelling the historically accepted and defined *chora* of *signifiance*, through the proposition of the representation of a different rela-tion to natural objects, to social apparatuses, and to the body itself. A subject of this type crosses through the linguistic network and makes use of it to indicate, as if via anaphora or hieroglyphs, that he or she is not representing a reality posed in advance and for ever detached from the pulsional process, but that he or she is experimenting or using the objective process through immersion in it and re-emerging from it via the drives. The subject of expen-diture is therefore not a punctual site, a subject of enunciation; it acts across the organization (the structure or finitude) of the text in which the *chora* of the process is figured. This *chora* is the *non-verbal semiotic articulation of the process*; music or architecture might provide metaphors better suited to desig-nate it than the grammatical categories of linguistics which it actually reorganizes. It is the logic of the 'concrete operations', of the 'motility' (which

Artaud refers to) which runs through and across the body in social space (transforming objects, relations to the family and to the social domain).

Expulsion and the drive

The Freudian theory of the drives enables a thinking of the negativity in question in relation to the body of the subject. Energetic but already semiotic charges, 'junctures of the psychic and the somatic', the drives extract the body from its homogeneous shell and turn it into a space linked to the outside, they are the forces which mark out the *chora* in process.[28]

It is important to note that in developing the notion of the inauguration of the symbolic function through the symbol of negation (in the article 'Negation' (1925)), Freud remarks that the inauguration results from a *repulsion* (*Austossung* or *Verwerfung*, in *Wolf Man*), but says nothing about the 'pulsional bases' of this gesture, of the drive which activates this 'kineme'. The consequence of this omission is that, via repulsion, the symbolic function will be opposed to *Einbeziehung*, the unification or incorporation which relates back to orality and pleasure; the symbolic function will thus be dissociated from any pleasure, opposed to pleasure, and set up as the paternal site, the site of the superego. The only way to react against the consequences of repression which are imposed under the constraint of the pleasure principle will be to renounce pleasure, through the medium of symbolization, through the institution of the sign and the corresponding absence of the object, expelled and lost for ever.

What seems to be left out of such an interpretation is the pleasure associated with the pre-symbolic, semiotic function of expulsion, a pleasure repressed by the symbolic, but which can return within it and, articulated with oral pleasure, disturb or even dislocate the symbolic function. In any case, it can transform ideation into 'artistic play', it can corrupt the symbolic through the return of the drive within it, turning it into a semiotic mechanism, a mobile *chora*. The drive in question is the anal drive: anal expulsion, the anality in which Freud sees the sadistic component of the sexual instinct and which he identifies with the death drive. We should emphasize the importance of anal expulsion, of anality, preceding the installation of the symbolic; it is at once its condition and its repressed. The process of the subject as the process of his or her language and/or of the symbolic function itself supposes, in the economy of the body which supports it, a reactivation of this anality. Artaud's texts, as we shall see, explicitly designate the anal drive acting on the body of the subject through the subversion of the symbolic function. Freud's relative silence on anality, like his silence in front of Signorelli's frescoes, is not only the symptom of a certain prudishness in relation to homosexuality, in which Freud, to his credit, saw the basis of the social organism; this silence is complicit with the silence of psychoanalysis in relation to the literary function inasmuch as it is a subversion of the symbolic function and a putting into process of the subject: psychoanalysis will speak about fantasy in literature, but never about the economy of the subject dissolving the symbolic and language through an activity understood as 'aesthetic'. If the return of expulsion in modern texts (and with exemplary clarity in Artaud), corrupting the symbolic and sublimation along with it, bears witness to the death drive – to a destruction of life as well as the subject – it is important also not to miss the pleasure [*jouissance*[29]] which this aggressivity or 'sadistic component' reveals. The *jouissance* of destruction (or, if one prefers, the 'death drive'), manifested in the text through language, passes by way of a resurfacing of a sublimated and repressed anality. This means that before arranging itself in a new semiotic network, before forming the new structure of the 'work', the not-yet-symbolized drive, the 'remains of first symbolizations' (Lacan), attacks, through a recovered anality and in full knowledge of homosexuality, all the static positions of the process of *significance* (sign, language, family structure or identificatory social structure).

We are led at this point to draw attention in more detail to the implications of expulsion and *jouissance* in the symbolic function and its putting into process. The sadistic component of the sexual instinct can also be seen, veiled, in the 'oral phase' as well as in the 'phallic phase', but it dominates the 'anal phase' and appears as an essential factor in the libidinal economy, to such an extent that Freud recognizes the possibility of a primary sadism directed against the self before any isolation of an object, thus of a primary masochism.[30] What we call *expulsion* is nothing other than the logical mode of this permanent aggressivity, and the possibility of its being positioned, and thus renewed. Though destructive, a 'death drive', expulsion is also the mechanism of relaunching, of tension, of life; tending towards a state of equilibrium, inertia and death, expulsion perpetuates tension and therefore life.

We should also note that what psychoanalysis calls the 'anal phase' is situated before the oedipal conflict and before the separation of the 'ego' and the 'id', according to the Freudian schema. It is a phase which ends a fundamental period for the infantile libido, the period described in terms of a predominant sadism before the onset of the oedipal; an oral, muscular, urethral and anal sadism. Under all these forms, of which the anal is the last to be repressed and in this sense the most important, drives or energetic charges give rise to an eroticization of the glottal, urethral and anal sphincters as well as of the kinetic system.

The drives passing through sphincters arouse pleasure at the very moment that substances having belonged to the body detach themselves from it, to then be expelled outwards. It is an acute pleasure coinciding with a loss, with the separation of objects from the body and the isolation of these objects outside the body. This is the fundamental experience of separation, before the position of an alterity detached from the body proper, before the real object: this is a separation which is not a lack but a discharge and which, although it deprives the body of something, provokes pleasure. The psychoanalyst supposes that this *jouissance* in loss is experienced as an attack against the expelled object, against any exterior object (mother and father included) and against the body proper. The problem becomes: how to restrain this aggressivity? In other words, how to restrain the pleasure of separation produced by expulsion whose ambivalence (*jouissance* of the body with loss of part of it), a paradox of pleasure and threat, is characteristic of the drive? The 'normal', oedipal path consists in an identification of the body proper with one of the parents during the oedipal phase. Simultaneously, the expelled object becomes definitively separate; it is no longer simply thrown out but suppressed as a material object, it becomes 'the other opposite me', with which only one kind of relation is possible, that of the sign, the relation to the symbol *in absentia*. Expulsion is therefore on the path from object to sign, this passage to the sign occurring when the object is detached from the body and isolated as a real object; in other words, and at the same time, expulsion is on the path towards the imposition of the superego.

However, as cases of infantile schizophrenia show, the violence of expulsion and of the anal pleasure provoked by it can be such that it cannot be absorbed by oedipal identification and the installation of a real, symbolized object. Expulsion returns, and the pleasure it provokes glues the body to it, so to speak, without the latter being able to defend itself through suppression or repression. Expulsion and the sadism which is its psychological representation return to disturb the symbolic chains constituted by oedipalization. The resulting 'disturbances' in behaviour are interpreted by Melanie Klein as the organism's 'defences' against danger and aggressivity. But the psychoanalyst recognizes at the same time that 'this defence . . . is of a *violent* character and differs fundamentally from the later mechanism of repression', which installs symbolism.[31] These defences are moments of resistance, thetic moments in the 'violent' pulsional process which, far from having a *preventative* psychological value, operate an *arrangement* of the 'sadistic' pulsional charge, an *articulation* of expulsion which is not subsumed by the construction of a superego (as occurs in the oedipal phase). The deformation or repetition of words or syntagms, hyperkinesis or stereotype bear witness to the establishment of a new semiotic network, a new *chora* which defines verbal symbolization at the same time as the formation of a superego modelled by the paternal law and sealed by the learning of language. Artaud writes: 'and life is what I did when I thought about working on the resistances to my motility'.[32]

The acquisition of language, and notably of the syntactic structure which constitutes its normativity, is in fact parallel to the mirror stage. The acquisition of language presupposes the suppression of anality; this derives from the fact that it is an acquisition of the capacity to symbolize via the definitive detachment of an object (no longer expelled but completely rejected) and via repression under the sign of this rejected object. Any return of expulsion along with the erotic pleasure around the sphincters associated with it disturbs the symbolic capacity and the acquisition of language which accomplishes it. In inserting itself into the system of language, expulsion delays the schizoid child's acquisition of language and can even prevent it. In the adult, the return of a non-sublimated or non-symbolized anality breaks the linearity of the signifying chain, 'paragrammatizes' it, 'glossolizes' it. In this sense, Artaud's interjections or expectorations translate the struggle of a non-sublimated anality against the superego.

Ideologically, such a transformation of the signifying chain attacks, provokes and reveals the repressed sadism (but what is commonly called sadism is in fact the repression of anality), the anality subjacent to social institutions and apparatuses.

Oralization can function as an intermediary between the fundamental sadism of expulsion and its sublimation via signification. The melody, harmony, rhythm, the 'sweet' and 'pleasant' sounds, in short, the musicality present in any of Artaud's sentences can be interpreted as an oralization of the returned expulsion.

> a body
> gobbling the infinite nothing
> where it tonsilizes its shit.[33]

Artaud uses the term 'expulsion' to designate both the logical principle of the negative movement (of separation) and the excremental and anal connotations of anything which appears as a 'creation' or a 'product', whether the world itself or the human activity which exercises the transcendent speculations of his contemporaries.

> The truth of the matter is entirely different from what the Kabbala claims to expound transcendentally.
>   The world was left to mankind not as a creation but as a reject, a foul-smelling turd that the Ancient of Days withdrew from when he made zimzoum, not in order to make room for it but because he just didn't want to risk touching it with a ten-foot pole.[34]

The superego and its linear language, characterized by the subject–predicate syntagmatic articulation, are attacked by a return of oral and glottal pleasure, in sucking or expelling. Fusion with the maternal breast or its expelled product seems to be at the base of this eroticization of the vocal apparatus and also at the base of the introduction into the order of language of a surplus of pleasure characterized by a redistribution of the phonemic order, of morphological structure and even of syntax (cf. Joyce's *mots-valises*, but even more so Artaud's *glossolalia*).[35]

Abundant orality and aggressive, negative orality are thus closely linked, particularly during the following anal stage which will allow an increase of aggressivity and will allow the body to detach itself and to establish a relation – always and already negative – to the outside. Thus, even if it is recognized as more archaic, positive and profusional, orality and the libidinal drive which it supports are carried forward and, in the genesis of the symbolic functioning of the subject, determined by expulsion.[36]

If, through dis-articulation or any other reason, there takes place an accentuation of the expulsional aspect of the drives, or more exactly of their negative charge, expulsion takes over the muscular apparatus as a channel.[37] The muscular apparatus discharges the energy swiftly in 'thrusts of brief duration'; pictural gesturality, or that of dance, is related to this mechanism. But expulsion can equally pass through the vocal apparatus, which seems moreover to be the only internal organ unable to retain bound energy: the buccal cavity and the glottis liberate the discharge in a finite system of phonemes, specific to each language. There follows an increase in the frequency of phonemes, their accumulation or their repetition, moving away from the linguistic code to determine a specific choice of morphemes,[38] or rather the condensation of several 'borrowed' morphemes in a single lexeme.[39] Expulsion, invested in the buccal cavity, thereby awakens in it and through it the 'unifying', 'positive' libidinal drive, which characterized the earlier phase, the initial profusion of the same cavity. Through the new phonemic and rhythmic network which it produces, expulsion becomes a source of 'aesthetic pleasure', without thereby leaving the field of meaning; it cuts it up and reorganizes it, imprinting upon it the trajectory of the drive across the body proper, from anus to mouth.

We can thus establish that expulsion is the return of negativity in the field of the subject constituted by *Austossung* as a subject of negation. Expulsion reconstitutes real objects, or rather it is the creation of new objects; in this sense it re-invents the real and re-semiotizes it. If it thereby echoes a destructive process of schizoid character it is nevertheless the positivization of the process, since it affirms it in reintroducing it into the domain of meaning. Meaning is thus separated, divided, multiplied, put into process. The semiotization of expulsion across the symbolic order is the site of an untenable contradiction which only a limited number of subjects attain. If expulsion includes the moment of 'excorporation', or 'expectoration' (in Artaud's words), or of 'excretion' (in Bataille's words), this motor discharge or corporeal spasm invest themselves in an already separated *other*, in language. Expulsion reintroduces and deploys within language the very mechanism whereby the separation of words from things is produced, and it has no other way of doing this than opening out, dislocating and readjusting the *vocal* register. Expulsion reintroduces and reiterates itself in language, which is already installed by a previous, forgotten expulsion.

The simplification characteristic of the formalist theory of symbolism consists in seeing only a text, rather than the process of *signifiance*, that is, seeing only a coded or deviant distribution of marks or signifiers without perceiving the pulsional, heterogeneous expulsion which produces these marks and which divides the semiotic between the corporeal and the natural, on the one hand, and the symbolic and the social, on the other, both in quite specific ways.

Taking account of this heterogeneity implies going further than a consideration of the symbolic function as supra-corporeal, supra-biological and supra-material; it implies seeing it as a product of a dialectic between two orders. Consequently, it is better to use the term *semiotic*, rather than *symbolic*, to refer to the space of this heterogeneity of meaning. From such a perspective it seems that it is expulsion – anal, sadistic, aggressive, morbid – which poses the 'object' and the 'sign' and which constitutes the real in which objective or phantasmatic realities exist.

Two possibilities thus become open to the subject. The first consists in passing beyond expulsion, to reality, suppressing for ever the trajectory of separation, scission and expulsion, to experience it only as a reified reality which one 'engages' with and in which the entire logic of the meta – meta-expulsion, meta-logic, meta-physics – is also reified; a subject of this kind places itself under the law of the father and assumes this paranoia, as well as the homosexuality which connotes it and whose sublimation is only too fragile: this is Orestes, the murderer of his mother in the name of the law of the city. The other trajectory consists in returning constantly to expulsion, and thereby attaining, underneath the paranoid homosexuality revealed by signifying production, the schizoid rhythm of division and of death. The painful, agitated or 'mummified' body of Artaud bears witness to this explosion of unity and its remodelling in the semiotic network which follows the passage of the drives.

An indelicate question cuts into the debate at this point. Inasmuch as she exists, is there a place for a woman in the social domain, in its stagnation as represented by bourgeois familial conventionality, as well as in the movements which accompany artistic or political production, or those of meaning, both positions being sutured by the homosexuality of warrior-brothers or the oralized homosexuality of poets (as shown in Renaissance or Florentine art, the latter particularly angst-ridden)? She is kept apart from schizoid expulsion, which cuts itself off from everything. She is effaced from the paranoiac group, an object of exchange for the brothers of the community, or a revered matriarch. As Hegel saw, she can only become an object of eternal irony within the fraternity, she can only take up the mask of a brother and, thus travestied, become an eternal Clorinda, and enter the play of negations, the only way to attain a voice in the cultural and social chapter. Far from a psychological detail, this factor is a burning social issue. Current political and cultural movements integrate women either little or not at all, and when they do it is at the cost of a masking and a self-effacing irony which seem to lend credence to Freud's affirmation that only masculine libido exists. Nevertheless, there is in the functioning of the 'hysteric' a process of multiplied ruptures which are inaugurated not by a unitary castration but by an unending multiplicity of separations, breaking the unity of the symbolic field, and as if plugged into a translinguistic rhythm: a multiplicity of separations which do not in this instance become integrated, without remainder, behind the irony of the fraternal masquerade. Such a functioning is nevertheless to be distinguished from expulsion. As a lethal and generative drive, an excorporation of excrement or of the child, an aggressivity and a binding, both a murder and a birth, a 'vagina in the service of the anus' (according to Lou Andreas Salomé), a chaining together of the positive and the negative, an effacement of the dichotomy but also of the heteronomy between expulsion and stasis, negativity and negation, a separation without rupture (without castration) and struggle, the hysteric's spasm resembles expulsion but should not be equated with it. The dark night of myths, the active but asymbolic matter of old beliefs, the 'diabolical', are figures for this spasm due to which the woman entertains an imagined recognition in schizoid expulsion. Artistic or political productions of meaning become her focal point, her fascination. A woman can identify with the process, take herself as the schizoid's other, twin or even as his substitute. Artaud himself recognized that such a fantasy is not without a certain basis in objectivity; that the asymbolic spasm allies itself with expulsion as the site of contradiction in the subject in process. In the most powerful moment of the contradiction, always to be understood as heterogeneity (any other kind of contradiction is either restricted to the field of logic or is a difference without struggle) when the loss of unity, the anchor of the process, cuts in, and when the asymbolic, semiotic *chora*, which can be mobile but which can also become immobile, appears – at that point the subject in process discovers itself as separated, and thus as feminine, since it grasps that the hysteric also, in her own way, goes through the experience of the asymbolic, even if she does not possess it. The subject in process discovers itself as bi-sexual, hermaphrodite, and, as such, as nothing. Artaud recognizes himself to a greater extent in the innumerable 'daughters' or 'sisters', real or imaginary, with which he surrounded himself, in order to reject them, but which he bears more easily perhaps than the kabbalistic societies of the male. The subject in process needs to see himself in a sister or a daughter so as not to become mad. His body is a text of flesh wracked by drives and multiple ruptures, repeated scarrings, all of which are characteristic of the behaviour of the (hysterical) woman: 'My stick will be the outrageous book called to being by ancient races now dead which are spoked into my fibres like my excoriated daughters.'[40] Expulsion, animating the process of the subject, can *identify* with the spasmodic, asymbolic functioning of a woman, and such an identification facilitates *control*, on the part of the subject, a certain *knowledge* of the process, a certain relative *arrest* of its movement, all of which are the condition for its renewal and are factors which prevent it from deteriorating into a pure void, which enable it to remain on the roof of heterogeneous contradiction. For the subject in process, woman represents that heterogeneous being who doubles up unity, who separates it, and who it is indispensable to control, struggling with her without sublimating her into a virgin-mother.

> By woman. Through woman. By woman indirectly enlightened and achieving her own duplicity. For it was by woman that the divider king was separated within himself and found in himself the means by which to separate all that should be separated.[41]

And further on:

> A natural force altered by woman will free itself against and by woman. This force is a death-force. It has the dark rapaciousness of the genital. It is provoked by woman but man directs it. The mutilated femininity of man, the enchained tenderness of men that woman had stamped on have revived a virgin on that day. But it was a virgin without body, without sex, one which only the mind can profit by.[42]

As for the hysteric, her identification with the process of the subject remains a problematic and completely ephemeral hypothesis. This is because the process, to the extent that it is not a catatonic collapse, follows the path of paranoia, and the woman, after an ephemeral moment of illusion, is thus drawn into an identificatory projection into the structural roles accorded her by the fraternity, described above. Subsequently, and this is quite common, she submits herself to the demands of the community, by masking herself, eluding, playing, lying, but always precariously, since the symbolic proposed to her does not absorb her spasmodic force. Or – and this is what is borne out by the recent women's movements, which should not be too hastily assimilated into the eternal feminism of the suffragette, the woman will try to gain lucidity in relation to the spasm represented by phallic culture (that of the present) as a castration, and will subsequently attempt to find practices appropriate to this spasm. One is nevertheless led to believe that if *logical unity* is paranoid and homosexual, then feminine demand, or the hysterical spasm, will never gain a symbolic representation *specific* to itself, but will continue to propose itself as a moment *within* expulsion, within the movement of ruptures and of rhythmic divisions. Insofar as she has a specificity a woman finds it in asociality, in the breaking of communal conventions, in a sort of asymbolic singularity. But at the same time, and as if in order to camouflage this truth, she spends her life in pretence, in playing out the roles of the nurse, wife, or idealized mother of artists, or the travestied companion of the brothers. When revolutions take place, she can recognize herself and place herself within them, in accordance with their rejections, but at the same time, and without hiatus, in accordance with their recuperation. Since such is the law of the city, capitalism included, a law which does not concern itself with her and which does not refer to her, she makes a pretence of obeying it.

To return to the drive, it seems that one might be able to think of it today as a kind of echo of the processes of separation inherent in bio-chemistry. Might expulsion be an equivalent of the separation and recombination with inversion ('the double helix'), specific to the living molecule in the process of reproducing itself? In any case, expulsion would be biological or genetic in only one of its determinations; it is always and already social or anti-social since it is negativity, *signifiance*, and relation to others.

The rotation of the *chora*

Biological, genetic expulsion is a mobile crossing of the organic body imprinting upon it a gesturality which will be structured by social needs and constraints. The return of the already kinetic pulsional expulsion, through the Freudian *Fort/Da*, projects biological, material expulsion into an expulsion constitutive of a space of practice. First is produced the separation from the object, the constitution of the real, *absence*; but subsequently, and across the latter process, through repeated expulsions the labile imprint of the first melodies which are vocal, gestural and signifying. The lability and mobility of these imprints are shown in the mobility of the body, a dancing, gesticulating body, a theatrical volume, but also in a paragrammatization which points to the dislocation 'into fragments' of the linguistic tissue:

> Everything is in motility, of which, like the rest, humanity only sees the shadow.
> . . .
> There is no tissue
> consciousness does not come from the weft
> but from the corridor of parietal cannon shots. . . .
> . . .
> and where nothing has value
> but from shock and counter-shock
> without which no virtue can be given to anything
> characteristically logical or dialectical for the movement
> pushes sight from mind and the scope of mind
> from which it takes form, volume, tone, force. . . . [43]

The struggle of the drives, of the 'two motilities', which recalls Freud's dialectical dualism, is evoked in Artaud's texts as dissociation, blow, shock, 'convulsions in the lower depths', 'pulsations of the atmosphere':

> You can hear a grinding of locks, a kind of horrible volcanic shock, cut off from the light of day. And from this collision, and this

151

tearing apart of two principles, are born all potential images, in a thrust more vital than a ground-swell.[44]

The struggle of the drives threatens the unity of consciousness, its 'aggregate', even if the 'mental beast', 'the intelligent beast which looks but does not look to see', is unaware of it: 'They cannot imagine the aggregate of their consciousness coming apart.'[45] The violence of expulsion tends to destroy the fragile equilibrium where heterogeneous contradiction (the condition of the process of *signifiance*) is maintained and tends to return to the state in which differences are effaced, dominated by the heavy, opaque, unified body – but a body which is dissociated, shattered into painful territories, parts larger than the whole. Artaud's texts explore this risk through the practice of a compacting and fragmenting of the body under the effects of expulsion, and through the production of discourse, that is, in keeping itself on the line between heterogeneity and verbal unification. He designates this form of expulsion as an 'aggressive will', as 'rapacity', 'bestiality', 'brutality', 'force', 'bearing', 'dignity', 'contradiction', 'privation', 'cupidity', 'detachment', 'disinterest', 'pain'.[46]

The return of the splitting, pulsional charge organizes the *chora* as a 'vertical rotation', splitting the body vertically, running around it, and binding it in repeated turns. This mobile, revolving *chora* has also been described by Lautréamont:

> After having piled a large part of the rope at his feet in the shape of superimposed ellipses, so that Mervyn is suspended half way up the bronze obelisk, the escaped forger with his right hand imparts to the adolescent a movement accelerated by a uniform rotation in a plane parallel to the axis of the column; and with his left hand gathers the serpentine entwinements of cordage which lie at his feet. The sling whistles in space; Mervyn's body follows it everywhere, always held from the centre by centrifugal force, always keeping his mobile and equidistant position in the aerial circle, independent of matter.[47]

But this pulsional mobility, after accumulating, reaches a moment of arrest which immobilizes the body. The fragmented body, of which each part is experienced as the whole, loses its structured unity, and, in clinical schizophrenia, also loses the signifying structure capable of reunifying it in the sign system.

> The vertical rotation of a constituted body (and which is in a state beyond consciousness) does not stop hardening and being weighed down by the opacity of its thickness and its mass. The criterium is the inert lead of the total contradiction of a pure state of detach-

ment, of a ferocious indifference which permits an insensitivity to
any idea, feeling, notion or perception.[48]

The violence of expulsion rejects the effects of delay, of signifying difference,
and tends towards a return to a state of 'leadlike' inertia; for the body,
become a receptacle of semiotic operations, is not based

> on sensation
> nor on thought
> and there is something else
> and it is precisely this other inert and insensitive thing which is the
> body.[49]

Corporeal expulsion acts as if accompanied by lightning:

> So it's a lightning flash of iron
> which comes out of his body,
> which to make this happen needs to be
> a solid cannon of resistance.[50]

This violent, pre-symbolic mobility, which is the condition of meaning and
is a force of rejection affecting even the unity of the signifier, appears in the
practice of the text. It is labelled as 'void' or 'nothing' by idealist discourse
and is without 'unity', 'being' or 'concept':

> There is no history,
> an infinite possibility,
> parabrahma,
> a non-being.
>   . . .
> I am the infinite.
> The stain of being is to always want to bring me back to being, to claim
> a notion when really
>   there is none.
>   . . .
> life made
> not of intellectual splendour
> nor of the spiritual beauty of simplicity,
> nor of simplicity itself
> but underneath and further on
> the carnage,
> without reason or conscience,
> where there is nothing,
> and which will *always* be thus.[51]

The dis-aggregation of consciousness is the dis-aggregation of the body: a body dispersed in the cosmos, enlarged to cosmic dimensions, enveloping them, merging with them and swallowing the 'world', 'the personal automat', the 'aggregate'. It excludes any identification and any transference with a human or natural *other*:

> The human body has had enough suns, planets, rivers, volcanoes, seas, tides without having to go and look in so-called external nature or in others for them.[52]

This shattered, cosmic body, linked to the elements of the natural process, returns through repeated separations to the immobility of a third person (he) which is more than impersonal, even inhuman and dead:

> My true state is inert, beyond life and human capture.
> It's the state of my body when it's alone.[53]

What discourse thus apprehends, since the text's force is to keep language as close as possible to its shattering by the drive, is, on the one hand, a shattered body of which each organ is separated from the whole, and a pulse traversed by painful spasms of a continual mass:

> My mind is open at the stomach and it's from below that it piles up a dark and untranslatable science, full of underground tides, concave edifices, and congealed agitations.[54]

Organic functioning, characterized by separated members, which invades the trans-corporeal, *choral* automaton, tends, therefore, towards immobility – expulsion will lead to arrest, if it is not subsumed by a language and if a fluid, critical and combative ideological system does not lever it up and insert it into stases (moments of positioning) adequate to its pulsation. It thus becomes an immobilized body, a 'congealed agitation', a 'mummy', a 'dead thing', at the moment when heterogeneous contradiction cedes before organic pulsation.[55]

'Description of a Physical State' represents this situation of the 'internal rupture' of a body emptied of any reality and stuck onto the multiplication of things themselves:

> One must speak now of the disembodiment of reality, of that sort of rupture that seems determined to multiply itself between things and the feeling they produce in our mind, the place they should take.[56]

This is how expulsion, returned to itself, to its fundamental heterogeneity, without voice or signs, can be verbalized, when the word, 'badly formulated' or 'confused', agrees to measure itself against the force of expulsion; it is a flesh without life, pulsating, seized up by death, rarefied, hollowed out, non-compact, traversed by gyrations of fire:

> This flesh that doesn't find itself in life,
> this language which doesn't get beyond its rind,
> this voice which doesn't take the route of sound,
> ...this multiplied death of myself is in a kind of rarefaction of my flesh...
> Have you seen the mummy stuck in the intersection of phenomena,
> this unknowing, living mummy which is ignorant of all the frontiers
> of its void, which takes fright at the pulsations of its death?

However, the material expulsion dissociating and mummifying the body, the *jouissance* of death, far from foundering in a clinical mutism, engages a process of *signifiance* capable of representing the most precise, not 'symbolic' but always 'semiotic', movements of expulsion.

Artaud frequently insists on the fact that the unifying, mastering, violently positive moment, or the 'paranoid' moment, to use a clinical language (which, I must add, is not mine), is the condition of the realization of the signifying process, a condition inseparable from that of expulsion:

> I eat,
> I drink,
> I sleep,
> I live,
> as I specified last night,
> in war.
> Moreover the discussion is closed
> I am the master
> And you are all in my body
> like the dead.
> . . .
> I have in me a force of life which has never contented itself to separate itself from me
> and which comes back to me, more and more, as to its master.[57]

The time of destruction, annihilation of subjective unity and of lethal anguish, or, more simply, of 'emotional disarray', cedes before the affirmation of a *productive unity*; or, rather, the two moments of the process are indissoluble. In itself, the second moment, affirmative and symbolizing, is openly designated as egodiastolic, a paranoid distention of the ego.[58]

> The same thoughts, the same involuntary impulses could, after all,
> just as well serve only to inflate the ego, to nourish it more

intimately, to increase its internal density, and so much the worse for works and creativity, since psychically the result is the same.[59]

The mastery and affirmation of expulsion is described as the result of a mobility complementary to that of destruction, in a series of positioning terms in which 'effect', 'domination', 'exaltation', are preponderant:

> a perpetual effort
> of domination
> exaltation
> abolition
> precision
> appetite
> desire
> all unformulated
> in transformation.[60]

The dissolution inherent in the process is a 'sovereign desolation'.[61]

The contradiction between expulsion and mastery engenders precisely the process of *significance* which traverses any finite formation and presents itself as passage, fluidity, effacement of the limits between inside and outside, assimilation of an 'object' in a 'self without contours':

> to keep myself at the insensitive limit of things . . . to be perpetually in the state in which things pass through, without holding onto them, or incorporating them.[62]

The process of *signifiance* is precisely that *va-et-vient* between mobility and resistance: expulsion itself pushing on and away its semiotic moments of stasis. It is their struggle which assures *life* and *text*: 'and life is what I did when I thought about working on the resistances to my motility'.[63] Expulsion works precisely on those elements of the natural and social environment with which the individual tends to identify under biological and social constraints. In the family structure, it is the parent of the same sex who is subject to expulsion.

In this struggle, the individual looks for the complicity of the parent of the opposite sex, a fact which leads to hasty conclusions about the fundamental role of the transgression of the incest taboo in free symbolic functioning (art, for example), while it seems more fundamentally to be a question of a transient alliance with the parent of the opposite sex, of a screen intended to facilitate the expulsion of the same. This occurs to such an extent that, if there is a fixation on the parent of the opposite sex, no renewal of the process of expulsion is possible, and this blockage not only prevents any signifying production, but can also arrest the process of *signifi-*

ance itself. In the inter-subjective structure, whose model is the family, expulsion becomes manifest across the basic homosexual relation and tends towards its rupture, or rather its renewal; the struggle against symbolism is the expression of this tendency. In other words, if expulsion corrupts the symbolic function, it does so in a struggle against the homosexual tendency to identification, and in this sense it supposes the latter, recognizes and assumes it, drives it back but at the same time is conscious of it. Inasmuch as it bears on sexual relations between individuals (sexuality being only one of the strata of the process of *signifiance*), the subject in process is aware of the homosexuality subjacent to these relations and fundamental to any inter-subjective and/or transferential relation. Subjective identification and unification, acting against the process, are a relation to the *same*, in the image of identificatory unity that the father, the mother, the family or the state assume in society; Lautréamont's 'And God Brought in a Pederast' is striking here. For Artaud, homosexuality is the sexual profile of this subjective unity which esoteric speculations tend to rehearse: homosexuality is their 'stupidly bleated out and repressed unspoken' − it is homosexuality which is hidden and unseen behind Unity:

> the reduction,
> the declassification
> of a One
> I say grotesquely
> of one One
> of the One
> imperceptible
> inaccessible
> in 3
> pederastically at the origin
> son and holy ghost
> and not family
> mother and father and little baby.[64]

To displace expulsion across the homosexual, symbolic field is to displace it across sexuality, to situate it outside the inter-subjective relations which are the moulds for family relations; it is to bring to bear the pulsional charges which are as if inverted in the process of transformation of nature and society.

We can therefore propose that the defensive structures of society, from the family to capitalist institutions, are there to intercept expulsion in identificatory, inter-subjective and sexual positions, sublimated or not: they fix the generality of expulsion in precise and specific points − those of the homosexual relation, the inter-subjective canvas of the thetic phase and therefore of the paranoid moment of the subject defending its unity against the process. Freud points to the homosexual mechanics of social relations even if he falters in several instances before an evidence which remains opaque to him (Signorelli's frescoes) or only comes upon it too late (the 'Dora' case). While pointing to homosexuality as the basis of normativity and social normality, psychoanalysis does not propose that the subject in process moves across and through this fixation in full knowledge of it, and transports, without sublimation, the charge of expulsion into the very movement which makes it move through social institutions and laws: the movement of (political, scientific or artistic) revolutionary practice.

The 'all too human' of human sexuality, this sexuality of parental identification and narcissistic gratification, this morass of inter-subjectivity where unitary subjects protect themselves against whatever might put them into question, is demanded by the law of social stability itself. Consequently, one can propose, as did Artaud, that sexuality is complicit with the scientific and linguistic laws of society. To tamper with grammatical taboos, and perhaps also with those of arithmetic, is to come closer to a proposition which identificatory sexuality is deaf to: revolutions in language are a movement across and through sexuality and all the social coagulations (families, sects, etc.) which are stuck to it:

> Let man waste time in making love, say the initiates of arithmetic and grammar, while we continue to hold the reins of a power which has never lived but on the parasitical proliferations of the act named orgasm, coitus, copulation, fornication, which amounts to giving man a huge pustulent and eucharistic sweetie to suck so as to keep power over man and even over that little more than man which we call the divinity.[65]

In contemporary society, hypostatized sexual desire, 'that huge pustulent and eucharistic sweetie', is one of the essential ways towards the awakening of the subject, its liberation from familial, state and symbolic oppression. But to fix the subject on sexuality, to orient its negativity only into the inter-subjective region which sexuality is limited to, has not only become the new myth of a society which proclaims itself more liberated after every new law, it also constitutes a space in which religion, occultation and all kinds of obscurantism are included, fed precisely by moments of arrest, knots, points of the collapse and identification of the process.

In this sense, the space beyond the pleasure principle is through and beyond sexuality if and only if it is through and beyond homosexuality, itself the truth of the heterosexual 'relation', and only if it is through and beyond the symbolic.

In a society for which the family has ceased to be the basic structure of production and is itself in dissolution, transgressed by a whole set of social relations which exceed it, expulsion finds its representative stases either in different articulations of social relations, in social practices (science, politics, etc.) and the social groups which are their basis, or even outside social structure, in the objects and structures of the natural world. The identifications or suppressions of the *other* which operate in this space to produce the jubilatory phases of the subject, who identifies with the objects of his or her desire, do not have the same constancy or tenacity as the familial structure, necessary to be able to sufficiently and efficiently maintain the identificatory lure, and with it the possibility of a desirable fantasy. In the movement of natural and social cross-currents, tested by social practices of destructuring and renewal, desire becomes a fragile element, exceeded by the violence of expulsion and its separating negativity. In such a social configuration, which capitalism is in the process of realizing, expulsion appears in all its precision and strength, destructive of any subjective, phantasmatic or desiring unity. Its ferocious negativity is no longer reined in by desire, but held by the *semiotic stasis internal to the process of practice*, the moment of position and positivity, opening the way for a practical realization or a production. What production? The whole range of social practice has to be rethought in this light, from aesthetics to science and politics. What provides the affirmative moment of expulsion and ensures its renewal is not the *object produced*, which is, in fact, a metonymic object of desire, a support of phantasy, but the *time of its production*, or its *productivity*, where the object appears only as a limit, not a delayed limit on the horizon, but one which permits the articulation of expulsion in social practice.

The metonymic slide of desire and of the signifier which commands desire is therefore only an already secondary logical consequence of the 'becoming One' of the subject within the specularizations available to him or her by the present state of the forces of production, that is, an intrafamilial specularization. *As concerns the logic of expulsion, it should be situated not only as anterior to this metonymic sliding of desire, but as its basis and perhaps even as the motor of a functioning characterized by the enjoyment and transformation of symbolic or directly social reality.* The pleasures, desires, bypasses and subterfuges of this functioning, as moments of the binding of expulsion, are produced and are a part of the process of the functioning itself; they ensure its provisional unity; they are representations compensating for the destructive violence of its renewal, the representative corollaries of the thetic phase. The subject of this practice invests desire and representation in *productivity* rather than in the *products* of his or her practice, but since these productions are part of the transformation of the real, he or she invests desire in the transformation itself. To identify with the process of signifying, subjective and social identity, to identify with an impossible identity, is precisely to engage in the practice of process, to put into process the subject and its stases, to act in such a way that the laws of meaning correspond to objective, natural and social laws.

The practices we are interested in here, those of modern texts, realize a subtle, fragile and mobile equilibrium between the two aspects of heterogeneous contradiction. The passage of 'free energies' is ensured as against the fragility of their marking and of the *representamen* which are generated by them and which bind them. But the latter, under the violent assault of heterogeneous contradiction, do not manage to enclose it in the symbolic stereotype of a linguistic structure or an ideology established according to the dominant social mould (family or state), or constructed locally (the analyst–analysand relation). Moreover, expulsion dislocates *representamen* without annulling their *markings*, as thoroughly as possible, and, from the heterogeneity of its practice or its experience,[66] produces new symbolizations. Here we come upon the mechanism of *innovation*, the displacement of the structures of the real, and this applies to social practice in all its domains but especially, and with most immediate violence, to the political. When heterogeneous, material expulsion, primary or free energy, erupts within the very structure of the *representamen*, when contradiction enters into its most acute moment, where the repeated pulsional movement of expulsion attacks what it has itself produced, and by which it is deferred, retained and tamed, that is, when it attacks language, the practice which is the condition and the result of this contradiction engages not only the loss of *representamen* (and thereby the loss of the contradiction) but also the most radical effects of this contradiction (which are readable in rhythms, paragrams, onomatopoeia, on the one hand, and in intellection, the logical exploration of the struggle between the two heterogeneous orders, on the other). With this practice we are at the most radical site of heterogeneity: on the one hand, struggle against the signifier; on the other, the subtlest differentiations of meaning. If the former, expulsion being maintained, brings us to the heart of *jouissance* and of death, the latter, through its subtle differentiation (in rhythm, colour, vocalization, or even semanticized through laughter or word play), keeps us at the surface of pleasure, in a subtle tension. The most intense struggle towards death, inseparably proximate to the differential binding of its charge in a symbolic tissue which is also, as Freud suggests in *Beyond the Pleasure Principle*, the condition of life: such is how the economy of textual practice appears. Its principal characteristic, distinguishing it from other signifying practices, is precisely to introduce heterogeneous rupture and expulsion, *jouissance* and death, through the binding and differentiation of life and of meaning.

Consequently, Artaud, while referring to it as 'the toxic state', distinguishes his practice through a 'will to meaning': he searches for a language, speaks to others. The function of 'art' as a signifying practice appears in this light: the reintroduction in society and under the appearance of a pleasing difference, acceptable for the community, of a fundamental expulsion, of divided matter.

A 'language' without exteriority

What happens to language in this process of expulsion and its resistant stases?

Artaud refuses the assimilation of his practice to any abstraction of meaning or of spirit, but also any assimilation of it to a purely linguistic function:

> Now I don't operate but by breaths,
> not by fluids
>   . . .
> but on the reality
> which you get into
> after the explosion of the compacted maché box.[67]

If the tissue of language is this 'compacted maché box', if it is indispensable to set up a resistance to expulsion, expulsion explodes it and it is at this point that it is possible to see the text as a *practice*:

> The question for me was not to know what would ensue if you insinuated yourself into the structures of written language.
>   but into the weft of my living soul.[68]

The Word is subordinated to a function: to translate the drives of the body, and in this sense it ceases to be a word and is paragrammatized, even to the extent of becoming simple noise: 'through what words could I enter into the thread of this scowling meat (I say SCOWLING, which means squinting, but in Greek, there is *tatavuri* and *tatavuri* means noise etc.).'[69] Language will seek out this proximity with the drives, with the heterogeneous contradiction where death is profiled, and with it *jouissance*:

> This flux, this nausea, this language, here is where the Fire starts. The fire of languages, the fire woven into the twists of language, in the brilliance of the earth which opens like a pregnant belly with entrails of honey and sugar.
>
>   . . .
>
>   I look in my throat for names and the vibrative filament of things. The stench of nothingness, a must of absurdity, the dung of total death. . . . [70]

A language of expulsion, murderous for the subject and his readers:

> I left because I realized that the only language I could have used with a public audience would have been to take some bombs out of

my pockets and throw them in its face with a characteristically aggressive gesture.

Because I don't think conscience can be educated or that it's worth bothering to try to educate it.

And violence is the only language I feel capable of speaking.[71]

These are not just words, ideas, or any other kind of phantasmatic bullshit, these truly are real bombs, physical bombs, but it is so naïve and childish of me, isn't it, to say these kind of things so innocently, so pretentiously.[72]

At the most violent moment of this rupture, where the drive invades and imprints itself on the binding of language, humour acts as intermediary, as the passage from meaning to non-sense: 'the dung of total death . . . light and rarefied humour . . . '.[73]

From the perspective of language, expulsion is principally a passage outside meaning, the shadow of non-sense through sense, which releases laughter; if it veers towards murder, it is the fault of circumstance:

The humoristic reality of poets, which circumstances themselves have led towards the dark side, sneers: this grotesque soufflé is all corrupt with rats underneath.[74]

Language and rhetoric are illusions (gestures of thought) to be penetrated so that in spite of them the process which crystallizes and exceeds them can pass:

And art is to bring this rhetoric to the necessary point of civiliza-tion so that it becomes one with certain real ways of being, of feeling and of thought. In a word, the only writer to survive will be the one who knows how to manage this rhetoric as if it were already thought, and not thought's gesture.[75]

Artaud is aiming for what metaphysics would call an exteriority of language, of the mark, that is, a deviated, signified operation; he is looking for a language susceptible of exteriority, in conflict and thus in dialectic with himself. This exteriority is fundamentally different from that specific to the Hegelian force (*Kraft*) which suppresses itself if it is not invested in the concept. But, as is apparent in the brief text 'Rimbaud and the Moderns', the 'exteriority' Artaud wants to introduce into language is the process of things itself, and in this sense it is interior to them, and this is precisely what the 'moderns' miss, preoccupied as they are with logical and syntactic relations, with 'folds' and 'slopes' and with a 'poetry of invented relations'. Artaud therefore reproaches Mallarmé, for example, perhaps underestimating the conflict which the Mallarméan text bears witness to, but doing so correctly as concerns the formalist and ornamentalist interpretations of the Mallarméan enterprise – he therefore reproaches the classificatory, purely semantic exteriority of Mallarmé's writings:

> in his eagerness to give each word its full burden of meaning [Mallarmé] classified his words as if they were values existing outside the thought that conditions them, and performed those strange inversions in which each syllable seems to be objectified and to become preponderant.[76]

This material heterogeneity (and not exteriority) passes through language in order to shift it towards the process which produces and exceeds it; it is itself subject to laws; it is precise, 'logical', but of a logic other than that of repressive rationality. Artaud emphasizes this:

> In the realm of the affective imponderable, the image provided by my nerves takes the form of the highest intellectuality, which I refuse to strip of its quality of intellectuality. And so it is that I watch the formation of a concept which carries within it the actual fulguration of things, a concept which arrives upon me with the sound of creation. No image satisfies me unless it is at the same time *Knowledge*, unless it carries with it its substance as well as its lucidity. My mind, exhausted by discursive reason, wants to be caught up in the wheels of a new, an absolute gravitation. For me it is like a supreme reorganization in which only the laws of Illogic participate, and in which there triumphs the discovery of a new Meaning. . . . But it does not accept this chaos as such, it interprets it, and because it interprets it, it loses it. It is the logic of Illogic. And this is all one can say. My lucid unreason is not afraid of Chaos.[77]

This passage, which echoes quite closely Hegel's reflection on force (*Kraft*), the logification of force and the loss of the reality of this force in this logification,[78] not only suggests a theoretical postulation, that the movement of signifying matter obeys laws which are yet to be discovered, obeys an objective regulation which functions without being thought, an asymbolic pulsation whose tremors are recorded on the body. It also suggests the workings of the impossible stakes of the text: if material heterogeneity were enounced, denounced, it would no longer be heterogeneous; only the 'noises of creation', cries, the diction or otherwise the dislocation of syntax, evoke, according to the new laws, the 'formation of the concept'. The aim, then, is to produce 'concept-texts' from the formation of concepts in the dialectic of matter, and in doing so allowing the 'impulsiveness of matter' to appear in these concepts, so as never to give the subject the impression of status and calm, that is, ultimately, to find concepts which correspond precisely to a real madness:

> The truth of life lies in the impulsiveness of matter. The mind of man has been poisoned by concepts. Do not ask him to be content, ask him only to be calm, to believe that he has found his place. But only the Madman is really calm.[79]

A certain logical mastery, through the return of the drive within language, is the way to overcome dementia. In this sense, the paragrammatic, syntactic or pulsional explosion of language is the condition of the maintenance of the heterogeneous as well as the condition of the overcoming of madness:

> But he is the Great Consciousness.
> But he is the pedestal of a breath which turns your bad demented brain, for at least it has won this – to have overcome dementia.[80]

In clinical schizophrenia, in order to reintroduce the signifying instance in the movement of the drive, pluralizing or immobilizing the body, one tends to attempt to include the subject in a relation to the other, to create a relation of transference which operates along the path of communication. This is never completely possible with so called psychotic patients: the transference in this case is a 'grafted transference' (to use Gisèle Pankow's term[81]). This graft is intended to provoke the subject's *desire*, through including him or her in an affective participation in relation to the body of the analyst. In transferring the violence of expulsion into a demand in which desire signifies itself, this 'graft' displaces the motility of expulsion from the body proper, language and the ideological system it clothes, into the sphere of interpersonal relations in which expulsion is not only deferred but retained, to end up enmeshed in the mechanics of social functioning (the work of modelling, manipulation, encounter with the other, etc.). Such a restriction of expulsion through 'grafted transference' significantly uses a non-verbal, kinetic or graphic functioning; the 'sick' are made to make models, drawings, and so on. These exercises seize the body and its *signifiance* at a pre-verbal level, thus at a level prefatory to the sign and representation, sites where expulsion fixes itself, and which are so far only marks, an absent object not yet having transformed them into *representamen*.

Expulsion has not yet dissociated subject and object, but runs across the body and the immediate environment in a logically a-representative rhythm. It binds, links, arranges and organizes, but does not attain a representation of the object opposite the coagulated presence of the subject. This pre-verbal logic structures the space in which the subject–object separation will be set up. But before this occurs, expulsion runs through the totalizing receptacle, the *chora* (Artaud's 'gyrations of fire'), fragmenting it, cutting it up, rearranging it, and traversing the subject who is present only in an 'absent point', a 'dead kernel', with 'total lucidity'. Gestural motility, fixed in marks or in modelled spaces, can then function as the relay which translates expulsion into the verbal signifying system or into the system of its pictural representation. However, the constraints of these signifying systems, through the injection of expulsion into them, are modified and made more supple. The rules of pertinence, of logical coherence, and so on, which are necessary in normative or scientific signifying systems, are thrown into disarray. It is as if expulsion accepts a compromise with representative stases and with the logic of information and its destructive destinatees, but only to deploy itself there with violence, displacing these stases and conserving only the marks and articulations of the *chora* determined by the logic of expulsion and objectively determined by the experience of the subject within the natural and social configuration. The mobile receptacle of all the objective determinations of expulsion, of its own workings, and its specific character relative to objective constraints can be considered as the trans-verbal mode of the process. This is what we call *signifiance*. It can also be called the topology of practical experience, since the trans-verbal mode is realized through a practice of transformation of matter, within the dynamic of expulsion, without there being a solid differentiation between subject and object.

'Grafted transference' tends to transplant this topology into the domain of representation, first of all to ensure its subjective and semiotic binding, and then to establish social and inter-subjective submission. However, the psychiatrist often doubts the success of this ruse: 'It is difficult to know if the structure of the illness is affected by this therapeutic intervention.'[82]

As textual practice is a struggle with language, and thus with communication, it does not choose the relay of 'grafted transference'. That such a graft might occur in the biography of the subject and ensure him or her the ephemeral moment of unity indispensable to the process is a question outside the realm of artistic practice. As a topological receptacle of expulsion, artistic production finds its identificatory moment, its 'pole of transference', not in the 'other' of transference but in the *modelling* of the receptacle, in the *movement* of expulsion and its *organization*, and these aspects can be figured, in inter-subjective relations, by the mother or the nurse. The *other* subject is pushed out of the movement, and it is the shattered plurality of the *same*, divided by expulsion, coincident with the plurality of the natural and social world, which intercepts and captures expulsion. This capture is always plural, therefore, but at the same time internal and external to the reversible subject.

The fragmented and reorganized *chora* is best realized in dance, gestural theatre or painting, rather than in words. Artaud's theatrical practice, and perhaps especially the Rodez paintings, or those which accompany the last texts, bear witness to this non-verbal but logical (in the sense of 'binding') organization of expulsion.

It is thus on the stage of a revolutionized theatre that the mobile *chora* of language is most completely liberated: the word becomes a drive which is thrown out in enunciation, and the text has no other justification than to give rise to this music of pulsions:

> For the purposes of this definition that we are trying to give of the theatre, only one thing seems to us unassailable, only one thing seems real: the text. But the text as a distinct reality, existing in itself, sufficient unto itself, not in terms if its spirit, for which we have very little respect, but simply in terms of the displacement of air created by its enunciation. This is all we care about.[83]

The above is a formulation *avant la lettre* of the attempts in which we are presently engaged to define the text not according to its signified, nor its signifier, Artaud would say its *idea [esprit]*, but according to the organization of expulsion within it, the oralization of expulsion, or for Artaud, 'the displacement of air created by its enunciation'.

Representations are the *substance* (in the Hjelmslevian sense) of this *chora*: However, if the *chora* moves and functions it is because expulsion returns to dissolve substance, to renew representation and thus to prevent it from closing up, immobilizing itself in fantasy. *In the mobile* chora *of the text there are no fantasies*: 'My lucidity is total, keener than ever, what I lack is an object to which to apply it, an inner substance.'[84] This renewal is produced in the topological mode through the logic of marks and of kinesis, or, in relation to language, through isolated, non-lexicalized, non-semanticized phonemes, or phonemes susceptible of a fluid semanticization through linguistic multiplicity. It is this expulsion and its mobile *chora* that Artaud's practice presents in all its purity, assigning representation and fantasy their subordinate place as guardians of a unity which is exceeded, as a cell of pleasure to be expelled in a movement towards *jouissance*.

The only use of language possible will thus be as a ridge between binding reason and the heterogeneity which produces it, which wedges itself into thought and splits it: the proximity of death renders this language sibylline, that is, receptive to pulsional shocks and splits.

> Our attitude of absurdity and death is the attitude of greatest receptivity. Through the fissures of a reality that is henceforth non-viable, there speaks a deliberately sibylline world.
>
> Yes, this now is the only use to which language can be put, a way of madness, of the elimination of thought, of rupture, a maze of madnesses and not a Dictionary into which the college scouts of the banks of the Seine channel their spiritual strictures.[85]

The same search for an extra-linguistic logic of the heterogeneous inspires the 'Letter to the Chancellors of European Universities':

> Enough playing on words, syntactic stratagems and formula-juggling. We must now discover the Heart's great Law, the Law which is not a Law (a prison), but a guide for the Mind lost in its own labyrinth.[86]

There is therefore what Artaud calls a 'will for meaning'[87] binding the ruptures of an intensely separated body and constituting, indirectly, a formula for it, which is itself separated, broken, 'badly put' and 'confused'. Language is a detour, a displacement of the drive and its topology: language is a substitute for expulsion, but one in which 'the mind lets its limbs show', a substitute (Logos) which perpetuates itself through chaining and binding expulsion.

The process, insofar as it is maintained, reaches a point where the signifier disappears under the attack of the death drive, which is not recuperable by any sign. But through a detour, the process blocks this loss, and, faced with lack, formulates and speaks. Expulsion in this instance is characterized by the tension of language: 'a perpetual erection of language, tension after lack, the knowledge of the detour, the acceptance of the badly put'.[88] Language, always and already a detour of expulsion, under the pressure of a renewed expulsion, becomes divided, fragmented, discredited; it is no longer language as such, and can only be understood by 'aphasiacs, and in general all the rejects of words and speech, the pariahs of Thought'.[89] But it is only in this way that it can take on the possibility of presenting matter in discourse: 'All matter begins with a spiritual disturbance.'[90] Spiritual can be read as 'of meaning' in this instance. For in the disturbance of meaning it is expulsion which returns, through the unconscious where it is supposed to remain repressed: 'The invisible treasures of the unconscious become palpable, directly leading language in a single thrust.'[91]

The body, having become mobile *chora*, cosmic and social mutation and essential site of natural and social operations, invalidates the contemplative mentalism which appears when writing shuts itself up in a purely linguistic state, or if it is thought solely in relation to linguistics. Linguistic structures are the blockages of the process. They intercept and immobilize it, subordinating it to semantic and institutional unities which are in deep solidarity with each other. The whole series of unities – linguistic, perceptive, conceptual and institutional (the ideological, political and economic apparatuses) – oppose this process, enclose it and aim to sublimate it, to 'put it under a spell', to destroy it through 'magic'. 'Magic' and 'spell-casting' are the effects of the unitary enclosures of the process, and are executed through social apparatuses but also, and to the same effect, through the structure of meaning, itself conceived as a simple, disincarnate sign, a Word beyond experience.

It is by magic that the abominable institutions
which enclose us:
country, family, society, mind, concept, perception,
sensation, affect, heart, soul
science
law, justice, right, religion, notions, verb, language,
don't correspond to anything real.[92]

Artaud's attacks on the Kabbala translate his refusal of any stagnation of the process in a 'formula' supposed to possess truth. Complicit in this with grammatical normativity and with formalism, the Kabbala represents any attempt at holding, blocking or fixing the process. Esoterism and formalism are found to be in solidarity with each other in their common gesture of censoring the *functioning* (of pulsional *signifiance* and of practice) and substituting

certain lost elements of a humanity in full flower, which betrayed its august form,
which was unformalized, and unfathomed,
for a handy grammatical form, because it did not wish to take the trouble of counting higher than 1, 2 and 3.[93]

Such an experience of the body as the mobile *chora* of the process of *signifiance* does not tolerate any Master of the *chora* other than the thetic-unifying phase of the subject itself. It is consequently foreign to any meta-linguistic or metaphysical approach to the process of *signifiance* and enters into ideological struggle with the essential guardian of unity: religion. A patient remarks that: 'Schizophrenia is synonymous with atheism.'[94]

Artaud's violent reaction to surrealism can be explained in this light; it is a reaction against the mentalism and religiosity that surrealism draws on. In a letter to Breton of 28 February 1947 Artaud writes of: 'the parallels between surrealist activity and occultation and magic. I don't believe in any notion, science or knowledge, and especially not in a hidden science.'[95] Against surrealist initiation Artaud proclaims the irreducibility of experience, and in insisting on its personal character he demands not a subjective enclosure of the individual in him- or herself but access, through the individual, to an 'authentic and universal' reality, which is non-uniform and anti-humanist, if humanism is the fraternity of the same, identical subjects:

All experience is resolutely personal,
and the experience of the other cannot serve anyone else outside myself without creating those sordid batterings of the alter ego which compose all living societies and in which all men are in effect brothers because they're cowardly enough to be so, so lacking in

pride as to think themselves each come out of anything other than
the same and identical cunt,
of the same stupid cow,
of the same irreplaceable and despairing stupidity . . . [96]

Artaud underlines the fact that this experience is a 'revolution' complementary to social revolution, against the worldliness of surrealist exhibitions, or
against their occultist doctrines:

And on this point there is always a revolution to effect, on condition that man doesn't think himself revolutionary only on the social
level, but believes that he must always and above all be revolutionary on the physical, physiological, anatomical, functional,
circulatory, respiratory, dynamic, atomic and electric level.[97]

As if to confirm this statement, the name of Lenin appears among those of
Nerval, Nietzsche, Villon, Lautréamont and Poe, all those who have been
victims of the 'frightening psychological dissimulation of all the hypocrisies
of bourgeois infamy'.[98]

The process of the subject and the representation of historical processes

Through running along the faultlines of this mobile and heterogeneous
chora, which is nevertheless semiotizable, where the process of *signifiance*,
rejecting stases, operates, the trans-subject leaves him- or herself open to
becoming the mechanism of this functioning itself, the 'mode' of its repetition, without his or her own signifying substance, without interiority or
exteriority, without subject or object, purely the movement of expulsion. To
be the logic of the mobile and heterogeneous *chora* is not to be, in the sense
of being a unitary subject, but to remain within the lucid functioning of
expulsion. The non-separation of the process of *signifiance* and the material
process prevents the isolation of an absent object as signified object; it also
prevents the positioning of the subject him- or herself and ends up in the
loss of the initially desired proximity to the material process. The absolute
expulsion of the thetic, subjective and representative phase is the very limit
of the experiment of the avant-garde. It opens into madness or into an exclusively experimental logic, in the sense of an inner, or mystical, experience.
We should look more closely, then, at this limitation of textual practice by
the *chora* of heterogeneous expulsion.

My lucidity is total, keener than ever, what I lack is an object to
which to apply it, an inner substance. . . . I would like to get
beyond this point of absence, of emptiness . . . My inner enthusiasm

is dead. . . . Try to understand this hollowness, this intense and lasting emptiness. This vegetation. How horribly I am vegetating. I can neither advance nor retreat. I am fixed, localized around a point which is always the same and which all my books describe.[99]

No ob-ject, and therefore no arrest of the re-ject, the thetic-positional phase does not produce any representation through absence, that is, through separation from the *chora*, that would fit the object. Reject, expulsion, in the excessive renewal of its scission, diverts presence and annihilates the arrest or the lack of the object as well as of the sub-ject; there is no lack 'opposite', or subordinate, only the motility of the *chora* itself. The 'referent' of such a text is solely the movement of expulsion.

Artaud's texts are thus also characterized by the arrest of the representative system in the very mechanism of heterogeneous contradiction which produces it, the incapacity of situating this contradiction as a 'determinate nothing', that is, as having a content which is always new according to the next object (natural or ideal) which contradiction traverses and causes to appear.

While thus exhibiting the repressed of philosophical knowledge and of metaphysics, the secret of their sacred, such a text condemns itself to becoming the complementary opposite of philosophical speculation, to the extent that it restricts its practical field to the experience of heterogeneous contradiction. The latter, whose function is as we have seen to close and open the process of *signifiance*, instead of throwing the process into a course through nature and society and producing out of it vast itineraries of the novelistic or epic type, wraps itself up in the discursive structure whose contradictions are the most compacted, the lyrical, and/or in the experimental evocation of its own hatching as the hatching out of the subject into the immobility of death. An 'inertia without thought', as Hegel called it, is imposed, which in effect relates to the preoccupations of the 'ego' alone, and which limits the possibility open to expulsion in its working on language, of giving a space to the violence of conflict, of not retreating under the blows but transporting them into the shock of socio-historical contradictions. The way to madness thus remains open. That this situation represents an ideological blockage, an impossibility of socially and historically objectifying the signifying process, is a topic for further discussion. But it nevertheless points to the fundamental level that textual practice reaches when it accedes to the translinguistic, pulsional and expulsional process, and the risks that it runs in fixing itself there.

This point which is 'always the same and which all my books describe' consists in keeping the closure of *signifiance* always open to the expulsion of matter, in preventing the total sublimation of expulsion and its repression, in reintroducing expulsion even into the tissue of meaning and its chromatic, musical and paragrammatic differences, and in thus disarticulating the field of pleasure in order to thrust heterogeneity or productive contradiction into it.

If such is the social, or a-social, function of art, can it limit itself to opening contradiction out into a tissue of meaning solely representing individual experience?

When social history itself breaks and reformulates itself, can the heterogeneous contradiction, of which the text is the privileged terrain, absent itself? This is not a secondary issue; the essential thing would be to hold heterogeneous contradiction in whichever binding tissue or ideological signified it appears. This in effect is the position of formalism, but also of the esoterism to which texts of the end of the nineteenth century, as well as practices as radical as those of Artaud, succumb when they abdicate themselves from the sphere of politics.

At this point it is necessary to reintroduce the unitary, relational and social approach to the subject which Marxism inherits from Feuerbach; to reintroduce, that is, the subject who thinks of him- or herself as a self, and who struggles in a social community, from a socialized position. We need to grasp this discourse and the historico-social contradiction that it represents in order to renew, in all of its representations, the heterogeneous contradiction suspended by 'class consciousness' but explored by the 'poets'. This is not the 'juncture' of two perspectives, supposedly constituting an idealized totality: it is a question of a mutual enlightenment, returning the subject its internal/external motility, and thus its *jouissance*, through the risk of social conflict, giving it back its freedom through the implacable logical constraints of political struggle. The question of the second moment of heterogeneous contradiction, that is, of *meaning* as *representation* and *ideology*, in which heterogeneous contradiction will erupt, is of primary importance. What is at stake here is the survival of the social function of 'art', but also, beyond this cultural preoccupation, of the maintenance in modern society of signifying practices potentially appealing to mass audiences, opening the closure of the *representamen* and of the unitary subject, and subsequently opening up the closure of ideologies. In capitalist society where the class struggle shakes all institutions, where any subject and any discourse are determined in the last instance by their position relative to production and to the political, to keep heterogeneous contradiction separate from the ideologies currently in place, and to have it erupt in a representation solely of the process of meaning, is to render this contradiction inaudible or complicit with the dominant bourgeois ideology. In fact, the latter can perfectly well accept experimental subjectivism but can hardly or not at all accept the critique of its own base through this experience. To join the textual mechanism of heterogeneous contradiction to a revolutionary critique of the social order is precisely what is intolerable for the dominant ideology and for the various defence mechanisms of liberalism and oppression. It is also the most difficult task. In other words, the moment of semantic and ideological binding of the expulsive drive has to be a binding in and through a revolutionary discourse, taking the subject out of the closed room of his or her experience to plunge him or her into revolutionary transformations of social relations, and amidst their protagonists. If heterogeneous contradiction, in order to realize itself as such, has to accept pauses, symbolic stases, these should be taken from the revolutionary practices and from the discourses which are shaking contemporary society. It is within this representative narration, itself witness to the historical process going on in the revolutionary class struggle, that the signifying process (whose acute moment is realized in heterogeneous contradiction) should inscribe itself, according to a historical logic. If narration is one of the forms of binding, sublimation or repression of the pulsional charge under the constraint of communal structures, this narration, inasmuch as the text is at stake in it, should probably propose a revolutionary project. For it is that aspect which will provide the defensive counter-charge, thwarting heterogeneous expulsion without stopping it but on the contrary ensuring the duration of the struggle within each of its two sides (pulsional and signifying), since it ensures the historical impact of their inseparability. Thus articulated, heterogeneous contradiction penetrates or runs alongside a critical discourse which represents a revolutionary social practice, it constitutes its motor: expulsion, heterogeneous contradiction, *jouissance* in the process. Without this proximity social practice has a tendency to repress expulsion in unitary and technocratic visions of the subject and of ideology. The always renewed return, distinct from a mechanic repetition, of the 'material' within the 'logical' ensures the permanence of negativity, a permanence which is never effaced under the stases of subjective desire or a group acting as obstacle. Heterogeneity is thus not sublimated, but opened within the symbolic which it puts into process, and in which it encounters historical process such as it is objectively produced in society.

Moreover, if certain of Artaud's texts refuse any merger between the experience of the text and political practice, others (often) underline their necessary complementarity. Thus, against the communist Revolution in which he saw a simple transmission of power from the bourgeoisie to the proletariat, a perpetuation of 'machinism as a way of easing the condition of the workers', and, consequently, a 'castrated revolution', accusations which confirm the machinic schizophrenization of 'socialist' societies as of capitalist societies, but which is to be inserted into a critical and scientific study of such social phenomena and specifically of the place which Marxism and the state organization which follows from it accord the subject, against this, Artaud proposes what he calls a 'regression': the only 'regression in time', a kind of analytic anamnesis which could only be achieved through semiotic tremors, through the violence of expulsion invested in verbal, scenic, pictural organization, such that the latter resembles a kind of 'police raid', a 'session with the dentist or surgeon',[100] an explosion 'of bombs to put anywhere but especially at the basis of the majority of habits of thought today, whether European or not'.[101]

The anarchism of this regression, which goes by way of the subject only to make itself felt in bursting the subject apart, only serves social positivity: the sadistic negativity of the avant-garde joins with 'collective fury' at the time of great social or artistic revolutions, and this divided juncture is the condition of great artistic enterprises.

> Art has a social duty to provide a tissue for the anxieties of its time. The artist who has not sheltered in the depths of his heart the heart of his time, the artist who does not know himself to be a scapegoat, who does not know that his duty is to magnetize, to attract, and to bring down on his shoulders the errant furies of his time so as to discharge it of its psychological sickness, he is not an artist. . . .
>
> Now all artists are not capable of arriving at this kind of magical identification of their own feelings with the collective furies of men.
>
> And the times are not all capable of appreciating the importance of the artist and the job of safeguarding that they undertake to the profit of the social good.[102]

One question, among others, persists: if there are moments when the only possibility is the safeguard, then there are perhaps others when it is not sufficient to safeguard. Is it possible, and how is it possible, for the artist to make himself understood by subjects transforming the process of history?

Translated by Patrick ffrench

Notes

1 This article was originally a paper given by Kristeva at the 1972 conference, 'Artaud/Bataille: Towards a Cultural Revolution'. It was published in *Tel Quel*, 52–3 (1973), and subsequently in Philippe Sollers (ed.), *Artaud* (Paris, 10/18, 1973), and Kristeva's *Polylogue* (Paris, Seuil, 1976).

> *Procès* can be translated as both 'trial' and 'process'. Kristeva's use of the French word plays on both of these levels, suggesting the elements of violence and struggle involved in the passage of subjectivity. The connotations of 'trial' should be heard underneath the word 'process' which we have used to translate the French *procès*.]

2 J. Lacan, 'Introduction au commentaire de J. Hippolyte sur la "Verneinung" de Freud', in *Ecrits* (Paris, Seuil, 1966), 372 [not in the English translation].

3 Gilles Deleuze and Félix Guattari, *Anti-Œdipus: Capitalism and Schizophrenia*, trans. R. Hurley, M. Seem and H.R. Lane (London, Athlone, 1984).

4 [*Signifiance*, in French, is used to suggest an active production of meaning, distinct from the noun 'signification'. It functions as a nominalization of the present participle *signifi*ant – suggesting 'the act of signifying' in the same way as *croy*ance suggests 'the act of believing' we have translated it as *signifiance*,

following the example of other translations of Kristeva, since the English 'signification' and 'meaning' suggest the fixity Kristeva endeavours to evade.]

5 [Kristeva's use of the word *différance* in French cannot but signal her wish to mark out the difference of her reading of Artaud from Derrida's, in *Writing and Difference*, trans. Alan Bass (London, Routledge & Kegan Paul, 1978). I have therefore kept the word *différance* in its original French, as it is overdetermined by this reference.]

6 We should briefly remind ourselves that in Plato's interpretation the *chora* (*Ηώρα*) designates a mobile receptacle of merging, contradiction and movement, necessary to the functioning of nature before the teleological intervention of God, and that it corresponds to the mother: the *chora* is a matrix or a source of nourishment in which the elements are without identity or reason. The *chora* is the *site* of a *chaos* which *is* and which *becomes* prefatory to the constitution of the first measurable bodies. While accessible to a 'bastard reasoning' or to 'reverie' this site exists in a state which is not yet a Universe, since 'God is absent from it' (*Timaeus*, 52–3). Thus: 'And there is a third nature, which is space and is eternal, and admits not of destruction and provides a home for all created things, and is apprehended, when all sense is absent, by a kind of spurious reasoning, and is hardly real – which we, beholding as in a dream, say of all existence that it must of necessity be in some place and occupy a space, but that what that is neither in heaven nor in earth has no existence . . . and the nurse of generation, moistened by water and inflamed by fire, and receiving the forms of earth and air, and experiencing all the affections which accompany these, presented a strange variety of appearances, and being full of powers which were neither similar nor equally balanced, was never in any state of equipoise, but swaying unevenly hither and thither, was shaken by them, and by its motion again shook them, and the elements when moved were separated and carried continually some one way, some another. As when grain is shaken and winnowed by fans. . . . ' Plato, *Timaeus*, 52–3, from *The Collected Dialogues of Plato*, eds E. Hamilton and H. Cairns (Princeton, NJ, Princeton University Press, 1969), 1179.

We should also note that the *chora* has a maternal connotation in many Roman and Byzantine, but also Chinese, religious ceremonies. By extension, the sovereign who assures the laws of the city provides the maternal function of supplying its *chora* (cf. D.A. Miller, 'Royauté et ambiguïté sexuelle', *Annales*, 3–4 (May–Aug. 1971), 646; M. Granet, *Chinese Civilization*, trans. K.E. Innes and M.R. Brailsford (London, Kegan Paul, 1930).

If our use of the term *chora* refers to Plato, who in this instance seems to follow the pre-Socratics, the notion that we will attempt to formulate concerns the organization of a process which, while being that of the subject, moves through the unitary cut-off which installs it and introduces into its *topos* the struggle of drives which makes it move and puts it into danger.

Jacques Derrida has recently focused on and interpreted this notion, with which, according to Derrida, 'Plato doubtless wanted to reduce [Democritean *rhythmos*] to silence by "ontologizing" it.' (J. Derrida, 'Interview with J.-L. Houdebine and G. Scarpetta', in *Positions*, trans. Alan Bass (London, Athlone, 1972), 75.

In our use of the term it is a question, as it is hoped will become evident, of an attempt to outline this site, as a certain organization, while giving back to it the voice and rhythm which compose it, and thus to extract it from the Platonic ontonology justifiably criticized by Derrida.

The path we have followed towards this end consists in not localizing the *chora* in any particular body, even in that of the mother who represents for the infant's sexual ontology, '[that] which contains all that is desirable, especially the father's penis' (M. Klein, *The Psycho-Analysis of Children*, trans. A. Strachey, London, Hogarth Press, 1969, 269). We see the *chora* as a play across and with the body of the mother – of the woman, but within the process of *signifiance*.

7 [I have translated the French word *rejet* almost exclusively as 'expulsion', except in those contexts where it is used in a different sense. The French word has the double meaning of both the act of repelling, or expelling, and the thing that is expelled.]

8 A. Artaud, 'Description of a Physical State', in *Selected Writings*, ed. Susan Sontag, trans. Helen Weaver (New York, Farrar, Strauss and Giroux, 1976), 65.

9 'Man is self consciousness', writes Feuerbach, *Sämtliche Werke*, vol. II, 242. My [Kristeva's] references to Feuerbach are taken from David McLellan, *The Young Hegelians and Marx* (London, Macmillan, 1969), 99.

10 'The essence of man is contained in community, in the unity of man with man.' Feuerbach, *Sämtliche Werke*, vol. II, 4 [see McLellan, *The Young Hegelians*, 100].

11 Feuerbach, *Kleine philosophische Schriften* (Leipzig, 1950), 34 [see McLellan, *The Young Hegelians*, 94].

12 Feuerbach: 'Man is the ground of the state. The state is the realized, complete and explicit totality of the human essence. . . . The head of state is the representative of universal man.' *Sämtliche Werke*, vol. II, 233 [see McLellan, *The Young Hegelians*, 114].

13 [Cf. McLellan, *The Young Hegelians*, 112.]

14 Man is above all a mastering, a 'solution to conflict'. Marx: 'On the one hand, it is only when objective reality everywhere becomes for man in society the reality of human faculties, that all objects become for him the objectification of himself. The objects then confirm and realize his individuality, they are his own objects, that is, man himself becomes the object.' *Frühe Schriften*, I, 600 [see McLellan, *The Young Hegelians*, 108].

15 *Frühe Schriften*, I, 505 [see McLellan, *The Young Hegelians*, 106].

16 As J. Hippolyte notes, 'The freedom of bourgeois society is demanded but in this case the individual is reduced to the particular, and the only escape is into the state or into religion.' *Etudes sur Marx et Hegel* (Paris, PUF, 1953), 94.

17 Hegel, *Science of Logic*, trans. A.V. Miller (London and New York, Allen & Unwin, 1969), 836.

18 Lenin, *Philosophical Notebooks*, trans. C. Dutt (London, Lawrence & Wishart, 1961), 229.

19 Hegel, *Science of Logic*, 91.

20 D. Dubarle and A. Doz, *Logique et dialectique* (Paris, Larousse, 1972), 36.

21 Philippe Sollers, 'The Roof', in *Writing and the Experience of Limits*, trans. P. Barnard (New York, Columbia University Press, 1983).

22 Frege, 'Negation', in *Collected Papers on Mathematics, Logic and Philosophy*, ed. B. McGuiness, trans. M. Black (Oxford, Blackwell, 1984), 378.

23 Cf., among others, J. Dubois, L. Irigaray and P. Macie, 'Transformation négative et organisation des classes lexicales', *Cahiers de lexicologie*, VII (1965).

24 R.A Spitz, *The First Year of Life: A Psychoanalytic Study of Normal and Deviant Development of Object Relations* (New York, International Universities Press, 1965).

25 Hermine Sinclair-de Zwart, *Acquisition du langage et développement de la pensée, sous-système linguistique et développement de la pensée* (Paris, Dunod, 1967), 130.

26 Ibid.

27 Frege, 'Negation'.

28 Sollers has proposed the first reading of a literary text uncovering through its language the drives which organize the translinguistic *chora* in 'La matière et sa phrase', *Critique*, June 1971.

29 [*Jouissance*, a familiar enough word by now in the context of the translation of French theory, has been translated variously by *jouissance* or 'pleasure' or 'enjoyment', according to the context, and the seam of meaning in the French word which appeared the most called upon in that instance.]

30 Cf. Freud, 'Beyond the Pleasure Principle', in *On Metapsychology: The Penguin Freud Library 11*, ed. A. Richards, trans. J. Strachey (Harmondsworth, Penguin, 1984).

31 M. Klein, 'The Importance of the Formation of the Symbol in the Development of the Ego', in *The Selected Melanie Klein*, ed. J. Mitchell (Harmondsworth, Penguin, 1986), 97.

32 A. Artaud, 'Note pour une lettre aux Balinais', *Tel Quel*, 46 (1971), 34.

33 Ibid., 29.

34 A. Artaud, 'Letter against the Kabbala', in *Artaud Anthology*, trans D. Rattray (San Franciso, City Lights, 1965), 113.

35 The oral cavity is the earliest developed of the perceptive organs, and permits the infant's first contact with the outside world. Its burgeoning character, intended simply to ensure contact, or, rather, the biologically indispensable fusion with the mother's body, attains a negative value after the sixth month; at this age the movement of the head suggests a refusal, prior to the abstract, semantic 'No' of the fifteenth month. Cf. Spitz, *The First Year of Life*.

36 'In my opinion, in the normal state of fusion of the two drives, aggression plays a role which is comparable to that of a carrier wave. In this way the impetus of aggression makes it possible to direct both drives toward the surround. But if the aggressive and the libidinal drives do not achieve fusion, or, alternatively, if a delusion has taken place, then aggression is returned against the own person; and in this case libido also can no longer be directed toward the outside.' Ibid., 288.

37 S. Freud, 'The Economic Problem of Masochism', in Freud, *On Metapsychology*.

38 Cf. effects of alliteration, assonance, and so on.

39 Cf. the *mots-valises*.

40 Artaud, 'Préambule', in *Œuvres complètes*, vol. I (Paris, Gallimard, 1970), 13.

41 Artaud, 'The New Revelation of Being', in *Artaud Anthology*, 89.

42 Ibid.

43 Artaud, 'Note pour une lettre aux Balinais', 11–17.

44 A. Artaud, 'L'automate personnel', in *Œuvres complètes*, vol. I, 147.

45 A. Artaud, 'Nouvelles lettres sur moi-même', in ibid., 272.

46 Artaud, 'Note pour une lettre aux Balinais'.

47 Lautréamont, *The Lay of Maldoror*, trans. J. Rodker (London, The Casanova Society, 1924), 317–8.

48 Artaud, 'Note pour une lettre aux Balinais', 11.

49 Ibid., 20.

50 Ibid., 25.

51 Ibid., 28, 32, 34.

52 A. Artaud, 'Lettre à André Breton', 28 February 1947, *L'éphémère*, 11 (1969).

53 A. Artaud, 'Lettre à André Breton', 2 February 1947, in *L'éphémère*, 11 (1969).

54 Artaud, 'Nouvelles lettres sur moi-même', 274.

55 Cf. Artaud, 'Invocation à la momie', in *Artaud le Momo, Œuvres complètes,* vol. XII (Paris, Gallimard, 1974).

56 Artaud, 'Description of a Physical State', 65.

57 Artaud, 'Note pour une lettre aux Balinais', 24, 19.

58 David Cooper points to this paranoid instance in poetic creation when he underlines the poetic instance in paranoia: 'All the metaphors of "paranoia" are a poetic protest against this invasion (of the family and of others). The poetry, which of course varies in quality, is, however, always unappreciated by society, and, if it becomes spoken aloud too much, it gets treated by psychiatry.' *Death of the Family* (Harmondsworth, Penguin, 1971), 11. Other psychoanalysts have also likened the 'subversion of words', the abandonment of their 'strict denotation to slip into a highly polysemic Witz effect, a particularly relished effect *beyond* meaning', with 'the luxurious vagueness of paranoid existence'. Cf. Pierre Dubor, 'Dissociation de l'économie et du sens chez les psychotiques: utilisation du réel dans l'agir', *Revue française de psychanalyse,* 5–6 (Sept.–Dec. 1971), 1068 (an *exposé* at the Conference on Psychosis).

59 A. Artaud, 'Letter to George Soulié de Morant, 17th February 1932', in *Selected Writings,* 290.

60 Artaud, 'Note pour une lettre aux Balinais', 19.

61 A. Artaud, 'L'osselet toxique', in *Œuvres complètes*, vol. I, 280.

62 Artaud, 'Note pour une lettre aux Balinais', 33.

63 Ibid., 34.

64 Cf. Artaud, 'Letter against the Kabbala', 118 [translation adapted].

65 Ibid. [translation adapted].

66 I analyse the notion of *experience* in relation to Bataille in my intervention on Bataille in this conference. Cf. 'Bataille: Experience and Practice', in Leslie Boldt-Irons (ed.) *On Bataille: Critical Essays* (New York, State University of New York Press, 1995).

67 Artaud, 'Note pour une lettre aux Balinais', 30–1.

68 Artaud, 'Préambule', 9.

69 Ibid.

70 A. Artaud, 'L'enclume des forces', in *Œuvres complètes*, vol. I, 141–4.

71 A. Artaud, 'Letter to André Breton, 28 February, 1947', trans. Yvonne Houlton, in *Interstice,* 2 (Autumn 1996), 33–4.

72 Ibid.

73 Artaud, 'L'enclume des forces', 144.

74 Artaud, 'Lettre à André Breton', 23 April 1947, *L'éphémère,* 11 (1969), 50.

75 Artaud, *Œuvres complètes,* vol. I, 193.

76 A. Artaud, 'Rimbaud and the Moderns', in *Selected Writings,* 26. [In this translation the subject of the sentence is mistakenly given as Rimbaud, not Mallarmé.]

77 A. Artaud, 'Manifesto in Clear Language', in ibid., 108.

78 Hegel, *The Phenomenology of Mind,* trans. J.B. Baillie (London and New York, Allen and Unwin, 1971), 179–213.

79 Artaud, 'Manifesto in Clear Language', 109.

80 Artaud, 'L'osselet toxique', 279.

81 G. Pankow, *L'homme et sa psychose* (Paris, Aubier, 1969), 26.

82 Ibid., 29.

83 A. Artaud, 'Alfred Jarry Theatre, First Season, 1926–7', in *Selected Writings,* 159.

84 Artaud, 'Letter to René Allendy', in ibid., 169.

85 Artaud, 'Dinner is Served', in ibid., 103 [translation adapted].
86 A. Artaud, 'Letter to the Chancellors of the European Universities', in *Collected Works*, vol. 1, trans. José Corti (London, Calder and Boyars, 1968), 179.
87 A. Artaud, 'L'activité du bureau de recherches surréalistes' in *Œuvres complètes*, vol. I, 271.
88 Ibid., 270.
89 Ibid., 271.
90 A. Artaud, 'A la grande nuit ou le bluff surréaliste', in ibid., 287.
91 Ibid., 288.
92 Artaud, 'Lettre à André Breton', 23 April 1947, 50.
93 Artaud, 'Letter against the Kabbala', 118.
94 Pankow, *L'homme et sa psychose*, 220.
95 A. Artaud, 'Lettre à André Breton', 28 Feb, 1997, *L'éphémère*, 11 (1969), 5.
96 Ibid.
97 Ibid, 8.
98 Ibid, 9.
99 A. Artaud, 'Letter to René Allendy', in *Selected Writings*, 169–70. ['Inner enthusiasm', here, does not capture the resonance of the French *noyau mort* ('dead kernel'), which Kristeva italicizes. 'Describe' is also better rendered by 'translate', given the context.]
100 A. Artaud, *Œuvres complètes*, vol. II (Paris, Gallimard, 1971), 14.
101 A. Artaud, 'Manifeste pour un théâtre avorté', in ibid., 25.
102 A. Artaud, *Œuvres complètes*, vol. VIII (Paris, Gallimard, 1971), 287.

Part III

ART

9

CHROMATIC PAINTING

Theorem written through painting[1]

Marc Devade

Not criticism but revolution is the driving force of history, also of religion, of philosophy and all other types of theory.

(Marx–Engels, *The German Ideology*)

A definite system by which the movement of colour passed along the long path of its culture.

(Malevich, 'Non-Objective Creation and Suprematism', Moscow, 1919)

The chromatic . . . is to the origin of art what writing is to speech.

(Derrida, *Of Grammatology*[2])

Generalities I

0 The volume of a body is the portion of space occupied by that body.

0.1 The surface of a body is that which separates it from the surrounding space.

0.2 A surface is the site of the positions of a line that varies according to a fixed law: this line generates the surface.

0.2.1 If this line is a straight line that applies to every point of the surface in every direction, this surface is a plane surface.

0.3 The historically determined surface of the pictural body (the canvas) is a plane surface.

1 In practice, every body has a certain density, indicates space.

1.1 The density of a pictural body can be thought of as negligible: it is an empty volume; from a geometric point of view it can be considered a surface.

1.2 The canvas, as plane surface, is an empty volume.

1.3 The practice of painting is the practice of the (theoretically 'negligible') density of the surface; it is the theoretical practice of the surface of the pictural body as empty space.

N.B. *chroma, chromatos* =
(a)   a body's surface.
(b)   the body's colour.

---

2 The 'chroma' is the sur-face of a body, i.e. something on, over, above the body's face: a face that has an upper part; it implies thereby a relation between a face and that which goes beyond it.

2.1 The face of a pictural body is its figure in space, its form, its format, the dimension of its volume: the plane as the rule that constitutes pictural practice.

2.2 The density of a body, the always already given upper part of its form, is that body's colour.

2.2.1 The pictural surface is not a transparent body (a window affording a glimpse of or displaying something deeper) but a coloured surface: a face that is immediately above.

Colours are attached to the density of surfaces.

(Newton)

2.3 There is no creation *ex nihilo* of painting; the face of the pictural body is always a surface of colour: a 0–2 limit always already a part of the practice of painting.

2.3.1 This limit is the basic double 'surface': the chromatic surface that is the 'always-already-begun' of pictural production.

2.3.2 The chromatic surface reaches its limits when the colour is either white or black (we shall call these surfaces non-chromatic surfaces):

– in the first instance the colour diffuses all the radiations it receives equally in all directions; it is the result of a synthesis by addition of the basic trichromatism (red, green, blue).

– in the second instance, the colour fully absorbs all the radiations it receives: it is the result of a synthesis by subtraction of the basic trichromatism.

2.4 The theoretical material practice of the surface, an empty space, is the practice of spacing that constitutes the articulation of the movement of production (time) and pictural space.

> Time-space (as Leibniz saw, before Einstein) is nothing but 'the order of the relation of things between themselves'.
> (Kristeva, 'The Engendering of the Formula', *Tel Quel,* 37)

> Yes, all things are part of a whole, each part receives its visual value from the other parts. Everything is constituted through relation and reciprocity. A colour exists only through another colour, a dimension is defined by another dimension, there is no position except in opposition to another position. That is why I say that the principal thing is relation.
> (Piet Mondrian, *Natural Reality and Abstract Reality*)

2.5 The articulation of a non-chromatic surface and a non-chromatic linear trace (a drawing that generates surfaces) is the production of a graphic surface.

2.6 A graphic surface opens onto a detour round the non-chromatic limits it imposes via chromatic colours.

2.6.1 The articulation of chromatic colours and a graphic surface is the production of a pictural surface.

2.7 The obliteration of the spacing of the surface (through a perspectival reduction) is, then, the obliteration of the articulation of production, and the desire for a final return to a substantial unity that is mono-chromatic or visual.

2.7.1 Materialist pictural production takes place only as the detour of limits, where the desire for unity is constantly subverted by the real practice of painting which demonstrates explicitly the non-existence of that unity, the illusion in its infinite differences (differ*a*nces: J. Derrida).

N.B. *Producere* = to lead forward, to bring out, to prolong, to defer; *proago*, in Greek = to lead before, to carry outside, to make distinct.

They themselves [men] begin to distinguish themselves from animals as soon as they begin to produce their means of subsistence, a step which is conditioned by their physical organization. . . . The way in which men produce their means of subsistence depends first of all on the nature of the actual means of subsistence they find in existence and have to reproduce.

(Marx–Engels, *The German Ideology*)

3 Pictural production is the doubling of a surface: since the material support is always already a coloured surface (a non-chromatic surface, at the very least), this coloured surface is doubled when at least one of chromatic infinity's colours is produced on this surface.

3.1 The real practice of painting is the production, the bringing forward, the *mise-en-scène* of a 'density', of an empty volume, of a surface that has been doubled, prolonged, deferred by the articulation of colours on the plane surface.

3.2 Colour (from its white and black limits to infinity) in (alternating) intervals effects a spacing: the spacing of an articulation that produces an empty volume.

3.2.1 The spacing of the surface (from its non-chromatic limits to its chromatic infinity) is the *mise-en-scène* of that surface: a differance that is the movement of production.

3.2.2 The sustaining of this differance between the production of chromatic colours and their limits is the articulation that produces the surface as surface above the surface, as doubled surface.

3.3 The production of a graphic surface is said to be simple.

3.3.1 The production of this graphic surface depends on formal operations.

3.4 The production of a pictural surface is said to be complex: the production of at least one chromatic colour on a surface of non-chromatic colour.

3.5 The theoretical practice of painting is the articulation of the graphic surface and the pictural surface that defers it; this articulation produces not a contradiction but an equivalence or identity of the chromatic and the non-chromatic: the colours black and white being the starting-point and the end of all colours, the site of disjunction/junction and of the absorption/diffusion of their 'potential infinity' (Kristeva).

3.5.1 The accumulation of chromatic colours across the graphic surface produces a qualitative leap. It suppresses the linear trace, prolongs or defers the non-chromatic graphic surface; it produces a chromatic surface.

3.5.2 This deferral of the empty volume (irreducible to the following terms: form–content, outside–inside, same–other, since one is the other, one is already the other, one only is through the other) is the material and real production of the surface, of a pictural surface.

The production of a 'chromatic surface': a pleonasm indicating the doubling of production that is at work in the painting effect.

Generalities II

'Hence the law is not beyond phenomena, but is immediately present in it; the realm of laws is the *quiescent* [Hegel's italics] reflection of the existing or phe-nomenal world.'
This is a remarkably materialistic and remarkably appropriate (with the word 'quiescent') determination. Law takes the quiescent – and therefore law, every law, is narrow, incomplete, approximate.
(Lenin, *Notebooks on Hegel's Dialectics*[3])

The material formation of the object will replace its aesthetic composition.
(*Lef*, 1923)

The adventure of the history of forms in reality.
(Pleynet, *Art International*, Oct. 1968)

The principle of structuration is to be found in the matter itself of that which is structured.
(Kristeva, 'The Engendering of the Formula', *Tel Quel*, 37)

4 The production-process of painting is indissolubly linked to the production of 'forms' across the plane. The plane–base structure is nothing outside of the formal effects it produces.

4.1 The plane is not the *mise-en-scène* of an expression or of a vision projected onto this plane (which would preserve the ideological division of spectator and actor, spectator and painting, 'artist' and painting), but the *mise-en-scène* of painting through the effects of its real production; as an object produced by its own structure: by its format.

4.1.1 Painting elaborates its real production, puts into play and exposes the formal operations initiated by the line that generates the surface in question.

4.2 The absence of 'cause' (subject–vision–author) within 'metonymic causality' (where the cause is the effect) (see Louis Althusser, *For Marx*) whose object would be the pictural structure therefore is not the result of the exteriority of formal elements in relation to the format; on the contrary, it is the form of the structure itself that elaborates its own effects.

4.2.1 This implies that these effects are not exterior to the structure, that they are not formal elements or segments of pre-existing planes that come from the exterior to leave their mark on the plane.

4.2.2 This implies that the structure produces its own formal elements, that these formal elements are immanent to the structure and that the entire existence of the structure consists in its effects.

4.2.3 Elements produced by the plane, forms generated by the format, are segments of the plane, parts of the structure as a whole, a whole to be found in each part.

4.3 The plane–base structure produces a specific combination of elements of this plane, which have effectiveness only as an account of the effects of the structure itself.

> 'Effect contains nothing whatever which Cause does not contain' (226) and vice versa.

> 'But we may here and now observe that, insofar as the relation of cause and effect is admitted (although in an improper sense), effect cannot be greater than cause; for effect is nothing further than the manifestation of cause' (230).
> (Hegel, *Logic*, 4, cit. Lenin, *Notebooks on Hegel's Dialectics* [4])

4.3.1 The effectiveness of a format is the regulation of its assembly; a mode of production that is painting's *mise-en-scène* of itself; *mise-en-scène* of the elements of the plane–base structure.

4.3.2 The format is therefore manifest as a dimension to be regulated; the elements it produces are the regulating dimensions thereof.

4.3.3 The relation between the dimension to be regulated and the dimensions that regulate constitutes the graphic matrix of painting.

4.4 The author-actor-spectator of this *mise-en-scène* is none other than its own structure elaborating itself, playing itself in a mechanical programme of which we are the contingent readers. A programme that is the sum of the painting's formal elements.

5 Given the plane–base structure, transformations of the elements derived from it can be effected.

5.1 The topological analysis of the laws for transforming figures produced by the base structure – the axis of rotation, changes regarding origin and unity, translation, divergence, disappearance, dispersal, intersection, reunification, inclusion, etc. – enable the determination, either empirically or algebraically, of the parameters of geometric solutions.

5.1.1 By varying these parameters cyclically, a given number of figures emerge through logical deduction.

5.2 The translation of topological analysis, either empirically or mechanically, enables the linear and continuous programming of formal combinations derived from the plane–base structure.

5.2.1 This programming, be it empirical or effected by calculation or logical means, shows on a numerical table the placing of those extremities to be situated on the plane.

5.2.2 Tracing curves, by hand or by mechanical means, is the direct inscription of these graphic solutions as a geometric drawing of the format. It establishes a graphic surface.

5.3 The resolution of the linear programme supplies the formal elements corresponding to any specific base structure, and to any specific variable of that base structure.

5.4 The formal pictural system, its mechanical programme, therefore amounts to the production of a logical writing, of a code that programmes a trans-finite and ordered number of formal sets and elements produced by a base structure and its variables.

5.4.1 If we take, for example, five plane-based structures, each with five variables, the number of possible solutions will be five to the power of five, i.e. more than 100,000.

5.5 These formal elements are not linked to any kind of phonetic writing, to a geometry or to numbers expressing the relation of these elements to the sound of the voice or to music, as has been the case throughout the pre-history of painting through Pythagoras, Orphism, Plato and the Renaissance all the way to to Kandinsky; they are not linked (in the way painting played with the codes of Old and New Testament writing) to the Writing [Scripture] of a divine and transcendent Word (Logos), but to a writing that is logical and universal, or on the way to becoming so; a logical writing with roots that stretch back to the Egyptian surveyors and their manual calculations (see the 'Calculator's Handbook' by Ahmosis, 1800 BC).

5.5.1 These geometric forms written by programme establish praxiological models, ordering the play of effects of the structure, of the graphic structure.

5.5.2 Linear, ordered, continuous (coded) determination is the scientific aspect of painting in its reference to an entire cultural system: it forms the ideological depth of painting playing on the scientific level of its period. It is a real ideological depth, in that painting programmed in this way does not imitate the machine, does not reproduce our vision of it, does not mimic its functions, but is produced by its actual functioning (by calculation); it uses its operations and integrates them into another system.

5.5.3 The double mechanism of brain and machine (analysis and programming) computes the totality of effects, of formal elements derivable from a given structure. This total sum, this complete computation, definitively cancels out the 'story', the 'narrative', the 'history', the 'meaning' of forms: forms are always already 'written' by the programmed code of the structures that renders them graphic.

(Without being prophetic, we can envisage that logical machines will calculate the sum of forms, that graphic surfaces will be defined, available for 'performance' by actual pictural practice. Pictural performance would then find itself blocked by the incomplete realization of that definition and by the arbitrary if ordered choice of definition to be performed. Here pictural production confronts the end of the history of forms.)

5.5.4 Graphic production simply re-produces, re-cites, re-counts the geometric forms, the formal elements that are the commonplaces of painting; graphic production constitutes the general grammar, the code, the system of rules to which painting refers and which amounts to the permanence of a cultural system. The graphic is manifest as the code for the development, for the transformation of painting; it directs the production of painting.

> The practical activity of man had to lead his consciousness to the repetition of the various logical figures thousands of millions of times in order that these figures could obtain the significance of axioms.
>
> (Lenin, *Notebooks on Hegel's Dialectics*[5])

5.5.5 The reproduction of structures and of the formal elements derived from them is manifest as the general mode of production of painting and as the permanence of its general conditions of production; it is the historical and cultural determination of pictural production in general by the permanence of structures and objective elements.

5.5.6 In this sense, we can say that painting that privileges formal research, despite its spectacular effects (and also because of these), is not revolutionary; it does not call the code into question; rather, such painting applies the code as strictly as possible and reproduces the code as a law governing it, without seeking to transform the code.

5.6 The graphic, produced by the structure (synchronic surface effect) is the 'inconsistent consistency' of painting up until the point where colour comes to affect it. The graphic constitutes the method of painting's production, its given law, the formative operation to be completed by the chromatic operation that will engage directly with it.

Generalities III

> But let us return to this subject: the destruction of form.
> (Mondrian, *Natural Reality and Abstract Reality*)

> There's only one road to a full rendering, a full translation: colour. Colour, if I may say so, is biological. Colour is alive, and colour alone makes things come alive.
> (Paul Cézanne to Joachim Gasquet[6])

> There's a logic of colour. (. . . The painter owes allegiance to that alone.)
> (Cézanne[7])

> At this juncture a kind of painting emerges that can be mastered by following precisely the laws of colour and its transference onto the canvas.
> (Larionov, *Rayonnist Manifesto*, 1913[8])

189

6 The accumulation of colours across the surface produces a qualitative leap: it establishes that formal limit, the non-chromatic graphic surface, as chromatic surface. Colour produces the spatiality of the surface as double, without being an accidental contingency of an already constituted space.

6.1 The process of pictural production confronts a synchronic effect, the graphic surface, opened up to the diachronic painting effect, the chromatic surface.

6.2 The infinity of colours is a complex effect introduced by a simple effect (the graphic surface, the limit and the point of departure of colours).

6.2.1 The always already given simple effect is the synchronic graphic structure opened up to the diachronic spacing of chromatic colours that produces a constantly renewed difference of the surface.

6.2.2 The doubling of the surface-effect by chromatic colours that is always already implicated in the simple effect opens up the simple effect to movement, to succession, to multiplication and to the serial alternation of colours by interval.

6.3 The primary difference, the graphic (non-chromatic and synchronic) surface and the second difference (the diachronic and chromatic surface) consitute the real conditioning of the dialectical materialist production of painting, the readable realization of its process of production.

6.4 Across the complex effect, spacing indicates the doubling of the process of generation and the very possibility of the painting-effect, the limit of the simple effect and the revelation of this simple effect's variations and mutations.

6.5 This articulation of the graphic surface and the chromatic surface produces a volumetric surface, defined by the concept of 'chromaticity'.

> 'This, which appears as the activity of Form, is equally the proper movement of Matter itself' (85–6).
>   Matter is not the Ground of Form, but the unity of Ground and Grounded.
>
> (Lenin, *Notebooks on Hegel's Dialectics*[9])

7 The plane forms of the base structure are indissolubly linked to the pictural matter (colour) of the painting-effect.

7.1 Chromatic colours establish a spacing that overturns the linearity and the continuity of the programmed code, of formal graphism, and produces a chromatic surface: this is the multi-dimensionality of the code, of the line, of the plane and of its consecutive forms.

> I see surfaces overlapping, and sometimes straight lines seem to fall.
>
> (Cézanne, *Letters*)

7.1.1 The infinity of colours perverts the code that it methodically plays on. This infinity is both the possibility of and the cancellation of the code; it reverses the effect of synchronic, non-chromatic synthesis to open it up to diachrony and to chromatics.

> There are no lines, there is nothing shaped, there are only contrasts;
> not of black and white, but due to the sense of colour.
>
> (Cézanne, *Letters*)

7.2 The production of painting, of the painting-effect through colours, is the consumption of its code, the consumption of the forms produced by the structure of the plane–base. It is a real production-effect of painting, whose structure determines forms that chromatic colours (the 'over-determination' of painting) deny by effacing the structure itself, the initial plane.

7.2.1 Colour then appears to be the proper nature of painting; colour transfers the surface from the graphic to the chromatic level, from the 'graphic programme' level to the level of the 'chromatic gram'.

7.2.2 The chromatic level is the originary level of painting, a level always already open in the simple non-chromatic effect, and it reverses the ideological relations of colour conceived of as instrument of a linear graphism (drawing), of an illusory depth; it engenders volume out of its own structure.

7.2.3 Through colour, graphism (the programme, form, geometry) has an infinite number of births (or birth-certificates) in which, each time, another birth is announced, while still being concealed.[10]

7.3 Geometry – form, graphism, the programme held in reserve – is always deferred by colour and discovers its possibilities as expansion, as account of its own history, as traced gram and not as a fixed term of a resolved programme in its graphic linearity.

7.3.1 Colour takes account of forms, a consumption by colour that makes readable the programme produced by its structure; a production of painting that paints colours indefinitely while consuming its programme.

7.3.2 Colours make readable those forms that make colours readable by cancelling/posing these same forms.

> 'The movement of the Determinate Relation of Causality has now resulted in this, that the cause is not merely extinguished in the effect, and with it the effect too (as happens in Formal Causality), – but the cause in this extinction, in the effect, becomes again; that effect vanishes into cause, but equally becomes again in it. Each of these determinations cancels itself in its positing and posits itself in its cancellation; what takes place is not an external transition of causality from one substratum to another, but this becoming other is at the same time its own positing. Causality, then, presupposes or conditions itself.' (235)
>
> 'In Reciprocity, original Causality presents itself as an arising out of its negation (or passivity) and as a passing away into it – as a Becoming. . . . Necessity does not become Freedom because it vanishes, but only because its identity (as yet an inner identity) is manifested.' (241–2)
>
> 'Considering a given content merely from the point of view of reciprocity, then such an attitude is in fact quite without concept; it is then merely a matter of a dry fact, and the requirement of mediation, which is the point of immediate concern in applying the relation of causality, still remains unsatisfied.' (The requirement of mediation (of connection), that is the point at issue in applying the relation of causality – Lenin's note.) 'On closer examination, the deficiency in the application of the relation of reciprocal action is seen to be that this relation, instead of being the equivalent of the Notion, has itself to be grasped first of all. And this occurs through its two sides not being left as an immediate datum but, as was shown in the two preceding paragraphs, being recognized as moments of a third, higher determination, which is precisely the Notion.'
>
> (Cited by Lenin, *Notebooks on Hegel's Dialectics*[11])

7.4 Painting produced by this means is archi-painting, so named because it announces the becoming of painting beyond the cut effected by its present production; painting as diagram of colours.

8 The system of formal combinations, synchronically programmed, always already given by the base structure, is affected by the impact of colours; an unmotivated affect, the active operation of colour that is produced by the pulsion of labour in pictural production.

8.1 Colour is not a 'value', does not valorize forms, it is not an instrument that supports forms; on the contrary, colour has the effect of effacing form and restoring it as discharge.

8.2 The combinatory and the formal sequences are established only under the constraint of the productive rule that constitutes the plane structure; this always already given effect of constraint necessitates changes of colour-scale, of tone, mutations, combinations and diachronic coloured sequences that accentuate the non-identity of the structure and its impermanence. The impermanence of the programme in its metonymic metamorphoses is its being bound to the chromatic colours that produce a diagram of colours.

8.2.1 The formal combinations produce the object of painting that colours affect, becoming thereby objects themselves; they account for their successive postures, the successive postures of pictural volume, of its history.

8.2.2 This non-identity and formal impermanence postulated by the spacing of the hollow volume is linked to the process of effacement, annulment/transformation of the graphic programme by colours.

8.3 Between the formal programme and the affect of colours intervenes a system of transference: colours produce a chromatic surface and develop the game of the infinite expansion of colours and of their non-chromatic term, of the hollow volume and the plane surface.

8.3.1 The vector of the plane surface is the non-chromatic (white and black term): a site of absorption and diffusion, a site of discharge and reserve of affect, transferred by the graphic programme of the base structure.

8.3.2 The vector of the hollow volume is the infinite expansion of colours: the place of this expansion is determined only by junction or disjunction with the site of discharge or reserve, a place constrained in its degrees of intensity by the quantity of space allowed it by the limits of the graphic programme.

> I make different surfaces with tones from the palette, you see. You have to see these surfaces. Clearly. But also harmonize them, make them merge. It has to turn and to insert itself at the same time. Only volumes are important.
>
> (Cézanne, *Letters*)

> There is a necessary proportion in tones that can lead me to modify the form of a figure or to transform my composition. So long as I have not found this proportion in every part, I look for it and continue my work. Then a moment comes when every part has

found its definitive relation, and then it would be impossible to add anything to my painting without beginning it anew.

(Matisse, 'Notes of a Painter', *La Grande Revue*, 1908)

The quantitative relations of colours used freely determine their quality.

(Matisse[12])

8.4 The chromatic surface, as site of junction and disjunction, of affect and discharge, is the only historically determined site of painting's dialectical-materialist production. It is the very possibility thereof, its renewal and continual transformation.

8.4.1 This is the production of a movement that, within the linearity of a methodically combined, sequentially programmed series, places colour-elements that transgress and contradict that series, while maintaining it, that negate the series while transforming it by their successive stances, combinations, sequences and scansion.

8.4.2 The primordial colour element (a non-chromatic limit), always already in place and maintained, is the basis of the pictural surface, transformed into volume (through the empty volume that is the pictural body) by the chromatic colour element (infinity), effacing the graphism of the plane–base structure: a 'chromatic surface' effect.

8.4.3 The chromatic element is the affect of the non-chromatic element which it establishes as foundation; the chromatic element is the discharge of chromatic colours which it establishes as a volume with foundation; this hollow volume is the force of labour of the surface which makes readable the material support of pictural production.

8.5 The movement of this sequence is the painting-effect, both arbitrary and ordered: colour arbitrates only through ordination and measure, and develops within a repetitive and productive space (that repeats a graphic programme and produces a chromatic surface).

9 The chromatic/non-chromatic relation is divided between expansion and term, infinity and limit, volume and plane, where the one ceaselessly spills over into the other, neither being able to propose itself as cause without being the effect of the other.

9.1 The term, founding instance of all colours, transgresses the sequences of colours that themselves transgress their term.

9.2 Chromatic and non-chromatic colours that negate while maintaining each other transport the plane surface to a higher level, transform it and produce a chromatic surface of annulment and transformation.

9.3 If the 'graphic' is the instrument of painting (writing, engraving, drawing), and the 'gramma' is the painted (written, engraved, drawn) character, we can see that this passage towards a painting of the signifier separates colour from instrumentality, from the graphism that has guided it through our culture. It opens it up to its obliterated real process of production: the grammatic generation of the pictural system.

9.3.1 The pictural programme, its graphic tracing made destitute by colour, constitutes a pictural trace or gram realized through colours.

9.3.2 The chrome/gram game, diagrammatic colour, the diachromatic trace, establishes a chromo-grammatic surface that offers painting up to be read with reference to nothing but itself, painting painting.

9.4 This chromo-grammatic surface lets us know painting (its mechanical programme) scientifically, by opening it up practically, through colours: the practical theoretical dialectic of the chrome and the gram; the subject of painting (colour) becoming object (trace-gram) and the object of painting (the trace) becoming subject (colour).

> There where it was I must go.
>
> (Freud)

10 The production of painting, until this point monopolized by the reproduction of an exterior subject, seizes those means of production expropriated in the service of representation and practises itself dialectically in an objective space which it makes readable as history.

10.1 By abandoning painting as image, as sign of a meaning, as representation or expression of a subject, as meaning offered up to the vision of a subject who recognizes himself therein, as sign-value (pictural surplus-value), this pictural production brings down its commodity value, its money-signification, the value to which, as representation, sign, reproduction and expression of a subjective real, painting attached itself; just as money is the sign of a commodity, a production, a labour that it obliterates, the sign of its hidden reproduction.

10.2 Insofar as the subject, the sign, meaning and representation fall radically, painting as sign and meaning bypasses its relation to capitalist economy, subverts it by openly reproducing its mode of production and exchange.

10.3 Insofar as painting is no longer a sign of value, a paper to be cashed in, it acquires a dimension other than that of a space of visual recognition, of representation or relation; it is itself the site of exchange as product of a social labour (painting) exposing itself to an equivalent labour (reading) and not subject to exchange. The value of painting here simply becomes the unveiling of its relation of production (painting–reading). (At this point, the problem is not that everyone can make a painting – 'do-it-yourself', ready-made, or multiple works are revealed to be diversionary operations, tactics of marketing or censorship – but that everyone can perform the painting–reading operation, everyone can read.)

11 This theoretical practice, of which we are the 'practitioners' and not the 'visionaries', plays painting as a body in the space wherein that body is worked upon; a body that affects us by its play and which we affect by playing it according to its rules.

> The artist is only a vessel of sensations, a brain, a recording machine.
>
> (Cézanne, *Letters*)

11.1 This confrontation of two bodies in space produces a discharge, a discharge of colours affecting the rules that transfer and inform them.

11.2 The painting-effect is the production of a hollow volume that is the site of a dialectical exchange, the realization of an encounter within the logical and unmotivated space of matter, of pictural matter.

11.3 The chromatic play is the matter of exchange and its transformation, opening up the possibility of the social inscription of the body in and through a matter that has been thought, that has been made dialectical.

12 A painting that exposes its material production, develops the pictural body through colours, lays bare the mechanical operations it provokes in a working upon the body that produces them, upon the thought that produces them; the work of history that it ceaselessly deconstructs and transforms: measureless painting of colours which allows us to become, voiceless.

Translated by Roland-François Lack

Notes

1 [This article was published in *Tel Quel*, 41 (1970), where it accompanied the first part of Derrida's 'The Double Session', an article by Jean-Louis Schefer on 'Representative Systems', an article by Roman Jakobson, and an excerpt from the work of Maurice Roche, thus seeming to focus on the articulation of the economies of writing and of the image.]

2 Marx–Engels, *The German Ideology*, ed. and trans. C. J. Arthur (London, Lawrence and Wishart, 1970), 59; K.S. Malevich, *Essays on Art 1915–1933*, vol. 1 ed. T. Andersen, trans. X. Glowacki-Prus (London, Rapp and Whiting, 1969), 120; Jacques Derrida, *Of Grammatology*, trans. G.C. Spivak (Baltimore, Johns Hopkins University Press, 1976), 214.

3 Hegel, *Logic*, cited by V.I. Lenin, 'Conspectus of Hegel's *Science of Logic*', in *Philosophical Notebooks*, vol. 38 of *Collected Works* (London/Moscow, Lawrence and Wishart/Foreign Languages Publishing House, 1961), 151. [We have replaced the word 'appearance' from the English translation with the word 'phenomena' used by Devade.]

4 Hegel, in ibid., 159, 160.

5 Ibid., 190.

6 Joachim Gasquet, *Cézanne: A Memoir with Conversations* (London, Thames & Hudson, 1991), 162, 161.

7 Ibid.

8 Mikhail Larionov and Natalya Goncharova, 'Rayonnists and Futurists: A Manifesto, 1913', in John E. Bowlt (ed.), *Russian Art of the Avant-Garde: Theory and Criticism* (London, Thames & Hudson, 1988 [1976]), 91.

9 Lenin, 'Conspectus', 145.

10 J. Derrida, *Edmund Hussert's Origin of Geometry: An Introduction*, trans. J. P. Leavey (New York, Hayes, 1978), 131.

11 Lenin, 'Conspectus', 161–2.

12 Matisse, letter to Alexandre Romm (January 1934), in *Matisse Peinture, Sculpture, Dessins, Correspondance* (Moscow/Leningrad, 1969).

10

HEAVENLY GLORY[1]

Marcelin Pleynet

to K.M and F.T

if she plays naked
>> *nubile nubilious*
>> *it's for him*
>> *it's that he wants her to show him*
>> *and show him nude*

she: with a tit (without it)
> *she has*
>> *she hasn't*
>>> *i have*
> *i do not know*
>> *i know*
>>> *she says it's god*

and if i say
> *i look on her as a nay*
>> *saying you see god and your mother*

> *'heaven play naked for you'*
> *'heaven play naked with my brother'*

with it
> *she is my brother*
>> *with my brother she has it*

he has his mother
> *he has my mother*
> *my mother has him*
> *naked it is the she she shows*
>>>> *the without it*
>>>>> *she plays there*

in the groin
            in the scene of love and hate
where sow to say
                sough mother-sear
                    good day my dear
                my mother-son
his argument amounts to this
                we find ourselves in this nothing there
                                        bent over you
                                        bent over nothing
she loves him
                there she loves him
                for my double
                she is her let her
                plus her a
                less my a
                my a my bone
                river without er
                                s river without water
                at home
                    to you
                i show her and see her
            come in my he
            come in my sheaf

    come in my mouth
    come in my law
                    my caressant
                    my poplar
                    my rondines
                    my swallow
heaven in the loins and on the you
                        on the starred one
        if she shows you
                if you ask her
                        holy drunkenness
                son's mother
                who is in she even what i am there
                heavy
most venerable
most honoured
            'I am compelled to tell you that it is not possible to take upon oneself
                the sentiment calling for what you understand'

199

she too wants to be my brother my son
    she dreamt she says
      god's woman   god's mother   god's name

if she plays naked
            nubilious mother
                because i write god's name
we lunch
    she tells she had this dream of a naked son
    and that he writes for her and thinks
    i think in her
    i think of you

she comes to me because i write god's name
                there where i write the has it
    sea of laughter
          behind the misty ocean
                   i dream
                 we eat

i write the place
       behind the ocean mother
       son's mother
       pearl and nimbus
          light of years
    she tells me all in the eyes
          she looks at me at all
    he is born the divine child
            in the hard of her at all
    'you come to bed'
          she has me from him: i hear
    hair   fork

                   'come in my fork
                   in play'
i love in play
      son's god mother's brother
      mother of gods
      father in play
      hours and edges
jongleurs troubadours
       c'una non sai loinhdan ni vezina
       si vol amor vas vos ne si aclina
         soul-cheats
       sham displayer

200

to the woman
to the mother

lovers loving in the river her jewel
her gold her cheek her o her a
mother marry
sea shored
at the he simulating water
at the i
'simile qui con simile e sepolto'
liey est magie

little mover
she comes to me
she is a friend's wife
her father is king
your father is dead
i know how to come she says
and i know that come lies
i am nature and appetite
you left me   i am belief
you left me
and released me

i am membrance
i am luna

'he is sweet as the birds that go to the temple'
sow am i
he is silken my friend
i am the virgin the temple and the life
i am the pillar
he is the dove
he is my blessed in heaven
i am space
he is the goad
i am the mere
and he is water

et del parlar materno
'ieu sui Arnaut que plor et vau cantan'
it's against him
beaten telling
it's for him he wants her to show it
and wants me
as i want it
thing of has it

snow and dew
fireless burning non rispose nulla
when all come naked to me for him
and all naked the night towards me
and he towards me lure all naked
once more you confide
dream-fear
fruit of Judaea

and he hidden
where she glistens

they have not finished moaning
i have not finished moaning
were i body
madonna si devoto
com'esser posso piu
i moan it
wandering in dream
to you i see her fruit in dream
'young he fought against his father
for this lady then'
as in dying
in slumber picking
the same flowers
the same herbs
in the same herbal
part of the same
glutton of the same
and of the beloved
singing feeling without her listening
in time's gold
truthless
scent of lure
mother of heaven
mother-work

i make
I
earth
vault of heaven
clamour-wall
wall of writ
to know without knowing
verily
i say

or   read   your   no
litany)

Translated by Jacqueline Lesschaeve and Henry Nathan

Note

1   [The French text of this poem appeared originally in *Tel Quel*, 71–3 (1977), the special issue on the US, and was included in Pleynet's *Rime* (Paris, Seuil, 1981). This translation by Jacqueline Lesschaeve and Henry Nathan appeared in *Tel Quel* 77 (Autumn 1978), one of only two translations into English to appear in the review, the other of which, from Sollers's *Paradis*, translated by Carl R. Lovitt, is also included here.]

11

THETIC 'MADNESS'[1]

Marcelin Pleynet

We know that the unconscious castration complex has the
function of a knot.

(J. Lacan[2])

I could begin: this is not my place, this is the place I do not occupy, or even:
I am not in my place, I occupy the place I don't occupy. But what place?
What place will poetic language not occupy at a conference on psychoanalysis?[3] And since one has to mark a date, I mean mark out a before and an
after, unpick the arrangement of this before and after, as this is where we
have to start in order to recognize what is at stake in psychoanalysis, I begin
by marking that place impossible to occupy, that place which is always occupied and impossible to occupy, the place of language. That's why it occupies
me. I would like in what follows to remain there, in my place, that is to say:
everywhere [*partout*] and nowhere [*nulle part*]. It is this nowhere [*nulle part*],
which could only be a null share [*part nulle*], which I would like to question
here. Here, under the theme 'sexuality and politics' as well, since it will be
necessary to define something of the organization of the city which concerns
psychoanalysis, and . . . language.

In *Memories, Dreams, Reflections*, Jung recalls a conversation he had with
Freud:

> I can still recall vividly how Freud said to me: 'My dear Jung,
> promise me never to abandon the sexual theory. That is the most
> essential thing of all. You see, we have to make a dogma of it, an
> unshakable bulwark.' He said that to me with great emotion, in the
> tone of a father saying, 'And promise me this one thing, my dear
> son: that you will go to church every Sunday.' In some astonish-
> ment, I asked him: 'A bulwark – against what?' To which he
> replied, 'Against the black tide of mud' – and here he hesitated a
> moment, and then added, 'occultism.'[4]

I will spare you Jung's commentary, and give you only his first free association: something to do with the church, dogma and religion is in question in the Freudian theory of sexuality. But Freud does not speak explicitly about religion, but of occultism – of the occultism (which can also become a question for psychoanalysis, Jung knows something about this) whose definition, according to Freud, we can glean from a reading of the *New Introductory Lectures on Psychoanalysis*, and which is not to be confused with how he describes religion, dogma and the church. It is in the space between religion and occultism that analytic discourse marks itself out, historically, relative to the question of the process constituting the relation of the subject to the law. Freud links, initially and interminably, the virtualities of analysis to the crisis of the religious institution: 'In our time, neurosis replaces the cloister to which all those who were disappointed with life and too weak to bear it used to retire' – this crisis is evidently also that of any institution. If the mediating organization of religion fails, in the relation of the subject to the law, any place becomes untenable, the crisis begins, henceforth history can only be its symptom. The question is opened: what is at stake in institutions? What is at stake in the institutional subject? What is at stake in the subject and its religious mediation to the law? What symptom, what truth, manifests the constancy of this trinity: law, religion, subject, the constancy of the organization of this three in one which, whatever its ordering (Father, Son, Holy Spirit), Georges Dumézil finds at the origin of the structure of Indo-European institutions: a priest, a hero, a king (law-maker)? A structure developed in monotheistic organization: Moses, Akhnaten, the people of Israel. An institutional model from which woman is excluded, even if femininity finds its place alongside the most replaceable instance: Moses, the priest, religion, the Holy Spirit, if, in this three in one, any of the instances is completely replaceable. What a strange Holy Family maintained by the law, bound together by the priest and realized by the hero! Not one of the representatives can be excluded from it since they form one social body, but how can the hero become hero without the support of the law and how can the law maintain itself without the binding of religion? While the three 'persons' are found within the church, neither the hero nor the law can represent religion.

From 1912 to 1939, from *Totem and Taboo* to his last work *Moses and Monotheism*, Freud continues to insist on the fact that religion arises from that which binds and legislates among the sons: the murder of the father. Murder of the father from which the moral and social order is sketched out, the moral order sublimating the will of the dead father, the social order tending to maintain the new order inaugurated by this sublimation – an order (legislation) without which a return to an anterior state (to murder) would become inevitable. An order, that is, in which the renunciation of the drives supposed by the equality of rights no longer acts as an obstacle to the murderous struggle for the possession of the women, sisters or mothers. It is at this point, writes Freud, that social laws become distinct and separate from other laws, which, it should be underlined, come directly from religion. A distinction whereby they exist only through being bound to what works within them, and exist only in this binding; to the extent that both have their basis in the murder of the father, and are more or less directly linked to the unconscious: society is built on a common crime. It is obviously this 'more or less' which will effect both separation and link. If the moral laws which come directly from religion remain associated with the originary murder, the laws called upon to maintain the new social order, supposed by the henceforth metaphysical character of interdiction (an interdiction which is, we should not forget, the incest taboo), tend, within the very function of the economy of conservation and under the pressure of diverse economic factors, to separate themselves from what determines them: the will of the father. But it is clear that for one and the other the subject is totally implicated, and for him the separation can only bind. A binding which in the organization of the passage from the murder of the father to its repression attaches the tribe to the mother, to matriarchy, and then, I suppose, through another displacement of the repression, to patriarchy.

The evolution implied by the economy of the social form determined by religious repression tends from the origin towards a separation with the forms of repression, but in a quantity–quality relation. A relation of the quantity of the investments in play to the quality of the forms of repression – with the quality which these forms have of binding economic investments. Moral and religious structures follow the 'evolution' of social laws according to a mode of separation which variously binds the subject to the investments implied by the new social structure. There we have, in a sense, in the binding effected by separation, the schema of a principle of civilization. Suppose that the form of repression is too binding, separation is accentuated, becomes a symptom, and puts the religious structure in question; suppose that it is not binding enough and the social structure regresses towards stages anterior to the form of repression; a situation neither too binding, nor not binding enough will guarantee social and religious stagnation. If one considers Christianity as a crisis internal to Judaism, it is easy to see how this crisis arises from the encounter between Jewish peoples and the Mediterranean world, from the conjunction of two civilizations, one continually in crisis through structures of repression which are too binding, the other in crisis through the insufficiently binding character of its religious dogmas. The passage from Judaism to Christianity (from the religion of the Father to that of the Son), and what we know of the compromises involved, bears out well enough that what was needed was a displacement of the moral law in relation to the social law – and this through an internal transformation of their relation: repression of guilt and fixation (fascination and terror) before whoever carries its symbolic trace. The community of sons develops, unites, binds itself with an implicit avowal: they, the others, the Jews, have

killed God. The initial interdiction is maintained but the new social structure is in this instance bound to an implicit avowal in the form of a
disavowal. Freud translates the whole text of the accusation that the
Christians bring against the Jews as follows: 'You will not *admit* that you
murdered God. . . . We did the same thing, to be sure, but we have *admitted*
it and since then we have been absolved.'[5] From moral laws to social laws a
new dialogue, a new discourse, is engaged, that of guilt and avowal. Avowal
incarnates the father in the son and disincarnates the father, which makes the
son effective (but not a father) in definitively stopping up the question of the
interdiction with what remains. The avowal, the religion of the son, in liberating certain affects of the feeling of guilt, adapts and thus binds the
interdiction to the conditions of the development of the social order which
can only control the forces in question thanks to this binding. At this point
there appears, in full clarity, the entry into the schema of representation and
the composition of spirituality in active life. New structures of separation
and binding, new religious and social forms, new discourses, but also, let us
not forget, new language. From the religion of Aton to the Judaic religion to
the Christian religion, the forms of the social link in the course of transformation change their language. Egyptian, Hebrew, Greek: at the level of
what occupies us here every new discourse entails a new language, since from
religious to social structure it is language which is bound. Thus, of the sons
of Noah building their city, Yahweh says: 'Here they are, one people with a
single language, and now they have started to do this; henceforward nothing
they have a mind to do will be beyond their reach.'[6] In the mediation
between the sublimation of the will of the father and the new order supposed
by this sublimation, the sons will never cease to successively have recourse to
a new language, with a diverse mode of interpretation, variously bound.

The question which opens today, and by today I mean since just over half
a century ago: religious crisis, crisis of institutions, crisis of the subject, is to
be approached from the side of the binding order of religion. For our
purposes, the following partition is in play: *religion of the father* – guilt –
repression of the initial murder, *religion of the son* – avowal – repression of the
father – definitive burying of the question of the inaugural murder –
occultism. Freud proposes on this subject that,

> with the strength which it derived from the course of historical
> truth, this new faith overthrew every obstacle. The blissful sense of
> being chosen was replaced by the liberating sense of redemption.
> But the fact of the parricide, in returning to the memory of
> mankind, had to overcome greater resistances than the other fact,
> which had constituted the subject-matter of monotheism.[7]

What is the status, today, of what binds the tribe: the murder of the father?
Where does the dead father of religion hold these bonds? It is usually

thought that this question of the binding of the moral law in the constitution of the social structure is above all a question of the place of the hero, the
subject – it is in these bonds that, in whatever light one considers the question, the place of the subject figures in all religions: 'A net is stretched over
all living beings', writes Rabbi Aquiba. In the Old Testament the bond is at
the same time the fact of God and of death, like god death binds, and god
binds to death. We are never as close to the truth of the relation that the
hero entertains with his god than when he speaks of the binds which unite
them: 'I tell you, God himself has put me in the wrong, he has drawn the
net around me.'[8] Binding and unbinding God, master of the relation
between the moral law and social structure: master of bonds. What we find
here bears upon the ambivalence of the relations with the father, with the
divine. To bind is as much the fact of God as of the Devil, binding belongs
to the 'sacred', to *sacer*, to the good as to the bad, to the saintly as much as to
the damned. As the Latin dictionary tells us: the guilty party consecrated to
the infernal gods is *sacer* (*sacer esto*), whence the meaning of 'criminal' (*auri
sacra fames*). In the New Testament Christ unbinds what Satan has bound:
'And here is this woman, a daughter of Abraham, who has been kept pris-
oner by Satan for eighteen long years; was it wrong for her to be freed from
her bonds on the Sabbath?'[9] The obligation determined by repression, the
obligation towards the god which (*uoti sponsio qua obligamur deo*) originally
entailed the wearing of a material bond, constitutes the very bond which
founds religion – *religio*, which certain authors attach (if I may) to *religare*,
which properly speaking would mean: 'the fact of binding oneself in relation
to the gods'. An etymology which is to be found in Lucretius at the very
same point where he is praising the qualities of his poem: 'This is my reward
for teaching on these lofty topics, for struggling to loose men's minds from
the tight knots of superstition and shedding on dark corners the bright
beams of my song . . .'[10] (*religionum anumum nodis exsoluere . . .* where he
derives *religio* from *religare*). Moreover, on this question we also find the
comparison that, on Ernest Jones's suggestion, Freud establishes between
Christ and the god Mitra, whose cult will contest with Christianity for a
time. And it is precisely on this point that if we follow Freud's remarks on
the origin of Judaic monotheism, that is, on the religion of Aton and the
reign of Akhnaten, around 1346 BC, it must be specified that the god Mitra
(whose name appears at the head of the list of Aryan gods on a document
from the fourteenth century BC) is contemporary with the religion of Moses,
and perhaps even older, inasmuch as Antoine Meillet interprets and proposes
to define 'the Indo-Iranian God *Mitra* as the Contract personified', inasmuch
as Dumézil links the word *mitra* to the root *mei*, to exchange, and groups it,
across the whole Indo-European domain, to other words with nuances as
diverse as the Sanskrit *meyate* (he exchanges), the latin *munus* (gift, service
rendered, obligation, duty), to the old Slav *mêna* (change, exchange,
contract). Dumézil writes: 'This word *mitra* must have originally denoted

the means or the agent of operations of the *potlatch* type – in other words, of "obligatory exchanges of gifts." '[11] Mitra is described as the one who 'must give back gift for gift'.[12] Exchange, obligation, contract, the word evolves until it signifies 'friendship'. We are still close to the root of *religio* and *religare*, and even more so to the extent that the god Mitra, also the god who binds, is associated under the ambivalent form of the sacred, as a double and in opposition, to the god Varuna, whose name has been interpreted as signifying the faculty of binding (Indo-European root *uer-skr. varatra*: belt, rope); he is moreover represented as holding a rope in his hand, a bond through which religion is founded, and in the ceremonies which concern him, 'everything which binds, starting with knots, is called Varunian'. Etymology, on the one hand, and the most archaic religious forms, on the other, allow us, it is clear, to run through, verify and interpret across a range of languages the constitution of one of the most pregnant symbolic investments that exists. If it is indeed the case that in the sinuous itinerary in which we are engaged this binding can take the function of interpretation.

On the question of the subject and institutions, the role of religion, of its separating and binding function, I can hardly be assured at the end of this itinerary by the notion that it is essentially a question of a bond, and more precisely of a rope. Should we speak of a rope in the house of the hanged man? However, everything which I have interrogated as a model of investment leads me back inexorably to this braid in which I am tied up, to this function of the psychic apparatus which Freud tells us is one of the oldest and most important, which consists in binding. Does not the knotted rope figure as one of the oldest systems of notation? The bond which is knotted prepares and consolidates the net of language thrown over what is guarded by the will of the father (access to the mother, to the sisters, to the women), and it is for this reason that it is ambivalent, sacred. The binding god (Varuna)

> is assuredly 'the terrible'; and as a result of his magic, of his *maya* as an *asura*, thanks to which, omnipresent as he is, he has the power of immediate comprehension and action everywhere and over everything, and thanks to which he also creates and modifies forms and makes the 'laws of nature' as well as their 'exceptions'.

The weapons of this magic 'are most often specifically in the form of whips, knots, material or figural bonds.'[13] It remains that if all this underlines the ambivalence of the sacred, which participates in the double will of the law and watches over the harvest, it does not for all that explain why the moral law (*religio–religare*) is crystallized through it in the symbolic representation of the rope and the knot; and what of the symbolic production of language of humanity is bound in this bond?

Bonds, nets, knots, rope and weaving: what is it that is hidden there which traces and guards the first note and unfolds across history, without delay, the shimmering tissue of languages? But if language is the place where this is hidden, why not interrogate it? What do we know of the moral sense which does not depend on, which does not engage the ubiquity of the symbolic and the law? And according to this order, what associations can we yet expect from these bonds? If, starting from the question of the institution and the relations that the subject entertains with religion and with the law, we encounter the symbolic representation of the bond, if we follow it up to its fixation as of the most archaic models for writing, the notation, perhaps initially numerical, of the knotted rope, should we conclude that since it is language itself which is knotted, that we cannot therefore unknot ourselves in language, undo our place in language? This applies without doubt to an apparatus which entertains extremely close relations with language, but doesn't this type of notation already participate itself in the diversity of languages, and in the activity which it supposes, is it not only a phase of a symbolic investment (a phrase) which precisely has to be unknotted? That which binds, is knotted, and is the note of a debt (that is, the gift or *potlatch*), obligation, the sacerdotal function (the relation of any subject to religion), is the rope, the braided fibre, the weave. The bond is bound and woven and in binding it weaves. Among the Dogons the word is assimilated to weaving. And are we not at this point on the threshold of Freudian interpretation when we learn that the Dogons say that: 'the foundation of the woman's corn loft is like the word of weaving'?[14] Freud suggests that woman discovered the technique of the weave which binds:

> It seems that women have made few contributions to the discoveries and inventions in the history of civilization; there is, however, one technique which they may have invented – that of plaiting and weaving. If that is so, we should be tempted to guess the unconscious motive for the achievement. Nature herself would seem to have given the model which this achievement imitates by causing the growth at maturity of the pubic hair that conceals the genitals. The step that remained to be taken lay in making the threads adhere to one another, while on the body they stick into the skin and are only matted together.[15]

Threads, fibres, in effect, and this is the point I wanted to make, concerning the possible meaning held by the bond. If I follow the dictionary, at *fibre* I obtain:

> lat. *fibra*. Each of the thin and flexible filaments which, grouped into bundles, constitute certain animal, mineral or vegetal substances . . . techn. *textile fibres* (wool, hair, silk) . . .

and from the Latin *fibra*:

> filament of roots, fibre, vein; in the language of the oracles, 'divi-
> sion of the liver, lobe', then the 'liver' itself, and by extension
> 'entrails', the first meaning could have been 'cleft', cf. *fibras radicum*,
> Cic. Tusc, 3,13 which must refer to the place where the root divides
> to give birth to other roots; this sense of 'cleft' is also in Pliny . . . [16]

This investigation is one in which nearly everything is worthy of more
detailed attention, starting from the presence of the word *fibra* in the
language of the oracles (those which cause things to grow through interpretation) to signify the 'liver' [*le foie*], right up to this initial meaning situated
at the place where the root divides to give birth to other roots, between the
legs where nature caused hair to grow on the genital organs, hair which
masks and reveals the cleft in that place where the little boy cannot believe
that the little girl does not also have one, and calms himself saying that it's
still *small*, where the little girl cannot believe that it will not grow. This
place where faith [*la foi*] is knotted in a woven lack, which notes and which
counts, net of language thrown over the cleft, net of the cleft got from the
dead father: religion, language of the subject knotted at the cortex, loose
tissue even so of the founding repression and the double law, of knowledge
and any occupied place. 'With this net bind and destroy' proclaims an
Assyrian incantation; and the Babylonian poem of creation: 'They were
thrown into nets, held in the hoop nets, were put into caverns.' Imagine this
braided 'tress', this lurking distress, constructing civilizations, history and
all the stories we are all familiar with.

The study which Freud devoted to Michelangelo's Moses (which as we
know appeared without the author's name) has been much commented
upon, as well as the study within that volume of the reciprocal relation of
the tablets of the law and the right hand and the beard of the patriarch in
Michelangelo's iconography. Might one not, in the perspective of the above,
and also taking into account the appendix to the study added by Freud in
1927,[17] call attention to the fact that Michelangelo's statue of Moses was
destined for a tomb (that of a pope, a humanist *papa*, a man of action particularly interested in power) – that Moses sits upon the tomb, and dare I say is
in his place, the place of death (– doesn't Michelangelo write: 'I realize I
have wasted my youth, tied to this tomb'[18]?) – that Michelangelo never
finished this tomb, that it remains unfinished and that the relation of the
tablets of the law to the arm, to the hand in the beard, outside the characters
and the ideas that the Old Testament as well as its interpreters attribute to
the patriarch, are justified by the hidden place which the dead father, the
dead *papa*, occupies in the artist's will: Moses as guardian behind his beard
of the *tomb* to which Michelangelo is bound (we know that Pope Julius II
commissioned his tomb in 1505, eight years before his death). Should we

conclude that there is always and already a death, binding the tombs where the dead will come to take their place? Do women know something of this empty place which must be occupied? What kind of woven matter is the statue (beard covering the mouth of Michelangelo's, or someone else's, Moses – the slaves and the so-called figures of *the night* on the same tomb); what language, sealed in the law which the artist of the Renaissance already knows he is only able to hold on to with his elbow? The form, the stopper of a generation and, moreover, a language and an accounting of the sublime, accumulated fetishes to which man binds himself as a slave to meaning, at any price (believing it to be a member, a limb, or a hiding place), slave also to a knowledge which wants to know nothing of it. There and nowhere – place of the null share – every time the bond (which is always of the father) institutes a language, only one (which means: the diversity of languages) in place of what has no place. The dominated place where the father binds the diversity of languages is the place without language; it is in language (the language of dreams, if you like) that the open place of the question of the free exchange of the place and of the object of the place takes place. At this point, resort, accident, formation of the bond, return of the repressed: the unity of language appeals to the analyst who treats much as the poet deals with the null diversity of languages. A double movement of interpretation, posing a thesis and in its infinity precipitating the viscera to the fixed heavens, carried away at any moment to nothing. Go and see for yourselves if you don't want to believe me. I say that nothing or something is always lacking. Since these woven lacks are born from what hides and reveals, as we know, and the rest stacks up again from that: I am there in not being there and from being there I am not.

Translated by Patrick ffrench

Notes

1 [This article originated at an International Conference in Milan, in 1975, on the subject 'Sexuality and Politics', organized by Armando Verdiglione, also featuring contributions by Sollers, Kristeva, Serge Leclaire, and others. It was published in *Tel Quel*, 65 (Spring 1976), and subsequently in Pleynet's *Art et littérature* (Paris, Seuil, 1977).]

2 J. Lacan, *Ecrits: A Selection*, trans. A. Sheridan (London, Tavistock, 1977), 281.

3 Milan, November 1975; International Congress of Psychoanalysis, 'Sexuality and Politics'.

4 C.G. Jung, *Memories, Dreams, Reflections*, ed. A. Jaffé, trans. R. and C. Winston (London, Fontana, 1961), 173.

5 S. Freud, *Moses and Monotheism*, The Pelican Freud Library, *13*, ed. A. Dickson, trans. J. Strachey (Harmondsworth, Penguin, 1985), 334.

6 Genesis, 11, ii: 6–8.

7 Freud, *Moses and Monotheism*, 384–5.

8 Job, 19: 6.

9 Luke, 13: 16. Cf. also when he gives the *keys* to Peter: 'I will give you the keys of the kingdom of heaven; what you forbid on earth shall be forbidden in heaven . . . ' Matthew 16: 19.

10 Lucretius, *On the Nature of the Universe*, trans. R. Latham (Harmondsworth, Penguin, 1951), 54.

11 G. Dumézil, *Mitra Varuna: An Essay on Two Indo-European Representations of Sovereignty* (New York, Zone Books, 1988), 69.

12 Ibid., 70.

13 Ibid., 67 [translation adapted].

14 G. Calame-Griaule, *Words and the Dogon World*, trans. D. LaPin (Philadelphia, Institute for the Study of Human Issues, 1986).

15 S. Freud, *New Lectures on Psychoanalysis*, *Pelican Freud Library 2*, ed. J. Strachey and A. Richards, trans. J. Strachey (Harmondsworth, Penguin, 1973), 166–7.

16 A. Ernout and A. Meillet, *Dictionnaire étymologique de la langue latine* (Paris, Klinksieck, 1967).

17 S. Freud, 'Postscript', in J. Strachey (ed. and trans.), *The Standard Edition of the Complete Psychological Works of Sigmund Freud*, vol. XIII (London, Hogarth Press, 1955), 237–8.

18 Michelangelo, Letter of 1542.

12

THE AMERICAN BODY

Notes on the new experimental theatre[1]

Guy Scarpetta

The 'immanence' of the Americans is undeniable (their being
is within themselves and not beyond).

(Georges Bataille)

The theatre

Where should one stand when writing 'about' the theatre? Which eye,
which ear, on which stage? In which language, which body in which
language – when in any case the theatre itself will perform, move, show,
display itself to the eye and ear, invent its own space, rhythm and bodies –
when in any case it will write its own text from an endlessly transformed
viewpoint, through a body and a language which are not 'on stage', on
display, but which can create scenes for themselves and perform them – and
all this will dance beyond all dances, scream beyond all screams, free up a
thousand spaces and a thousand rhythms, without end . . .

What I wish to suggest here is that it is neither a question of being 'in
front of' the theatre, as a silent or talkative, hallucinated or 'distant' spectator; nor one of being behind or beside the theatre in search of a hidden
secret or mastery. *Across* is a better term, as distinct both from illusory identification and safe 'distanciation' – both within and without, in the position
where writing takes place as *transference*.

A transference where our presence is 'called upon'. In that moment,
theatre for me represents that which provokes and defies language, inviting
it to go beyond the limit of aphasia, beneath which bodies move on stage. A
relief of codes, connections, disconnections – a shifting stratification of
bodies, voices, colours, words, songs, dances and images, forcing the written
text to explore its own dimensions, its 'polyphony', its *play*. Calm zones, *soft
machine**[2] or violent outbursts. Without forgetting that the history of
theatre is *also* the history of its relationship with writing, the way in which

theatre performs writing, integrates it or becomes integrated therein, 'represents' it or reduces it, and confronts itself through writing and through its own elaborate process.

Amongst all these different elements, the main question raised is the passage from aphasia to language, from visual and auditory perception to *meaning*. In one way or another, every effect which the theatre can call upon – display, voyeurism, scopic 'passion', hysteria, fetishization, fragmented bodies, 'motility' – will have to negotiate this passage, regardless of whether the passage is 'processed' theatrically. So writing 'about' the theatre is meaningless unless it tests-records-inscribes this passage (which always involves the question of that *other* passage in the experience of each subject, between 'visual' and 'verbal' representations).

So *repression* is an issue here. Repressed theatre may be seen as pre-symbolic regression, a refuge of sound/colour/movement, an ancient ground where 'perception' and 'representation' are one. Beyond repression lies a new space, which no longer denies time (or death or negation); in other words, a space 'beyond hallucination'.

Writing, here, presupposes such a *crossing*.

The code and its investment

Here in Europe, however, there is no sign whatsoever of any engagement with such an experiment: outdated conventions, academicism, formalism, pedagogical treatment of 'classics', hyper-inhibited or hyper-hysterical bodies, uninspired texts, uninteresting spaces, a general lack of invention and imagination. All of which is sustained by a right-on leftist morality, which is narrow-minded, deaf and blind, and ready to mature into the Official Art of some future regime (already, in many instances, the official art of the present one).

In fact, the theatre carries on as if it had never registered the consequences of the radical break at the beginning of this century with practices dating from the Renaissance.[3] Or rather, as if the theatre had deliberately *reduced* this break to its most 'formal' (and narrowly technical) effects, without in any way taking into account the cultural and ideological disruption which constituted its most significant aspect. Thus any theatrical 'innovation' is condemned to be inscribed in a *tradition* (let us say, schematically, from Brecht to Artaud). A new academicism, undividedly triumphant. A general mood of mummification-sanitization only slightly nuanced by a few *minor* perversions.

The 'Italian-style stage' established its dominance during the Renaissance, linked as it was to the emergence of the code of single-perspective in painting.[4] Thanks to the fiction of the transparent 'fourth wall' as representative illusion, it represented from the outset the subordination of both the signifier to 'narrative' and the semiological 'depth' of theatre to the identificatory trap of univocal meaning (at the same moment in time, on *another scene*, Shakespeare was getting to the sublime 'rub' of power and madness, and was foregrounding its unconscious 'backstage'). The Italian-style stage basically signalled the passage from feudal ideology (religious, symbolist) to bourgeois humanism and reason. The theatre did try to break the mould, at the beginning of this century, with Appia, Craig, Russian playwrights like Meyerhold and the Proletkult, the scenographic experiments of the Bauhaus (Moholy-Nagy) and then more profoundly with Artaud and Brecht – but the break worked at a strictly *formal* level, without really succeeding in reaching the cultural 'decentring', the radical change in thinking which were implied by such a break (in which respect theatre is *way behind* the disruption introduced into modernity by the experiments in breaking out of rhetoric, from Lautréamont to Joyce).

But Brecht and Artaud signified something quite different. For Brecht it was the inscription of dialectics into a signifying process, the foregrounding of the contradictory stage, of 'non-Aristotelian' theatre, of 'theatre for the scientific age' (but Brecht, trapped within the limits of Marxist 'reason' and its impasses, succeeded in little more than 'perverting' the technical means of illusion and identification, without reaching their unconscious mechanisms). As for Artaud, whilst it is clear that his gesture (of which theatre is only one 'opportunity'[5]) directly touched upon the calculation of life and death, the repressed genetic basis of the species, reproduction, the emergence of a new body, the possibility of 'being born otherwise' – it should be noted that his experiments in the transgression of limits and the overcoming of Western 'reason' and the subject forming part of that tradition gradually shifted towards *language* as a symbolic 'ground', following on from the *practical* failure of his theatrical experiments. This went so far as to theatralize language, multiplying it, pluralizing its points of enunciation, injecting into it the pulsional negativity and organic rhythms which it is designed to repress.

It seems clear henceforth that for forty years European theatre has been happy to exploit 'formally' the possibilities opened up by Brecht and Artaud, without ever returning analytically to the break they introduced. Hence the worn-out, repetitive state of the theatre at present, the astonishing stereotyping of academic 'distanciations' and gesticulating hysterias. In other words, the 'Italian-style stage' is *denied* rather than surpassed, precisely in the sense that its unconscious (sexual) *function* remains untouched, unbreached, unanalysed.

Hence the perpetuation of a signifying chain (a 'supplementary' symbolic order) in which the actor is called upon to be a 'sign' or indeed an 'organ'. The imaginary repetition, *ad infinitum*, of the split subject. The hystericization of the actors in the service of the directors' fetishism (in an atmosphere of traumatic denial of sexual differentiation: travesty being the latent truth of all theatrical 'play-acting'). The mechanical flattening-out of bodies and their *dépense*, [expenditure], whereby the frustrated relationship between the actors and directors is resolved (through the infinite conflict of hysteria and mastery) into a desperate *exhibition*, i.e. the search for an illusory *recognition* supposedly to fill up a yawning gap which is never accepted as such. Thus we have a theatre *shot through* with neurosis and perversion. As Lacan remarks: 'To love the truth – even the truth incarnated by the hysteric – is certainly to devote oneself to a form of theatre which, we know, can no longer be anything other than a charity gala.'[6]

It is becoming clearer by the day that no *dépense*, no transgression, may any longer take place *in that place*. What I wish to suggest here is that renewal, linked to another *history* of the code (more relaxed than the breaks of the 1930s), will henceforth come to us, in this field, principally from the United States.

The United States

Let us rapidly outline a few points which will allow us to identify the *specificity* of the current situation in America – and its potential repercussions in the 'theatrical' field.

Firstly, a segmentation and compartmentalization of the social fabric (functioning 'by ghetto', especially noticeable in New York) allows 'zones' of negativity and *dépense* to exist on the margins of the productive and institutional machine (zones in which 'everything is permitted and nothing is possible', as Julia Kristeva puts it). Places of creativity, invention, withdrawal, contestation, spaces for a *different* rhythm and 'way of life'* compared to the official model. One might call it the underground in the 'open air'*. Within the very *play* of the capitalist machine, artistic (for example, theatrical) experimentation can experience the pressure of the existing institutions in a far less oppressive manner than here (in France, where they separate and paralyse any theatrical activity).

Secondly, a mode of sexual organization which is less oppressive and certainly less *religious* than in Europe. A mixture of freedom of circulation, of 'positions' (the official Puritanism, linked 'ethically' to the world of work and business, tolerates areas of *dépense* often linked to religious minorities, Catholic or Jewish) with a certain sexual *deflation* (no doubt linked, contradictorily, to that same Puritanism).

Thirdly, the omnipotence, in spite of everything, of a certain matriarchal 'base' (clinically x-rayed 'in reverse' by Burroughs) allowing for the exploration, through 'aesthetic' experiments, of a whole pre-symbolic field (as if directly plugged into the maternal body) consisting of rhythm, music, space and colour. In the very same place where the access to language, to meaning, and to the symbolization of these experiments seems blocked (with certain exceptions), there is an active proliferation of practices within the 'visual arts'* (painting, theatre, dance): breaking of limits, invention of spaces and

217

rhythms, deviations (voyeurism, exhibitionism) exaggerated to a perverse, quasi-psychotic degree – the vertiginous exploration, in any case, of a 'silent continent'.

Fourthly, the relaxed attitude which we remarked upon above in respect of a 'tradition' which, in Europe, too often bogs us down. Whilst the arbiters of meaning and truth (psychoanalysis, literature) seem virtually absent from the cultural horizon, at least in their radical form, we should nonetheless note a direct, free, immediate 'treatment' of something which, over here, remains bound within a sclerotic ideological straitjacket. Surrealism, for example, seems to have developed into a practical sense of limit-inscription and excess-gesture,[7] which has nothing to do with the precocity and mythological figuration which constitute its derisory posterity over here. All of these remarks determine in part the singularity and the *advance* of American theatre in its recent transformations, compared to the exhaustion of its European counterpart.

American theatrical experience

It does in effect appear difficult to understand what is taking place at the moment in American theatre (the extent and the *stakes* of the transformation) without taking a little time to discuss the history of the code over the last fifteen years, and the divergence this history demonstrates in relation to the exhausted, repetitive character of the development of European theatre during the same period.

Let us go back, therefore, to the beginning of the 'sixties': what seems most clearly symptomatic, of course, is the Living Theater (Julian Beck, Judith Malina). In the Living Theater we can see Artaud's influence (at least the Artaud of The Theatre of the Absurd) with the emphasis placed on the physical, concrete character of the directorial code, the escape from its 'illustrative' function, the rehabilitation of the body and of gesture, the mistrust of rationality, the exploration of theatrical space through its mobile, organic dimension. An aesthetic of excess, of the scream. Then, more or less in concordance with the vast movement of cultural-political contestation in the mid-sixties and the underground 'counter-culture' to which it gave birth, we see an attempt to deal with the question of 'breaking out of the stage' by a mythical, communitarian appeal to the removal of the stage-barrier, the fusion of actors and audience, unmediated *contamination*, etc. The ideological background to all this was a mixture of communitarian and pacifist anarchism and neo-Oriental spirituality. To put it simply: the theatre at that point discovered its utopian, mythical phase, a reflection-symptom (without analysis or 'rethinking') of the general utopianism of the forces of contestation within American society at the time.

But the important point is that *at the same time*, in a more surreptitious, discreet way, and inspired by quite different cultural 'influences' (Cage,

Cunningham), a *different* process was getting under way (which did not 'only' concern the theatre), essentially around the Judson Church Dance Theater, whose whole history from 1962 to 1966 would need to be examined and looked at more closely: the influence of Cage and, beyond that, Duchamp; the relations between theatre, dance and the plastic arts, the role of Yvonne Rainer and Trisha Brown (who was, as few people know, one of the *founders* of the Judson Church Dance Theater); the workshops of Robert Dunn and Ann Halprin; the links between the 'experiments' which took place and the *happening** which was developing at the same time in the margins of a certain impasse in painting; the role of the 'literalist' and neo-structuralist ideologies, etc. In any case, it does appear to be here, in this fertile experimental laboratory, where some of the young participants included Meredith Monk, for example, or Robert Wilson, that the principal features were formed and developed of what would become, after a short assimilatory phase, the renewal of contemporary American theatre. Schematically, the two essential characteristics of what happened at the Judson, through experimentation, confrontation and exchange, we can describe as *dissociation* and *decompartmentalization* of the codes.

Dissociation: basically this involved, for the participants, establishing a *tabula rasa*, returning to the minimal 'cells' whose combination had represented the traditional theatrical code. As John Howell points out,[8] in the *events** at the Judson, the 'theatre' as such was rejected, and it was theatrical 'techniques' which were to be examined and appropriated. An echo of 'minimal' art (Judd, Morris, Stella). Hence the return to simple questions: What is a body, a gesture, a movement, a space? What is a body *in* a space, what body produces what space, what space what body? How may we *break down* a movement *between* body and space? What is theatrical *time*? Are there 'autonomous' codes? How can we foreground them? So a 'minimalist'-style interrogation was begun along with the formation of a scenic 'vocabulary' at the heart of an explosion of theatrical coherence (indeed, it was less a question of producing 'shows' than of identifying the 'atoms' of a process which could break them down: an analytical gesture in action).

Decompartmentalization: this gesture seems effectively inseparable from what was going on, at the same time, in music, cinema, painting. The same search for a 'real time', a coincidence between the time of expression and the time of representation; in other words, 'immanence' and *refusal of any realm beyond process*. This means we can relate the theatrical and choreographic 'minimalization' of the Judson Church with the practice of the 'shaped canvas'* in painting, Michael Snow's research into the space–time relationship in cinema, where the movement of the camera becomes the *subject* of the film (*La Région centrale*), or the research into musical *time* based on the reversal of the traditional notes–rhythm relationship (Philip Glass), etc. It is the period when Richard Foreman wrote a famous article on 'Glass and Snow', when even Robbe-Grillet's 'literalism' may be integrated into this broad movement. In 1966, Yvonne Rainer spoke of a 'close correspondence between the parallel developments in dance and the plastic arts'. The watchword, significantly, is 'structure as subject'.* The confrontation of different codes based on a common literal demystification: languages no longer 'express', they rather *explore themselves*, starting with their basic elements, which are isolated and utilized without recourse to any arbitrary 'choice'.

All of which may of course be seen as 'formalism' and repression of the question of the subject and of the 'irrational' at work within these practices. It is clear, however, that this formalism never became bogged down in formulas and stereotypes, that new spaces were created, a different, 'atomic', divided *perception* was introduced, subjects and bodies were thereby transformed, finding a new, experimental, reinvigorating dimension – and that all this was not without consequence in the later development of American theatre, including its 'overcoming' of formalism.

Amongst all the 'performances' I have seen recently, it is the work of Trisha Brown which no doubt best encapsulates the principles, perspectives and discoveries coming out of the Judson Church. The exploration of new dimensions: *Roof Dance*, a piece taking place on the roofs of fifteen 'blocks'* in Manhattan (an 'all over'* gesturality, questioning the space between bodies, the effect produced by their distancing, and preventing any unifying, centred point of view) *Walking on the Wall*: an experiment in horizontal dance (bodies stretched out on the floor or hanging perpendicularly from the columns of a loft*); other pieces where the dance is developed from arbitrarily imposed 'limits' (a steel bar held fifty centimetres from the ground by two dancers, around which the dance takes place; or fictional 'cubes' indicating the dance space with the dancers 'inhabiting' the surfaces of the cubes, and with repetitions, echoes and permutations between the surfaces). The infinite combinations of the dance's *dépense* (generally made up of 'simple' movements, jumps, twists, off-balance gestures) takes place not so much 'against' the limits of a rhetoric as developed *out of* an arbitrarily chosen pattern (the dance precisely foregrounding and 'denouncing' this arbitrary aspect). Movements 'continuing' whilst bodies are carried by 'manipulators' or placed from the outside in sitting or lying positions, etc. What Trisha Brown's choreography shows us (in a powerful and disturbingly effective way) is that the *limit* (the law) is not that which determines or subjugates the dance (the *dépense*), but that which engenders it: the distance between the internal rhythm of the bodies and the external pattern of figures eventually disappears, in the immediacy of the movement which, by making the dance follow an abstract combination, questions negatively any traditional dance aesthetic and any illusions that the ('animated' or 'inspired') body might be anything other than a certain movement in a certain space. That a genuine beauty should emerge from this cold, almost mathematical aesthetic (a 'beauty' born out of the disorientation and unbalancing of classic dance space) is not the least significant paradox of such an experiment.

In the same 'vein' of experimentation as we find at the Judson Church, we could also cite a certain number of 'performances', often solos, which one can see almost anywhere in Manhattan (a very significant development) and which each in their own way examine the 'basic cells' of what *used to* constitute the theatre. Thus Scott Burton's 'Behavior Tableaux', a few of which I saw in April 1976 in the auditorium of the Guggenheim Museum: two bodies move in silence, extremely slowly, on a stage far removed from the spectators, performing very simple representational gestures (walking, sitting down, raising an arm, crossing paths, etc.), the effect of 'strangeness' stemming from the specific temporality of the performance (as if the space, in its withdrawal, created its own time) and from the long moments of complete darkness which periodically punctuate, like a hollow, the unfolding of the piece). All of this in complete, blank silence. A combination of the most *abstract* gestures and real, 'concrete' presence, precisely at the point where there is nothing left to 'represent' (as Linda Shearer remarks, 'just as the distance maintains physical formality, the extended and unnatural duration of the action strains the dramatic accessibility'). Another bodily perception seems to emerge, occasionally reminiscent of the dilations, distortions or 'losses' of time produced by an LSD *trip** – but without any of the 'expansiveness' or irrationality: something like the cold, sober, immediate, detached hallucinatory relief born out of the 'minimal' exploration of scenic gesturality and temporality.

Amongst many possible examples, we could also mention the work of Connie Beckley insofar as it represents a certain experimental continuity in relation to what was going on fifteen years earlier, even though it is no longer part of the Judson Church generation (Connie Beckley is 25). In many different ways, all her work stems from a desire to be situated between *vision* and *listening*: work based on a 'sketch' taken from the rolls of a pianola (the visual materialization of a piece of music), use of a portable tape-recorder (simultaneous movement, echo, dialogue, counterpoint, crossing-over), movement of the body based on tapes (recorded voices) arranged on the ground like a big keyboard and inserted one by one in three 'tape-machines' hung around the stomachs of the dancers, setting up a *changing mechanical polyphony* which is contrasted with the *stable organic voice* of the woman 'manipulating' the tapes, etc. – something is happening here which is close to visualizing a musical modulation or listening to a dance step. So: an osmosis, an exploration of intermediary zones, a gesture, in other words, of significant *translation* (bringing out the arbitrary nature of any *a priori* delimitation of codes) linked to the emergence of a different perception, de-automated and endlessly *displaced* from one register to another. This work clearly indicates a dimension distinct from minimalist 'stripping down' or a simple decompartmentalization: it is the confrontation of the 'organic' and the 'mechanical' with reciprocal intensities, contamination, splitting of stable 'units' in a *reversible* arrangement; this does not mean,

however, that one cannot legitimately relate this to the fundamental preoccupations of the 'minimalist' period, notably regarding the questioning of
the *limits* of the codes involved and their zones of contact and effects of
reciprocity or *translation*.

The 'minimal' gesture of these *performances* can therefore be seen as the
critical de-composition of the theatrical code, linked to analogous concerns
in other practices, as well as to the exploration of the 'intersections' of the
different languages which it brings into play. The main point seems to me
to be that at this moment the experimental gesture has discovered a
continuation and a new dimension in a 'renewal' of the theatrical code itself
(although the term 'theatre' is no doubt too limiting here given the importance of this new phase which is perhaps more profoundly a 'post-minimal'
reinvention of *opera*): a non-synthetical re-confrontation of codes, an open
dialectic, in which dance, theatre, voice, music, cinema and visual 'tableaux'
are rearticulated differently, 'in progress'.*

The kind of work carried out by the Mabou Mines troupe (director: Lee
Breuer) is quite typical of this continuity and transformation. As Diane
Nadone puts it: 'the process orientation of conceptual art is both Breuer's
method and intention, but Breuer, unlike most conceptual artists, does more
than initiate a process; he weaves the process into and realizes a product.'[9] In
the work of Richard Foreman, for example, we find the same sense of over-
coming/integrating conceptual or minimalist negation, both drawing
strength from its questioning and taking account of the point of no return
that it represents:

> At first I thought I was part of the same movement as certain
> people working in cinema, music, painting and dance. Then I real-
> ized that in a deep sense my structures were different. . . . Let's say
> that minimalism was for me 'therapeutic', like a necessary process of
> clarification. I think I use the same type of *principles* as minimalist
> or post-minimalist art – but I use them in isolated cells of my work.
> The difference is that my work is made up of thousands of these
> cells, and it's their combination and confrontation which provides a
> richness and a complexity within the composition – something
> which doesn't really interest the minimalists. For them, they stick
> to the cells, it's the cell which is the work of art. Whereas the same
> cells treated in a more or less minimalist manner, and then
> combined, brought together, related to each other, that's what
> represents the significance of my work.[10]

I would add to this that the gesture of integration of the basic formal questioning also represents an opening onto the *irrationality* of the code and onto
its articulation with the unconscious and its signifying or intensive 'forces' –
something which minimalism had pushed aside or even repressed.

To return to Mabou Mines, we can identify certain lines of investigation. Work on the 'decomposition' of code-and-actor: 'exterior' manipulation of the actor, from 1971 onwards, in the manner of Bunraku puppets; the same 'story' (*Play*) told and acted out three times by three different actors. Invention of a new space: actors performing *lying down* (*The Red Horse Animation*) organically producing shifting 'designs' on the ground, whilst their movements and gestures on stage produce, through a series of mikes and amps, the rhythmic *sound* of the piece itself; or a piece (*The Lost Ones*) involving little figurines a few centimetres tall which an actor, David Warrilow, manipulates and 'directs' whilst reciting/performing Beckett's text; the 'twisting' effect derives from the fact that the actor can, at certain moments, 'become' one of the characters, thus producing a vertiginous disorientation of space (and of the perception the spectator will have of it): a gesture of contraction and dilation, and a play between 'microcosm' and 'macrocosm' in which the contradiction between *representation* and *mise en scène* is both reinforced and abolished, in a space *without reference points*.

Let us now turn to some of the recent pieces representative of this gesture of reinvention of theatrical space and rearticulation of signification which I indicated above.

Richard Foreman: *The Book Of Delights*

Richard Foreman occupies a particular place within this new theatre: both by the 'multiplicity' of his involvement (Foreman being at once playwright, director, *writer*, decorator, technical 'manipulator' and in some sense actor) and by the fact that he has always dialectically complemented his theatrical activity with theoretical reflections (manifestoes, essays[11]) which occasionally 'break out' of the specifically theatrical field.

1959–1962: School of Dramatic Arts at Yale 1962: member of the writers' group at the Actors' Studio in New York; then influences from 'minimal' art and underground cinema. 1969: foundation of the 'Ontological Hysteric Theater', which staged more than twenty of the forty or so pieces Foreman has written. The Foreman 'style' takes the form of an indirect experimentation, 'in progress', upon the *heterogeneity* of the code (as opposed to any 'realism' or 'expressionism'). The *mise en scène* becomes at once a reading (distortion and 'multiplication', therefore) of a text which is itself fragmentary, broken, shattered. Points of articulation between text and theatre: the stage architecture (the staging of space) and the *tape* on which the text is *recorded* with noises and musical sequences, out of which the staging (the introduction of bodies) may be developed.

A piece by Foreman (such as *The Book of Delights* performed last year at the autumn festival in Paris) may be perceived as the disintegration of *all* the elements of the dramatic art (stories, events, gestures, voices, sounds, lights, movements) until one reaches what he calls the 'smallest components, the basic cells of experience' – the staging consisting of a re-composition bringing together abstraction (the reference to the 'real' exterior-anterior to the code reaches an almost absolute degree of dissolution) and the fore-grounding of the most *material* character of the code itself (as the filmmaker Jonas Mekas puts it: 'it is this mental aspect which is the unique particu-larity of Foreman's theater. . . . He reaches this level by a very formal and very controlled direction; so formal that it attains the opposite of formalism: reality itself').

Hence an aesthetic of constant 'starting from zero' (no stability: what we see and hear is swept away as soon as it is expressed in a productive, genera-tive movement, which exposes a *process* whereby the 'results' – the 'signs' – endlessly disappear). 'I invariably choose', writes Foreman, 'to express how I feel about the preceding moment of generated text. Mostly, how I feel about the energy that generated that preceding moment. Or rather, the relation-ship between that energy and the one out of many possible ways it chose to crystallize itself.'[12] Hence the absence of an axis or even a centre (Foreman says: 'Trying to be centered . . . on the circumference'[13]); incessant, contra-dictory passage from one perception to another developing to the maximum the *virtual* potentialities of the writing and the direction: 'the generated sentence, the gesture that results from fold layed upon fold, the idea that appears as a wrinkle where one line of input stumbles over another – those are the agents of the "act"', 'the irony is in the very *field* of discourse . . . each "item" in that field is now perceived as ironically meaning its opposite, causing its opposite to "be" the minute it is performed.'[14]

This 'irony', born out of a distortion internal to the code rather than a specific treatment of the referent, takes us into a heterogeneity of 'tableaux', without apparent links: thus, in *The Book of Delights*: stripped or 'entangled' bodies, a rotating bed, 'grotesque' scenes, a scene with a 'dentist', a scene with a lesbian prostitute, kidnapping of young girls, dances, cars, the whole thing backed up by a tape playing 'absurd' aphorisms, 'meaningless' frag-ments of conversation, snippets of jazz, etc.: laughter arises from the dissociation itself, which is seemingly gratuitous (playing on the nonsen-sical) but is carried out with the most extreme scenographic *rigour*. This has nothing to do with a new form of the theatre of the absurd or with the inte-gration of the irrational ('chance') into the theatrical performance: Foreman is trying to escape both from a theatre in which the action would be perceived logically, according to a 'rational' causality (one element *leading* to another), and a theatre introducing chance and spontaneity into the process (under the influence of John Cage), where Foreman is suspicious of the appearance of a 'new rhetoric'. 'What interests me', he says, 'is something which evades the satisfaction of hopes by chance, and which escapes any causality. This third way has a relation to the *disjunction* of elements.'[15]

One could no doubt define Foreman's gesture more profoundly as the elaboration of a new form of *distanciation*, which owes as much to the aesthetic of a Gertrude Stein ('syncopation', 'beginning again and again'*) as it does to that of Bertolt Brecht (although Foreman does refer to 'a post-Brechtian alienation technique of theatre, applied to spiritual rather than social concerns' – and staged in April 1976 in New York *The Threepenny Opera*, in a quite new and startling way compared to the conformist academi-cization of Brecht in Europe). Whatever the case may be, numerous 'distanciation' techniques are noticeable in his performances: pre-recorded text which the actors 'pick up' by repeating some of the words in a different rhythm to that of their mechanical 'playing' (autonomization of the voice-code, 'mechanical' segmentation preventing any coincidence of the actor's words with his 'role'); actors 'becoming' technicians during the performance itself; constant reminders, in the text itself, of the theatrical *hic et nunc*; the constant presence of bells and metallic sounds to mark out materially and perceptibly the rhythm of the performance and to mark also its exteriority; an arrangement of wires across the acting-space hampering the actors' move-ments or indicating the lines of their positions in the space and thus making manifest the latent architecture of their movements; perceptible movement of the scenery; without forgetting the presence of Foreman himself sat at a control panel which the spectators can see, like a conductor visibly controll-ing the entrances and exits, the unfolding of the dialogue, the playing of the tape, the rhythmical sounds and the lighting: no possible 'illusion' and an end to the dichotomy between workspace and acting-space, return *on stage* of that which the stage has usually served to obscure: the 'backstage', the work required before the performance.

Thus Foreman *denies* the traditional theatrical code by *accentuating* the conditions of its deployment. The 'tyranny' of the director over the signs which he manipulates is not pushed aside (in the utopian manner) but rather is displayed for what it is, and exposed (this is the decisive reversal he has introduced) as an *element* of the performance (and not as a shameful secret). The actor, contrary to any mythology of 'initiative' or 'improvisation', is clearly displayed as being manipulated, indeed fragmented, within a signi-fying chain, employed as a sign amongst others, including, as Foreman notes himself, the utilization, within the planning of the show, of some of the 'frustration' which necessarily stems from a *thwarted* exhibitionism (Foreman's principal actress, Kate Manheim, told me one day that this type of theatre could bring together narcissistic exhibitionism *and* masochism). The important point here is that such a manipulation-fragmentation of the actor, far from being a hidden 'condition' of the performance, becomes one of its major driving forces (a possible echo of the Bunraku), as if Foreman were operating upon the code a veritable *return of the repressed*, making manifest its latent content.

Which is to say that to some extent there is an issue of *censorship* here as well as the different sexual investments of the code. What seems striking, when one reads the existing commentaries of Foreman's theatre, is that the emphasis is placed uniquely on the *formal* aspects of the experiment (thus, recently, a presentation of Foreman by Robbe-Grillet which clearly tended to *reduce* the dramatic experience to a handful of 'principles' which it supposedly had in common with the *nouveau roman*) to the detriment of what is going on sexually in such a process. No doubt what Foreman is revealing is too *real* (that is to say, too 'mortal' for any formalism) not to be immediately censored by all those who have a vested interest (subjectively as well) in seeing that the questions treated, integrated and raised by the theatre should *remain* essentially 'formal'.

Now Foreman's theatre does precisely 'deal with' censorship; the word 'hysteric' appearing spelt out in the 'title' itself; and the 'sexual' scenes (their articulation on stage prevents them from being reduced to mere fantasies) are clearly visible. So the deep, fundamental point of Foreman's theatre is, once again, to make manifest and *inevitable* the latent sexual content of *any* theatrical gesture: that is, the complicit, 'blocked' (i.e. infinite) relationship between *hysteria* and *obsessionality*, as it is formed in the link between the actor (bodily exhibitionism) and the 'manipulation' (or 'mastery') of the *mise en scène*.

Thus we find in *The Book of Delights*, on one side, the exhibition of stripped and, at a certain point, 'blocked' female bodies; sado-masochistic fantasies; the evocation of the devastating relationship *with the mother*, counter-invested with 'prostitutional' scenes; the recurring thematics of female homosexuality as repressing the relationship to men and to sexual differentiation (all of which might represent the 'hysterical' side of theatre, occasionally reaching its schizophrenic limit: fragmented body, dissolution of language, and the body subjected to primary processes); opposed to this, something we can only define as an *obsessional counter-investment* of this hysterical 'appeal': a detailed, calculated, implacable *ritual* aimed at preventing any markedly noticeable evocation of sexual pleasure [*jouissance*], and 'cutting off' any traumatic appearance of affect, a barrier against anything which might signify sexuality (thus the naked bodies which the 'tyranny' of the direction forces into a 'grotesque', de-eroticized position); or indeed a system of *defence* against anything which might, on stage, represent castration too strongly (this 'obsessive' dimension might also be confronted with its paranoid limit, for example in a fantasy of 'omnipotence' over the signs employed). The *mise en scène* is thus exhibited in a perceptible manner as the repression of a repression.

Let us recall Lacan's comment on the 'relation' of the hysteric to the obsessive: 'one identifies with the spectacle, the other puts one on'. Or indeed:

> For the hysterical subject, for whom the technical term *acting* out takes on its literal meaning since he is acting outside himself, you

have to get him to recognize where his action is situated. For the obsessional neurotic, you have to get him to recognize you in the *spectator, invisible from the stage* [my emphasis], to whom he is united by the mediation of death.[16]

This link, whose theatricality is here indicated by Lacan (and which perhaps *is* theatricality), is inscribed by Foreman and for the first time *laid bare*, bringing out the buried content of any theatrical enterprise. The fact that he should have indicated clearly the element of *resistance* ('ritual as anti-doing', writes Foreman, which is the very definition of obsessionality; or again: 'generate gesture as a defence against input', 'real perception is *resistance* to perception.'[17]) and that he should even have spoken unambiguously of 'staging . . . obsessive theoretical excesses' and employed the term 'hysteric' to describe the very material of his experiment – all this indicates that *something quite different* is at stake here relative to a 'technique of distanciation' or a 'perversion of meaning'. We could say that what such a theatre stages, both dramatically *and* comically, within a pre-determined, enclosed, blocked, and yet infinite space, and through the deliberate suppression of any imago-role and any fetishism (one could say that theatrical fetishism succeeds precisely where Foreman *decides* to 'fail'), is indeed the intricate conflict between an anxious mastery haunted by death and an incessant somatization persecuting that same mastery – a game in which truth and identification are at stake, along with everything which the spectator projects onto it (the only question, which must for now remain unanswered, being *who*, on this stage, is 'pulling the strings').

The fact that this exhibited 'relationship' involves sexual differentiation seems self-evident, in the sense that *any* theatre is built around such an involvement (one can see how this appears even at the level of the signifier: 'Foreman', for example, may also be read as 'for man', whilst 'on the other side' we can read 'Manheim' as something like 'man I'm' – which is probably no 'coincidence' in this *mise en scène* of castration as the dead-end of *mise en scène*). Foreman's significant contribution is to *show this fact* in an exemplary manner (no 'theatre' should survive his work intact).

There are of course many other features of this work one could discuss: notably the way in which it *plays* with painterly references to Hieronymus Bosch and Max Ernst – and how can one avoid, for example, recalling Marcel Duchamp's use of a space covered with intertwined cords (the title of one of Foreman's pieces – *Dr Selavy's Magic Theatre* – pays a discreet homage to Duchamp) . . . Here I have chosen to concentrate on the aspect which 'curiously' seems to have been the most ignored in the standard commentaries on this type of theatre, because it is this aspect which makes Foreman's work both a point-of-no-return and an exemplary analytical moment in the history of the code.

Robert Wilson: *Einstein On The Beach*

The problem with trying to discuss Robert Wilson's theatre is no doubt the neo-surrealist label which lazy critics have employed, no doubt to 'situate themselves', ironically, in an art which *disorientates* most of our current indicators. Wilson's 'treatment' of surrealism appears to involve both a characteristically 'relaxed' attitude (no apparent fascination for surrealist *ideology*) and an exploration of limits (notably in the treatment of *perception*) which surrealist *figuration* (Magritte, Delvaux, Dali) never seemed to attain. Need one add that this is of course *theatre* (or opera), i.e. a multiple, polyphonic process in which painting might possibly play a part (even if only as a *feeling**), but where it would be hazardous to say the least to transpose mechanically from one code to another elements of a 'style' or 'aesthetic' which function according to the specificity of *each* code? Need one recall that surrealism has always *distanced* itself from the theatre and that if there is a 'surrealist theatre' (Vitrac) it is 'on the edge' of the movement, strictly 'illustrative' in approach, and has little to do with the gesture of *dépense* and transgression which typified surrealist culture? It remains true that surrealism forms the 'grounding' of much of post-war American culture (Pollock, Motherwell), but once again in a specifically free manner, and that it is important to study closely the *specificity* of each code if one wishes to grasp in what way, and within what limits, surrealism played a part in their transformation.

Wilson's importance, beyond the phantasmatic elements with which his theatre deals (and to which it is too often reduced), appears to me clearly to be the emergence of the question of *time* in the theatrical code and how this might be inscribed within the gesture of rearticulation of practices derived from the minimalist 'stripping down' which I evoked earlier. In other words, the appearance of time (of that 'function of time' of which Lacan says that it is the moment 'in which the symbolic and the real come together'[18]) *as specific material of the code*. At a stroke, the theatre goes beyond the 'human' (nothing less 'anthropomorphic' than Wilson's work; a reminder here of one of his press-conferences: 'My mother wrote me a letter two months ago, saying that a nine-year old boy died of old age' – laughter in the audience – 'It's not funny'). A disorienting temporal and spatial over-connection, or invention of a *different* space-time, underlined in *Einstein* by the clocks and gyroscopes, transparent horizontal and vertical 'elevators', eclipses, spaceships seen *at once* from within and without, or indeed the 'technical' gestures of the calculating *hand* which serve as a kind of a base to certain movements and seem to indicate (like the hands drawn 'in negative' on the walls of Pech-Merle) a new mutation of the species: there is a becoming-time and a becoming-space of the Wilsonian 'machine' which cross over and interpenetrate and whereby *all* our usual perceptual reference points are redirected, in a quasi-hallucinatory manner, towards a realm 'beyond the human'. Einstein: a 'voyager'.

The function of time is inscribed in most of the pieces created or staged by Wilson since 1965: a hypnotic-dreamlike time (twelve hours in *Deafman Glance*, 1970, or *The Life and Times of Joseph Stalin*, 1973) sometimes implicating the whole theatrical space within its *dérive* and disproportion (*Ka Mountain and Guardenia Terrace*, in 1972, lasted seven days and seven nights – 'biblical' time – and took place all over a mountain, denying any centred, unified, impartial point of view). If *Einstein on the Beach* (1976) returns to more 'human' proportions, it is nonetheless true that the way in which the space changes the meaning according to the 'point of view' employed (along an explicit metonymic axis) and the way in which the dance and the music are 'produced' by time as much as they produce it – all this implies an extraordinary *perceptual* leap, comparable perhaps to the 'mutation' ('fourth dimension') introduced by Einstein into our intellectual apprehension of space-time.

Einstein on the Beach: One must therefore *enter into* the opera of Philip Glass and Robert Wilson as if into a *different* mode of perception: nothing will happen unless one allows oneself to be taken into its rhythm, its duration, its vast zones ('beaches') of changing and isolated movements, if one does not allow oneself to be carried away in its repeated *dérive*, and submerged, free-floating, in its continuous 'atomic' process, with its own space and time. The space here, even in its 'relief', produces its own visual, rhythmic, disjunctive temporality, whilst the time of the piece implies, in its musical treatment and its harmonic 'colours', the need for a *volume* (Philip Glass: 'When I look at a space now I see it as a volume of air which is going to move around and produce sounds').

This is an *opera*. Therefore, as I indicated above, after and developing from the period of 'minimal' dissociation, we see a *non-hierarchical re-confrontation of codes*. A reminder here of Eisenstein examining the theatre in the light of a study of ideogrammatic writing: 'sound, movement, space and voice do not accompany each other in parallel – but function as elements of the same signifying range'. Note that within this dialectical 'range', the prior stripping-down of each code (its escape from any expressive or rhetorical functionality) allows for an ease and a *freedom* of rearticulation which is quite without precedent. Between the dancing, the music, the voices and the visual *mise en scène* (the 'tableaux'), there develops therefore a necessary and relatively autonomous relationship (this can be located in the very elaboration of the piece: areas of autonomy for each code based on a common rhythmic and temporal pattern, retroactive effects, problematization of integrity, etc.).

This is not a question of 'escaping' from the Italian-style stage by denouncing its arbitrariness (techniques of 'distanciation') or by trying to do away with the stage-barrier in the name of a mythical 'community' between actors and spectators (as the Living Theater had hoped to do). In Wilson's case, on the contrary, the Italian-style stage can perfectly well be retained to the extent that its illusionist function (open window on a 'slice of life') is undermined *from within* by the play of the codes employed: time, space, sounds, tableaux, all live their own life, which is irreducible to any 'representation' of everyday life whatsoever. Hence the effect of continual perceptual *decentring*.

It is therefore less of an opera 'about' Einstein, in the anecdotal sense (the reference to Einstein is a form of stereotyping, or mythical image, allowing, in an associative manner, a complete freedom of interpretation), than an *Einsteinian* opera: 'relativization' of our habitual or logical perception of space and time, and of their relationship. Working out of a new dimension: here, theatrical representation experiences its *fission*. The whole operates as a vast *slowing down of (signifying) particles* (*accentuated* by the acceleration of sound, and the chaotic downpour of notes, figures and atoms which floods onto the stage and drowns out the movement).

The rhythm is an effect of structure: the beat established by the 'kneeplays'* (interludes, 'linking' scenes) unfolds according to a double temporal pattern, dialecticizing 'repetition' and 'transformation': the pattern of the four acts and the pattern of the transformative return of the three basic scenes: (1) a train with characters around it (forward and backward movement, 'waiting', a child on a bridge launching paper planes, etc.) (2) a court with a bed in it (referring metaphorically to the *lit de justice*), which in the second scene splits in two to reveal a prison; (3) movements of bodies and of luminous signs perceived from a spaceship (dance sequences). The last act, as if inspired by a veritable *dreamwork*, 'displaces' these scenes along a metaphorical axis (the train 'becoming' a building – where Einstein is working, writing out figures – whose form resembles that of the train) or a metonymical one (passing through the inside of the spaceship) – or 'condenses' them (the court is reduced to the neon bar of the 'bed', which is slowly rising. In other words, therefore, the following broken rhythm:

I (1a,2a); II (3a, 1b); III (2b, 3b); IV (1c, 2c, 3c)

– a structure in which the last act (IV) brings together and transforms the preceding tableaux. If one realizes that this double broken rhythm (which transforms the homogeneity of time into a heterogeneity of temporal layers) may also be found in the rhythmical variation of the musical continuity, and indeed that this structural disruption functions within that as the driving force of 'infinite' harmonic combinations; and if one realizes that Andy De Groat's choreography is the site of a similar type of variability, between the movements (forwards, backwards, turning around) and the 'design' which

they form in the spatial volume through their incessant ('Brownian') movement – then it is clear that it is both *within* the articulations of these codes
and between the codes that theatrical *time* (and the new perception it creates)
is treated.

So: the art of the rhythmic interval, or transformational gap, within
which the dialectic of 'slowing' and 'accelerating' can unfold with all its
effects, including the trans-hallucinatory dizziness which the piece inspires
in us, as in an atomic and multiplied current in which nothing would ever
become fixed.

The 'tableau' is no longer, therefore, a frame (a decor), but an element of
the signifying process treated *as such* (with its own temporal dimension) in
the contradictory rhythmic ensemble of all the other elements. We should
note that this form of *mise en scène* (as opposed to European theatre, bogged
down in its worn-out baroque or expressionist aesthetics) presupposes an *eye*
which has been 'affected' by recent American painting, in its most radical
aspects. The play of covers and transparencies, the division of space, the
examination of *edges*, the treatment of colours, the role (in the 'kneeplays') of
large 'empty' zones restricting the action to a square on the side, all this is
redolent of Rothko, Motherwell, Olitski, Noland – or rather implies the *new
perception* which their work produced (although it is clearly not a question of
'references'). Let us say that the 'surrealist' dimension of Wilson's early
pieces (their Delvaux influence, if you like) occasionally reappears here in its
rhetorical aspect (notably in the two train scenes) – but mainly dominated,
framed and integrated within a less directly expressive or anecdotal visual-
ization. Shifts, vibrations, 'disconnections', visual heterogeneity, all these
effects one could describe as *open* opera.

A musical-rhythmical accumulation (described wrongly as 'repetitive' –
better to say 'modulated transformation'): Philip Glass speaks of a 'rapid
current of notes carrying rhythms', as if the traditional relationship between
rhythm as 'support' and notes as 'variation' were here radically reversed. The
way in which the sound-dimensions are stratified (ensemble alone, ensemble
and voices, voices alone) means that Philip Glass succeeds in integrating
into this continuous-multiple bombardment both elements issuing from
repetitive Oriental chants (Indian music) and elements of Western harmony
(canons, counterpoint, echoes of Bach and Gregorian chant). It is all as if the
music were *saturating* the regularity of the rhythm and the constancy of the
harmony in order to dissolve them, by excess, into the avalanche of notes
and figures which weave and bring together the whole of the process.

Let us at this point recall Freud: 'The manifestations of a compulsion to
repeat exhibit to a high degree an instinctual [*pulsionnel*] character and,
when they act in opposition to the pleasure principle, give the appearance of
some "daemonic" force at work.'[19] We may add that if the *repetition* in
Einstein does indeed present these 'highly pulsional' characteristics the
important point is not that it contradicts the pleasure principle but that it

constitutes *one of its major driving forces*. How should we perceive it then? Perhaps as a 'diabolical' pleasure.

Hence the spinning bodies, atoms infused with the calculated rhythm (repetition, amplification – transformation) which, playing upon the 'simple' gestural cells (forwards, backwards, turning around) pushes them to the heady, vertiginous limit, at which point it is the whole space which is transformed by the bodies therein inscribed. The actor-dancer becomes a luminous sign, both *within* the music and radically outside it, in its *dérive*, its intoxication, its 'relaxation'. Andy De Groat: '360 degrees. Sight, sound, balance. Concentrate your hearing. Listen with all your body.' Thus the movement is both rigorous and free (with its margins of improvisation integrated into the calculation of the choreographic architecture), an 'atomic' rush from which there emerge fantastical bodies: Ritty Ann Burchfield, a calm whirlwind carrying off the whole space in her infinite rotations; Sheryl Sutton, a fluid machine, a sort of black astronaut descended from another physical dimension; Lucinda Childs, a worn-out, jerky, disarticulated body, still capable of expressing a paroxysm of lightness and suppleness. A trampled-twisted-pushed-pulled-repeated-unleashed-ramified movement: Andy De Groat achieves in *Einstein* the horizontal equivalent of what *weightlessness* is vertically.

Note to what extent the perfectly *free* integration of scientific or 'mechanical' elements into this movement of signifying, excessive *dépense* represents a mode of imaginary circulation seemingly directly connected to technology. A sign of modernity, whereby the traditional division between 'art' and 'science' falls away, like that between *dépense* and 'calculation'. Wilson has succeeded magnificently in seeing and inscribing the *symbolic displacement* produced by a scientific mutation (and the court-sequence illustrates very well the question of transgression *of the law*, and of the opening out onto that which exceeds the law), and the imaginary or phantasmatic material can only be profoundly transformed by this fact. Eclipse, machines, clocks, computers, control panels, dashboards, mechanical gestures, all of this is swept up in this beautiful, hallucinating *dérive*. Everything indicates this 'passage', from the movements whereby the machine-like gestures can develop, at any point, into the extreme intoxication of the dance, through to the bodies floating outside of any gravitation in the last scene – without forgetting the astonishing voice of Joan La Barbara, capable of passing unnoticeably from a metallic, even mechanical timbre (at first barely discernible amid the sounds produced by the synthesizers) to the most affecting and vibrant modulated singing.

This stratification is heard-seen-perceived 'as' the passage from one perceptual mode to another, a transfer played out a hundred times in each instant: *Einstein on the Beach* can no doubt be understood as one of the summits of modernity. If hallucination represents a surplus of the symbolic in the place of a 'hole' in the real, this kind of theatre, on the contrary (but with the same effects of 'dissociation' of the self and of the coherence of its perceptual system) proposes a surplus of the real 'in relief' within the hole of the symbolic (the 'stage').

If the unconscious does not recognize time, the theatre which treats time *differently* can *play with* time and carry you off in its infinite dizziness. The infinite in this instance is not that which denies the limit, but the 'infinitesimal' difference which can transform itself and endlessly transform the visual-auditory 'volume' wherein it intervenes as an atom or a number. An infinity of unnoticeable cuts in the intensity of the flux: a movement without end and without borders. To recreate opera is to *play on* the interstice, the shift, the atom, the void, within the continuous signifying bombardment. Quantitative accumulations (repetitions, rotations) producing a qualitative leap in perception: *Einstein on the Beach* can be defined as the theatre of the *passage* from quantity to quality, at every level. And that is no doubt what gives it its strange beauty.

Meredith Monk: *Quarry*

If Meredith Monk is indeed part of this movement of the re-confrontation of codes discussed above (reinvention of opera), what constitutes the singularity and interest of her latest work (*Quarry*, staged in April 1976 in New York) is that this 'experimentation' has for the first time been reconnected with a precise historical and sexual signified: Fascism. The 'critical' dimension in action.

Meredith Monk's résumé is in this respect exemplary: her *marginality* is marked from the very beginning of her biography (Jewish, daughter of a cabaret singer, born in Peru whilst her mother was 'on tour'); studied dance, music, drawing, spent time at the Sarah Lawrence College (where she worked with Bessie Schoenberg); then the Judson Church Dance Theater, where she produced *Blue Print* (an exploration of extra-theatrical techniques, involvement with the cinema); finally, the creation of her own troupe, 'The House', and a series of shows: *Barbershop* in April 1969 in Chicago; *Juice* in November–December of the same year in New York; *Vessel* in October 1971, then the *Goldchild* series (from 1972 to 1975), various 'performances', either solo-pieces or with a limited number of partners (*Anthology*, *Roots*, *Small Scroll*, *Our Lady of Late*) and finally *Quarry*.

A constant interest in the *shattering* of theatrical space (Robb Baker has spoken of a 'multi-levelled experience' in this regard), an exploration of the multiplicity and heterogeneity of the code, even to the point of 'fragmenting' the very notion of spectacle. Already *Barbershop* was performed in three different places, without any 'order' or hierarchy. *Juice* was presented as an ensemble of three distinct pieces, performed on three different days in three different places (the 'spiral' of the Guggenheim Museum, along which the actors were arranged in 'tableaux', the audience moving along to view them successively; the Playhouse of Columbia University, an Italian-style stage implying a 'classical' relationship between actors and public; and Meredith Monk's loft, where the actors were replaced by a 'decor' – costumes, musical instruments – and by tape-recordings). A similar pulverization (but 'the other way round') for *Vessel* (performed successively in a loft, a garage and a theatre). The different variants of *Goldchild* (ranging from a solo-piece to a 'group' *mise en scène*, with repetitions and transformations of the theme) also taking place in different locations, theatres, garages, cathedrals. An exploration, therefore, of the deferral of meaning, of a non-unitary language, which, in *Quarry*, affects the way in which the codes employed (song, dance, theatre, lighting, 'marches', film) are seemingly articulated 'in suspense', in a surprising, disturbingly disconnected series of 'moments' and spaces (necessitating a simultaneously microscopic and 'overall' perception at once). Indeed Meredith Monk is the first person to treat the theatre *as* a fragmented body, in a constant state of combustion and 'passage'.

Meredith Monk's *body*, in the way in which it can be inscribed into different spaces, itself represents some sort of combustion: light, supple, fragile and yet dense, indefatigable, without 'age' and, in a very perceptible manner, *nomadic*, rootless. A strange, vibrant voice, capable of becoming 'volume', multiplying itself, reaching extraordinary timbres, rhythms and registers. Once again, nothing very 'human' about all this: Meredith Monk herself refers to her experience as having come *from far away*;[20] 'started dancing at the age of three because she could not skip'; or indeed: 'I was singing back tunes before I could talk.'* It is a body which is way beyond (because delving way beneath) the gendered, stable, demarcated, fixed bodies with which we are familiar. Dancing, singing, rhythms, spaces, iridescences from *before* the arrival of the speaking-standing subject – staged and transmitted on a different frequency from that of our standard perceptions.

What is most clearly at stake is, of course, the relation to the maternal body. The relevance of Meredith Monk's work (once again 'marginal' to matriarchal America and to its male communities haunted by figures of phallic mothers) lies in the fact that she has *both* managed to explore, in every direction and in excess, these pre-symbolic languages, connected to the maternal body, bringing out their pleasure [*jouissance*] – *and* has signalled, in her latest pieces, the *link* that the mother maintains, everywhere and always, with power. The fact that this conflict, in its virtualities and its often dramatic productivity, has involved myths of denial of sexual difference ('androgyny', for example), or neo-Jungian references (the search for an 'originary', archetypal language, as an illusory space *before* the determination of the subject in and by the Symbolic order – i.e. always through 'lalangue'), should no doubt be interpreted as the *indication* of the 'maternal continent' whose gently oppressive character Meredith Monk has examined elsewhere (in *Goldchild*), along with its capacity to develop into Fascism (in *Quarry*) when that which determines links, meaning and 'reason' has fallen apart.

In other words, it is through her practice's calculated pulverization, and the ambiguous form of *jouissance* which thereby unfolds its virtualities and its testing-of-limits, that Meredith Monk clearly indicates the realm prior to the symbolic where Fascism originates as pulsional *dérive*, 'insane matter', fragmented body captivated by the maternal image. Her singing at that point sounds like a cry, and maybe a cry of alarm.

Quarry may be seen as the shattering of the scenic space into different poles of interest, simultaneous and autonomous, the 'pivot' of which is represented by Meredith Monk herself, playing a sick little girl, stretched out, calling upon the fragmented signs of her history as so many brief, flashing hallucinations, perceived through a feverish haze. Disconnected, rearticulated moments whose only 'logic' would be that of an 'infantile' delirium. Meredith Monk claims to be 'apprehending the beginnings of something that will later come to be understood as the Fascist mining of victims or "quarrying" '. An intensity of fragments: a vaguely hysterical mother, in forties costume, an actress or newscaster, distant with her child; an old Jewish couple, in Hasidic costume; a couple of old American 'intellectuals', transfixed. A few wild movements: a photographer 'killing' the characters he photographs; cloud-carriers becoming aircraft-carriers; slow-motion, almost funereal dances. Some 'dramatic' scenes: a parade of megalomaniac dictators, grotesque, pathetic caricatures – all of whom are in the end killed by another dictator (the 'photographer') whose link to the mother-newscaster has been clearly indicated; the 'speech' of this dictator, with its military-automatic gestures, shouting inaudible words, almost psychotic violence; groups of heterogeneous movement-dances, moments of rhythmical *dépense* – which finally 'come together', little by little, in an ordered Fascist march, invading-pounding the stage, while the Jewish couple, overwhelmed, attempt to escape from or make their way through the unstoppable advancing crowd, and end up being knocked to the ground (a symmetrical scene represents the flight of the American couple out of this nightmare). A 'dreamlike' film-sequence, slow, haunted by death, projected three-quarters of the way through the show, during which we sense that the actors are crawling through the dark: rocks, a quarry (the title also referring to the 'quarrying' and persecution of the Jews), shadows floating in a dark, dirty liquid in the centre of the quarry, a slow almost dreamy drowning. A final 'requiem', with grand procession and singing in the round. The whole rhythm of the piece *measured out* by the gestures and songs of Meredith Monk (the 'child') around her bed, a strange, animal, strangled or piercing voice, a material vibration in excess, serving as a link between the different codes employed, and almost withdrawn from them.

The powerful unconscious impact of this piece stems no doubt from the fact that through this *suspended* play of articulated codes (song, dance, mime, theatre, movement, light, film) – fragmentary, erratic, latent – it is the *relief* of the Fascist nightmare which is made visible. Its terrifying and *grotesque* dimension – feverish, deadly and almost hallucinated. What Meredith Monk makes palpable is the sense in which the *family romance* is part of what 'gives rise' to Fascism; that there is a link between maternal hysteria and the *desire* for *death* implicit in power; and that *childhood* is perhaps a privileged point from which to perceive its delirium. A slow-motion combustion, as if the whole theatre were breaking up into dispersion and *diaspora*. Throughout all this, something like an 'extraction' ('quarrying'*) of fragments of historical memory, grasped-projected 'transparently' in the fever which *expands* them and yet brings out their organic, pulsional base. To an angst-inducing degree.

Mutation

I have, of course, only been able to signal in cursory fashion the principal aspects and implications of this 'renewal' of American theatre. A crucible of inventions, breakthroughs, renewed spaces and rhythms – and a new *jouissance*, too. To return to the questions I raised at the start of this article, although it is true that this theatre (in the whole range of its experiments, each uniquely irreducible) still falls way *short* of that which determines meaning and language – it does nonetheless highlight for us the urgent need to confront the radical novelty of this process, and its exploration of *another dimension* of human space and time. To confront, in other words, the modernity which it implies, the mutation in perception which it inscribes, and the new bodies emerging from it.

Only, of course, if we *want* to escape from our archaic, nineteenth-century world. But this 'escape', this liberation (more *urgent* than ever now that, 'religion' and 'reason' having collapsed, intense pulsional forces are emerging which, historically or 'genetically', nothing will necessarily prevent from becoming the breeding ground of Fascism) can *also* take place through our perception, our bodies, and the apprehension we can have of space and time – this is what Monk's theatre appears to be indicating. A mutation in progress, through the eye and the ear: the American experiment continues, multi-faceted and 'in advance'. We shall have to return for another look.

Translated by Michael Temple

Notes

1 [This article was originally published in *Tel Quel*, 71–3 (1977), a special issue on the United States. The issue also featured interviews and articles on painting (Motherwell), dance (Merce Cunningham) and film (Michael Snow), which are interwoven with images of Cunningham, the dancer Trisha Brown, and images from the work of Robert Wilson, among others.]

2 [An asterisk in the text indicates where the preceding phrase or word was in English in the original, an important stylistic effect given the context of the article in the special US issue of *Tel Quel*.]

3 This can be compared to the analysis undertaken by Marcelin Pleynet of the treatment, within modern painting, of Cézanne's breakthrough. See *Painting and System* (Chicago/London, Chicago University Press, 1984); 'Eloge de la peinture', *Art Press*, 6, 1974; 'Georges Braque et les écrans truqués', *Art Press*, 8, 1974.

4 Cf. Pierre Francastel, *La réalité figurative* (Paris, Gonthier, 1965).

5 Cf. Marcelin Pleynet, 'La matière pense', in Philippe Sollers (ed.), *Artaud* (Paris, 10/18, 1973).

6 Lacan, unpublished seminar, 'D'un discours qui ne serait pas du semblant'.

7 Cf. William Rubin, 'Notes on Masson and Pollock', *Art News*, November 1959, and *Dada and Surrealist Art* (London, Thames and Hudson, 1969); Marcelin Pleynet, 'La peinture par l'oreille', in *Art et Littérature* (Paris, Seuil, 1977).

8 *Art-Rite*, 10, Autumn 1975.

9 *Alternative Theatre*, January–February 1976, [Translation our own; source unidentifiable].

10 Interview with Richard Foreman by Guy Scarpetta, *Art Press International*, 2.

11 See Richard Foreman, *Plays and Manifestoes*, ed. and introduced by Kate Davy (New York, New York University Press, 1976).

12 Richard Foreman, 'The Carrot and the Stick' *October*, 1 (1976), 24.

13 Ibid, 24.

14 Ibid, 25–6.

15 Interview with Foreman by Scarpetta.

16 Jacques Lacan, 'Function and Field of Speech and Language in Psychoanalysis', in *Ecrits: A Selection*, trans. A. Sheridan (London: Tavistock, 1977), 90.

17 Foreman, 'The Carrot and the Stick', 29.

18 Lacan, 'Function and Field of Speech and Language in Psychoanalysis', 95.

19 S. Freud, 'Beyond the Pleasure Principle' in A. Richards, ed., J. Strachey, trans. *The Pelican Freud Library, vol. II* (Harmondsworth, Penguin, 1984), 307.

20 Cf. Philippe Sollers: 'There are bodies in a state of development, decomposition, explosion, involving any orifice you can think of, but that's not what's involved here. It isn't the image of the body, nor the image of the sexual body as it is perceived in pornography; it's a body which has come from further away, which goes further, which traverses the form of the body and even the form of the sexual body' ('Réponses' in *Minuit*, 17, January 1976).

13

PARADIS[1]

Philippe Sollers

we designate henceforth by the name orthosexuals all sexes not having their other in themselves and consequently incapable of finding it anywhere there will therefore be the ortho hetero-homos and the hetero homo-heteros women and men taking their tickets off the treadmill listen to me now like apples of gold on a silver thread such is the word said according to its two sides maskiyyôth chiselings links sphere plump polished the cut of the exterior hints at the interior read this here the thread here there right here it's written outside without remission but inside volume nothing ever gained vain smoke vaporous vapors one generation comes another departs the earth rests in its breast the sun rises it sets slides and restarts the wind turns goes returns and the waters never part the sea is not filled it swallows itself the torrents recede disperse themselves it all works beyond the aimless words the eye opens views reviews the ear listens harkens what was is will be and what is done will be redone will flee nothing new no thunder clap no cat a time to be born a time to digest i was wise and then mad and wise again and again mad i awake wise mad i slumber madder but wiser debility habilitates me my buffoonery refines me the fuller i am of shit the more i spin on the spit and the closer i get top the pit of the attic insipience rejoins insight what is coitus definitively if not an autocriticism but tell me could i still advance with veil of blood on my head my face buried in the blood could i hold out much longer in this blood and say you my other aren't you ever going to answer me you fluster me i lust for you i dream of you for you against you answer me your name is a diffused perfume your colour bursts among the thorns bring back my heart with wine make me a blanket of sunshine i'm smothering beneath this mask my skin drained basted nothing exists but desire wasted young in haste the old say they know they feel themselves out we are always too dutiful towards them and the more they wither the more they twitter and the more they expire the more they expound terror of vigour repression tutor they try to rethread their rejects sounds myths droopy lids faulty digestion the girls love that long leer behind the peepers hand fumbling at fly oh yes vacillating papa aren't i terrific and hyposons are also girlies and the mothers same with the fathers all the same the great secret that's it fizzling fright small change sacrificed crafty retallied defence of the original repressing pressing pinioned conflict of gold of silver metal cast in coins peru mexico egypt genova seville amsterdam where have the indians gone the carolingians or even the greeks the romans our god moves on in christian clothing dominican charles quint credit titles females black fleet brazil transferred slaves briefly there is no brevity i'm only trying to wake up and sometimes i believe in it but i fall oh how we pledge as fledgelings to reach the naked edge how we race straining towards the mark how we are drawn what how we are drawn remarkable regaining strength brilliant black blade awaiting the shave each awaiting secret rendezvous as if were awaited yes unique experience not twice the same hole in this can no man broken in man woman dissolved in woman drapery of legends thrown overboard how many years universes 16 billion so few not possible and us our oldest remains scarcely 3 million where's that folds of africa rift afar kenya sahara ghana thus little by little less little delicate skeleton vase of bones crushed under pathos call cry grumble mumble arrows throat and here's miss bovary split hairy diaphonous isis sailing over the float i return i return passage moulded in reverse mild trauma mind aspirated manageable grind of air curled irons entered centred behind the mask baby drowsy langôsha langôsha mournful train my resurrection is spoken i arise from the dead vertically from the dead empty tomb that is empty cradle too and empty as well the inner womb of the human nommy which is why we see her erect at the foot of the cross thrown for a loss which is why their only choice is to pose her as virgin otherwise the foundation's displaced time space geometry biochemistry face it discovering the disgrace leaves them all unemployed naked out in the streets nothing to follow borrow blazing point overwhelming void now you're only a breath a trace vestigium pedis in pelvis they draw away from you men feel it women seem to know it best in their hollow but take heart i am here i am with you will drink for you your hemlock will clot i ate your meal for you simply make yourself more of a sleeper ameboid infusor unveiling pancaked your fabric close shaved a running dog's worth more than a dead lion for where you're going there are not works no discourse no science ivory vault pit of ovaries here that are lined up nephews aunts nieces cousins of uncles two in the afternoon legs mosquitoes flowers ovulary capital of women 700 two children that's always it passing by fresh breeze path of ants in the grass moment of mirages if i lose my cock sliced from midsection if i try to retape it to the nape fibroid crater mucous how to replace it now separated meaty how to hook it staple it planted rocket wave utero-sacred squall salpinched armed follicle of the yellow corpuscle as if we advanced cut by cut a bit further prostrate postated as if we backed up just like that without budging all the while advancing turning fixed as if we permutated curbed by the carbide the child jumps on the bed babbles and bawls here he is leaning spinning without axis little vertebrate awaiting his cake muscle encased

239

child at the very edge of the nights he's always there in each man-woman always been there bung of gaps i don't judge i describe i invent nothing i follow you jumbled boiling bubbles of memories thus we now arrive in the plain the motor heats we're half asleep first it's the secreted odour green sombre tide of sprayed orangetrees i am stretched out smashed in behind with the bags beside the rosy blonde englishwoman it's the moment when she sings a little and her blue left eye's going to hook it seems onto the branches she stays like that with this ejected eye aiming at the mountains and the mountains are blue violets and they're already far to the west and there are water spouts all about swollen ziff and rooves of leaves everywhere doused here's the smoke we're getting there she says

Note

1   [The English translation by Carl R. Lovitt from which this excerpt is taken appeared in *Tel Quel*, 70 (1977). The original French appeared in issue 62 (1975).]

Part IV

DISSEMINATION

DISSEMINATION

Patrick ffrench and Roland-François Lack

Dissemination as a figure of influence is conveniently measurable, when it is a question of a discourse in a different language, by translation. Our own activity as translators can thus be included as a feature of *Tel Quel*'s dissemination. Translation, however, is, as we know, an ambivalent term covering a plurality of modes of 'passage'. *Tel Quel*'s dissemination is on one level measurable by the translation of texts originally published in or by the review. However, its role as a location committing the writer to a certain programme or project is more often than not effaced in the course of this translation; *Tel Quel* becomes a mere site of publication, erased in the move from one site to another. A number of texts published in the 'Collection *Tel Quel*' have been translated into English: Derrida's *Writing and Difference*, *Dissemination*, Barthes's *Critical Essays*, *S/Z*, *The Pleasure of the Text*, *Sade / Fourier / Loyola*, *A Lover's Discourse: Fragments*, *The Responsibility of Forms*, Kristeva's *Séméiotiké*,[1] *Polylogue*, *Powers of Horror*, *Revolution of Poetic Language*.[2] The erasure of the name '*Tel Quel*' from these translations, and of the hallmark brown edge which framed all books produced under the label '*Tel Quel*', functions in such a way as to blur the specificity of *Tel Quel* as a name, and leads to its association with textual or poststructuralist theory in general. *Tel Quel*'s dissemination occurs, then, in a veiled and specific sense (translation of texts) and an explicit, generalized manner (the association of the name with 'textual theory'). Again, the star-names of the period function as relay of *Tel Quel*'s activity as site of a programme and as foyer welcoming like-minded work from the context.

This relay is conditioned, however, by a proliferation of material from 'around' *Tel Quel*, by those names who published in the journal but were not part of the committee, the 'group' *stricto sensu*, and a singular lack of material from within the group, from Philippe Sollers, Marcelin Pleynet, Jean-Louis Baudry, Marc Devade, Jean-Pierre Faye, Denis Roche, Pierre Rottenberg and Jacqueline Risset. The obvious exception is Kristeva, whose work in any case, though it takes off from the context of *Tel Quel*, is separated from it in the passage into English. Her important essay on Sollers, 'L'engendrement de la formule',[3] is significantly not included in any of the extant compilations of her work. This situation is more markedly the case when it comes to the fiction and poetry produced by the group. While there is a singular lack of translated fiction or poetry by, say, Pleynet, Roche, Sollers and Baudry, the English-speaking reader can access translations of Maurice Roche, Pierre Guyotat and Severo Sarduy, all writers for whom *Tel Quel* was a decisive influence, who published in the review and were at various times grouped with *Tel Quel* at conferences, but who were not part of the committee itself. *Tel Quel*'s influence is relayed via its periphery.

A different figure of dissemination, one which it is more difficult to substantiate, is *reading*. *Tel Quel* was curiously subject to an inflationary effect whereby its influence was exaggerated in relation to the relatively small number of copies sold. 'Reading' as a figure, as opposed to translation, leaves no visible trace, no inscription, and so is something of an unquantifiable element. It seems pertinent, nevertheless, to point to the influence of *Tel Quel* on certain forms of fiction and poetry – auto-referentiality, typographic play, permutation; one might identify Christine Brooke-Rose, Walter Abish and, in a more generalized sense, Juan Goytisolo, Umberto Eco, Paul Auster, as writers whose work bears the trace of *Tel Quel*, but it is difficult in this case to separate *Tel Quel* from a more generalized category of ludic fiction, also practised by the *nouveaux romanciers*, or the Oulipo group, for example.

More immediately identifiable is a particular instance of the relay of *Tel Quel*, measured by both translation and reading, in the powerful influence it has had on English-language film theory and film practice. Periodicals such as *Screen*, *Film Quarterly* and *Camera Obscura* featured translations from *Cinéthique*, the film journal once allied with *Tel Quel* where Sollers, Kristeva, Pleynet and Baudry published important articles. It is Baudry's essays on the apparatus which are taken up with most resonance in this film theory, influencing structural-materialist film practice (cf. the films of Peter Gidal). Baudry's critique of the filmic apparatus as premissed on *quattrocento* perspective and constructing the viewer as transcendental subject functions, once again, as a translation of Althusserian and Derridean theory into a different space from writing, the centre ground of *Tel Quel*'s concerns.[4] So *Tel Quel*'s dissemination seems marked by an emphasis on its margins, through a metaphoric displacement or projection of a theory of writing into other fields and practices.

This is not the case with another aspect of dissemination; a major part of *Tel Quel*'s activity is the foregrounding of a previously repressed canon of limit texts, and canon-formation also functions as a measure of dissemination. Though rarely translated (into English), critical accounts of writers of *Tel Quel*'s canon have become major, if contested, contributions to study on those writers. *Tel Quel*'s exploration of Joyce, mainly emphasized in the seventies, is a good example.[5] Contemporary writing on Bataille seems marked by a repeated and somewhat knee-jerk rejection, as overly politicized or theoreticized, of *Tel Quel*'s accounts of him, overlooking *Tel Quel*'s major role in Bataille's rise to prominence. The importance of *Tel Quel*'s analysis of Sade (specifically the 1967 special issue) is signalled by Pasolini's prefacing of his film *Salo* with remarks from Barthes and Sollers on Sade. Either as authority or as counter-example, *Tel Quel*'s critical mass in contemporary criticism of these writers, as well as of Mallarmé, Lautréamont, Céline, and others, is indisputable.

A different approach to *Tel Quel*'s dissemination can be traced in the punctual relations it entertains with the star-names of the 'time of theory' – whose work has, as outlined above, been translated. Our sense, as Anglophone readers, of *Tel Quel*'s importance goes by way of the relay of its influence via figures such as Althusser, Lacan, Foucault, Derrida and Barthes, perhaps the Ur-figure of this relay. Some associations are limited, however, to a defined context, and go no further. This is the case with Irigaray's text 'Le v(i)ol de la lettre',[6] her only contribution to the review, as yet untranslated. Irigaray has commented that her text is to be seen in the specific context of work on language, and that it does not signal her allegiance to the programme of *Tel Quel* as such. Within *Tel Quel*, in contrast to texts by, say, Derrida or Barthes, Irigaray's text does not have any resonance beyond the issue in which it appears. The publication of interviews with René Girard, however, do get taken up in *Tel Quel*'s analysis of theology and ethics, or 'radical evil', in the late seventies. Writers such as Cixous (writing on Joyce) and Umberto Eco (also on Joyce) contribute work around a specific object, such that their function as relays of *Tel Quel*'s dissemination is circumscribed, while playing a part in *Tel Quel*'s dissemination via its canon.

Another kind of interaction occurs with a writer like Foucault, who plays a crucial role in the early sixties, writing 'Distance, Aspect, Origin' on *Tel Quel* fiction, publishing an article in the review, and chairing the 'New Literature' conference. If there is benefit for both parties in this exchange, *Tel Quel* serving Foucault with an example of an anti-humanist writing as 'exteriority', before Derrida, and Foucault in some sense enabling *Tel Quel* to displace the 'centrality' of Robbe-Grillet, ironically Foucault's place is eventually occupied by Derrida, as *Tel Quel* distances itself from what appeared as a Blanchotesque nostalgia for an absent presence. Foucault is reaffirmed, though, in the late seventies, as *Tel Quel* moves away from the apparent 'hegemony' of philosophy. Foucault, however, is not the origin or master of a discourse of theory which is appropriated by *Tel Quel*, while this is the case for Derrida and (to a lesser extent) Althusser. The imprint of the 'Collection *Tel Quel*' marks this appropriation, in Derrida's case, and this goes a lot deeper than reference limited to specific works (such as Foucault's book on Roussel, reviewed affirmatively by Sollers, or Sollers's affirmative review of Deleuze's *Proust and Signs*, in 1964[7]). The trace of Derridean theory is translated into the very fabric of *Tel Quel*'s critical perspective, such that even in Scarpetta's 1977 article on performance, translated in this volume, the resonance of Derrida is evident. This 'use' of Derrida is highly stylized, and partial, however, differing significantly from Derrida's 'influence' on Anglo-American 'deconstruction' (making for a spectacular silence on both sides in relation to the other). The aspects of Derrida's work highlighted by *Tel Quel* privilege his critique of idealist logocentrism (as evident here in Goux's annexing it to a critique of exchange, prefiguring Derrida's *Given Time*[8]) and the fetishistic celebration of writing as material inscription, hieroglyph, giving rise to the visually seductive look of the journal.

Derrida's *Dissemination*,[9] with its final text on Sollers's *Nombres*, and 'The Double Session', the trace of an (already written) performance at *Tel Quel*'s Group of Theoretical Studies, is perhaps the most effective marker of *Tel Quel*'s relay through the name. Paradoxically, its 'Outwork' marks out in the complex weave of its argument an implicit resistance to what is emerging as the persistence of Hegelian dialectic, albeit overturned, in *Tel Quel*'s writing. It is contemporary to the interview, in *Positions*, with *Tel Quel* associates Scarpetta and Houdebine, who press Derrida on the question of dialectical materialism. Derrida's insistence on the necessity of an analysis of the philosophical lineage of Marxism before being able to commit himself contrasts with *Tel Quel*'s effacement of *difference* underneath the concept of *contradiction*, from 1971 onwards, whence the subsequent estrangement of the two parties. The hidden effect of *Tel Quel*'s dissemination via Derrida's reputation is nevertheless marked by Derrida's response to Scarpetta and Houdebine that a 'theoretical elaboration' around the question of Marxism remains 'yet to come' (*encore à venir*), projecting the appearance, much later, of *Specters of Marx*. While Derrida is the name signifying a discourse explicitly inherent in *Tel Quel*'s 'pro-gramme' (the word itself echoing *Of Grammatology*) from 1967 to 1972, and implicit subsequently, *Tel Quel* functions for Derrida as a space of ambiguous articulation with a creative textual practice (not visible anywhere else) and an intervention into the context of the politicized avant-garde.

Roland Barthes's text on *Tel Quel* in *Roland Barthes by Roland Barthes* gives a subjective, psychoanalytical version of the review's role as a space of collective commitment, commitment to a language spoken 'with the same body'.[10] *Tel Quel* is Barthes's superego, a space where, in a quite visible manner, his writings take on a more radical edge than they would outside that space, but he affirms that he does not have 'the same body' as his colleagues on the review. Barthes's presence in *Tel Quel* is thus that of a 'different body', and this tension – between collective body and the body as 'irreducible difference' – is what characterizes Barthes's relations with *Tel Quel*. This emerges in specific symptoms: Barthes's Japan, affirmed as the space of the neutral in *The Empire of Signs*, which was not published by *Tel Quel*, contrasts with *Tel Quel*'s China, to which Barthes's self-mocking reaction is 'Alors la Chine?' ('What about China, then?'). *Tel Quel*'s influence is certainly present in Barthes's shift from high structuralism to a psychoanalytically informed reading of himself as reader, from *S/Z* onwards. Barthes, for *Tel Quel*, on the other hand, is the Zen master who teaches by example the art of withdrawal from the hysteric space of the avant-garde, so that *Tel Quel*'s long-term dissemination via the name Barthes can mark out a continuity beyond the image of a review at the mercy of intellectual fashion. *Tel Quel* occupies the role of the superego which commands *jouissance*, in relation to Barthes's more subtle, hesitant enjoyment of private pleasures. Barthes is, then, the Ur-figure of *Tel Quel*'s dissemination, the relation representing a tension between literary community and exceptional subject. Issue 47, the first special issue on Barthes, is the major symptom of this tension, marked by the emphasis on Barthes as 'the anti-hysteric' (Sollers), and closing with the hysterical exclamation mark after the stereotypical 'Vive la pensée mao-tsetoung!' In his exchange with Jean Thibaudeau, Barthes provides an analysis of his entry into the space of *Tel Quel* that bears out the tension we have described. Our volume ends with this interview-text, emphasizing the receptivity of *Tel Quel* as perhaps its lasting legacy.

Notes

1 The translation of Kristeva's works is curiously partial. Only a few articles from her first book *Séméiotiké*, and her collection *Polylogue*, were included in the two collections *The Kristeva Reader* and *Desire in Language*; included here are two of the crucial articles omitted. The translation of *Revolution of Poetic Language* features only the 'theoretical preamble' of the book, not its analysis of Lautréamont and Mallarmé's work.
2 See Bibliography for a full list.
3 *Tel Quel*, 37–8 (1969).
4 For a discussion of the apparatus and textuality, see R.-F. Lack, 'Screen as Figure', *Paragraph*, 19:1 (1996).
5 Cf. G. Lernout *The French Joyce* (Michigan, Michigan University Press, 1990), which contains a chapter on *Tel Quel*.
6 *Tel Quel*, 39 (1969).
7 P. Sollers, 'Logicus Solus', *Tel Quel*, 14 (1963); 'Proust et les signes', *Tel Quel*, 19 (1964).
8 In which Derrida 'responds' to Goux, and obliquely to *Tel Quel*, in a note on Goux's analysis of Gide's *The Counterfeiters*. J. Derrida, *Given Time: I Counterfeit Money*, trans. P. Kamuf (Chicago and London, University of Chicago Press, 1992).
9 *Dissemination*, trans. B. Johnson (Chicago and London, University of Chicago Press, 1981).
10 Cf. R. Barthes, *Roland Barthes by Roland Barthes*, trans. R. Howard (London, Macmillan, 1977), 175.

14

RESPONSES

Interview with *Tel Quel*[1]

Roland Barthes

(Jean Thibaudeau had the kindness to prepare for me a long, precise, direct and well-informed questionnaire, bearing at once (as was the rule) on my life and work, for a series of televised interviews, recorded under the generic title 'Archives of the 20th Century', which will probably never appear, unless perhaps in the event of the death of the author. Of course it was a game, which neither Jean Thibaudeau nor myself, deriving from a theoretical space where biography is not taken so seriously, were taken in by. The interview took place, but it was only possible to reproduce a few of the numerous questions asked. The responses were rewritten – which does not mean that we are dealing with writing, since, given the biographical material, the 'I' (and its litany of verbs in the past tense) must be taken as if the person speaking were the same (in the same place) as the person who had lived. It should thus be remembered that the person whose birth date is the same as mine, 12 November 1915, becomes, due simply to the effect of enunciation, an entirely imaginary and continuous first person; the quotation marks which are pertinent for any naively referential statement should thus be implicitly re-established in what follows: any biography is a novel which dares not speak its name. R.B.)

The usual opening questions: birth, class origins, childhood . . .

I was born during World War I (at the end of 1915, 12 November) in Cherbourg, a town I don't know since I have, literally, never set foot there, being only two months old when I left. My father was a navy officer; he was killed in 1916, during a naval combat in the Pas-de-Calais; I was 11 months old.

The social class I belong to, is, I would say, the bourgeoisie. So that you can judge for yourself, I'll list my four immediate forebears (as the Vichy regime did under the occupation to determine the degree of a person's Jewishness): my paternal grandfather, a white-collar worker in the railways, the *Compagnie des Chemins de Fer du Midi*, came from a family of lawyers living in a small town in the Tarn region (Mazamet, I was told); the parents of my maternal grandmother were impoverished provincial nobility (from around Tarbes); Captain Binger, my maternal grandfather, from a family of master glass-makers, was an explorer – he explored the Niger region in 1887–9; as for my maternal grandmother, the only wealthy one in this constellation, her parents came from Lorraine and had a small foundry in Paris. My father's side was Catholic, my mother's Protestant; since my father was dead I was given my mother's Calvinist religion. In short, my social origins amount to one quarter landed bourgeoisie, one quarter old nobility and two quarters liberal bourgeoisie, the whole mixed together and unified by a general state of impoverishment: this bourgeoisie was either tight-fisted or poor, a poverty that was sometimes acute; which meant that, being a 'war widow', and since I was a 'pupil of the state', my mother learned a trade, book-binding, from which we scratched a living in Paris, where we had moved when I was ten.

I consider my homeland to be the South-West: it's the land of my father's family, the land of my childhood and my teenage holidays (I often go back even though I have no family or friends there now): Bayonne, the town where my paternal grandparents lived, played a Proustian role in my past – a Balzacian role, too, since I heard there, over many visits, the discourse of a certain type of provincial bourgeoisie, which from an early age I found more diverting than oppressive.

More biographical questions: your adolescence? your studies?

I spent my teenage years in Paris, always in and around Saint-Germain-des Prés (which was then a rather provincial area), rue Jacob, rue Bonaparte, rue Mazarine, rue Jacques-Callot, rue de la Seine; I still live not far from there. But during the three school holidays I always went to Bayonne, where my aunt and grandmother lived in a house with a big garden, part of a former rope factory, in the Allées Paulmy. In Bayonne I read a great deal (whatever novels I came across, mostly from a lending library in the rue Gambetta) but above all I played a lot of music; my aunt taught the piano so I heard it played all day long (even scales didn't bore me), and as soon as the piano was free, I'd be there, playing by sight; I was composing small pieces long before I could write; and later, before I became ill, I took singing lessons with Charles Panzera, of whom I am still in awe and who is kind enough not to have forgotten me; today still, when I attempt to clarify notions of literary theory which can seem far removed from my youth and from classical music, I sometimes find Panzera within me, not his philosophy but his precepts, his way of singing, of enunciating, of *taking hold* of sounds, destroying psychological expressivity through the purely musical production of pleasure: so many revelations that are still relevant to me. If I want to know what is language (the French language), I only have to play his record of 'La Bonne

Chanson',[2] sadly only a transfer from 78s. It was Panzera's misfortune that he stopped singing before the LP era, leaving a void that for the present generation is filled, unjustifiably, by Fischer-Dieskau.

I first went to school in Bayonne, and in Paris I went to the lycée Montaigne, then to the lycée Louis-le-Grand. Two months before sitting the philosophy baccalaureate, 10 May 1934, I suffered a haemoptysis and went on a rest-cure in the Pyrenees, at Bedous in the Aspe valley. This incident put paid to my 'vocation': being good at literature I had planned, up until my illness, to go to the *Ecole normale supérieure*; but when I returned to Paris in 1935 I settled for a degree in classics: a meagre investment for which I compensated by forming the Classical Theatre Group of the Sorbonne with Jacques Veil, a friend now gone (murdered by the Nazis); I was actively involved in this (to the detriment of my studies) until about 1939.

What 'milieu' shaped you?

What is a 'milieu'? A space of language, a network of relations, of supports, of models. In this sense I had no 'milieu'; I spent my teenage years alone with my mother, who was herself socially 'un-assimilated' (though not *déclassée*), maybe simply because she was working; we had no 'acquaintances'; my only milieu was school, the lycée; I only spoke to my classmates; my grandparents' background in Bayonne was probably in some sense a milieu, but I have already said that for me this milieu was a kind of spectacle. This doesn't mean I wasn't shaped by a certain lifestyle, a bourgeois lifestyle, despite its poverty: the way you are brought up is enough, especially when this upbringing is solely maternal (you may read my answer in this way: the Mother is separate from the milieu; she is innocent of it, she isn't a party to its habits; she is in herself a 'good' milieu, or at least she serves as a filter; in a sense, then, she forestalls social alienation). As for my cultural milieu, it was mostly made of books: those found at home, literary classics, some Anatole France, some Proust, Gide, Valéry, novels of the twenties and thirties; no surrealism, no philosophy, no criticism, certainly no Marxism. We read *L'Oeuvre*, a newspaper that was radical-socialist, pacifist and anti-clerical, rather 'leftist', in fact, for the period.

How did you perceive the war? Who are you, intellectually and politically, at the time of the Liberation?

I more or less spent the entire war in a sanatorium-bed. I was exempt from military service because of my initial tuberculosis; at the outbreak of war I was appointed teacher at the lycée in Biarritz; back in Paris after the defeat, I was prep-master at the lycée Voltaire and the lycée Carnot. I then had another tuberculosis attack and went to recover at the *Sanatorium des Etudiants* in Saint-Hilaire-du-Touvet, in the Isère region, then after a short stay in Paris and yet another attack in 1943 I went to Leysin, in Switzerland, until 1946. That whole period more or less coincided with the Occupation. At the sanatorium, apart from towards the end, when I felt saturated, over-come by the system, I was happy: I read, and I spent a great deal of time and energy on my friendships. For a while I thought about giving up literature to study medicine (I wanted to be a psychiatrist); I started a course [the PCB] but stopped after a minor relapse and finished off my classics degree instead (before completing my degree I had done my *diplôme d'études supérieures* on incantations and invocations in Greek tragedy with a man I was very fond of, the Hellenist Paul Mazon). During my time in sanatoria I wrote a few articles for *Existences*, the journal of the *Sanatorium des Etudiants*, notably on Camus's *L'Etranger*, which had just come out and where I first found the idea of 'blank writing', i.e. the degree zero of writing. At the university clinic in Leysin, where about thirty of us were being treated, a friend of mine, Fournié, talked to me convincingly about Marxism; he was an ex-typographer, a Trotskyist militant returning from deportation; the intelligence, flexibility and strength of his political analysis, his irony and wisdom, a certain moral freedom, in short the fullness of his character, free from any political *excitedness*, gave me a very high notion of Marxist dialec-tics (or, rather, what I saw in Marxism, thanks to Fournié, was dialectics); I only ever found this seductiveness again in reading Brecht. On the other hand, 1945–6 was the time when we were discovering Sartre. After the Armistice, to answer your question as directly and as briefly as possible, I was a Sartrian and a Marxist: I tried to 'engage' literary form (of which I had a deep sense from Camus's *L'Etranger*) and to Marxicize Sartrian engagement, or at least – and maybe this was a limitation – I tried to give it a Marxist justification: this dual project is quite apparent in *Writing Degree Zero*.

How did you come to literary criticism?

Have I in fact reached it? Or at least, is it really literary criticism that I came to? – I shall simply describe the circumstances. The friend I spoke of, Fournié, knew Maurice Nadeau, who then was the editor of the literary section of *Combat* – the importance of which at the time is well known. Around 1946, it must have been, I showed a short text to Nadeau about the idea of blank writing and the engagement of form. Nadeau asked me for two articles for *Combat*, which I gave him (in 1947): this was the origin of *Writing Degree Zero*. A little while later, after a stay as French Lecteur in Bucharest and Alexandria, returning to Paris as a (rather free) bureaucrat at the *Direction générale des relations culturelles*, I developed this same theme in further articles for *Combat* (in 1950). Besides Nadeau, to whom I owe my all-important start, two men were interested by these early texts, and they asked me to make a book out of them: Raymond Queneau (although

Gallimard refused the manuscript), and Albert Béguin, who, with Jean Cayrol, got me taken on by Seuil, where I am today.

Your first book is, in 1953, Writing Degree Zero. *This brief volume constitutes a 'beginning' of extraordinary power. Were you, subjectively, 'sure' of yourself (sure of your means, of your plans)?*

The 'subject' (something not really known at the time) is 'divided'; hence, 'subjectively', so was I. As subject of a struggle, or of what I saw as such – demonstrating the political and historical engagement of literary language – I was sure of myself; but as subject producing an object to be publicly offered up to the scrutiny of others, I was ashamed, rather; I remember one evening, after it became certain that *Writing Degree Zero* would be published by Seuil, walking along the Boulevard Saint-Michel and blushing at the idea that the book could not be called back. This feeling of panic still fills me today after writing certain texts (and I am not even talking about my reluctance, which is in truth a fear, to reread my old books); suddenly the power of words seems outrageous, their responsibility unsustainable: I feel too weak faced with my own writing. Still I carry on, throwing the text into circulation, because I tell myself that this is just a false moment in the labour of writing, the perhaps unavoidable phase when you still believe that, like speech, writing is an exposed piece of your own body – and also because of the kind of philosophical thinking that convinces me that writing cannot avoid being a terrorist act (a terror that can turn against its author), and that it is ridiculous to want to recover it: at most I might correct what in my text seems to hold too great a risk of being stupid or aggressive: I allow some of its traits to *drift*.

To which critical systems or theories of literature is Writing Degree Zero *indebted? Did Paulhan, Blanchot and Sartre contribute to your formation? And on the Marxist side, did you know the work of Lukács?*

I knew of no critical system or theory of literature ('system' and 'theory' were, anyway, unknown words in those existentialist times); I had read neither Paulhan, nor Blanchot or Lukács, and I probably did not even know their names (except maybe Paulhan). I knew Marx, a bit of Lenin, a bit of Trotsky, whatever was known by Sartre at the time, and I had read a lot of literature in the sanatorium.

Would you like to justify the 'exclusions' made by Writing Degree Zero *(for example, Artaud, Bataille, Ponge . . .)?*

These 'exclusions' were due to ignorance: I knew neither Artaud, nor Bataille or Ponge. You may indeed transform such ignorance into 'exclusions', but you then have to refer to my unconscious or my laziness, something which I leave to my future critics. It seems that, in these problems of intellectual chronology, you unduly project the present into the past: to know nothing of Bataille in 1950 doesn't mean the same thing as it does today; the same applies to Lukács: who knew Lukács after the war besides Lefebvre and Goldmann? It seems that in your opinion there is some sort of intellectual morality which obliges the essay writer to be systematically curious about intellectual production around him. My writing has always been more opaque, much less dependent on reading, than you think: injustice, partiality, chance, inadequacy, even, in one's reading-choices does not impede writing, even about contemporary things.

Describe your life up to your book on Michelet.

I remained with the *Service de l'enseignement des relations culturelles* for two or three years: I was dealing with doctorates *Honoris Causa* and with travel arrangements for teachers in religious schools. In 1952 I obtained a grant from the CNRS to complete a lexicology-thesis on the vocabulary of social issues in France around 1830. I must add that during my stay in Alexandria in 1950 I had met Greimas, who was a teacher like myself; thanks to Greimas I studied linguistics and through him I got to know Matoré: then I became interested in lexicology, in lexical sociology.

In 1954 you published your book on Michelet. Was it a completely voluntary choice? Or did external circumstances provoke this book?

When I was a student I used to see a man who was in many ways fascinating, Joseph Baruzi, the brother of the religious historian, the John of the Cross specialist. Joseph Baruzi had an extraordinary 'marginal' culture: he knew how to reveal the mystery of the outmoded. It is he who made me read Michelet's work, some of which I admired straight away (notably, as I recall, some pages on the egg), presumably because of their baroque forcefulness. Later, in Leysin (Swiss universities lent their books to tuberculosis patients, whereas the French universities didn't, for fear of contagion) I was able to read the whole of Michelet's work. I copied out onto index-cards sentences that, for whatever reason, pleased me, or simply sentences that were repeated; by classifying these sentences, the way you toy with a pack of playing cards, I necessarily ended up with a thematic analysis; then, when Seuil (Francis Jeanson, I believe) asked me for a book in their 'writers of all time' series, I just had to get it down on paper. This thematic analysis owed nothing to Bachelard for the simple reason that I had not read him – which did not seem like a valid enough reason for protesting every time the *Michelet* book was linked to Bachelard: why would I have *refused* Bachelard?

Would you like to talk about your involvement with Théâtre populaire?

Théâtre populaire had two distinct phases. During the first, we (Voisin, Dort, Dumur, Duvignaud, Paris, Morvan Lebesque and myself) were keen to defend, and even to criticize, Vilar's *Théâtre National Populaire* on the grounds that, in the end, it was good popular theatre: Vilar tried to break the institution of bourgeois theatre while insisting on a degree of aesthetic refinement within the conception of the stage show; but he did not have or did not want to have any ideological culture. The second phase of the *Théâtre populaire* was initiated by the arrival in France of Brecht and the Berliner Ensemble (in 1954). The – for us – radical struggle that we (especially Voisin, Dort and myself) engaged in on behalf of Brecht, of Brechtian theory and dramaturgy, created much bad feeling towards us; some left the group, others spent their time denying the *difference* we saw in Brecht's theatre, ironizing about the supposed intellectualism of Brechtian concepts ('distanciation', 'social gest,'[3] 'epic' theatre, etc.) – the French dislike mixing intelligence and art – or else they protested against the 'dogmatism' and 'terrorism' of French Brechtianism.

You have never stopped (see 'Literature and Signification', 1963) referring to Brecht. Why? Is the exemplarity of Brecht linked, for you, to his Marxist basis?

I have twice described (albeit briefly) the shock I felt from Brechtian theatre and the reasons why, as soon as I was aware of this theatre, it became difficult for me to like or even to watch any other; I may come back at some length to Brecht in a forthcoming work; Brecht is still very present for me, all the more so as he is not fashionable and still has not penetrated within the axiomatic field of the avant-garde. His exemplarity, in my eyes, derives in truth neither from his Marxism nor from his aesthetics (even though both have great importance), but from the conjunction of the two: i.e. from the conjunction of a Marxist reasoning and a semantic thinking: he was a Marxist who had reflected upon the *effects of the sign*: a rare thing.

You have not published a book on theatre. Your writings about theatre are either scattered through Mythologies, Sur Racine *and* Essais critiques, *or else have not been published in a book. Why is that?*

Simply because no one has asked me to.

Mythologies *came out in 1957. It is a collection of short texts published from 1954 to 1956, principally in the journal* Les Lettres Nouvelles. *First question: what part does a critical journal play in your work, in your* écriture?

One of the first effects of writing (whether feared or wished for) is not knowing *to whom one is speaking: writing* is not transferential (this is why many 'orthodox' psychoanalysts refute the idea of psychoanalytical literary criticism). In the process of writing, the journal represents a sort of intermediary stage between speech, which has specifically *ad hominem* aspects, and the book, which no longer does. Writing a text for a journal you don't really think about the readership of this journal (the readership is in any case not very 'thinkable') but about its group of editors; they have the virtue of constituting some sort of collective, but not really public, addressee: it is like a workshop, a 'class' (the way we speak of the violin class at the Conservatoire): you write for the class. Besides tactical considerations of struggle, of solidarity, which are not what I mean here – the journal is a stage in writing: the stage where you write to be liked by those you know, the careful, reasonable stage where you *begin* to relax, without breaking, the transferential umbilical cord of language. (This stage is never truly over: if I have no friends, if I was not writing for them, would I still have the courage to write? We come back to the journal.)

In the 1957 foreword to Mythologies *you present the text as an attempt to 'track down, in the decorative display of* what-goes-without-saying, *the ideological abuse which, in my view, is hidden there.'*[4] *Would you specify your political position in the fifties?*

The purpose of *Mythologies* is not political but ideological (paradoxically, at this time and in this France, ideological events seems more common than political ones). What defines *Mythologies* is a systematic and tireless assault on a type of monster that I called *la petite bourgeoisie* (to the point of turning it into a myth); the method is not very scientific and did not pretend to be so; that's why the methodological introduction only came later, after reading Saussure. The theory of *Mythologies* is treated in a *postface*; it is only a partial theory, by the way, because, though a *semiological* version of ideology was indeed sketched out, it should then have been completed, and still should be, with a political theory of the petty bourgeois as phenomenon. Since the petty-bourgeois element within myself is still being dealt with (far more so than the bourgeois element), I sometimes think about working on, if not a great book, at least some substantial enterprise on the petty bourgeoisie, where I would discover from others (political theorists, economists, sociologists) what, politically and economically, the petty bourgeoisie is and how to define it according to criteria that are not strictly cultural. My (highly ambivalent) interest in the petty bourgeoisie derives from the assumption (or working hypothesis) that today culture is almost no longer 'bourgeois' but 'petty-bourgeois'; or at least that the petty bourgeoisie is attempting at the moment to develop its own culture by *degrading* bourgeois culture: bourgeois culture returns within History but as a *farce* (you remember Marx's scheme); this 'farce' is so-called mass-culture.

You have often insisted on the importance in your 'evolution' of the essay 'Myth Today' (1956) that ends Mythologies. *But you published no book for five years after* Mythologies. *Even though later books take up texts written during that time, does this silence indicate a 'crisis', certain 'poetic' or scientific 'difficulties'?*

1956–63: I went through a period of instability, at the professional level. As I said, I had started a thesis in lexicology but I soon experienced some methodological difficulties that I couldn't resolve and that at the time I didn't even consider 'interesting' (briefly, I had difficulty with classifying, not words, which lexicology does very well, but syntagms, stereotypes – for example: 'Commerce et Industrie' – which was a way of posing the problem of what we might call associative semantics); I was not getting anywhere and my CNRS [Centre national de recherche scientifique] grant was withdrawn. At that point Robert Voisin helped me out by taking me on at the Arche publishing house; then, thanks to the support of Lucien Febvre and Georges Friedman, I came back to the CNRS but this time in sociology: I started a sociological, or more exactly a socio-semiological, analysis of clothing – which later led to *The Fashion System*[5]. A few years later (I don't recall the date) I again lost my CNRS grant, but again, thankfully, I was rescued when Fernand Braudel took me on at the *Ecole des Hautes Etudes* as supervisor. In 1962 I became director of studies there by proposing a seminar on the 'sociology of signs, symbols and representations': this title was a compromise: what I wanted to do was semiology (hence 'signs' and 'symbols') but I did not want to cut myself off from sociology (hence 'collective representations', a term from Durkheimian sociology).

Intellectually, I don't think there was any 'crisis' at that time, on the contrary; moreover I'm not sure whether the production of books is halted by a 'crisis' or by one's confidence, drive and enthusiasm for the gathering of information; in my case it was rather the latter. Thanks to Saussure, I could (or so I thought) define ideology through the connotation-scheme of semantics, I firmly believed I could become part of a semiological *science*: I lived through a (euphoric) dream of scientificity (of which *The Fashion System* and *Elements of Semiology* are the residue). Writing books did not matter to me then, I had time; besides, as you have said, I wrote many articles which sustained my writing (my desire to write). What followed, at least until now, has shown that my 'truth' resided in the second postulation, not in the first, even though I often still have to sanction this truth as a 'semiologist', an authority in some circles, contested in others.

Two of your books have a name as title: are Michelet and Racine particularly important writers for you, either as signifiers of classical or nineteenth-century literature, or in themselves? And are they, for you, 'favourite' writers? What is a 'favourite' writer? And who are 'your' favourite writers?

I have explained the personal origins of the *Michelet* book. *Racine* was a straightforward commission. Grégory, from the *Club Français du Livre*, had asked me for an introduction to the *Mémoires d'outre-tombe*. I liked it very much but the professor who had established the 'correct' text wouldn't allow Grégory to use it; Grégory needed a *Racine*, so he asked me to do it ('they needed an accountant, the man who got it was a dancer'[6]). As much as I like Michelet, I dislike Racine; I could only get interested in him by introducing personal problems of alienation in love. As for the 'favourite' author question, I think it's simply whomever you regularly reread: in which case, to stay with the classics, my 'favourite' authors are, above all, Sade, Flaubert and Proust.

What works on linguistics or other scientific disciplines have influenced your semiological research?

It's the whole of culture, the infinity of our readings, our conversations – even hurried, half-understood fragments – in short the inter-text, which acts upon your work, knocking on the door to be let in. To name names I would say that in my case the semiological push comes from Saussure, read in 1956 (though, by 1947, I had read a 'minor' structuralist called Viggo Brøndal, from whom I took the notion of 'degree zero'); I owe much to my conversations from 1950 onwards with Greimas, who, among other things, introduced me early on to the Jakobsonian theory of shifters and to the formal weight of such figures as metaphor, metonymy, catalysis and ellipsis; Hjelmslev enabled me to push further and formalize the schema of connotation, a notion which always been very important to me and that I cannot do without, despite the risk in presenting denotation as a natural state and connotation as a cultural state of language. As for Chomsky, it's really only now, very late, that I've been interested in him. I read Propp in English, I don't know when, after a tip from Lévi-Strauss, and, before the appearance of Todorov's anthology, I read Erlich's book on the Russian Formalists[7]. But of all the linguists I have read, Benveniste comes first, so shamefully forgotten and abandoned today: the surface of his linguistics simmers, poignant in its discreteness, like water that's about to boil: this strength, this heat that makes science rise (even as rigorous a science as Benveniste's) towards *something else*, is, as you know, what I call writing. Here we enter a very modern history (Lévi-Strauss, Lacan, Todorov, Genette, Derrida, Kristeva, *Tel Quel*, Sollers), the subject of the seminar I want to work on for 1971–2. If it is linguistics that set up the operative frame of semiology, semiology was only modified and developed under the glare of other disciplines, other ways of thinking, other demands: ethnology, philosophy, Marxism, psychoanalysis, theories of writing and of the text (and it would be wrong to 'recoup' these disciplines as semiology, on the grounds of being a 'semiologist': there is a general dislocation towards *something else*).

In 1965, a pamphlet by Professor Picard, Nouvelle Critique ou nouvelle impos-ture, *violently attacked the* nouvelle critique *and especially you. This attack received the 'uncritical, unqualified, undivided support' of much of the press. Since 1953, what hostility have you provoked? Did this 'Picard affair' have any antecedents, or did it take you by surprise?*

I shall answer by referring to the future, rather than to the past. If the Picard affair is closed, it is not forasmuch *foreclosed.* Which means that on the historical stage of the signifier it can return; I would even say that within an unchanging society, through a simple repetition compulsion, it *must* come back. The actors will be new but the *site* will be the same. I have always been struck by the fact that Picard's arguments, or rather his turns of phrase, though apparently coming from an over-aestheticizing view of literature, could just as well have come from, and so could still come from, an opposite direction: from historicism, positivism or sociologism, for example. In fact, these sites are all one, i.e. a site of a *blindness to signs [asymbolie]*: on the other side of psychoanalysis, there is only one place, whose occupants (the 'actors') may change, but not its topological function. Without wishing it, of course, I wouldn't be surprised if one day, for example, a certain kind of university came to replace the traditional university, and that Picard was reborn in the guise of some positivist, sociologist or 'Marxist' censor (I put it in inverted commas to indicate that it would only be a *certain kind* of Marxism): such places already exist.

The Fashion System *came out in 1967. You have presented this book as a 'quite naïve type of stained glass window' where one must read 'not the certainty of a doctrine, nor even the unchanging conclusions of research, but rather the beliefs, temp-tations and trials of an apprenticeship'. Why this naïveté, in 1967, ten years after* Mythologies? *Is your work obstinately bound to the 'trials' of a never-ending apprenticeship?*

I had first thought of developing a serious socio-semiological analysis of clothing, of clothing as a whole (I had even begun some of the research); then, after a private comment from Lévi-Strauss, I decided to homogenize the corpus and to content myself with *written* clothing (as described by fashion magazines). Because of this change, *The Fashion System* was published much later than it was conceived and for the most part worked out. In those years intellectual history evolved quickly, the unfinished manuscript became anachronistic and I even had second thoughts about publishing it. It may also be because I expected nothing (let's say: I expected no pleasure) from the publication of the book: my pleasure was entirely in the development, in assembling the system, working hard at it, with enthusiasm, the way you work at solving a problem in physics or at putting together a complex and useless object. There was barely any pleasure in announcing the result of this work – something that shows in writing-up (proving once more that the *imaginary* of science dispenses with writing but also misses it – and misses truth)./*The Fashion System* obeyed a scientific impulse; I believed then that once the semiological theory was laid out, one had to build specific semiotics, semiotics *applied* to pre-existing constructions of cultural objects: food, clothes, narratives, the city, etc. This deductive view is what later seemed to me 'naïve': the 'good sense' which appears to dictate such an enterprise derives rather more from the *imaginary* of the scientist (I always use 'imaginary' in the Lacanian sense). In other words, the naïveté was the belief in metalanguage.

As for the infinite nature of my apprenticeship, I would say this: it's not the apprenticeship that is unending, but desire. My works seems to consist in a series of 'disinvestments'; there is only one object from which I never have disinvested my desire: language. Language is my *objet petit a*.[8] Since *Writing Degree Zero* (and probably since my adolescence, when I perceived the discourse of the provincial bourgeoisie as spectacle), it is language that I have chosen to love – and of course to hate at the same time: I am entirely trusting and entirely mistrustful of it; but as for my methods of approach, dependent as they were on whatever was being said all around me, whatever was exerting a particular fascination on me, they can have changed. They can be tried out, be found to please, be transformed, and be abandoned: as if you still loved the same person but were trying out some new forms of eroticism with them. *The interminable apprenticeship* cannot be understood as a kind of humanist programme, as if you were never satisfied with yourself and had to progress ('mature') towards some Olympian image made of knowledge and wisdom; it is, rather, as the fateful stream of what Lacan calls 'the revolution of desire'.

The dedication to S/Z *(1970), thinking about the concerns of many teachers, particularly within the 'arts and humanities', has an air of provocation about it: 'This book is the trace of a work done during a two-year seminar (1968–9) held at the Ecole pratique des Hautes Etudes. I hope that the students, auditors and friends who took part in this seminar will accept this dedication of a text which was written according to their attention (écoute) to it.'[9] Don't you think that these sentences might irritate some professors whose teaching is challenged?*

I am certain that students and teachers already create working communities between themselves; in any case this is the norm at the *Ecole des Hautes Etudes*. If this dedication contains a paradox, it is not the one you are driving at, it is another which is not usually noticed: some people have thought that *S/Z* arose out of *discussions* between students and the director of studies; they haven't seen that the dedication (besides its genuinely friendly character) is there to introduce the term 'listening' [*écoute*]. The paradox, mindful of academic and contestatory discourses, is the following suggestion: I see no interest in opposing the 'lecture' to the 'seminar'; liberation does not consist in giving the student the right of speech (a minimal measure), but in attempting to modify the circuit of speech – not its physical circuit ('speaking up') but its topological circuit (referring here, of course, to psychoanalysis). In other words, attempting to become conscious of the true dialectic (in the Lacanian not the Platonic sense) within the teaching relationship. According to this dialectic, listening is not only active – which doesn't mean very much in itself – *listening is productive*: by returning to me – in silence, possibly, but through a renewed presence – the analysis of *Sarrasine* I was engaged upon, the auditorium, to whom I was bound by a transferential relation, ceaselessly modified my own discourse.

On the other hand, why spend two years on a novella by Balzac, when, according to your own declarations, 'the exigence' of "ideological critique" 'brutally reappears'?

To follow on from what I said about 'listening': two years might seem a long time to 'explicate' a few pages out of Balzac, but that's a good length of time for a transference. What fundamentally differentiates a seminar from a lecture – and this is why I like seminars and dislike lectures – is that in the first instance a dialectic can be developed, in the second instance it's just a show of force by language: a seminar, *because it lasts*, and deals with a single object, features many hidden 'adventures' (I always speak of the adventures of the signifier); for me the principal object of a seminar is not its programme ('produce a textual analysis of a novel by Balzac'), but lies in the knowledge of language sought after and tacitly practised within the seminar.

As for ideological critique, everybody agrees that's the new university's obsession; the difficulty is deciding where ideology is, or rather *if there is a place where it is not* (this place is not necessarily the one from which the critic of ideology speaks). I don't think that ideology stops *before* Balzac (in relation to us), or rather (since the object of my work was not Balzac but the text) *before* the classical Narrative. It is precisely because the demand of ideological criticism has brutally resurfaced these past three years, as I said in the introduction to *Mythologies*, that we must resist the temptation to reply brutally, with declarations *on* ideology. The stronger the demand, the more subtle the response: otherwise it would run the risk being merely opportunistic, or just functionally descriptive: we would declare ourselves to be outside of ideology without *first* asking where ideology is – and where is it not.

How can one distinguish, using Kristeva's concept of intertextuality, the 'fiction author' and the 'critic'? Can S/Z be read as the 'rewriting' of Balzac?

The notion of *inter-text* has first of all a polemical value: it serves to counter the Law of *context*. We all know that the context of a message (its material surroundings) reduces its polysemy. If you speak of *jumelles*, a word with two meanings in French, it is the remainder of the sentence that is responsible for eliminating one of the two possible meanings and for determining the signified as either 'binoculars' or 'sisters born at the same birth'. In other words the context restores the signification, or rather, to be both more general and more precise, restores the signifying process to communication. To 'take account of' the context (in philology, in criticism, in linguistics) is always a *positive*, reductive, legalistic enterprise, premissed on the evidence of rationalism: the context is, in the end, an asymbolic object; take anyone who invokes context, go far enough and you will always be met by a resistance to symbols, an asymbolism. The inter-text – which is not the bench of 'influ-ences', 'sources' and 'origins' before which a work or an author is summoned – is, more broadly and at quite another level, the field where is effected what Sollers (in his article on Dante)[10] brilliantly and unforgettably called *the traversal* (traversée) *of writing*: it is the text *as it crosses and is crossed* (you can recognize, in this equivalence of the active and passive voices, the speech of the unconscious). This means that the inter-text does not recognize any divi-sion of genre. Putting aside, of course, the question of value, the commentary in *S/Z* seeks *equality* with the Balzac text (*equal* as when a canal-lock brings two planes of water to the same level). So it isn't wrong to say that *S/Z* is a rewriting of *Sarrasine* – as long as one adds straight away that it is not 'I' who wrote *S/Z*: it is 'we': everyone I consciously or uncon-sciously cited, called upon, and which are 'readings', not 'authors'.

As for the more specific opposition between fiction and criticism, I have often said that this opposition breaks down within the present crisis of the novel, within the crisis of criticism, and in respect of the advent of the Text. In the transitory state of present production, the roles are simply confused, without yet being abolished. As far as I'm concerned, I don't see myself as a critic, but rather as a novelist, a *scripteur* not of the novel [*le roman*], it is true, but of the 'romanesque': *Mythologies* and *Empire of Signs* are novels *without* a story, *On Racine* and *S/Z* are novels *about* stories, *Michelet* is a para-biography, etc. This is why I could say that my own historical position (one should always ask oneself this question) is to be at the *rear-guard of the avant-garde*: to be avant-garde one must know what is dead; to be rear-guard, one must still love it: I like the romanesque but I know that the novel is dead: this is, I think, the exact place of what I write.

Some of the pages of the Empire of Signs *are reminiscent of the 'realism' of texts in* Mythologies. *A Utopia today, a satire in 1957: to use the formula you applied to Voltaire, it would be tempting to say that you are – very paradoxically, since for you the questioning of literature is central – 'the last happy writer'. What do you owe to the eighteenth century (Voltaire, Montesquieu, Diderot . . .)?*

The little tableaux in the *Empire of Signs* are happy mythologies: maybe this is because, on top of certain personal reasons, in Japan my highly artificial position as a tourist, as a lost tourist, as an ethnographer, in short, allowed me to 'forget' the Japanese petty bourgeoisie, the influence it certainly has over morals, the art of living, the style of objects, etc.: I was spared the mythological nausea. One of my projects (requiring far greater effort) would be precisely to *forget* the French petty bourgeoisie and to itemize the few 'pleasures' I can enjoy while living in France. If I ever produce this book, it could be called *Our France*, a reference to Michelet, to whom a book of the same title is apocryphally attributed. It would of course demand a dialectical analysis, because I wouldn't, as I could for Japan, be able to separate modern France from its political history; moreover, as I am French, I would have to 'psychoanalyse' myself in some way, to know what I am abolishing, assuming or transforming as regards my origins.

As for the eighteenth century, I've not been much inclined to read its authors – which means I still have to read them. This is a pleasure that I am quite deliberately *keeping in reserve*, especially regarding Diderot. The reason can seem artificial, frivolous, but I think that it follows the logic of my desire: a text touches me directly, in some kind of intimate way, through its language; the language of the eighteenth century (except Sade's, for reasons I've tried to show in a recent text[11]), to my eyes, is not marked: I cannot see the code, its codes (this is probably why it is said to be 'elegant'): it comes at that moment in History when class-language becomes *natural*. Things criss-cross: the language I relish is not the language of progressive time (the language of the – intellectually – already empowered bourgeoisie) but the language of authoritarian time, the clumsy coded, *jointed* [*coudée*] language (with its vast articulations) of the rising intellectual bourgeoisie, the prose of the seventeenth century: I have read (sadly, no doubt) more Bossuet than Diderot.

You wrote in Empire of Signs: *'Writing is after all, in its way, a* satori; satori *(the Zen event) is a more or less powerful (though in no way formal) seism which causes knowledge, or the subject, to vacillate: it creates* an emptiness of language. *And it is also* an emptiness of language *which constitutes writing . . . '*[12] *What is this 'writing' in relation to that of* Writing Degree Zero?

From the writing of *Writing Degree Zero* to writing as we understand it today, there has been a shift and, so to speak, an inversion of names. In *Writing Degree Zero*, writing is a rather sociological, or at least socio-linguistic, notion: it is the idiolect of a collectivity, of an intellectual group, a sociolect situated on the scale of communities between language, the system of a nation, and style, the system of a subject. Today I would rather call this writing *écrivance* (with reference to the opposition *écrivains/écrivants*[13]), as writing (in today's sense) is specifically absent from it; and writing, according to the new theory, tends to fill the place of what I then called style. In its traditional sense, style refers to a matrix of utterances; in 1947, I had tried to existentialize, to 'put flesh on' the notion. Today we go much further: writing is not a personal idiolect (as style was), it is an uttering (not an utterance) through which the subject plays out its division through dispersal, casts themselves obliquely across the scene of the blank page. This notion owes little to the old idea of 'style' but owes much, as you are aware, to the double revelation of materialism (through the idea of productivity) and psychoanalysis (through the idea of the divided subject).

What 'plans' your work? Do you always have some work 'ahead of you'?

I have only once ever written a text 'for nothing', my first text, the one I showed Nadeau around 1946, which was not published but determined the requests that followed. Beside this first zero text, all my texts have been written according to requests (when I am left free to choose the subject) or according to commissions (when the subject is given, which I don't necessarily mind). In short, I've always written in response to someone's prompting. Which means that, since life brings me into an increasing number of relationships and situations, I have more and more work 'ahead of me' – and hence I am always behind. I spend my time writing out 'plans' (in the magical hope that to write down a project is to have realized it) which I pin up in front of me and then have to rework when they go out of date. Within the intellectual 'profession' (since it is a profession) there is a familiar vertigo arising from the contradiction between the pressure of demand, which creates an illusion of vitality, as if you were someone *necessary*, and the gratuity of the practice of writing, from which, as Lacan might say, we protect ourselves [*se remparder*] by repeating that writing is a political task, is counter-ideological, etc.: a labour demanded of us by History. One way of limiting this vertigo without entering the imaginary of false reasons is to *functionalize* [*fonctionnariser*[14]] the practice of writing, to regularize it through an ascetic approach to time-keeping; I try to reserve every morning, *whatever may happen*, for the labour of writing.

Writing in response to a request (or to a commission) is a 'task'. I proceed from task to task, which in no way precludes the pleasure [*jouissance*] of writing, nor even its 'dreams'. A dream of writing is not necessarily compact; an idea for a book doesn't come about in an organized, deliberate, justified way, but through scraps of desire, fragmentary wishes, that arise from any kind of contact with life, and do not necessarily bear upon important ideas. Before conceiving of a book, before having the slightest idea as to what it could be, or even that it might one day exist, you can conjure up an ultimate detail of the book, a phrase *for which* the book will be made, or a typographical layout that you can *see* (I think a text has no chance of ending *happily* – beyond any sense of 'obligation' – unless you *see*, almost *hallucinate*, the typographical – the written – object into which it will be transformed). Lately I have often formulated these two dreams: to write a 'free' text, conceived beyond any sense of demand (as far as one as its origins go), and thereby opened up to experiments with form (it is never a *form* that is asked for: the age is gone when you would be asked for a 'sonnet'), experiments conducted *at my level, within my own limits*, not according to models generated by the avant-garde. The other dream is to devote myself to acquiring some new form of knowledge: learning a language, a science, or even simply knowing a particular subject 'thoroughly'. But this would need an object that wasn't too detached or futile (not a hobby, like stamp collecting), nor too close to the language of today, that didn't require its modernity or its importance to be perceived *too quickly*. These are not impossible dreams; the impediment would be my awareness in the end that they depend upon an 'imaginary', and that the 'truth' of my work tends to be located there where a quite specific *request*, issuing from the collectivity *as it is* (a *commission*, in effect), immediately and in some sense naïvely introduces into my plan, without pause, detour or transcendence, the desire of the Other: this is the condition on which, given my own neurotic structure, I can remain *close to the signifier* and not be too soon disappointed by its constant fits and starts: it is during this very brief *reprieve* that I write.

What is this 'interview'? What is the 'posterity' to which, in its televisual guise, it would appear to be destined?

I would like to use your question to put the interview on trial – not this particular interview, as its aim is biographical, hence acceptable; it alone makes use of the first person of the past historic, whereas writing cannot. Nor do I mean written interviews, questionnaires where the answers are entirely generated by writing. I am speaking of the everyday interview, spoken, recorded and then transcribed (but not written). This kind of interview is very much in vogue. The reasons are presumably economical (if not directly financial): the interview is a cheap article. 'You don't have time to write a text? Well give us an interview.' The old rivalry between thought and form resurfaces, or rather their economy, their false complicity (as old partners in crime): *thought* has the reputation of being immediate, it is assumed to require no preparation, it costs nothing, it can be *directly* dispensed: that's the interview. *Form*, on the other hand, is labour intensive, needing time and effort, it's expensive: that's the article. Thought doesn't get amended, but style does. An entirely bourgeois view, literally, since the law of the bourgeois state (dating from the Revolution) protects the ownership of the form, but not of thought. It's a curious trick: the thought is devalued, it becomes anonymous, at the same time as it is being evoked and framed during the interview as *personal*. The mechanism of this practice is entirely theatrical: the interview is an emphatic sign that the author *thinks*; speech is supposed to be thought in its purest state. To note speech (without writing it) sanctions it as a responsible, consequential act: I shall countersign your speech, hence you are thinking. During the interview the author *acts as if* he is thinking. (I am questioning an institution, not the performances; I don't deny that some interviews are well thought out, and in some circumstances useful. Moreover, to systematically refuse interviews would be to play another role, that of the secretive, wild, unsociable thinker.) In relation to writing (which does not mean style), the interview seems even more vain, to the point of being absurd. Its practice supposes that the writer, having *written* (a text, a book), still has something to *say*: what? some 'oversight'? some 'leftovers'? Unless he is asked, as is often the case, to repeat himself, or, worse, to spell out 'clearly' what was written 'densely'. Those things that constitute writing – the ambiguity of meaning, of meanings, ellipsis, ambivalence, figure, word-play, anagram – are not matters of style, but the enunciatory practice whereby the subject engages with language. Writing is precisely what exceeds speech, it is a supplement wherein is inscribed not another unconsciousness (there aren't two of them) but another relationship between the speaker (or the listener) and the unconscious. Hence speech cannot add to writing. What I have written is then *prohibited from speech*. What more could I say? What could I say better? One has to persuade oneself that speech is always *behind* writing (and therefore behind one's 'private life', which is only the unfolding of a word: 'I' am always, by necessity, more stupid, more naïve, etc., than what I write). Strictly speaking, the only kind of interview which one could defend would be one in which the author would be solicited to say what he could not write. The good interviewer would then be someone who, giving up the task of re-presenting to the author the usual subjects of his work, would have a conscious awareness of the way speech and writing were *shared out*, and would interrogate his partner on the very thing which writing disallowed him to write. What writing never writes is 'I'; what speech always says is 'I'; what the interviewer should solicit is thus the author's *imaginary*, the list of his phantasms, inasmuch as he can reflect upon them, speak them in that fragile state (which would thus be specifically that of *interviewed speech*) in which they are articulated enough to be spoken and so insufficiently dissolved so as to be written (for example, as far as I am concerned: music, food, travel, sexuality, work habits).

As for 'posterity', what can I say? It's a dead word for me, which is giving it its dues since its validity is only established on the basis of my death. I consider that I have lived well up to now (I mean: happily, in a distracted manner, in a state of enjoyment) *within a small part of my time and my country*. I am entirely taken up in this simultaneity, in this concurrence, I am no more than a *particular contemporary*, which means: destined while I live to the exclusion of a large number of languages, and subsequently destined to an absolute death; buried in the archives (of the twentieth century), perhaps one day I will re-emerge, like a fugitive, one witness among others, in a broadcast of the Service for Research on 'structuralism', 'semiology' or 'literary criticism'. Can you imagine me living, working, desiring, for that? In any case, the only eschatological thought I can have would not concern my 'survival'; if one day the relations between the subject and the world were to be changed, certain words would be dropped, like in a Melanesian tribe in which at each death a few elements of the lexicon are suppressed as a sign of mourning; but it would be rather as a sign of joy; or at least if those words were to join the museum of social and burlesque archaeology of which Fourier dreamed for the distraction of the children in the phalanstery: this would happen doubtless to the word 'posterity', and perhaps to all the 'possessives' of our language, and, why not, to the word 'death' itself. Cannot one conceive of a community (undreamed of even in religions) such that the terrible solitude of death (experienced first of all in the fear of losing a loved one) would be impossible? Could there not one day be a *socialist* solution to the horror of death? I don't see why death should not be a socialist problem. Someone (Gurvitch, I think) quoted Lenin or Trotsky (I don't remember which, but it was at a time, in the middle of the October Revolution, when the distinction was not important): 'And if the sun is bourgeois, we will stop the sun.' This is a specifically revolutionary statement (which could only be produced in a revolutionary period); what Marxist would dare to proclaim today: 'And if death is bourgeois, we will stop death'?

In your article on Julia Kristeva's Séméiotiké *('The Stranger', 1970) you write that 'in a society deprived of socialist practice, thus condemned to "discourse", theoretical discourse is temporarily necessary'. Do you mean to say that your work is an awaiting and a preparation for 'socialist practice'?*

Your question runs the risk in my opinion of reducing the plural of the subject in representing it as tending towards something unique and full; your question denies the unconscious. I accept it, however, and I will answer this: if it is absolutely necessary, to live and to work, to have a representation of an end (which is sometimes curiously called a Cause), I would just remind you of the tasks that Brecht suggests for the intellectual in a non-revolutionary period: liquidate and theorize. These tasks are always coupled together by Brecht: our discourse can represent nothing, prefigure nothing; we only have a negative activity at our disposition (Brecht called it *critical*, or even *epic*, that is, interruptive [*entre-coupée*], interrupting [*qui coupe*] history), at the end of which shines only, like a distant glimmer, intermittent and uncertain (barbarism is always a possibility), the ultimate transparency of social relations.

Translated by Vérène Grieshaber

Notes

1 [This interview, as Barthes remarks, was originally destined for television broad-cast. It is published in issue 47 of the review (1971), as part of a special issue on [Barthes, the first of its kind, alongside articles on Barthes by Sollers, Kristeva, François Wahl, Severo Sarduy and Annette Lauers, and a poem by Pleynet dedi-cated to Barthes. It also included Barthes's article 'Writers, Intellectuals, Teachers'. In the final, editorial section, the issue also includes the 'Positions of the Movement of June 21st', a Maoist splinter group within *Tel Quel*, which would eventually assume control, and a chronology of the review's history up to that point, 'rewritten' from a Maoist perspective.]

2 [Fauré's settings of Verlaine, recorded by Panzera in the 1930s.]

3 [Gest: 'a gesture or set of gestures (but never a gesticulation) in which a whole social situation can be read', from 'Diderot, Brecht, Eisenstein', in *Image – Music – Text*, trans. Stephen Heath (London, Fontana, 1977), 73–4.]

4 Roland Barthes, *Mythologies*, trans. Annette Lavers (London, Cape, 1972), 11.

5 [R. Barthes, *The Fashion System*, trans. M. Ward and R. Howard (London, Cape, 1985)].

6 [Barthes quotes here from Beaumarchais, *The Marriage of Figaro*, Act V, Scene 3, Figaro's monologue.]

7 [See T. Todorov (ed.) *Théorie de la littérature* (Paris: Seuil, 1965) and V. Erlich, *Russian Formalism: History and Doctrine* (New Haven: Yale University Press, 1965)].

8 [*Objet petit a*: a term from Lacanian discourse: little other object, the small a differentiates it from the Other (*Autre*). Malcolm Bowie, in *Lacan* (London, Fontana, 1991), qualifies it as 'anything and everything that desire touches, [which] cannot exist where desire is not' (166).]

9 From the dedication to *S/Z*, trans. R. Miller (Oxford, Blackwell, 1974), x.

10 [See P. Sollers, 'Dante and the Traversal of Writing' in *Writing and the Experience of Limits*, trans D. Hayman and P. Barnard (New York: Columbia University Press, 1983.]

11 *Sade, Fourier, Loyola*, trans. R. Miller (London, Cape, 1977). [French version 1971.]

12 *Empire of Signs*, trans. R. Miller (London, Cape, 1975), 4. [French version 1975.]

13 [*Ecrivain*: the writer for whom writing is a problem in itself; *écrivant*: the writer for whom writing is a means to an end. See *Critical Essays*, trans, R. Howard (Evaston, Northwestern University Press, 1972).]

14 [I.e. to treat as would a *fonctionnaire*, a white-collar worker.]

BIBLIOGRAPHY

TEL QUEL IN ENGLISH

(Articles or books originally published in or by the review; other material by members of the group.)

Barthes, R., *Critical Essays*, trans. R. Howard (Evanston, IL, Northwestern University Press, 1972)
——*Criticism and Truth*, trans. K. Pilcher Keunemen (London, Athlone, 1987)
——*A Lover's Discourse: Fragments*, trans. R. Howard (New York, Cape, 1979)
——*The Pleasure of the Text*, trans. R. Miller (Oxford, Blackwell, 1990)
——*The Responsibility of Forms: Critical Essays on Music, Art and Representation*, trans. R. Howard (Berkeley, University of California Press, 1986)
——*The Rustle of Language*, trans. R. Howard (Oxford, Blackwell,1986)
——*Sade, Fourier, Loyola*, trans. R. Miller (New York, Cape, 1972)
——*The Semiotic Challenge*, trans. R. Howard (Oxford, Blackwell, 1988)
——*Sollers Writer*, trans. P. Thody (London, Athlone, 1987)
——*S/Z*, trans. R. Miller (Oxford, Blackwell, 1990)
Baudry, J.-L., 'The Apparatus', trans. J. Andrews and B. Angst, *Camera Obscura*, 1 (Fall 1976)
——'Ideological Effects of the Basic Cinematographic Apparatus', trans. A. Williams, *Film Quarterly*, 27: 2 (Winter 1974–5)
Boulez, P., *Stocktakings from an Apprenticeship*, trans. S. Walsh (Oxford, Clarendon, 1991)
Derrida, J. *Dissemination*, trans. B. Johnson (London, Athlone, 1981)
—— *Positions*, trans. A. Bass (London, Athlone, 1981)
——*Writing and Difference*, trans. A. Bass (London and Chicago, Routledge & Kegan Paul, 1978)
Eco, U., *The Open Work*, trans. A. Cancogni (London, Hutchinson Radius 1989) [Eco's articles in *Tel Quel* on Joyce were a version of some sections of this book.]
Foucault, M., *Language, Counter-Memory, Practice*, ed. D.F. Bouchard, trans. D.F. Bouchard and S. Simon (Oxford, Blackwell, 1977) [Contains Foucault's article 'Language to Infinity', originally in *Tel Quel*.]
Genette, G., *Figures of Literary Discourse*, trans. A. Sheridan (Oxford, Blackwell, 1982)

Goux, J.-J., *The Coiners of Language*, trans. J.C. Gage (Norman and London, University of Oklahoma Press, 1994)

——'Discourses of Impossibility: Can Psychoanalysis Be Political?', trans. E.J. Bellamy, *Diacritics: A Review of Contemporary Criticism*, 23:1 (1993)

——'General Economics and Postmodern Capitalism', trans. K. Ascheim and R. Garelick, *Yale-French-Studies*, 78 (1990)

——'Lacan Iconoclast', trans. J.C. Gage, *Stanford Literature Review*, 8:1–2 (1991)

——'Luce Irigaray versus the Utopia of the Neutral Sex', in C. Burke, N. Schor and M. Whitford (eds), *Engaging with Irigaray: Feminist Philosophy and Modern European Thought* (New York, Columbia University Press, 1994)

——'Politics and Modern Art – Heidegger's Dilemma', trans. M. Sharp, *Diacritics: A Review of Contemporary Criticism*, 19:3–4 (1989)

Guyotat, P., *Eden, Eden, Eden*, trans. G. Fox (London, Creation, 1996)

Hollier, D., 'The Dualist Materialism of Georges Bataille', *Yale French Studies*, 78 (1990)

Kristeva, J., *About Chinese Women*, trans. A. Barrows (London, Boyars, 1977)

——*Desire in Language: A Semiotic Approach to Literature and Art*, ed. L.S. Roudiez, trans. L.S. Roudiez, T. Gora and A. Jardine (Oxford, Blackwell, 1980)

——*The Kristeva Reader*, ed. T. Moi (Oxford, Blackwell, 1986)

——*Language, the Unknown*, trans. A.M. Menke (Hemel Hempstead, Harvester Wheatsheaf, 1989)

——'My Memory's Hyperbole', *New York Literary Forum*, 12–13 (1984)

——*Powers of Horror*, trans. L.S. Roudiez (New York and Guildford, Columbia University Press, 1982)

——*Revolution of Poetic Language*, trans. M. Waller (New York and Guilford, Columbia University Press, 1984)

——*The Samurais* (New York, 1995)

——*Tales of Love*, trans. L.S. Roudiez (New York and Guilford, Columbia University Press, 1987)

Pleynet, M. *Giotto* (Milan, 1985)

——*Motherwell*, trans. M.A. Caws (Paris, Editions Daniel Papierski, 1989)

——*Painting and System*, trans. S.M. Godfrey (Chicago and London, University of Chicago Press, 1984)

Ricardou, J., 'Nouveau Roman, Tel Quel', trans. E. Freiberg, in *Surfiction: Fiction Now . . . and Tomorrow* (Chicago, Swallow, 1981)

Risset, J., 'Joyce and *La moglie del sordo*', in Carla de Petris (ed.), *Joyce Studies in Italy* (Rome, 1988)

Roche, M., *Compact*, trans. M. Polizzotti (New York, Dalkey Archive, 1988)

Sarduy, S., *Cobra, Maitreya*, trans. S.J. Levine (New York, Dalkey Archive, 1995)

Scarpetta, G. 'Kundera's Quartet (On *The Unbearable Lightness of Being*', *Salmagundi* (New York), 73 (1987)

——'Richard Foreman's Scenography: Examples from his Work in France', trans. J. Dolan, *The Drama Review* (Cambridge, MA), 28:2 (1984)

Schefer, J.-L., *The Enigmatic Body*, trans. P. Smith (Cambridge, Cambridge University Press, 1996)

Schneidermann, S., *Jacques Lacan: The Death of an Intellectual Hero* (Cambridge, MA, Harvard University Press, 1983)

Screen Reader I (London, BFI Publications, 1977)

Sollers, P., *A Curious Solitude*, trans. R. Howard (London, Eyre & Spottiswoode, 1961)

——*The Park*, trans. A.M. Sheridan Smith (London, Calder & Boyars, 1968)

——*Watteau in Venice*, trans. A. Manguel (New York, Scribner's, 1995)

——*Women*, trans. B. Bray (London, Quartet, 1984)

——*Writing and the Experience of Limits*, ed. D. Hayman, trans. D. Hayman and P. Barnard (New York, Columbia University Press, 1983)

Thibaudeau, J. 'The Novel as Autobiography', trans. J. Goodwin, *Denver-Quarterly*, 13:3 (1978)

——'Novels, Not Philosophy', trans. W. Guyman, *Yale French Studies*, 52 (1975)

——'Preliminary Notes on the Prison Writings of Gramsci: The Place of Literature in Marxian Theory', trans. M. Malet, *Praxis: A Journal of Radical Perspectives on the Arts*, 3 (1976)

MATERIAL IN ENGLISH ON *TEL QUEL*

Bann, S. 'The Career of *Tel Quel*: *Tel Quel* becomes *L'Infini*', *Comparative Criticism*, 6 (1984)

——'Introduction to Marcelin Pleynet: Painting and 'Surrealism and Painting'', *Comparative Criticism*, 4 (1982)

Benoist, J.-M., *The Structural Revolution* (London, Weidenfeld & Nicolson, 1978)

Brandt, J., *Geopolitics: The Politics of Mimesis in Poststructuralist French Poetry and Theory* (Stanford, Stanford University Press, 1997)

——'The Theory and Practice of a "Revolutionary Text": Denis Roche's *Le Mécrit*', *Yale French Studies*, 67 (1984)

Britton, C., 'The *Nouveau Roman* and *Tel Quel* Marxism', *Paragraph*, 12 (March 1989)

Descombes, V., *Modern French Philosophy*, trans. L. Scott-Fox and J.M. Harding (Cambridge, Cambridge University Press, 1980)

Dews, P., *Logics of Disintegration* (London, Verso, 1987)

Elliot, G., *Althusser, the Detour of Theory* (London, Verso, 1987)

ffrench, P., '*Tel Quel* and Surrealism: A Re-evaluation', *Romanic Review*, 88:1, January 1997

——*The Time of Theory* (Oxford, Clarendon, 1996)

ffrench, P. (ed.) *From* Tel Quel *to* L' Inhini: *The Avant-guarde and After*; Parallax, S (1998).

Fletcher, J. and Benjamin, A. (eds), *Abjection, Melancholia and Love: The Work of Julia Kristeva* (London, Routledge, 1990)

Greene, R.W. 'Poetry, Metapoetry, Revolution: Stages on Marcelin Pleynet's Way', *Romanic Review*, 68 (1977)

——*Six French Poets of Our Time* (Princeton, Princeton University Press, 1979)

Guerlac, S., *The Impersonal Sublime* (Stanford, Stanford University Press, 1990)

——'The Sublime in Theory', *Modern Language Notes*, 106 (1991)

Harland, R., *Superstructuralism* (London, Methuen, 1987)

Harvey, S., *May '68 and Film Culture* (London, BFI Publications, 1978)

Hawkes, T., *Structuralism and Semiotics* (London, Methuen, 1972)

Heath, S., *The Practice of Writing* (London, Elek, 1972)

Hedges, I., 'The Cinematographic Writing of Maurice Roche', *Visible Language: The Research Journal Concerned with All That is Involved in Our Being Literate* (Cleveland, OH), 12 (1978)

Hill, L. 'Julia Kristeva: Theorizing the Avant-Garde?', in J. Fletcher and A. Benjamin (eds), *Abjection, Melancholia and Love: The Work of Julia Kristeva* (London, Routledge, 1990)

——'Philippe Sollers and *Tel Quel*', in M. Tilby (ed.), *Beyond the Nouveau Roman* (Oxford, Berg, 1990)

Hobson, M., 'On the Subject of the Subject; Derrida on Sollers in *La dissémination*', in D. Wood (ed.), *Philosophers' Poets* (London, Routledge, 1991)

Hollier, D., '1968, May', in D. Hollier (ed.), *History of French Literature* (Cambridge, MA, Harvard University Press, 1989)

Kao, Shushi, 'Paradise Lost? An Interview with Philippe Sollers', *Sub-stance*, 30 (1981)

Kerr, T., 'A Postmodern Novel', *Paragraph*, 12 (March 1989)

Klinger, B., 'In Retrospect: Film Studies Today', *Yale Journal of Criticism* (Baltimore), 2:1 (Fall 1988) [on Baudry and Mulvey]

Kuappi, N., *The Making of an Avant-Garde: Tel Quel* (Berlin and New York, Mouton de Gruyter, 1994)

La Charité, V., *Twentieth Century Avant-Garde French Poetry* (Nicholasville, KY, French Forum, 1992)

Lack, R-F., 'Intertextuality or Influence?: Kristeva, Bloom and the *Poésies* of Isidore Ducasse', in M. Worton and J. Still (eds.), *Intertextuality, Theories and Practices* (Manchester, Manchester University Press, 1990)

——'Screen as Figure', *Paragraph* 19:1 (1996)

Lavers, A. 'Healing Words: Dr. Lacan's Structuralism', *Times Literary Supplement*, 3439 (25 January 1968)

——'In Revulsion is Our Beginning', *Times Literary Supplement*, 4047 (24 October 1980)

——'Logicus Sollers', *Times Literary Supplement*, 3484 (5 December 1968)

——'On Wings of Prophecy', *Times Literary Supplement*, 4074 (1 May 1981)

——'Rejoycing on the Left', *Times Literary Supplement*, 3681 (22 September1972)

——*Roland Barthes: Structuralism and After* (London, Methuen, 1982)

Lechte, J., *Julia Kristeva* (London, Routledge, 1980)

Lernout, G., *The French Joyce* (Ann Arbor, University of Michigan Press, 1990)

Marx-Scouras, D. *The Cultural Politics of Tel Quel* (Pennsylvania, Pennsylvania State University Press, 1997)

——'The Dissident Politics of *Tel Quel*', *L'Esprit créateur*, 27 (Summer 1987)

——'Requiem for the Post-War Years: The Rise of *Tel Quel*', *The French Review* (Champaign), 64:3 (February 1991).

Mathy, J.-P., *Extrême-Occident: French Intellectuals and America* (Chicago, University of Chicago Press, 1993)

Michelson, A., 'The Agony of the French Left', *October*, 6 (1978)

Reader, K., *Intellectuals and the Left in France since 1968* (Manchester, Manchester University Press, 1987)

Rose, J., *Sexuality in the Field of Vision* (London, Verso, 1986)

Roudiez, L., 'Readable/Writable/Visible', *Visible Language: The Research Journal Concerned with All That is Involved in Our Being Literate* (Cleveland, OH), 12 (1978)

Roudinesco, E., *Jacques Lacan and Co.: A History of Psychoanalysis in France*, trans. J. Mehlman (London, Free Association Books, 1990)

Sturrock, J., *Structuralism and Since* (Oxford, Oxford University Press, 1979)

Suleiman, S. R., 'As is', in D. Hollier (ed.), *History of French Literature* (Cambridge, MA, Harvard University Press, 1989)

Turkle, S., *Psychoanalytical Politics* (New York, Burnett, 1978)

INDEX

New York University
Bobst, Circulation Department
70 Washington Square South
New York, NY 10012-1091

Web Renewals:
http://library.nyu.edu
Circulation policies
http://library.nyu.edu/about

THIS ITEM IS SUBJECT TO RECALL AT ANY TIME

NOTE NEW DUE DATE WHEN RENEWING BOOKS ONLINE